The Codification of Public International Law

R. P. DHOKALIA

MANCHESTER UNIVERSITY PRESS
U.S.A.: OCEANA PUBLICATIONS INC.

221638

kW 5

Published by the University of Manchester at
THE UNIVERSITY PRESS
316–324 Oxford Road, Manchester M13 9NR
UK standard book number 7190 0404 7

U.S.A.
OCEANA PUBLICATIONS INC.
75 Main Street, Dobbs Ferry, N.Y. 1 522
US standard book number 379 00264 7
Library of Congress catalog card number 66 11927

Distributed in India by
N. M. TRIPATHI PRIVATE LTD
Princess Street, Bombay 2

Printed in Great Britain by Butler & Tanner Ltd, Frome and London

CONTENTS

FOREWORD by Professor B. A. Wortley, O.B.E., Q.C.,
LL.D.   ix

PREFACE   xi

ACKNOWLEDGMENTS   xiii

ABBREVIATIONS   xv

PART ONE
THE HISTORICAL BACKGROUND OF THE
MOVEMENT TOWARDS CODIFICATION

I   THE PROGRESS OF MANKIND TOWARDS WORLD   3
    ORGANIZATION

    INDIVIDUAL VISIONS OF WORLD ORGANIZATION   5
    Pierre Dubois; Dante; Emeric Crucé; Hugo Grotius;
    Sully's 'Grand Design'; William Penn; John Bellers;
    Saint-Pierre; Jean Jacques Rousseau; Jeremy Bent-
    ham; James Mill; Immanuel Kant; William Ladd;
    William Jay; Leon Levi; Johann Caspar Bluntschli;
    James Lorimer

    THE ORGANIZED PEACE WORK   19
    The First Phase 1815–1867; The Second Phase
    1867–1900; The Movement in the Twentieth Century

    FROM THE LEAGUE TO THE UNITED NATIONS   31

PART TWO
THE MOVEMENT TO CODIFY PUBLIC
INTERNATIONAL LAW

II PRIVATE EFFORTS AT CODIFICATION   37

    CODIFICATION PROJECTS BY INDIVIDUALS   37
    Jeremy Bentham; Abbé Grégoire; Early nineteenth-
    century Advocates of Codification; Project of Domin-
    Petrushevecz; Project of Johann Caspar Bluntschli;
    David Dudley Field; Pasquale Fiore; E. Duplessix;
    Jerome Internoscia

    CODIFICATION BY SCIENTIFIC ORGANIZATIONS   62
    The Institute of International Law; International

Law Association; The Harvard Law School; The American Institute of International Law; The American Society of International Law

III OFFICIAL EFFORTS AT CODIFICATION   76

EFFORTS OF GOVERNMENTS ACTING INDIVIDUALLY OR IN CONCERT   76
Initiative of Individual Governments; International Conferences; International Regulation of Social and Economic Problems

THE WORK OF THE HAGUE PEACE CONFERENCES OF 1899 AND 1907   87
The Hague Peace Conference of 1899; The Hague Conference of 1907; Appraisal of the Hague Conferences

OTHER EFFORTS BEFORE THE FIRST WORLD WAR   109
APPRAISAL OF THE CODIFICATION BEFORE THE FIRST WORLD WAR   111

CODIFICATION EFFORTS UNDER THE AEGIS OF THE LEAGUE OF NATIONS   112
Appointment of the Committee of Experts 1924; Preparatory Committee for the Codification Conference; The Hague Conference of 1930; Appraisal of the Work of the Conference

CODIFICATION OF INTERNATIONAL LAW IN THE INTER-AMERICAN SYSTEM   133

CODIFICATION OF THE LAWS OF WAR AS A RESULT OF TWO WORLD WARS   140

PART THREE

CODIFICATION SPONSORED BY THE UNITED NATIONS ORGANIZATION

IV THE INTERNATIONAL LAW COMMISSION AND ITS ORGANIZATION   147

PRELUDES TO THE ESTABLISHMENT OF THE ILC   147
The Dumbarton Oaks Conference 1944; The San Francisco Conference and Article 13 of the UN Charter; The implementation of Article 13(1)(a) of the UN Charter; The Committee on Progressive Development of International Law and its Codification; The Report of the Committee of Seventeen

THE ADOPTION OF THE STATUTE OF THE INTER-
NATIONAL LAW COMMISSION   160

THE WORKING MACHINERY OF THE INTER-
NATIONAL LAW COMMISSION   165
    The composition of the Commission; Organization
    of the Commission's work

V THE FUNCTIONS OF THE COMMISSION AND ITS
   METHODOLOGY   201
      Functions; Distinction between codification and pro-
      gressive development of international law

   METHODS, PROCEDURES AND TECHNIQUE OF THE
   COMMISSION'S WORK   217
      Methods; Procedures; Selection of topics; Technique
      and working methods of the Commission

   CO-OPERATION WITH INTERGOVERNMENTAL
   ORGANIZATIONS   266
      The Inter-American Council of Jurists; Asian-African
      Legal Consultative Committee; European Com-
      mittee on Legal Co-operation

VI THE ACHIEVEMENTS OF THE COMMISSION   271
    WORK COMPLETED   271
      Special assignments by the General Assembly;
      Matters forming part of the Commission's own pro-
      gramme of codification; UN Codification Con-
      ferences

    TOPICS UNDER STUDY BY THE COMMISSION   321

VII FUTURE PROSPECTS   333
     METHODS   334
     EXTERNAL FACTORS BEARING ON CODIFICATION   339
     SOURCES OF INTERNATIONAL LAW   341
     'THE GENERAL PRINCIPLES OF LAW'   344

    INDEX   351

FOREWORD

Dr. Dhokalia's work is based on a thesis prepared in the years 1962 to 1964, and since then steps have been made in the codification of international law, notably the Vienna Convention on the Law of Treaties.

The great value of Dr. Dhokalia's work, however, is in fact that he deals with the story of codification from the beginning, and has been led in his researches to discover little-known authors and codifiers, of whom he gives an account not otherwise available. In addition, Dr. Dhokalia deals with the work and achievements of the International Law Commission and with the perennial problems that face all attempts to enunciate and develop international law by international agreements.

I am glad to recommend this work to students of international law and politics, as well as to the general reader interested in the progress of international law, which now not only deals with the problems arising on land, sea and in air space, but is beginning to deal with the problems of outer space, where many of the old formulae are inappropriate.

November 1969

B. A. WORTLEY
Faculty of Law
University of Manchester

Dedicated to my mother
and to the memory of my father

PREFACE

The most notable fact in the history of public international law has been the movement towards the substitution of codified rules for unwritten customs. Indeed, nothing is more damaging to the prestige of a system of law than its uncertainty or doubtful existence. The more a system of law is precise, definite, detailed and up to date, the more is it likely to be perfect and effective. In view of the fact that international law has suffered from lack of precision and certainty because of its decentralized creation and consequent complexities and scattered character, the codification process represents the most substantial progress towards realizing fully the idea of a legally ordered society of states governed by a global law.

The idea and the movement of the codification of public international law, like other ideas and movements which have come to fruition in objective institutions, had their roots in earlier periods and were the result of the culmination of an historical and evolutionary process. The movement can be satisfactorily studied and understood only by examining its history.

This study attempts to trace the history of the codification of public international law. The subject matter has been presented in three principal divisions.

Part One deals with the background of the movement towards codification. It deals with the concept of the unity of mankind and its progress towards world organization. It shows that man's quest for peace and order led to two interlinked movements for a régime of law and world organization. These two movements—for a world organization and for the development and codification of international law—are shown to have culminated in our times in the establishment of the United Nations and the International Law Commission. The ultimate object of both movements has been to substitute for force and violence a régime of law and justice as the basis of international conduct.

Part Two of the study gives in some detail an account of attempts at the codification of international law made by individual publicists in their private capacity, by scientific bodies of non-official character, and by governments acting individually or in concert. It shows how the idea of codification pioneered by Bentham was transformed into a world-wide movement leading to the concerted efforts on the part of governments, and how it eventually matured into the organized work undertaken by the League of Nations.

A detailed study of the codification sponsored by the United Nations is made in Part Three. The organization, functions, method of work and achievements of the International Law Commission up to the end of 1966 are examined, and the future prospects for the codification of public international law are assessed, taking into account the difficulties and problems involved in the task.

Ever since Grotius enunciated a system in which the totality of international relations were to be subjected to the rule of law, the history of international law has been the story of a struggle between the idea of a legally ordered society of states on the one hand, and the idea of a mere juxtaposition of sovereign states on the other. Whilst the progress of international law has been more pronounced during certain periods than during others, its recent history shows a marked extension of its domain to new relationships, the adaptation of old rules to new conditions, and the reaching of agreement upon matters about which there has been a divergence of opinion among states. Furthermore, whilst in the period before the second World War, developments in international law were related much more largely to the law of war than to the law of peace; in the post-war period, on the contrary, the discussions provoked, the solutions sought, the efforts put forth to codify and improve the law, and the conventions formulated have concentrated mainly on the perfection of the law of pacific relations.

Whilst rapid changes in the international community—the appearance of many new states of widely differing cultural backgrounds and levels of development; the rise of new ideologies and systems of public order; rapid technological progress and a growing demand for social reform; and the increase in the number of international organizations—have, on the one hand, tended to decrease the relevance of some traditional legal norms, they have created, on the other hand, new areas for legal regulation. The acceleration of the process of change in the international community and the necessities of international life continue to demand a large measure of uniformity of basic rules of international law. This strengthens the trend towards law-making by multilateral treaties and the quasi-legislative process of codification in which new states with their numerical preponderance seem to insist on having their voices heard. These tendencies are indicative of a process of universalization and democratization of international law on which codification is likely to exercise an abiding influence.

ACKNOWLEDGMENTS

This study originated as a doctorate thesis submitted in 1964 to Manchester University. I am deeply grateful to the University not only for the generous award of a research grant for the period of my stay at Manchester but also for honouring this work by publishing it.

My two years' work in the Faculty of Law under Professor B. A. Wortley's guidance was indeed a rewarding experience. His constant guidance at every stage of the preparation of the manuscript and of its improvement with a view to its publication has been more than I can adequately acknowledge here. I am furthermore deeply indebted to him for kindly writing the foreword.

I gained much from discussions with Dr. D. W. Bowett of Queens' College and Dr. Clive Parry of Downing College, both of Cambridge University, for which I am very grateful. To Dr. W. H. Balekjian of the Vienna Law School, then Simon scholar at Manchester, and Mrs. J. Hoyle my sincere thanks are due for much help with French and German sources. Mr. Edward Reid-Smith kindly helped me by undertaking a patient reading of practically the whole manuscript and making many suggestions for improvement in its literary style.

In the preparation of the thesis, especially in the search for elusive League of Nations and United Nations documents and verification of source material, I received valuable and ungrudging aid from the staff of Manchester University and the Manchester reference libraries. My thanks are also due to the Director of the Codification Division of the United Nations, Miss Margret Mcfee of the U.N. Information Centre, London, and Mr. Gonzalo J. Facio of the Organization de los Estados Americanos for much valuable information sought by me.

No author can properly thank everyone for the assistance extended to him, directly or indirectly, in the preparation of his work. However, special thanks go to Messrs. R. K. Mukherji, Masud Khan, N. R. Kazmi, and Surendra Nath for much help in the correction of the typescript. To my parents-in-law, Mr. and Mrs. J. L. Beohar, who completely relieved me of worries about my family back at home, I am immeasurably indebted. Mr. and Mrs. W. W. Woollett and Miss Valerie Woollett of Sale, Cheshire, deserve my special gratitude for making my stay in the U.K. homely and full of happy memories.

Finally, I wish to express my grateful appreciation to Manchester University Press for all the scholarly care which they have bestowed upon their arduous task of bringing out the book while my continuous co-operation with them could not be possible owing to the distance between us. For any shortcomings and errors in the book, of course, I remain solely responsible.

Varanasi, India   R. P. DHOKALIA

ABBREVIATIONS

A.J.I.L.	American Journal of International Law
B.Y.B.I.L.	British Year Book of International Law
Col. L. Rev.	Columbia Law Review
C.L.P.	Current Legal Problems
ECOSOC	Economic and Social Council of the United Nations
GA	General Assembly of the United Nations
H.L.R.	Harvard Law Review
I. & C.L.Q.	International and Comparative Law Quarterly
Int. Con.	International Conciliation
ICJ	International Court of Justice
I.L.A. Rep.	International Law Association Report
ILC	International Law Commission
I.L.Q.	International Law Quarterly
Int. Peace Year Book	International Peace Year Book
L.Q. Rev.	Law Quarterly Review
L.N. Doc.	League of Nations Document
L. of N. Offl. Jnl.	League of Nations Official Journal
N.Y. Univ. Law Rev.	New York University Law Review
PCIJ	Permanent Court of International Justice
Proc. Am. Soc. Int. Law	Proceedings of the American Society of International Law
Trans. Grotius Soc.	Transactions of the Grotius Society
T.L.R.	Tulane Law Review
UN	United Nations
UNCDIIOR	United Nations Conference on Diplomatic Intercourse and Immunities Official Records
UNCIO Doc.	United Nations Conference on International Organization Documents
I UNCLSOR	First United Nations Conference on the Law of the Sea Official Records
II UNCLSOR	Second United Nations Conference on the Law of the Sea Official Records

U.N. Doc.	United Nations Document
UNGAOR	United Nations General Assembly Official Records
Y.B.I.L.C.	Year Book of the International Law Commission
YB of the UN	Year Book of the United Nations
Y.B.W.A.	Year Book of World Affairs
Yale L.J.	Yale Law Journal

PART ONE

THE HISTORICAL BACKGROUND OF THE MOVEMENT TOWARDS CODIFICATION

CHAPTER ONE

THE PROGRESS OF MANKIND
TOWARDS WORLD ORGANIZATION

In order to appreciate fully the feasibility of a universal legal system and the significance of the connection between the movement for the codification of international law and mankind's aim to replace the rule of force by the rule of law in a world community, it will be profitable to analyse briefly the main ideas, theoretical concepts and historical links underlying various attempts to organize the community of mankind through an association of independent states and to evolve a system of law common to all.

Concepts of a world society, of a common law of mankind and of equality of man are fundamental to the existence of both the state and the international community. Such concepts may be seen as a synthesis of the ideals of philosophers, jurists, theologians and far-sighted statesmen of different countries at different periods of history. Nearly every civilization—the Chinese, the ancient Indian, the Mesopotamian, the Islamic and the Christian—has developed the myth and the symbol of a unified world. However, as Europe pre-dominated during the last five centuries in the world of ideas and of thought as well as in the social, political and economic fields, it is relevant here to confine our account to the concept of a world society as it grew in Europe to be powerful enough to have attained world-wide significance. If we speak today of 'one world', it is certainly a world made one by European methods and European techniques.[1]

The concept of a free union of humanity—a real commonwealth of mankind—has developed in the course of history through various efforts to organize international life and has been embodied in recent times in the Covenant of the League of Nations and in the Charter of the United Nations as intrinsic to general peace and security. It is the product of a historical pattern of thought which expected that an international organization, which was not a world state, would inaugurate an era of universal peace, security and order, even though such thought has at times emphasized freedom, at times unity.[2] Typically, however, there is always the thought of

[1] G. Pearson: *Towards One World*, 1962, p. vii; Sir Ernest Barker, Sir George Clark and P. Vaucher (eds.): *The European Inheritance*, 3 vols, 1954.
[2] See Franciscus Suarez: *De lege et dei legislatore*, ii, c. xix, para. 9, cited by T. E. Holland, *The Elements of Jurisprudence*, 13th edn. 1924, p. 393.

unity in variety and of the necessity and possibility of organizing the world legal order. The elements of the concept of unity of mankind seem to appear throughout the course of history from Greek and Roman times, with important links in the chain of thought in the writings and theories of many scholars who contributed to the formation of a general pattern of common thought and thereby provided a theoretical basis of world organization schemes. Emerging from Greek and Roman times of the greatest glory, these elements came through the Middle Ages and, moulded by the Christian philosophy, ideals of life and conduct, have, in reaching the modern era, been slowly matured through centuries of theoretical presentation.[1] Although man's perception of these concepts of unity may have been dimmed from time to time, to disregard them altogether would be perilous to his welfare and his future.

Greek philosophers first discerned that reason, controlling and co-ordinating the diverse and often rebellious elements of human life, pointed to the ideal that only by common action and community of thought could the growing variety and richness of human life be developed towards its natural end.[2] They conceived the whole universe as a cosmos or ordered whole governed by a creative force, called by them Nature, or God, or the Universal Law. Man, being part of Nature, could achieve his highest purpose and attain true happiness only by ordering his life according to the Laws of Nature. They conceived the whole universe as a single intelligible unity pervaded by reason, and their belief in a world state was simply the political aspect of their general philosophic conception.[3] The philosophies of Plato, Aristotle and the Stoics saw a rational design in the universe manifested, however imperfectly or partially, in the material world. The natural law of the Greeks implied the idea of a common law which was natural to humanity.[4] Greek ideas ultimately became the most potent means of human unity and the notion of the law of nature became one of the most creative forces and one of the most constructive elements of western civilization.[5] It became the foundation of a system of Roman law in the hands of

---

[1] Sir R. W. Carlyle and A. J. Carlyle: *A History of Mediaeval Political Theory in the West*, vol. I, 1903, p. 2; F. S. Marvin (ed.): *The Unity of Western Civilization*, 1915, pp. 17–34.
[2] J. A. Smith: 'The contribution of Greece and Rome' in Marvin (ed.), *Unity of Western Civilization*, pp. 69–90.
[3] See R. W. Livingstone (ed.): *The Legacy of Greece*, Oxford, 1921.
[4] See for a valuable study of Greek legal thought and institutions J. Walter Jones: *The Law and Legal Theory of the Greeks*, 1956, pp. 3–16, 37–72; also Heinrich A. Rommen: *The Natural Law*, trans. T. R. Hanley, 1947, pp. 3–26.
[5] F. S. Marvin (ed.): *The Evolution of World Peace*, 1921, p. 15; W. Friedmann: *Legal Theory*, 1960, pp. 47–50.

the practical Roman jurists. Moreover, the philosophy of natural law had a perfectly continuous history through the Middle Ages, down to what Sir Frederick Pollock called 'the date of its greatest and most beneficent achievement—one might almost say its apotheosis—in the foundation of the modern Law of Nations by Grotius'.[1] Thus we may say that 'reason' applied to the phenomena of the world, however imperfectly, has tended to point out some possible reconciliation of human passions and interests under the aegis of international law.[2]

INDIVIDUAL VISIONS OF WORLD ORGANIZATION

After the birth of the modern nation state systems various schemes were conceived, from time to time, to urge the need for a world organization to guarantee peace.[3] The better-known early movements for peace, world organization and the codification of international law which both stimulated and impressed the superior minds of Europe and America were interrelated throughout the course of history. All peace projects represent the efforts directed towards the attainment of the same goal—the abolition of war. Also, the similarity of the basic assumptions, apparently resulting from the characteristic combination of certain historically developed ideas and moral values, seems to emphasize a general pattern of thought and a definite concept which underlies the theoretical basis of world organization schemes and of international legal order.

The better-known projects of peace and international confederation are associated with the names of Pierre Dubois, Dante Alighieri, Emeric Crucé, Grotius, Sully, William Penn, John Beller, the Abbé de Saint-Pierre, Jean Jacques Rousseau, Jeremy Bentham, Immanuel Kant, William Ladd, William Jay, Leon Levi, Johann Caspar Bluntschli and James Lorimer. Their projects were designed to find out the ways and means by which a number of independent communities, or sovereign states, could live side by side in harmony, without acknowledging a common superior or, failing that, to find out the methods of settling their differences or conflicts of interests without recourse to the arbitrament of war. They therefore urged upon an unwilling and unappreciative world the desirability of an international confederation, or international conferences and of international tribunals.

---

[1] Sir Frederick Pollock: 'The history of the Law of Nature' in *Essays in the Law*, 1922, p. 31.

[2] C. Phillipson, *The International Law and Customs of Ancient Greece and Rome*, vol. 1, 1911, pp. 30, 63–4.

[3] A Dutch jurist, Jacob ter Meulen, gives an account of individual international plans written or proposed between 1300 and 1800 in his book *Der Gedanke der Internationalen Organization in einer Entwicklung*, The Hague, 1917.

Pierre Dubois

To France is due the credit for the origin and development of pacifist ideas, as well as for the first project for a world organization and the first plan for an international court of justice. The mediaeval herald of peace projects for world organization was Pierre Dubois, lawyer and adviser to Philip le Bel, king of France in the early fourteenth century. In his chief work, *De recuperatione Terre Sancte*, written between 1305 and 1307, he advocated a federation of Christian sovereign states in which he expected France to play a leading rôle.[1]

Dubois was thus a pioneer—the first to propose an international court of arbitration. He urged that a state waging war be boycotted and a concerted military action be taken against it—a recommendation that received notice only six centuries later, in the Covenant of the League of Nations. He advocated that the money that would be saved through the abolition of wars should be used for the establishment of international schools, and was thus one of the earliest proponents of international education.[2]

Dante

Dante Alighieri's political essay *De Monarchia*,[3] which Lord Bryce considered to be the 'epitaph of the Holy Roman Empire' in Italy,[4] was indeed a cry of despair and a plea for unity in the divided world of the fourteenth century. In contrast to Dubois, Dante found his remedy in the establishment of a world state under an all-powerful emperor.[5] His concept of the organization of humanity, in which he insisted on the harmonious co-operation of the several members of the universal body politic for the attainment of peace and well-being of the world, while conserving their particularisms and autonomy, approached very closely to present-day thought. It is not unrealistic to assume that, for the attainment of peace, Dante intended the organized forces of all nations to pay allegiance to a

[1] First published in 1611 it made him one of the most famous men in the history of the peace movement. See W. S. M. Knight: 'A mediaeval pacifist—Pierre Dubois', *Trans. Grotius Soc.*, vol. IX, 1924, pp. 1–15; Elizabeth V. Souleyman, *The Vision of World Peace in Seventeenth and Eighteenth Century France*, New York, 1941, pp. 2–3; F. Melian Stawell, *The Growth of International Thought*, London, 1929, p. 67.

[2] Sylvester J. Hemleben: *Plans for World Peace through Six Centuries*, Chicago, 1943, p. 3.

[3] Not published until 1559, at Basel. Some held that it was produced between 1308 and 1314, others between 1318 and 1321. See *The 'De Monarchia' of Dante Alighieri*, Aurelia Henry ed., 1904, pp. xxxii–xlvi.

[4] James Viscount Bryce: *The Holy Roman Empire*, 1904, p. 264.

[5] See E. Sherwood Smith: 'Dante and World Empire' in *Social and Political Ideas of Great Mediaeval Thinkers*, Hearnshaw ed., 1923, p. 128.

universal emperor, thereby contemplating a monopoly of force in international society in order to eliminate war.[1]

Emeric Crucé

The peace project of Emeric Crucé appeared during the period of the Thirty Years War.[2] In the records of history it was the first proposal for an international organization that was also a proposal for maintaining peace. Crucé seems firmly to have grasped the principle that the function of a league of nations must not be merely to adjudicate in disputes but also to foresee and dissipate the causes of hostility.[3] He embraced the whole human race in his concept and showed foresight in not confining the family of nations to Christian states alone. To have thought of an international body comprising members of different races and creeds on equal footings, testifies to the unusual breadth of his mind, at that period. Crucé condemned war and could see no excuse for bloodshed among men. In contrast to other writers on peace projects, he sought no special advantage for his own country and laid stress upon internal peace within each country as a foundation to peace between countries.[4] Moreover, because of his grasp of related fields and his recommendations on such diverse subjects as currency laws, administration of justice and the nature of sovereignty, Crucé occupies an important position in the history of peace literature.[5] Long before Cobden, Crucé advocated free trade and commercial co-operation between nations.

Hugo Grotius

The Thirty Years War provoked new thought and discussion along the lines taken by Crucé, to whom it is likely that Grotius was indebted, for he had found refuge in Paris in 1621, just two years before the publication of Crucé's work. Grotius's great and immortal work, which appeared in Paris in 1625, commanded an instant and permanent reputation and became for centuries a leading textbook.[6] It envisaged the possibility of sovereign states living together

---

[1] Bryce, *op. cit.*, p. 280; Hemleben, *op. cit.*, p. 11. See for detailed commentary on Dante's project Elizabeth York: *League of Nations, Ancient, Mediaeval and Modern*, 1919, pp. 37–80.
[2] *Le Nouveau Cynée*, or *The New Discourse of the Occasions and Means to establish a General Peace and the Liberty of Commerce throughout the Whole World*, appeared in 1623. See T. W. Balch (ed. and trans.): *Emeric Crucé, The New Cyneas*, 1909; W. Evans Darby, *International Tribunals*, 4th edn., London, 1904, pp. 22–3.
[3] G. G. Butler: *Studies in Statecraft*, 1920, p. 102.
[4] Hemleben, *Plans for World Peace*, pp. 30–1. Butler called him a most daring speculator in the realm of international relations among the French thinkers of his age: see *Studies in Statecraft*, p. 92. For contrary view, see A. Nussbaum, *Concise History of the Law of Nations*, 1954, p. 78.
[5] Souleyman, *Vision of World Peace*, pp. 16–17.
[6] See William Whewell's translation, *Hugonis Grotii, 'De Jure belli et pacis'*, 1853.

in a family of nations governed by a Law of Nations, based on contract and justice, that would regulate war even if it did not guarantee peace. Only a passing reference is made here to Grotius, for he is widely acknowledged as the 'Father of International Law' for the reason that his work remains perhaps the most complete that the world has yet owned, at so early a stage in the progress of any science, to the genius of one man.[1] He attempted to apply to the relations between states the principles which govern under municipal law the rights and obligations of individual citizens.[2]

For Grotius human reason—right reason—became the basis of the laws and institutions of society. Since his times the principle of sociality and solidarity of independent states, not necessarily equal, founded on the interests of humanity at large and discoverable and applicable by human reason, has become the foundation of the science of the jurists of the Grotian school.[3] His sole concern was that war should be waged only as a last resort and for a just cause alone; even in war, law must stand above force. He neither demanded a permanent assemblage of nations nor insisted upon a permanent tribunal, and was satisfied with periodical conferences for the adjustment of international difficulties. The main interest of Grotius was, therefore, to humanize warfare and to develop the principle of the pacific settlement of disputes.

Sully's Grand Design of Henry IV

It was during that period of confusion when Europe underwent a series of religious wars, culminating in wholesale massacre and widespread disorder and threatening the very existence of states, that Maximilien de Béthune, duc de Sully, Minister of Finance, confidant and friend of Henry IV, prepared an imaginative and comprehensive scheme for the federation of Christian republics of Europe.[4] The Grand Design was published in two volumes in 1638, many years after Henry IV's death, and its third and fourth volumes were printed in 1662, after the death of Sully.

Sully's plan contemplated an arbitrary division of Europe into approximately equal parts and conceived of a congress of nations which was a paternalistic organization. Since he understood the

[1] Hamilton Vreeland: *Hugo Grotius—the Father of the Modern Science of International Law*, 1917, pp. 71–2. See for contrary view C. H. McKenna: *Francis de Vitoria, Founder of International Law*, 1930, p. 7; James Brown Scott, *The Catholic Conception of International Law*, 1934.
[2] C. van Vollenhoven: *The Law of Peace*, W. Horsfall Carter trans., 1936, p. 192.
[3] W. S. M. Knight: *The Life and Works of Hugo Grotius*, 1925, pp. 191–223; H. Lauterpacht: 'The Grotian Tradition in International Law', B.Y.B.I.L., vol. 23, 1946, pp. 48, 51–2.
[4] *Sully's Grand Design of Henry IV:* Introduction by David Ogg, 1921; also *The Great Design of Henry IV*, ed. and intro. by E. D. Mead, 1909.

value of moral as well as physical force, he realized that the latter could not be dispensed with. So he was the first European statesman to suggest adequate sanctions for the federation of Europe, and to recognize that the efficacy of these sanctions would be dependent upon public opinion. The Grand Design carried a high prestige and influenced similar subsequent projects.[1]

William Penn

Renewed interest in plans seeking to prevent war was prompted by the wars of the later seventeenth century. The War of Devolution 1667–8 was followed by the Dutch War of 1672 and that of the League of Augsburg 1688–97. The signs of the approaching War of the Spanish Succession were also casting their shadow. William Penn, who is remembered as the founder of the colony of Pennsylvania and for his experiment in Quaker government there, offered his plan for world peace in *An Essay towards the Present and Future Peace of Europe* in 1693.[2] His plan had two sources of inspiration— Sully's Grand Design, and the practical example of the Confederation of the Netherlands.[3] He argued that, as in a municipal society citizens established order out of chaos by instituting government, so the sovereign princes of Europe could also evolve a European order by establishing a European parliament composed of their representatives.[4] The sovereign or imperial diet or parliament of nations of Europe was to meet annually, or at least every two or three years to formulate rules of justice to be observed by the sovereign princes in their relations with one another. He contemplated the use of military sanctions to enforce, in case of need, the decisions of the European parliament. His plan therefore, regarded the provision of sanction as an important factor for the success of his scheme and thereby it contained the germ of the idea of an international police force for the enforcement of peace. Penn's project was perhaps one of the first to look forward to disarmament and to the application of funds usually spent on military preparedness to better advantage.[5]

[1] W. A. Phillips: *The Confederation of Europe. A Study of European Alliance 1813–1823* . . . ., 1914, p. 20. David Ogg, *op. cit.*, p. 10, traces direct inspiration by Sully in the peace projects of Bentham and of more obscure writers like Bellers and Rachel. See also Phillips: 'Historical survey of projects of universal peace' in Edith M. Phelps: *A League of Nations*, 2nd edn., 1919, pp. 15–22. See for the influence of the Grand Design J. B. Scott (ed.): *An Essay on a Congress of Nations by Ladd*, 1916, pp. xx–xxii.

[2] An edition of this was published by the American Peace Society in 1912.

[3] V. J. Lewis: 'William Penn', *New Commonwealth*, vol. II, no. 12, 1934, p. 177.

[4] William Penn: *An Essay* . . ., American Peace Society edn., pp. 1–9; Darby, *International Tribunals*, pp. 56–64.

[5] American Peace Society edn., p. 13. See for critical appreciation of the plan, Hamleben, *Plans for World Peace*, pp. 52–3.

John Bellers

Another Quaker, John Bellers of Gloucester, followed closely in his tract the line laid down by William Penn. The work, generally known by its shortened title *Some Reasons for an European State*, appeared in 1710 during the War of the Spanish Succession and was proposed to the British Parliament for a peace league. Like Penn, Bellers also conceived of an annual congress of all the federated states of Europe, including Russia and Turkey. Bellers's scheme divided Europe into one hundred equal provinces, each to supply to the league one thousand soldiers or an equal value in ships or money.[1] Evidently, like Penn, he also accepted the inevitability of force as the ultimate sanction of an international award.

Saint-Pierre

At the close of the War of the Spanish Succession another scheme to guarantee peace was devised by Charles François Irenée Castel de Saint-Pierre (1658–1743) in 1713; it was titled *Projet pour rendre la paix perpétuelle en Europe*.[2] He expressed his debt to the Grand Design of Henry IV and thereby hoped to obtain a hearing for his project. He envisaged the formation of a permanent Grand Alliance or European Union of the twenty-four states of Christian Europe. The first part of the project put forward some important propositions and the second answered probable objections to the plan. The plan was drawn up in the form of a treaty, and was recommended for the signature of European powers. It contemplated a union of all Christian sovereigns represented by their deputies in a senate of peace. The union was to be a voluntary one and each state was to have equal representation in the senate of peace, which was to sit permanently at Utrecht.

Saint-Pierre indicated four essential requisites for the preservation of peace: first, formation of a union or league of states on the basis of a fundamental treaty signed by the greatest possible number of states; secondly, prompt settlement of interstate disputes through conciliation, mediation or compulsory arbitration; thirdly, attainment of considerable diminution of armies, military equipment and expenses; and lastly, establishment of an international force sufficient to compel obedience to the decrees of the international tribunal and

[1] A. Ruth Fry: *John Beller, 1654–1725. Quaker Economist and Social Reformer*, 1935, p. 93; Darby, *International Tribunals*, pp. 64–9; see also G. W. Knowles: *Quakers and Peace*, Grotius Soc. Pubn. no. 4, 1927, pp. 30–1.

[2] First published in Cologne in 1712 and reprinted in two volumes at Utrecht in 1713, the third in 1717, and an abridgement was issued in 1729. An English translation (*A Project for Settling an Everlasting Peace in Europe* . . .) was published in London in 1714. See H. H. Bellot (trans.): *Selections from the Second Edition of the Abrégé du Projet de Paix Perpétuelle*, Grotius Soc. Pubn. no. 5, 1927.

to enable it to function effectively for the preservation of peace. He conceived a strong federation in which all the member states renounced war as an instrument of national policy wherein arms could be taken up only against a country that did not live up to its covenant or which was declared by the union to be an enemy of European society. Over-anxious to ensure perpetual peace, Saint-Pierre endowed his Union with functions from which, even in the twentieth century, the framers of the Covenant of the League of Nations and the Charter of the United Nations have recoiled. He defined aggression by a state as the launching of a sudden attack or refusal to conform to 'the regulation of the Union' or to an arbitral judgment of the senate. His plan bound in advance, without reservations, every league member to make war upon the recalcitrant state at the instigation of the senate, and engaged in advance all their military resources to be employed in an international police force which was based on the quota system.

Saint-Pierre showed great foresight and practical vision in the realm of ideas by sowing the seeds of the future League of Nations or the United Nations, international court of arbitration, and international police force. His basic ideas have found their place in experiments of world organization in our time. Although no standing army of the United Nations has yet been created, the need for this kind of army has been strongly felt. His project was the first and incomparably the most complete and coherent scheme ever formulated for ensuring perpetual peace and for the avoidance of war. It was more broadly planned, more firmly knit, more precise in detail and more practical than any plan that preceded it; and those which followed were probably all influenced by it.[1]

The main provisions of his plan were reproduced by the internationalists of the nineteenth century, such as Fiore;[2] they were incorporated in the Germanic Confederation of 1815 and in the Holy Alliance;[3] and they formed more or less completely the basis of the League of Nations Covenant and the U.N. Charter. Saint-Pierre's ideas on the union of nations, on disarmament, on peaceful settlement of disputes, on open diplomacy, on respect for frontiers established by treaties, and on an international police force seem to have much in common with what the Covenant attempted to envisage,[4] and with what the Charter is attempting to develop.

[1] For illustrations of the influence of Saint-Pierre see Souleyman, *Vision of World Peace*, pp. 92–5, 176–81; see also *A.J.I.L.*, vol. 7, 1913, pp. 87–107, for Cardinal Alberoni's project, and M. R. Vesnitch's article on Alberoni, pp. 51–83.
[2] P. Fiore: *Il Diritto Internazionale Codificato e la sua Sanzione giuridica* (1890), trans. E. Borchard: *Fiore's International Law Codified*, New York, 1918.
[3] H. Wheaton: *History of the Law of Nations in Europe and America*, New York, 1845, p. 263; Phillips: *Confederation of Europe*, pp. 24, 27, 29, 34–5.
[4] Hemleben maintains that Saint-Pierre went farther than the League in

The project of the Abbé de Saint-Pierre was a natural conclusion to a century of war—the age of Louis XIV. In the subsequent period, up to the conclusion of the Holy Alliance of 1815, war was the normal condition of Europe and it is not surprising that serious thinkers resorted to the contemplation of schemes for securing world peace. Among them Rousseau, Bentham and Kant are pre-eminent.

Jean Jacques Rousseau

Rousseau and the group of writers who shared his philosophical outlook approached the issue of war from a moralistic point of view. They felt themselves citizens of one vast universe and conceived of universal peace as the outcome not of a fraternal union of princes but of the brotherhood of an enlightened humanity. Rousseau, who was personally acquainted with the Abbé de Saint-Pierre and had a great admiration for him and his project, realized that the good Abbé's work, despite its merit, did not attract general attention because of its cumbersome and careless style.[1] He therefore re-edited the Abbé's work and not only rescued the gist of the author's arguments from the morass of verbosity but also provided them with a philosophy.[2]

For Rousseau, international anarchy was similar to the state of nature prior to social contract. He thought that, for the abolition of war, the nations should follow the same course as that followed by individuals. They should attempt to pass to the next stage of civilization and order by means of an international contract to establish a union of peoples. He conceived of a real community of an enlightened humanity wherein the component states would subject themselves to the general will of a congress of nations.

Rousseau's plan for a constitution of Europe based upon that of the Abbé involved five articles:[3] 1, a perpetual irrevocable alliance between the contracting powers envisaging a meeting of plenipotentiaries, where all differences were to be terminated by arbitration or judgment; 2, details of the number of members and method of control of the proposed diet; 3, confederated guarantee of the possessions and government of each confederate state, renunciation of all anterior pretensions and regulation of all future disputes

---

many respects: *Plans for World Peace*, pp. 68–71; see also Baron David Davies, *The Problem of the Twentieth Century*, 1930, pp. 78–81.
[1] See Introduction to *A Project of Perpetual Peace*, trans. E. M. Nuttall, 1927, p. vii.
[2] *A Project of Perpetual Peace: Rousseau's Essay*, trans. E. M. Nuttall, 1927; C. E. Vaughan: *Introduction to Rousseau, A Lasting Peace through the Federation of Europe and the State of War*, 1917.
[3] Nuttall, *op. cit.*, pp. 45–51.

by arbitration, without violence being resorted to under any pretext; 4, cases under which a violator would be put under the ban of Europe as a common enemy; 5, the majorities necessary to reach the conclusions in the diet, but the articles themselves not to be changed without the unanimous consent of all parties. He did not believe that it would be easy to find a favourable moment to carry the plan into effect merely through a congress of nations, and declared that 'it is no longer a question of persuading but of compelling, and instead of writing books we must raise troops'.[1]

Jeremy Bentham

Bentham's project entitled *A Plan for a Universal and Perpetual Peace* differed from Rousseau's in many respects. Since it remained in unpublished form until 1843 when it was given to the world in Bowring's edition, it remained practically unnoticed and exercised no influence upon passing events. But Bentham deserves a close study, particularly for his pioneering of the codification movement and his strong advocacy of the international court of judicature. A more detailed assessment of his contribution to the codification and peace movement is given in the next chapter.

James Mill

Bentham's disciple James Mill faithfully reproduced Bentham's main proposals in his article 'Law of Nations' in a supplement to the *Encyclopaedia Britannica*.[2] His was not a peace plan. His article dealt with the rights of nations, which he regarded as the basis of international law. It restated with admirable force and clarity Bentham's central argument that war was avoidable by independent civilized states with the aid of public opinion and a rational body of international law. He thought that the combination of nations to vindicate the law of nations was impossible and so approbation or disapprobation of mankind was the only power to operate the sanction of that law. Two factors raising the efficiency of the sanction were: i. a strict determination and certainty of the law of nations, and ii. a tribunal to yield prompt and accurate execution of the law. To that end, two practical and indispensable measures were, first, the construction of a code; and second, the establishment of an international tribunal.[3]

---

[1] Nuttall, *op. cit.*, pp. 111, 113; see also pp. xiv, xxii.
[2] 5th edn., 1820. Reprinted in James Mill: *Essays on Government, Jurisprudence, Liberty of the Press and the Law of Nations*, privately printed, n.d.
[3] For his Scheme for a Federal Supreme Court, see Darby, *International Tribunals*, pp. 182–3; Mill, *op. cit.*, pp. 28–33.

Immanuel Kant

The German philosopher Kant published his famous treatise *Perpetual Peace* in 1795[1] during the reign of Frederick William III and at a time when Prussia had just made peace with the revolutionary government in France after three years of war. The Treaty of Basel, 1795, doubtless influenced Kant in the same way that the Treaty of Utrecht moved Saint-Pierre to formulate his peace project. Kant welcomed and admired both the French Revolution and the American Revolution. His work aroused such interest that it went successively through several editions.

Kant's treatise was very brief and had a more democratic basis than that of Saint-Pierre. In his view, the moral idea and pure practical reason could only be developed fully under republican institutions because the people will never vote for war. He began by laying down in the preliminary articles general international maxims, most of which have long been accepted by practical workers for peace, e.g. that no peace treaty must contain the germ of future wars; that no independent state shall be disposed of by other states; that standing armies shall be abolished in course of time; that national debts for war shall be forbidden; that states shall not interfere in the domestic affairs of others; and that brutal methods of warfare shall be prohibited.[2]

Kant did not work out in detail the schemes of a congress of nations nor did he suggest the establishment of an international court to administer law. But he cherished a hope for a universal domain of cosmopolitan law that would eventually be realized through a gradual and continued progress. He assumed that all men had a general interest in peace which would constitute the strongest bond uniting the world. Kant struck at the roots of war and enunciated ideas which were very modern. His proposals in respect of disarmament, open diplomacy, national indebtedness, prohibitions of hostilities, colonialism and league of nations, if carried out, might have prevented two world wars. But his philosophical arguments, at times, appear strange and illogical. They had two premises: i. that the categorical imperative[3] enjoined men always to act on a

---

[1] *Kant's Perpetual Peace*, trans. Benjamin F. Trueblood, 1897; trans. N. M. Butler, 1939.

[2] Kant's plan, like that of Saint-Pierre, was in the form of treaties, ready for the signature of the nations. See Helen O'Brien (trans.): *Perpetual Peace, A Philosophical Proposal*, Grotius Soc. Pubn. 1927, pp. 19–23; also York, *League of Nations*, pp. 267–8.

[3] The categorical imperative expressed generally what constituted obligation or the Principle of Duty, what reason absolutely and therefore objectively and universally laid down in the form of a command to the individual as to how he ought to act. See W. Hastie: 'Kant's Philosophy of Law' in Clarence Morris: *The Great Legal Philosophers*, 1959, p. 241.

maxim of respect for human beings as ends in themselves; and ii. that the juridical principle underlying the dynamics of government was that men, as rational beings, ought to seek to extend the reign of law. It has to be admitted that Kant's essay had no influence whatsoever on contemporary events.

The projects of peace and world organization proposed by social philosophers from Pierre Dubois to Immanuel Kant had been looked upon chiefly as international utopias. Their authors seemed to have taken no pains either to work out the practical details of their measures or to get their views adopted. The contemporary monarchs and statesmen, preoccupied with national and dynastic ambitions, paid little attention to these schemes which would in effect have curbed their freedom of action. The nineteenth century, however, ushered in by the Napoleonic era and largely as a reaction to that period, was to witness an unprecedented surge of internationalism and pacifism which was a continuation of the great body of intellectual speculation of the previous centuries. There resulted well-organized peace movements in several countries.

William Ladd

In America the desire for peace found expression in the formation of peace societies, such as the American Peace Society founded in 1828 by William Ladd. A group of Americans led by William Ladd and Elihu Burritt inaugurated a campaign for the establishment of a congress of nations and worked indefatigably to induce the government of the United States not only to act upon their proposal but also to propose its adoption to all the governments of Christendom.

Ladd's most celebrated and influential scheme for peace was written for the American Peace Society in 1840. He proposed the creation of two distinct international bodies, a congress of nations and a court of nations, and thus separated entirely the diplomatic and legislative from the judicial functions[1]—his one original contribution to his subject and one of the principles which determined the attitude of the U.S.A. towards the League of Nations in due time. Like Bentham and Mill he left the executive function of the international government to public opinion.

A very important feature of Ladd's plan was that it recognized

[1] William Ladd: *Prize Essay on a Congress of Nations for the Adjustment of Universal Peace*, Boston, 1940, published in England by Thos. Ward and Co., London, 1840 as *An Essay on a Congress of Nations for the Adjustment of International Disputes without Resort to Arms*. In the advertisement to the essay he claimed originality in regard to the separation of the legislature and the court in a government of nations, Boston edn., p. iv.

that the preparation of an international law code was indispensable if wars were to be prevented. The primary function of the congress of nations would be to establish the principles of international law with the unanimous consent of all the member nations and ratified by their respective governments. Thus, every principle of law established by the congress would resemble a treaty so as to produce permanent results. The first concern of the congress, after organizing the court of nations, was the codification of international law for defining the rights of belligerents towards one another, for settling the rights of neutrals, for endeavouring to abate the horrors of war and to abolish war between nations, and for taking measures of general utility to mankind. The submission of each statute for separate ratification would not be necessary; the completed code was to be submitted to each nation as a whole. Those articles unanimously adopted by the various governments were to be considered as enacted international law; the remaining articles could await further investigation. But until the code was completed the court of nations was to decide the cases brought before it in accordance with the principles of law generally known and acknowledged.

Ladd's plan exercised considerable influence on the peace movement in England and it was introduced by his disciple, Elihu Burritt, in the peace conferences of Brussels (1848), Paris (1849), Frankfurt (1850) and London (1851). His project obtained a practical vindication when the first Hague Conference was convened as a Congress of Nations, which brought into existence the Permanent Court of Arbitration at The Hague, although this differed in composition from Ladd's proposed Court of Nations.[1]

William Jay

William Jay offered his plan *War and Peace* in 1842.[2] It envisaged an agreement in future treaties not to resort to war and to submit the disputes between states to arbitration whose award would be binding. According to the author, war could be eliminated by the gradual rousing of public opinion against it and by the creation of agencies for settling controversies between nations. In course of time he thought it would be possible for Christian nations to establish an international tribunal for the adjudication of national differences, and also to prevent all forcible resistance to its decrees.

As an active member of the American Peace Society and its president for a decade, Jay shifted the emphasis of the peace movement from establishing a congress of nations and a court of nations

[1] Schwarzenberger: *William Ladd I.E.T.*, 2nd ed., 1936.
[2] *War and Peace: The Evils of the First and a Plan for Preserving the Last*, N.Y., 1842.

to the cause of arbitration.[1] The arbitration clause proposed by him made its way into treaty after treaty. The movement led to the successful settlement of the Alabama claims by arbitration in 1872, which was hailed in both America and England and immeasurably strengthened the cause of arbitration.[2] But arbitration continued to constitute only a component part or one of the elements of the more inclusive plans for an international congress.[3]

Leon Levi

Another important plan for world organization which was influenced by the success of arbitrations during this period was that of Leon Levi, professor of International Law in King's College, London, and a vice-president of the London Peace Society. His scheme was that the Peace Society and the International Arbitration League should invite the governments of the civilized world to join in appointing a Permanent Council of International Arbitration, which should be composed of appointees of various states, sitting as international judges and not as nationals. The Council was to be summoned by the secretaries to offer mediation or arbitration at the outbreak of any dispute involving members or non-members. It was to function as in Ladd's scheme, dispensing a code of international law as soon as such a code was drafted. As regards sanctions, the scheme did not contemplate the exercise of physical force to compel compliance with the awards of the council or court. It relied on moral rather than on physical force.[4]

Johann Caspar Bluntschli

Bluntschli's plan of peace was entitled *Europa als Staatenbund*—Europe as a confederation—and formed part of a chapter of his *Gesammelte Kleine Schriften*, published in 1879.[5] He criticized projects submitted up to that time on the grounds that they aimed to establish either universal monarchies or universal republics and ignored the fundamental problem of European organization, which was the preservation of the independence and freedom of the confederated states.

---

[1] See for the petitions to the governments of the civilized world, The General Resolutions adopted by the Peace Convention held in London on June 22, 1843. Published by Johnston & Barretts, London, 1843.

[2] Richard Cobden, an influential advocate of arbitration movement in England, made his famous motion in the House of Commons in favour of arbitration in 1849. It was lost; but a motion in favour of the reform of international law and arbitration was adopted by the House on July 8, 1873. Similar actions were taken by the legislatures of other countries. See *Advocate of Peace*, June 1874, pp. 41–5.

[3] See Christina Phelps: *The Anglo-American Peace Movement in the Mid-Nineteenth Century*, New York, 1930, p. 151.

[4] See Darby: *International Tribunals*, pp. 216–23.

[5] See Darby: *International Tribunals*, pp. 194–212.

c

Hence, he conceived of a confederation of specified states taking care to preserve their independence and freedom. He advocated the establishment of a code of international law[1] and an international legislature. The latter was to be bicameral; both houses were to promulgate international law by a majority decision, but their chief work was to enact a code of international law. On the one hand, he brought his international legislature into direct contact with the national legislatures of separate states, and, on the other, saw the codification of international law as an essential function of that international body.

James Lorimer of Edinburgh

The best-known project of the later part of the nineteenth century was that of Professor James Lorimer of the University of Edinburgh. In his work, *The Institutes of the Law of Nations*, he gave his scheme of international government.[2] He was critical of the tendency to take for granted a congress of ambassadors or plenipotentiaries as forming a congress of nations to represent the will of nations. He believed that a trustworthy international legislation must be the expression of the will of the respective nations rather than of diplomats representing only the administrative departments of the national governments. This he thought very necessary in the context of the course of events that had changed the relations between the governing and governed classes as a result of the growing strength of public opinion. In the danger of rearmament he saw the real and permanent obstacle to an international organization, and maintained that, until an effective substitute for separate action could be found, separate action would continue; questions of international disarmament and of international organization appeared to him to act and react on each other at every point and in every direction. He favoured, therefore, the creation of a central force—an international army—so extensive as to exceed any single force or combination of forces. He stood for the formation of a self-vindicating international government or organization with an international legislature, judicature, executive and exchequer. This government would essentially need a class of officials devoted to international affairs and rising above national prejudices and traditions of exclusive self-interest and patriotism. In other words, he conceived of an international civil service analogous to a national civil service. His ideas concerning the ways and means towards lasting peace were not without influence on the practical affairs of his time, inasmuch

---

[1] Discussed below in Chapter II.

[2] *The Institutes of the Law of Nations: A Treatise of the Jural Relations of Separate Political Communities*, 2 vols., Edinburgh, 1884. See vol. II, pp. 279–87.

as the government of the Netherlands presented his opinions at the Hague Conference in 1899.

The study of the most noted peace plans offered by individuals demonstrates a variety of ideas conceived as panaceas for world peace. But most of their authors attempted to build their schemes upon the political order of their times and in conformity with the historical development of international co-operation up to that stage. The mediaeval plans reflected the idea of the unity of Christendom; the projects of the era of emerging nation states conceived of a federation of kings and rulers whose representatives were to run any proposed international government. The schemes of the age of democracy, on the other hand, thought of a congress of nations representing the national governments which in many cases were elected by the people. And, as the democratic or parliamentary form of government in theory and practice came into use through the world, the force of public opinion came to be recognized as a powerful factor in ensuring peace. Continuing failure to ensure peace, the recurrence of war and the failure of governments to settle their disputes by pacific methods persuaded the internationalists and the pacifists to place increasing reliance upon world public opinion and, to that end, to organize a widespread peace movement.

THE ORGANIZED PEACE WORK

The organized peace movement had its beginnings in the first half of the nineteenth century. The ideas about world peace promulgated by individual thinkers, although they did not move effectively the leaders of their day, did not pass into oblivion. They inspired the pacifist doctrine and banded men together in their faith or defence and amalgamated to become a cause to live for, work for, and even to die for.[1] And as the frightfulness of the catastrophes of war increased in all dimensions, as the risks to peace multiplied, thoughtful men were driven together to reflect and to find a remedy. The organized peace work gained momentum in consequence of widespread disillusionment and continuous setbacks to the hopes of establishing a general and lasting peace. The rising tide of democracy, the recognition of the daily press as a potential tool for the cause of peace in educating the masses and influencing them towards peace, and the growing faith in the efficacy of world public opinion—these were the factors that inaugurated a new era of organized peace movement.

[1] See G. W. Knowles: *Quakers and Peace*, pp. 13–14.

THE FIRST PHASE: 1815 TO 1867

Peace Societies

The organized peace efforts began in 1815 with the founding in the United States of three peace societies—independently and in ignorance of each other's initiation. The world's first peace society, in New York, was founded by a local merchant of non-resistant principles, David Low Dodge, in 1805.[1] Another was founded in Massachusetts by Dr. Noah Worcester in 1814[2] and a third by two Quakers in Ohio. In England also, in 1816, the British Society for the Promotion of Permanent and Universal Peace was founded in London by William Allen with the support of his Quaker friends.[3]

The American Peace Society, into which the local American societies were merged, was precise in its aims from the start. It stood for one cause—international peace—and to that end sought the co-operation of all in the abolition of war. Its notable contribution was in campaigning for arbitration and a congress of nations as vital means to achieve lasting peace.[4] It urged the legislature of Massachusetts to establish some mode of just arbitration for the amicable and final adjustment of all international disputes instead of resorting to arms. On the basis of the petitions both privately signed and issued by the Massachusetts Peace Society,[5] the legislature resolved on April 28, 1838, to call a congress of nations for the purpose of forming a code of international law and establishing a high court of arbitration—perhaps the first such positive direction in the world given by a state legislature.

In England the peace and free trade movements persistently endeavoured to have the virtues of arbitration aired in Parliament. The first petition of the Peace Society was presented to both Houses in 1842. During the Anglo-American boundary dispute in 1839, resolved by the Webster–Ashburton Treaty, the British and Ameri-

---

[1] He published two pamphlets: *The Mediator's Kingdom not of this World*, New York, 1805, and *War Inconsistent with the Religion of Jesus Christ*, New York, 1812. See *Encyclopaedia of the Social Sciences*, vol. XII, 1934, p. 41.

[2] Dr. Worcester published *A Solemn Review . . . of the Custom of War . . .*, Boston, 1814 (reprinted by J. Lomax, Stockport, England, 1816). The American Peace Movement was distinctly religious in origin; it began with Christian men and membership of the New York Peace Society was confined to members of the Christian Church. See E. D. Mead: *The Literature of the Peace Movement*, World Peace Foundation Pamphlet Series no. 7, part IV, 1912, p. 4.

[3] For full account see Tracts of the London Peace Society no. 1 (undated), p. 17; C. S. Miall: *Henry Richard M.P.—A Biography*, 1889, pp. 29–30.

[4] Phelps: *Anglo-American Peace Movement*, pp. 45–50; for history of the American Society and development of peace propaganda see E. L. Whitney: *The American Peace Society—A Centennial History*, Washington, 1928.

[5] Petitions filed in 1835 and 1837. See J. H. Ralston: *International Arbitration from Athens to Locarno*, 1929, p. 128.

can Societies co-operated for the first time and the links between them steadily strengthened, to culminate in the Peace Convention in London in 1843.[1]

Although both American and British Peace Societies were preponderantly religious, they were internationally minded and influenced the creation of a public opinion on both sides of the Atlantic. Their positive achievements lay in enriching the pacifist literature, in sponsoring practical suggestions in several articles and in submitting a number of petitions to Congress and Parliament which led to a peace resolution endorsing Ladd's proposal for a congress of nations being adopted by both Houses of the Massachusetts Legislature in 1837–8,[2] which recommended that the President of the United States open negotiations with foreign governments to that end.

Under the influence of the American and British societies, the pacifist movement took root on the continent of Europe. The French Peace Society (Société des Amis de la Morale Chrétienne et de la Paix), whose honorary president was the American judge William Jay, was founded in Paris in 1821. In 1830 the Geneva Peace Society was formed by the Count de Sellon. Their objectives corresponded with those of their English and American counterparts, with whom they collaborated closely by sponsoring resolutions in the legislatures.

The peace congresses

The international peace congresses, an offshoot of the peace societies, helped to direct public attention to peace ideas. The first congress was held in London in 1843; others followed at Brussels in 1848, Paris in 1849, Frankfurt in 1850, London in 1851 and Edinburgh in 1853. Victor Hugo, Henry Richard, Cobden, Elihu Burritt and John Bright were the great figures associated with these events.[3] The congresses provided a common platform for advocates on both sides of the Atlantic to deliberate the best means of preserving peace, to further the active co-operation of the peace societies, to extend their joint spheres of influence, to capitalize the period of international calm by urging upon governments and the people the advantage of peace and the need to find alternatives to war—and to furnish

[1] See F. H. Hinsley: *Power and the Pursuit of Peace*, Cambridge, 1963, p. 93. He notes the direct influence of Bentham on the American Peace Society, whose constitution was drafted by William Ladd in 1828 and which was directly inspired by Mill's essay.
[2] A. C. F. Beales: *The History of Peace. A Short Account of Organized Movements for International Peace*, New York, 1931, p. 1; M. E. Curti: *The American Peace Crusade 1815–1860*, 1929, p. 29.
[3] Beales: *op. cit.*, pp. 54–5.

people with full information about the peace movement.[1] Their deliberations aroused wide popular interest in the peace cause.[2] As a result of the peace congresses, the peace societies embarked on a campaign to utilize every outlet for propaganda to form new auxiliaries to present addresses to the governments and rulers, and to submit petitions and memorials to the legislatures. Most of the petitions—and particularly in the United States—pleaded for the establishment of a congress of nations and for a code of international law.

Alas, the deep impression made on an inert world by the work of the peace societies and the congresses was obliterated by the Crimean War. The denunciation of war by peace societies earned for the peace advocates a reproachful epithet 'pacifist'. The Crimean War in Europe, the Civil War in America, the so-called mutiny in India, and rebellious and national upheavals in China and Persia clouded the period between 1853 and 1867, years of trial and decline for the peace movements. But in England the crusade against war was continued[3] and its triumph consisted in its being instrumental in obtaining the inclusion of protocol 23 in the Treaty of Paris, 1856, expressing the wish that states resorting to arms should have recourse to the good offices of friendly powers, which served as a precedent for later arbitral provisions. This was a landmark inasmuch as it was probably the first time that the assembled representatives of the principal nations of Europe gave an emphatic utterance to sentiments which at least contained a qualified disapproval of a resort to war and a recommendation to submit disputes to arbitration.

THE SECOND PHASE: 1867 TO 1900

The first phase of the organized peace movement was that of the preparatory work. It was the period of insistence upon the dogmatic principle that war was un-Christian in character. The peace efforts then had a predominantly religious colour. A curious mixture of Christian and humanitarian philosophy essentially conditioned the ideals and activities towards concerted action for peace among the pioneers of the peace movement. In other ages only individuals had dreamed of universal peace.

The religious nature of the crusade for peace was, however, on the wane[4] during the period of the peace congresses, when free trade,

---

[1] Miall: *Henry Richard*, pp. 53-4.
[2] See Official Reports of the Peace Congresses, London, 1861, and Miall: *op. cit.*
[3] Miall: *op. cit.*, pp. 100-18.
[4] The fundamental weakness of the movement was pointed out by J. T. Shotwell: *War as an Instrument of National Policy*, 1929, p. 16.

internationalism, the theory of congress of nations and of stipulated arbitration were fast becoming the major themes. The new trend mentioned imperialism, tariff barriers and irredentism as the principal menaces to peace; and a plea began to be made to discard abstract problems, to concentrate on economic realities and to stipulate arbitration clauses in international treaties.[1]

The second phase of the peace movement, beginning with the years leading to the outbreak of the Franco-Prussian War in 1870, witnessed the inauguration of annual universal peace congresses and inter-parliamentary conferences, and its culmination was the Hague Conference of 1899. Judged by the achievements of this period from the point of view of their motives, direction and quantity, it must be recognized as the most fruitful part of the whole history of the peace movement. Its most outstanding feature was the increasing influence exercised by the peace movement of the world upon government policies. During this period the peace movement launched by the peace bodies of Britain and America expanded throughout the world and was at last linked up within and outside legislatures. Despite their fundamental differences all sections of the peace movement combined by the end of the nineteenth century to pursue the common aim of realizing a condition where the adequate power of the world community would maintain common law and common justice, and public order would replace the prevailing anarchy.[2]

Countless peace organizations, formed all over Europe and America and even in the Far East, provided a new life and impetus to the peace movement.[3] They gave preference to active peace work rather than to mere non-resistance and anti-war propaganda. But they appear not to have possessed a common objective or a unified programme. Whilst the peace movement emanating from Europe prophesied a narrower ultimate idea of a United States of Europe in contrast to a Congress of Nations advocated by the older peace

---

[1] See R. Cobden: *Speeches on questions of public policy*, ed. J. Bright and T. Rogers, 2 vols., 1870, vol. II, pp. 179–89, 191–210. Also Helen Bosanquet: *Free Trade and Peace in the Nineteenth Century*, 1924.

[2] P. B. Potter: *International Organization*, 1928, p. 268.

[3] The following peace societies were founded: Ligue de la Paix in 1867 (changed to Société Française de l'Arbitrage entre Nations in 1883); Union de la Paix in 1867 at Le Havre; International League of Peace and Liberty in 1867 at Geneva; Netherlands Peace Society in 1870; Peace Committee of Berlin in 1874; International Law Association at St. Petersburg in 1880; Spanish Royal Academy of Moral and Political Science in 1884; Scandinavian Peace Society in 1882; Swedish Peace and Arbitration Association in 1883 at Stockholm; Norsk Union against War in 1883 in Norway; Peace Societies in Australia and Japan in 1888; Universal Peace Union in 1866 at Boston; and International Arbitration and Peace Association of Great Britain and Ireland in 1880 at London. See Beales: *History of Peace*, pp. 176–83.

societies, the emphasis in America was on arbitration, disarmament and the international unification of the American continent.[1] Nevertheless, the tactics adopted by the peace societies all over the world coincided sufficiently to allow a concerted and simultaneous action in the direction of disarmament, arbitration and the improvement of international law.

Another theme of the movement during this period was a universal campaign for arbitration. This received much impetus from Henry Richard's success in England. The passage of his famous bill in the House of Commons in August 1871, asking the British government to take initiative in the improvement of international law and in the establishment of the permanent system of arbitration, was a great achievement indeed.[2] In fact a wave of similar arbitration motions followed in the legislatures of several European countries[3] and also across the Atlantic. The conclusion of the Treaty of Washington of 1871, leading to the Geneva Arbitration of the Alabama claims and other awards which successfully settled long-standing Anglo-American disputes, may be regarded as vindication of the practicability of arbitration in the settlement of international disputes.[4]

In the United States, too, several motions of the legislature urged the government to initiate measures for a permanent system of arbitration as a substitute for war in determining state differences. This led to the adoption of arbitration as a principle of international law among the eleven American nations who signed an arbitration treaty on April 28, 1890, the first agreement to make arbitration obligatory for a Great Power. The Anglo-American Arbitration Treaty of 1897 was the first treaty in which Great Powers pledged themselves to pacific settlement in mutual disputes, though much of its value was lost because of reservations.[5]

The American Peace Society took the initiative in yet another direction. Maintaining that arbitration was not a panacea for all types of disputes, it stressed the need for judicial settlement in accordance with the rules of international law universally recognized and adopted in the form of a code and administered by a permanent

---

[1] The idea of pan-American collaboration received concrete form when the First Pan-American Congress met in 1889. See Whitney, *American Peace Society*, pp. 154–8.

[2] Miall: *Henry Richard*, pp. 192–201.

[3] See L. Appleton: *The Gradual Progress of International Arbitration*, 1882, pp. 20–3. Also Ralston, *International Arbitration*, pp. 133–6.

[4] J. B. Moore: *International Arbitrations*, 1898, is the repository of the history and awards of the principal arbitrations of the nineteenth century; see vol. I, pp. 495–678. See also R. L. Jones: *International Arbitration*, 1907, pp. 182–9; and *Herald of Peace*, 1884, p. 117, 1885, p. 165, and 1886, p. 71.

[5] For an account of arbitration between the United States and other countries see Ralston, *International Arbitration*, pp. 203–39.

body of jurists. Hence the Society adopted a series of resolutions seeking early steps towards the adoption of an international code and the formation of an international tribunal. David Dudley Field, the renowned American jurist and a pioneer in the codification of international law, embarked upon a crusade for producing such a code.[1] He formed in 1873 an International Code Committee of America to formulate a series of proposals, and, with Dr. J. B. Miles (the secretary of the American Peace Society, who travelled all over the continent of Europe to enlist support from jurists and leaders of the peace movement), inspired the establishment of two academic juridical societies in Europe at the end of 1873. These were *L' Institut de Droit International* at Ghent and the Association for the Reform and Codification of the Law of Nations (now the International Law Association) at Brussels.

Supported by the concern shown in international problems by the publicists, political scientists, jurists and other professional men and their organizations, the peace movement embarked on a more practical and positive search for some durable form of international organization. By the end of the nineteenth century it had developed, from the aspiration of idealists and religious mystics, into a movement favouring the creation of an actual international legal system and a political machinery. It sought co-operation with the legal profession for the reform and codification of the law of nations. It had sought co-operation with parliaments and governments, which was greatly facilitated by the inter-parliamentary conferences on peace, first held in 1889, and by the Inter-Parliamentary Union, formed in 1892. The Union, composed of members of parliaments who advocated peace, organized yearly meetings and aimed to bring before parliaments questions concerning the improvement of international relations and to discuss the most practical means of organizing world peace by simultaneous concerted agitation within all parliaments.[2]

The peace movement also sought to carry with it world public opinion in favour of peace through a series of Universal Peace Congresses in different countries, a series that has continued since 1889. The first Universal Peace Congress of 1889 revived the old series of congresses (1848-51) which was suspended since the Crimean War crisis. Whereas the Inter-Parliamentary Conferences assailed governments from within on disarmament and war preparations, the Universal Peace Congresses carried on an extensive propaganda to create an organized world opinion. While the approach of the

[1] Discussed below in Chapter II.
[2] For notable dates in the peace movement see *Peace Year Book*, 1910-11, pp. 96-7.

former was practical, that of the latter was idealistic. But both, engaged on the same problems, were complementary to each other. Both began by stressing the theme of the settlement of differences by an arbitral tribunal and, eventually, came to discuss also other questions of public international law, the organization of a society of nations and an international tribunal, law of war and neutrality, disarmament, private international law and other contemporary international questions.[1] The establishment at Berne of the Inter-Parliamentary Bureau in December 1892 (at Brussels since 1909) and of the International Peace Bureau in January 1892 (at Geneva since 1925) provided for the peace movement a permanent secretariat and well-knit organization for world-wide communication.[2] Thus by the end of the century the peace movement had taken firm root in Europe.

The peace movement was also strengthened by the formation of federations of national peace societies in France, Germany, Sweden, Switzerland and the Balkans[3] and of women's peace associations in England, Sweden and elsewhere. The Nobel Peace Prize was set up in 1897. The century closed with over four hundred peace organizations in different countries, linked through annual reunions as well as permanent secretariats. Along with other societies sympathetic to the movement, they steadily built up a world-wide body of men and women who were seeking a saner and better way for the establishment of some organization for the settlement of international differences. These people were the pioneers of humane and enlightened ideals in international politics and should be given the credit for heralding a new era—that of the League of Nations and the United Nations—in the twentieth century.

The peace societies had prepared much ground by the time the Hague Conference met in 1899 on the initiative of Czar Nicholas II of Russia. The most conspicuous achievement of this conference was the successful establishment of the Permanent Court of Arbitration, which fulfilled the dreams and aspirations of the peace advocates. Its great convention on the pacific settlement of international disputes was to a large extent based on the convention drafted by the Inter-Parliamentary Union.[4] When the century closed, therefore,

[1] For differences among the peace societies see Hinsley, *Power and Pursuit of Peace*, pp. 131–3.
[2] For the aim of the Berne Bureau see *Peace Year Book*, 1910, pp. 3, 4.
[3] French Peace Bureau in 1889, German Peace Union 1894, Swedish Peace Society by 1911 and Swiss Peace Society in 1894. In Latin countries the trend was towards multiplication, and in Anglo-Saxon countries towards individual and local multiplication but striving for alliance.
[4] For some connection between the Inter-Parliamentary Union and the Hague Conference, see *The Times*, December 16, 1898, and H. Evans, *Sir Randal Cremer, His Life and Work*, 1909, pp. 177–80. See also *Peace Year Book*, 1911, pp. 63, 64.

the advocates for peace had the satisfaction that out of two essentials
for a world organization—a legislature and a judiciary—the second
had been secured.

THE MOVEMENT IN THE TWENTIETH CENTURY

Before the first World War

Up to 1914 there were no spectacular achievements by the peace
movement. National and international congresses passed strictures
on wars, discussed current political problems and thrashed out projects for an international press union, for an international auxiliary
language, a general arbitration treaty of universal scope and
application, and an international university.[1] They concentrated on
popular peace propaganda and the exposure of the military and
naval expenditure of the Great Powers. Their work tended towards
the creation of actual political machinery and co-operation with the
legal profession in the reform and administration of international
law. They favoured an organized society of nations having four
bases: legislative council to draft a code of international law; a
judicial authority to apply it; an executive to watch over common interests; and a reduction of armaments to a police minimum.[2]

The marked revival of the idea of a federal union of independent
sovereign states was one of the chief characteristics of international
thinking in the early twentieth century. This was probably the outcome of the failure to make governments accept an effective system
of universal arbitration which, because of its voluntary nature and
the narrow interpretation of 'legal disputes' that it covered, did not
provide a guarantee of settlement of all international disputes. The
increasing popularity of the concept of Pan-America and the
Central American Court of Justice (1907) was another factor in this
revival.[3] The developments in the Pan-American Union were
believed to inaugurate the first step towards the federation of the
world. After 1890, one notes a marked revival of the popularity of
two main goals: the federation of nations, and the public or democratic control of foreign policy.[4] Other subjects touching on most of
the basic problems of international life were the principle of the
equality of nations, unconditional compulsory arbitration, peaceful

[1] See the *International Peace Year Book*, 1915, pp. 10–18.
[2] See Resolution X, official report of Seventeenth Universal Congress of Peace,
1908, pp. 171–8, 359.
[3] P. S. Reinsch: 'The concept of legality in international arbitration', *A.J.I.L.*,
vol. 5, 1911, pp. 604–12; see also pp. 451–9.
[4] Phelps, *League of Nations*, pp. 32–3. The Berne Peace Bureau endorsed in 1910
the idea of Pan-Europe on behalf of the World Peace Movement.

sanctions, a permanent international tribunal, territorial waters, and even the question of the organization of an international police system.[1]

Wartime (1914–18) and after

Neither the efforts of the peace movement nor the much-heralded plans of international socialism to prevent a general European war proved strong enough in the crisis of 1914. The vast majority of members of peace societies succumbed to the patriotic propaganda of their governments, the peace congresses ceased and the societies became disorganized.[2] Even most of the leaders of the Second International as well as of the International Federation of Trade Unions capitulated; in America, apart from the Quakers, the bulk of the American peace movement ranged behind the government in support of the war.[3]

Nevertheless humanity's great crisis aroused a sense of responsibility and pacifist thought moved new elements and organized groups among internationalists to apply themselves to the idea of international organization.[4] Sentiments for peace found articulation in a powerful movement by women sponsored through the Hague Congress of Women,[5] in non-resistance and anti-war movements[6] and in the formation of several new organizations to carry out an active programme and advocacy for the formation of a League of Nations. The conscientious objection movement of the pacifists turned into the No More War Movement which was founded in 1921, with affiliated societies in many countries and later developed into the War Resisters International—a universal pacifist organization.[7]

The new peace-planning groups—or the League of Nations societies—which took over a large part of the work formerly done by the peace societies departed from the pre-war piecemeal approach and stressed the need for more comprehensive machinery for world peace. The definite beginning of a practical movement towards a league of nations was the foundation in 1915 of the American

---

[1] The 20th International Peace Congress discussed these subjects at The Hague in 1913; see *International Peace Year Book*, 1914.

[2] *International Peace Year Book*, 1919.

[3] A. W. Humphrey: *International Socialism and the War*, 1915, pp. 34–103; also Whitney: *American Peace Society*, p. 293.

[4] See, for example, *Outline of the Plan by Henry Ford Peace Expedition*, 1915.

[5] See *Report of the International Congress of Women*, Int. Women's Cttee. for Permanent Peace, Amsterdam, 1915; also *International Peace Year Book*, 1921, pp. 62-3.

[6] *Int. Peace Year Book*, 1921, pp. 65–86.

[7] *Encyclopaedia of the Social Sciences*, vol. XII, 1934, p. 47. The International Conference on the History of Resistance Movements, 1958, deals with European resistance movements from 1939 to 1945.

League to Enforce Peace.[1] Its lead was followed by associations with like aims—The World Court League (New York, 1915),[2] The League of Nations Union (Britain, 1918),[3] the French Association for a Society of Nations (1918),[4] the International League of Women for Peace and Liberty,[5] the Central Organization for a Durable Peace,[6] the Union of Democratic Control,[7] and the League of Free Nations Association.[8]

The projects conceived at this time are too voluminous for full treatment here, but they were indicative of the fact that the war had welded national groups together to plan a league of nations along lines already well-explored by pacifist theorists in the past and to seek, under the pressure of the reality of the interdependence of states, the limitation of state sovereignty. Among the most noteworthy unofficial projects were those offered by: 1, the American League to Enforce Peace, led by William Howard Taft, former President of the U.S.A., and Theodore Marburg, a former U.S. minister in Belgium; 2, the British League of Nations Society, closely allied with a group centred on Lord Bryce and G. Lowes Dickinson; 3, The British Fabian Society, its most active member or draftsman being Leonard Woolf; and 4, the Central Organization for a Durable Peace sponsored by the Netherlands Peace movement.[9]

In the wartime projects it is true there existed no unanimity with regard to the fundamental details of an international community, such as a legislature to enact and codify international law, a system of arbitration and judicial settlement of disputes, provision of adequate sanctions to implement awards or decisions, universal reduction of armaments, or provisions for altering the *status quo* when necessary. But they all favoured the formation of a league of nations binding states to use agreed channels for settlement of all kinds of disputes in preference to resorting to war. Yet none provided for

[1] J. E. Harley: Documentary Text Book on International Relations, Los Angeles, 1934, pp. 35–6; also *Int. Con.*, vol. 1, no. 134, 1919, pp. 48–50.

[2] *Int. Con.*, vol. 1, 1919, pp. 51–2.

[3] Resulting from a merging between the League of Nations Society and the British League of Free Nations Association. See J. H. Latané (ed.): *The Development of the League of Nations Idea*, vol. 2, 1932, pp. 815–16, 818–19. Also Phelps, *League of Nations*, pp. 48–50, and L. S. Woolf: *The Framework of a Lasting Peace*, London, 1917, pp. 65–6.

[4] Phelps: *op. cit.*, p. 54, and Latané: *op. cit.*, pp. 822–4.

[5] *Int. Peace Year Book*, 1921, pp. 62–3.

[6] Led by the Netherlands Peace Movement. See Beales, *History of Peace*, pp. 298–301.

[7] *Int. Peace Year Book*, 1915, pp. 82–3.

[8] *Int. Con.*, vol. 1, 1919, pp. 37–46. For important societies down to 1921 see Sir F. Pollock: *The League of Nations*, 1922, note D, pp. 84–6.

[9] See Latané, *Devt. of League of Nations*, vol. 2, pp. 767–828; also Woolf, *Framework of Peace*, pp. 59, 61–125.

the *abolition* of war. In fact these projects were attempting only to co-ordinate existing methods of settling international disputes—judicial tribunals, councils of conciliation, commissions of inquiry, conferences for defining, altering and establishing international law —which had all reached a considerable degree of development through past state practices. Their value lay in upholding the principles and the philosophy which later flowered in the Covenant of the League of Nations.

Amongst all the peace movements during and after the first World War, the organized labour movement was most powerful as the world's greatest body of pacifically organized public opinion. Nationally and internationally it was able to bring its influence to bear on government policies. Irrespective of the failure of the socialist and labour movement to prevent war, of the breakdown of the Second International and of the divisions and dissensions of international labour, organized labour made a positive contribution towards peace.[1]

The labour movement as represented in the trade unions and socialist parties was not content with mere formulation of a peace programme but also sought an early conclusion of peace by democratic negotiations and put pressure on governments to state their war aims.[2] In parliaments and legislatures the socialists and labour parties assumed the rôle of government opposition to make their voices heard and publicized. The acceptance of their peace programme by President Wilson 'lent the prestige of his great authority to their demands, thus bringing them into the field of practical politics'. President Wilson's Fourteen Points and his diplomatic policy echoed the socialist and labour conceptions of peace by negotiation and of open and democratic diplomacy.[3] As far as the labour movement is concerned, the recognition of the just claims of labour, more strongly organized economically and, to a rapidly increasing degree, politically throughout the western world, had been a potent factor in stimulating the incorporation of Article XXIII of the Covenant of the League of Nations.[4] It marked a definite step

[1] See L. Lorwin: *Labour and Internationalism*, New York, 1929, pp. 73–96, and *International Labour Movement*, New York, 1953, pp. 45–6. Also R. P. Dutt: The Two Internationals, 1920, p. 3. For an account of labour's wartime peace programme see A. van der Slice: International Labour, Diplomacy and Peace 1914–19, Univ. of Pennsylvania (dissertation), 1941.
[2] G. D. H. Cole: *A History of Socialist Thought:* vol. IV, *Communism and Social Democracy 1914–31*, 1958, pp. 296–7.
[3] See van der Slice, *International Labour*, pp. 2, 208–57.
[4] 'The high contracting parties will endeavour to secure and maintain fair and humane conditions of labour for men, women and children both in their own countries and in all countries to which their commercial and industrial relations extend, and for that purpose establish and maintain the necessary international organizations.'

towards international co-operation for recognition of the need for the improvement of industrial conditions for which the labour movement had striven. The very inclusion of a Charter of Labour in the Treaty of Versailles and the formation of the International Labour Organization—a labour law-making or a labour convention-drafting body, representing, in addition to governments and employees, workers as well—attested to the powerful although indirect influence of the working class and to the widespread conviction that labour problems are international.[1]

The League of Nations emerged out of several official projects on January 10, 1920.[2] Despite its elaborately integrated structure, far in advance of any previous plan, it failed to rule out private war entirely and left nations free to go to war in certain sets of circumstances.[3] There was no code of international law for the Permanent Court of Justice to apply; the Court was precluded by its own statutes from making binding precedents. The League was neither a super-government nor an absolute guarantee of international peace. It remained, as it began, a league of governments and not of peoples.

Although this first great modern experiment of quasi-international government failed, the roots of the League of Nations were too deep and far-reaching to be destroyed. The whole League movement remains a matter of overwhelming importance in the history of mankind. It marked a stage in the development of a system of international government and created a consciousness that only as peoples and governments become willing to accommodate national policies to a world society of order and harmony can that system be perfected. The experience of the League and of other international organizations that functioned during the inter-war period (1918–39) provided a foundation for new international institutions after the second World War.

FROM THE LEAGUE TO THE UNITED NATIONS

The peace movement between the two World Wars was not a definitive movement. It expressed itself in a series of gestures. First, through the classic pacifism of Universal Peace Congresses (revived in 1921) and of international conferences of the International Federation of League of Nations Societies (held annually since 1919)

[1] The International Labour Code (1951) which is the work of the I.L.O. resulted from continuous and concerted international effort on the part of the labour movement as well as of national governments. See C. W. Jenks: *Law, Freedom and Welfare*, 1963, pp. 101–36.
[2] See D. H. Miller: *Drafting of the Covenant*, 2 vols., London, 1928.
[3] See Hinsley: *Power and Pursuit of Peace*, p. 149.

it strove to spread the League of Nations spirit.[1] The movement
believed in humanistic universalism based primarily on the faith
that human reason would build a better world; it urged the abandon-
ment of the traditional dogma of national sovereignty and the
doctrine of state omnipotence which it regarded as irreconcilable
with the organization of an enduring peace and with a spirit of
cosmopolitanism. It also contributed to the constructive study of
central issues in international affairs. Secondly, the religious pacifism, popularized by the International Church Peace Union of
America (1928), by the Pope and by the churches of the Christian
world, stood for Christian universalism. As an integrating force
towards peace in western society it conceived of no universalism
outside the spirit of Christ. Lastly, communistic pacifism professed
by the Third International and the communist-controlled labour
organizations was opposed to militarism and war, as an integral
part of the struggle of the proletariat to overthrow capitalism. It
demanded international control of the manufacture of armaments
and the gradual establishment of a supreme, democratically run,
international authority.[2] But the Workers' Movement, which at one
time was in the vanguard of internationalism and had an international executive and a commonly accepted policy, tended, during
the post-war period, to strengthen the state unit more than ever
before.[3]

After the Ethiopian débâcle, when the failure of the Covenant
opened the gates once again to rabid nationalism, rearmament and
war, and after the first shocks of the second World War, it was
because of the League experiment that public opinion all over the
world accepted almost as a matter of course that the first and most
indispensable need, after the war was ended, would be to rebuild
the institutions of the League of Nations.

The United States played a dominant part in planning the United
Nations organization. The formal completion of this, mankind's
most ambitious international structure, took place on June 26, 1945,
with the signing of the Charter which was a result of a series of conferences and preliminaries carried out between 1941 and 1945.[4] The
United Nations system drew heavily upon the pre-existing complex
international machinery and special purpose agencies of the League

[1] *Peace Year Books*, 1936–1940, for an account of the peace movement. See also
Quarterly Bulletins of the Int. Fed. of League of Nations Societies.
[2] Jane Degras (ed.): *The Communist International 1919–43: Documents*, 2 vols.,
1956, for resolutions against war and armaments.
[3] G. E. Lichtblau: 'Current trends on the international labour scene', *Year
Book of World Affairs*, 1963, pp. 195–218.
[4] L. M. Goodrich: 'From League of Nations to United Nations', *Int. Organization*, Feb. 1947, pp. 3–21.

which had proved to be durable enough for continued operation. It was also profoundly influenced by the dominant rôle played in its creation by the three Great Powers, the United States, the U.S.S.R. and the United Kingdom, whose collaboration during the war had offered a potential basis for an Allied Powers coalition. Small states also considerably influenced the Charter by successfully exerting themselves over amendments and modifications to proposals, thereby challenging the monopoly of the Great Powers. World public opinion was also a formative factor in the establishment of the United Nations; this was the reason for the U.N. being an organization of mankind: the expression 'we the Peoples of the United Nations', used in the Charter's preamble, denotes that the people rather than states were to constitute the basic elements of the organization. The preamble avers their determination 'to save succeeding generations from the scourge of wars' and 'to unite our strength to maintain international peace and security'.

In order to maintain a prohibition against the use of armed force it is imperative to substitute legal means for that force. The goal of human development, as the historical pattern of thought shows, and now so familiar and persuasive in large parts of the world, seems to be the gradual transformation of the world into a perfect legal community, where problems which formerly had been political could find a legal solution.[1] In the words of Professor B. A. Wortley, 'in this modern age every attempt at international co-operation for peace with justice must be regarded as more than ever desirable and, indeed, if humanity is to avoid the consequences of the destructive potentiality of modern science it is essential that social scientists and international lawyers should go forward with their unspectacular but essential task of promoting a blueprint for a peaceful and lawful future'.[2] The programmes sponsored by the United Nations and other organizations for the promotion of human rights and the progressive development and codification of international law offer the most likely means by which the experts may work towards the achievement of that future.

[1] W. Schiffer: *The Legal Community of Mankind*, 1954, pp. 3–4.
[2] B. A. Wortley (ed.): *The United Nations—The First Ten Years*, Manchester 1957, p. vii.

PART TWO

THE MOVEMENT TO CODIFY
PUBLIC INTERNATIONAL LAW

CHAPTER TWO

PRIVATE EFFORTS AT CODIFICATION

The movement for the codification of international law evolved, like the peace movement, out of a spirit of protest against the ravages of international anarchy. It was only indirectly a method of fighting for peace inasmuch as its primary object was the improvement of the laws of war and the regulation of conditions of warfare. It shared, however, with the peace movement the belief that the developing and perfecting of international law was the surest way to maintain peace. The codification movement was an expression of a natural impulse on the part of those who were interested in international relations to remedy the failure of national governments and to promote the law-making process itself in the community of nations in which the appropriate institutional forms had been rather vague, indistinct and irregular. This movement has proceeded along several lines.

The first has been in individual efforts by men whose natures moved them, in protest against the nightmare of international lawlessness, to conceive of the possibility of evoking order out of confusion by the publication of the law of nations in the form of precise and definite rules. This set in motion another process—the growth of a number of voluntary international associations which devoted themselves to the scientific study and discussion of international law. This second phase of codification—the organized movement sponsored by the scientific bodies dealing with international law—was responsible for the drafting and adoption, after mature deliberation, of model codes on a number of subjects. This work rendered great service to the study of international law from the historical, philosophical and scientific points of view. As the strength and influence of this widespread unofficial action grew, governments (which alone could really implement it) responded, though they did so cautiously and within narrow limits. They made official efforts at codification, either individually or in concert, and continued the process under the auspices of international organizations.

CODIFICATION PROJECTS BY INDIVIDUALS

JEREMY BENTHAM

The idea of codifying the whole of international law was first proposed by Jeremy Bentham, in the last quarter of the eighteenth century. He was unquestionably the first theorist to propose the replacement of international custom by a written code of law.

Generally regarded as the philosophical lawyer of his age, Bentham made his principal contribution in the field of jurisprudence; what he wrote on international law occupied only a comparatively small part of the eleven bulky volumes of his collected works.[1] But he was in his time the main influence in revolutionizing the science of international law and, at various stages in his life, he discussed the subject of codification.

In his *Principles of International Law*, comprising four essays written between 1786 and 1789,[2] Bentham first set out his proposals for the construction of an international code: i. revolutionary reforms in the regulation of interstate relations, renunciation of all colonies, rejection of offensive or defensive alliances, and disarmament; ii. the institution of a common court of judicature to settle differences between the several nations; iii. the establishment of a common legislature between states and of an international police force for the enforcement of the decrees of the court. Bentham did not conceive of a strictly judicial international institution. The functions of his proposed diet or congress were in fact similar to those of the Security Council of the United Nations of our own day.[3]

Bentham's proposals to establish a true international order were very relevant to codification because they provide the reasons on which a body of law and its accompanying arrangements in a society are grounded. These reasons appeared to be very startling at that time, but the subsequent experience of nations during the two World Wars eventually led them to pursue, in concrete terms, Bentham's postulates. The concrete steps taken in our times to bring about disarmament and the codification of international law not only attest the realism of Bentham's judgment but are also a tribute to his vision. Bentham's proposed diet or court of judicature and international police force may appropriately be described

---

[1] *Bentham's Works*, intro. by J. H. Burton, published by Dr. J. Bowring in 11 volumes, Edinburgh, 1838–43 (hereafter cited as *Bentham's Works*). For an assessment of his contribution to the science of law, see G. Keeton and G. Schwarzenberger (eds.): *Jeremy Bentham and the Law: A Symposium*, London, 1948.

[2] *Bentham's Works*, vol. II, pp. 535–61. The four essays are: 1, On the Objects of International Law; 2, On the Subjects or personal extent of the dominion of the laws of any State; 3, On War, considered in respect to its causes and consequences; 4, A Plan for An Universal and Perpetual Peace. The last is also published by the Grotius Society under the title *Jeremy Bentham's Plan for an Universal Peace*, introduction by C. Colombos, 1927.

[3] While Dr. Colombos, *op. cit.*, p. 7, maintained that Bentham contemplated both a common court of judicature and legislature, Dr. Schwarzenberger holds the view that his proposed court of judicature and the congress are one and the same organ (Keeton and Schwarzenberger, *op. cit.*, p. 82).

as forerunners of the present-day International Court of Justice, United Nations, and United Nations Emergency Force.

His views on codification

It was Bentham who coined the word 'codification'[1] and invented the term 'international law'.[2] The meaning he attached to codification is found in his 'General View of a Complete Code of Laws', published in 1802.[3] According to him, the object of a code is that anyone may be able to consult the law as he stands in need, in the least possible time; he was convinced that 'to be without a code is to be without justice'.[4] The code was conceived by him to be complete and self-sufficing, and in style to be characterized by force, harmony and nobleness. Once prepared it was not to be developed, supplemented or modified except by legislative enactment.[5] It must remove the inconsistencies of law and the uncertainties and complexities of customary or judge-made law. He recommended a competition for drafting codes, each, if possible, to be the work of a single hand. The existing codes of municipal law he criticized generally, saying that 'of all the codes which legislators have considered as complete, there is not one which is so'.[6]

Notwithstanding the fact that most of Bentham's ideas regarding codification—such as this last—have been discarded and that he never himself came within measurable distance of completing a code, he was acknowledged as the chief apostle of codification at the beginning of the nineteenth century. He offered to draw up complete legal systems for one country after another; although his offers were not accepted, nevertheless it is quite certain that his ideas had a great deal of practical influence.[7]

His views on an international code

For him the utility of the law consisted in its certainty, and the object of an international code was 'the greatest and common utility of all nations taken together'. He conceived of two parts to an international code: 'the laws of peace would be the substantive laws of the international code; the laws of war would be the adjective laws of the same code'; the task of the codifier would be 'to set

---

[1] See Sir Courtney Ilbert: *Legislative Methods and Forms*, 1901, p. 122.

[2] *Bentham's Works*, vol. I, p. 149 and footnote.

[3] *Ibid.*, vol. III, pp. 154–210.

[4] *Ibid.*, vol. X, p. 597 (letter to Daniel O'Connell); see also vol. V, p. 6, and vol. X, p. 429.

[5] *Ibid.*, vol. III, p. 210.

[6] *Ibid.*, vol. III, p. 206.

[7] *Bentham's Works*, vol. IV, pp. 535–94; see also Keeton and Schwarzenberger: *Jeremy Bentham and the Law*, chapters by S. G. Vesey-Fitzgerald, C. W. Everett and K. Lipstein.

himself to prevent positive international offences, to encourage the practice of positively useful functions'.[1] He regarded peace as normal, war as abnormal, and thought of devising means for preserving peace as well as for preventing war. For the prevention of war he suggested: i. 'Homologation of unwritten laws which are considered as established by custom'; ii. 'New conventions—new international laws to be made upon all points which remain unascertained; that is to say, upon the greater number of points in which the interests of two states are capable of collision'; iii. 'Perfecting the style of laws of all kinds, whether internal or international'.[2]

The code of international law Bentham had in mind would be complete in itself, requiring no commentary and consisting of the fewest possible general rules in which a whole system of law could be expressed in a logical order and in an unambiguous terminology. These ideas were elaborated in his work *Traité de législation civile et pénale*, published in Paris in 1802 by Etienne Dumont.[3] The twenty-third chapter of that work contained a *Plan du Code International*, which comprised a collection of the rights and duties of sovereigns to each other and was divided into a universal code and particular codes. The former was to embrace all the duties of the sovereign imposed upon himself and all the rights which he possessed in his relations with other sovereigns. The particular code for each state was to provide for recognition of the rights and duties possessed by that state, whether based upon express conventions or by reason of reciprocal utility. The laws composing a particular code were to be of two kinds: i. executed or executory;[4] ii. laws of peace and of war. The method employed for municipal codification was recommended.

Maritime and military codes were discussed in chapters 24 and 25 of the *Traité*. In the first of these codes Bentham apparently conceived the basic principle of the law of piracy, of the freedom of the high seas, of fishery rights, of innocent passage, of registration of vessels, and of the prevention of collisions. In the military code, he recommended the prescription of rules for the mitigation of the

---

[1] *Bentham's Works*, pp. 538–9. [2] *Ibid.*, p. 540.

[3] According to Dumont 'Bentham regarded this work as a sketch for his own guidance, and as too little developed to be offered to the public. . . . The spirit of philosophy and invention have not yet been applied in this general geography of the law. It is a subject upon which there have as yet been no human traces.' See *Bentham's Works*, vol. III, p. 156.

[4] Laws executed, according to Bentham, were 'those which regard the two sovereignties in their character of legislators—when in virtue of their Treaties they make conformable engagements in their collections of internal law', and the laws to be executed were 'those which were fulfilled by abstaining from the establishment of certain internal laws, or by exercising or abstaining from the exercise of a certain branch of sovereign power or those whose fulfilment concerned the personal conduct of the sovereign.' *Bentham's Works*, vol. III, pp. 200–1.

horrors of war, the protection of the civilian population, the maintenance of armies, and the operation of warfare.

But notwithstanding the magnitude and profundity of these plans, Bentham could not himself produce a single, comprehensive code following his own methods and technique. Probably his zeal for perfection, and a restless pursuit of one enterprise after another, prevented the completion of any code of law.[1]

However, Bentham's proposed code of international law of 1827 is very interesting. The manuscript is in the British Museum. Ernest Nys made its details known in the *Law Quarterly Review* of 1885.[2] The project was contrary to Bentham's elaborate concept as outlined in his *Plan du Code International* (1802), wherein he recommended a detailed code, containing not only the existing unwritten laws established by custom, but also provisions on all points which remained unsettled. His code of 1827 consisted of only eight articles, and it was intended to be adopted by the nations of the world acting on a plane of equality. It underlined certain fundamental principles to be agreed to by all states: i. universal equality—no state to pretend any authority over any other state on land or on sea, and all states to participate in any international congress on the basis of equality, whatever be its form of government (Articles 1, 2 and 3); ii. tolerance towards heterogeneity in religion and political structure of states (Articles 3, 4 and 5); iii. international peace, and friendly relations and co-operation between all states (Articles 6 and 7); iv. identity of national and international interests under the convincing force of utility (Article 8). These basic principles have a greater value for the present-day world, faced with dangerous antagonism between two major power agglomerations, than they had in Bentham's day. May not these principles provide a basis for the norms of international law on coexistence and for the strengthening of peaceful relations between states?

For Bentham the value of the international code consisted not only in removing international law from the sphere of merely conjectural law by transforming it into a binding code embodying the rights and duties of states, but also in serving as a directive to public opinion.[3] With that end in view the code was to be framed by a congress of civilized states, since it was only by the express

---

[1] A friend of Bentham's, George Wilson, reproached him in 1787 thus ' . . . your history since I have known you has been to be always running from a good scheme to a better. In the meantime life passes away and nothing is completed, *Bentham's Works*, vol. X, p. 171, Correspondence from Russia, letter of February 26, 1787.

[2] E. Nys: 'Notes édites de Bentham sur le droit international', *L.Q. Rev.*, vol. 1, 1885, pp. 225–31. Bentham's Code of 1827 is reproduced in the *Proceedings of the American Society of International Law*, 1910, pp. 223–4.

[3] *Bentham's Works*, vol. I, p. 75.

consent of states that effective codification of international law could be carried out—a truth that has been confirmed by the experience of the international community throughout the nineteenth and twentieth centuries.

Bentham regarded international institutions as the primary means of approximating interstate relations to the rule of law within the confederation of civilized states. His guiding principle was the transcendental one of utility,[1] which required a state to do the greatest possible good to other nations, implying the negative duty of not inflicting any injury on other states.[2] It offered a good pragmatic guide to international action with the possibility of transforming peace from the negative state of the mere absence of war into a state of 'mutual good will'.

Bentham saw no reason why the drafting of an international code should not include the 'adjustment and preappointed definition of all rights and obligations that present themselves as liable and likely to come into question'. For him, codification would be easier if it were resorted to at a time 'when no state having any interest in the question more than any other has, the several points may be adjusted by common consent of all, without any such feeling as that of disappointment, humiliation or sacrifice on the part of any', and at a time 'when no detriment to self-regarding interest, on the part of any having or by the part of any supposed to have place, no such cause of anti-social affection will have place in any of the breasts concerned'.[3]

His impatience with the vagueness, *a priori* reasoning, and inconsistencies of the natural law writers led him to attack the whole concept of natural law and the naturalistic school of international lawyers.[4] It inspired his numerous and vigorous legislative efforts to relate his practical legal propositions to definite social purposes and a balance of interests, and to stress the need for and to develop a technique of conscious law-making by codification as against evolution by custom or judicial law-making. He gave pride of place to treaties as a source of international law[5] because of the certainty they ensured in comparison with customary international law[6] and natural law as applied to international relations. Today international treaties are recognized as a principal source of international law[7]

---

[1] For a detailed study of his philosophy see Bentham: *Theory of Legislation*, 1931.
[2] Both duties were, however, subject to an important proviso—'saving the regard which is proper to its (states) own well-being'; *Bentham's Works*, vol. II, p. 538.
[3] Article 7 of Bentham's Code of 1827.
[4] He attacked Grotius, Pufendorf and Vattel. *Bentham's Works*, vol. III, p. 220.
[5] *Bentham's Works*, vol. XI, p. 34, his letter to Jabez Henry, January 15, 1830.
[6] *Ibid.*, vol. III, p. 162.
[7] Statute of the International Court of Justice, Article 38.

and as a powerful instrument for the codification and development of that law.

But Bentham's dynamic concept of law required it to be responsive to the needs of the community to which it was being applied and to reflect a consensus of the entire community rather than protecting only vested interests. He wanted the codifier to keep in view the main functions of law which consisted in: providing subsistence, aiming at abundance, encouraging equality, and maintaining security.[1] Thus emphasizing the protective function of law and laying the basis of a new relativist tendency in jurisprudence, which later came to be known as sociological jurisprudence, Bentham related international law to definite social purpose and a balance of interests. He wanted the categorical imperative—the greatest common utility of all nations—to be applied to the international code, since he never contemplated the code being based upon the existing law of nations. To him, to the extent that international law achieved the union between national interest and international duty for the eventual common good on the basis of the rational calculation of interests, it would attain perfection and become self-executing. Evidently, for Bentham, the reasonableness of international law was identical with its utility applied to interstate relations on the basis of reciprocity, which meant the 'greatest and common utility of all nations taken together'. For, 'the line of common utility once drawn, this would be the direction towards which the conduct of all nations would tend—in which their common efforts would find least resistance—in which they would operate with the greatest force—and in which the equilibrium once established, would be maintained with the least difficulty'.[2] Any codification keeping in view these premises would include progressive development of law and would not be restricted merely to the systematization of existing rules.

Bentham believed that once international legislation was based on rational principles,[3] a complete scientific codification binding the entire human race would be possible notwithstanding national, historical, political or cultural differences. It could provide a criterion which would be conducive to the peaceful settlement of disputes between nations on the basis of law. In other words, there would not arise a situation confronting a world court with the necessity of pronouncing a *non liquet* on the ground that there was no norm of international law applicable to a particular dispute.

[1] *Bentham's Works*, vol. I, p. 302.
[2] *Ibid.*, vol. II, p. 537.
[3] He believed in the possibility of rational legislation at national and international level: 'the law-giver should be no more impassioned than the geometrician. They are both solving problems by sober calculations.' *Ibid.*, vol. II, p. 19.

Bentham's views are undoubtedly not merely of historical interest. They transformed the abstract into the concrete, and the idealistic into the materialistic, and thereby laid the foundation of the doctrine of the codification of international law. Although he was the moving spirit behind the codification movement and law reform, the full value of his immense contribution has not been much appreciated. Schwarzenberger writes:[1]

Power and vested interests, irrationalism and emotionalism, official secretiveness and timidity on the part of scholars are nowhere more strongly entrenched than in the field of international affairs. It is, therefore, not surprising that Bentham's rationalist and uncompromising approach to the problem should be punished by being ignored or subjected to scathing criticism. In the words of one of the foremost authorities on Bentham in our time, 'No part of Bentham's teaching has had a reception at the hands of his critics more pathetic than his efforts to aid the cause of Peace.'[2]

For Ernest Nys, however, Bentham was unquestionably the first theorist to affirm the benefit that would result from the substitution of international custom by a written international law; he was the first to touch on the subject of Bentham's activity and constructive influence on the domain of that subject.[3] One cannot trace the progress of codification in England, in the United States, on the continent of Europe or in the Asian countries directly affected by European thought without concluding that the whole movement in favour of a clear, simple and concise law began with the criticisms made by Bentham very early in the nineteenth century, and that the soul of the great utilitarian and codifier marches on in the domain of national as well as international law.[4] Whereas codification of municipal law occupied public attention much earlier in the nineteenth century, it was not until the last quarter of that century that the same process in international law came to be seriously discussed in legal circles.

ABBÉ GRÉGOIRE

Like the philosopher Bentham, the philanthropist abbé and revolutionary bishop Grégoire also proposed the codification of inter-

---

[1] Keeton and Schwarzenberger, *Jeremy Bentham and the Law*, p. 152.
[2] C. K. Ogden (ed.), *The Theory of Legislation by Bentham*, 1931.
[3] E. Nys, 'The codification of international law', *A.J.I.L.*, vol. 5, 1911, pp. 871–900. *Idem*, *L.Q.Rev.*, vol. I, 1885, pp. 225–31.
[4] Assessments of Bentham's influence are found in: W. S. Holdsworth: 'Gibbon, Blackstone and Bentham', *L.Q. Rev.*, vol. III, 1936, p. 59; C. N. Gregory: 'Bentham and the Codifiers', *H.L.R.*, vol. 13, 1899–1900, pp. 344–57; F. N. Judson: 'Modern view of the law reform of Jeremy Bentham', *Col. L. Rev.*, vol. 10, 1910, pp. 41–54.

national law towards the end of the eighteenth century, also without sensible or material effect at the time. In post-Revolution France the work of reconstruction proceeded parallel with the work of destruction. The popular desire for new institutions, after the overthrow of the old régime, offered conditions which proved to be highly favourable to codification and the erection of a logical and harmonious structure. The French Revolution gave to the world the Declaration of the Rights of Man and the Citizen, a document which was to instal individualism as the dominant feature of the world. The Revolutionaries also realized that, as man lived in a society, nations could not live in a state of complete isolation. In June 1793, therefore, when the National Convention discussed chapter 25 of the Constitution, Henri Grégoire presented a *Déclaration du droit des gens*.[1] Containing only a brief enumeration of general rights and certain principles of international law in 21 articles, this was intended as an immutable code of laws, to be accepted by all people, and, therefore, to govern international intercourse and procedure for all time to come. It was not, however, adopted by the French National Convention though the author presented it anew on April 20, 1795.

The French Revolution, pacific at first, was so much cornered by the antagonistic and haughty demands of Austria and Prussia that war became inevitable. In face of the hostile, threatening attitude of the European Powers towards the Revolution, the National Convention could not accept the abbé's *Déclaration*. On its eventual rejection, Abbé Grégoire said: 'It is perhaps the first declaration of the law of nations which has been made. . . . . I had consecrated therein the eternal principles of the liberty of nations. The Committee of the Public Safety thought that these principles proclaimed in the face of Europe would irritate the despots with whom it was intended to enter into negotiations. . . .'[2]

The abbé was not a jurist. He was a natural law philosopher and his draft was, like Bentham's, in the nature of a general statement of the principles or just maxims, which should underlie a code of international law. The proclamation of the principles of the independence, liberty and equality of nations incorporated harmless truisms (Articles 1, 2, 10, 17 and 21). But the other provisions were not only much in advance of their time but also utopian and revolutionary in character—for instance Article 5, requiring subordination of the private interests of a nation to the general interest of humanity; Article 6, recognizing the right of every nation to organize and to

---

[1] Abbé Grégoire's Draft is rendered in English in the *Proceedings of the American Society of International Law*, 1910, pp. 226–7.
[2] See Nys: 'Codification of international law', p. 893.

change the form of its government; Article 7, questioning the right of a nation to meddle in the government of others; Article 8, stipulating that the only governments in conformity with the rights of the people were those based upon equality and fraternity; Article 15, laying down that an attack upon the liberty of a nation was an attack upon all others; and Article 16, providing that the leagues of states formed with the objects of offensive war, and treaties and alliances injurious to the interest of another country, would be deemed to be an attack against the human family. Several principles set forth in the *Déclaration*, in consonance with the spirit of the Revolution, challenged the divine right of kings, sought to change the idea of sovereignty by transferring it from the king to the people, and questioned the military alliances and the practice of intervention of the Great Powers in the affairs of other states.

The abbé's propositions resembled Bentham's doctrine in having a rational basis. The French Revolution was indeed the child of eighteenth-century philosophy, which was liberal and individualistic. Some have maintained that the codification movement in Europe was already in full swing before Bentham's time and that he was not greatly influenced by the continental movement.[1] On the other hand, Ernest Nys arrived at the conclusion that 'the project proposed in 1793 and 1795 by Henri Grégoire the constitutional Bishop of Blois, goes hand in hand with the teaching of the eminent Jurist'.[2] Possibly it was under the influence of Bentham's works that the French National Assembly commissioned Abbé Grégoire to draft the Declaration of the Rights of Nations.[3] If this was so there exists some link between Bentham and the draft of the abbé. Although Grégoire's draft was not by nature an international code, it has historical importance because it was the first attempt to present a declaration of a law of nations to the national legislature of a country.

EARLY NINETEENTH-CENTURY ADVOCATES OF CODIFICATION

No serious efforts towards the codification of international law appear to have been made during the disturbances that followed the French Revolution. Only a few incidental proposals for codification

[1] For C. S. Lobingier's view, see *Encyclopaedia of the Social Sciences*, 1953 edn., vol. 3, p. 609.
[2] Nys: 'Codification of international law', p. 876.
[3] Bentham was constantly in touch with the principal French reformers like Talleyrand and Mirabeau, Brissot and Lafayette. He addressed the French National Convention in 1793 (*Bentham's Works*, vol. IV, pp. 407–18). The National Assembly honoured him on August 26, 1792, with the title of Citizen of France (*ibid.*, vol. X, p. 281) and charged its Committee of Legislation with the examination of his works.

were made, which did not forward the movement but have been of some historical interest.[1]

Lorenzo Coline, a Florentine lawyer, prepared a draft code, *La Codice de guia delle gente in terra et in mare*, in 1815; 25 copies were prepared and sent to the leading powers represented at the Congress of Vienna, but the work apparently received no consideration.[2] In 1825 James Mill, one of Bentham's intimates, in his collected volume which contained his articles subscribed to the *Encyclopaedia Britannica* between 1816 and 1823, suggested an international code to be framed by some one person appointed by the delegates of civilized nations and subsequently to be sanctioned by them.[3] In 1846–7, a Spanish jurist Don Esteban Ferrater published at Barcelona a work entitled *Código de Derecho Internacional*, a two-volume collection of Spanish treaties with a short theoretical survey of international law, in the form of articles, and of the conflict of laws. This survey, under the title *Règles de droit international*, contained 414 articles, 'a veritable code' which made Ferrater 'the precursor of his many successors, whose names will one day be legion'.[4] In 1851 an Italian author Augusto Parodo published from Turin his *Saggio de Codificazione del diritto internazionale*, which dealt with the conflict of laws and only incidentally with international law (maritime law, the principles of diplomacy, and sanitary affairs).[5] In 1852, Louis Bara in his work *La Science de la Paix* proposed an assimilation of international legislation with national legislation in order to establish among nations similar rules of justice, as had already been established under national legal systems. He suggested the formulation of a civil code as well as a criminal code of nations.[6] A great service to the science of international law was rendered by Professor Katchenovsky, a Russian, when in two papers read before the Juridical Society of London in 1858 and 1862 he attempted to prove by reasoning and facts the real existence of international law and its authority, and thereby refuted the erroneous opinion of sceptics about international law.[7] Whilst holding that the view regarding the non-existence of a general code of nations as a great evil was very exaggerated,

[1] Nys: 'Codification of international law', *op. cit.*
[2] *Ibid.*, p. 881; see also Note on Private Codification of Public Int. Law, prepared by U.N. Secretariat (U.N. Doc.A/AC.10/25, May 16, 1947), also reproduced in *A.J.I.L.*, vol. 41, 1947, suppl. pp. 138–47, at p. 140.
[3] Nys: *op. cit.*, p. 882.
[4] J. B. Scott: 'The codification of international law', *A.J.I.L.*, vol. 18, p. 267; Nys: *loc. cit.*
[5] Nys: *op. cit.*, p. 885.
[6] *Ibid.*, pp. 884–5.
[7] 'On the present state of international jurisprudence', read on June 21, 1858, Papers read before the Juridical Society (1858–63), June 1859, vol. II, pt. II, pp. 99–110; 'On the present state of international jurisprudence', read on May 5, 1861, *ibid.* August 1862, vol. II, pt. V, pp. 553–76.

Katchenovsky recognized the value of codifying parts of international law, e.g. private international law and other doubtful and uncertain points of its public branch.

None of these works provided a specimen of international codification; it cannot be said that they created sentiment in favour of codification.

THE PROJECT OF DOMIN-PETRUSHEVECZ

The first attempted codification worthy of the subject and of very considerable value appeared in 1861, when a young Austrian jurist, Alphonse de Domin-Petrushevecz, published at Leipzig his *Précis d'un code du droit international*.[1] This project consisted of 236 articles and dealt with both public and private international law. Part I covered public international law and was subdivided into the Law of Peace (Articles 1–105) and the Law of War (Articles 106–175); in the second part, dealing with private international law, there were two sections: civil law (Articles 176–218) and criminal law (Articles 219–236). The code was conceived in a strictly juridical spirit and was written in a clear style.

The method of codification and the system of distribution of the matter were described in the introduction. The author claimed that his code was no platonic construction since it took account of the realities of international life. According to his views, since there existed no supra-national authority to enact law, an international code should pretend no more than a treaty validity based upon the free consent of states. The acceptance by states of an international code could be possible if the similarity between it and existing treaties could be established. The author was impressed by the fact that even in his day there was only a very small part of international law which had not been dealt with in some degree by numerous conventions between different states. These conventions showed the existence of principles often not only uniform but also expressed in largely identical terms. Wherever diversities of rules existed the author also found a tendency among states to make reciprocal concessions and to reach an agreement upon common rules. Where treaties failed to supply matter the author relied on widely prevalent opinions of the publicists. His conclusion was that the formulation of a code of common rules for the regulation of the relations between states, which could be acceptable to them all, was quite possible. He recommended preparation of such a universal code by an international commission which should edit, compile and codify

[1] A copy of the original edition, published by F. A. Brockhaus, Leipzig, is in the Edward Fry Library of the London School of Economics.

the rules found in the various conventions in force as well as in the promulgations of different countries, regulating reciprocal interests by harmonizing the divergencies and reconciling the conflicting opinions.

The Code of Domin-Petrushevecz represented an attempt to state the then existing rules of international law as well as to summarize the general principles which were found in contemporary treaties. It was only in the matter of maritime law that, owing to a striking diversity of opinion, the unequal distribution of forces and the actual preponderance of certain states, the author followed his own judgment. But in the code no reference was made to authorities, and no notes or explanations of any kind followed the articles.

THE PROJECT OF JOHANN CASPAR BLUNTSCHLI

In the same decade the renowned German–Swiss jurist, Johann Caspar Bluntschli, undertook the ambitious task of drafting a complete code of international law. He was not merely a jurist and a scholar of vast erudition but was also by turn legislator, publicist, philosopher, historian, friend of humanity, great teacher of law, counsellor of princes and a seasoned public figure.[1] It was he who had formulated the Zürich Civil Code, adopted by the Great Council of that city almost without a change in 1853. The codes of many other Swiss cantons were thereafter modelled on the pattern of the Zürich Civil Code. In 1866, Bluntschli codified military law for Germany—*Das moderne Kriegsrecht*—as Francis Lieber had codified for America in his 'Instructions for the Government of the Armies of the United States in the Field'.[2] Francis Lieber became the guide and friend of Bluntschli,[3] and it was on his suggestion[4] that Bluntschli prepared an international code which was published in 1868 as *Das moderne Völkerrecht der civilisierten Staaten, als Rechtsbuch dargestellt*.[5]

[1] H. B. Adams: *Bluntschli's Life Work*, presented to the Seminary of Historical and Political Science, privately printed at Baltimore, 1884, p. 23.

[2] See pp. 77–8 below. To Bluntschli, Lieber's work appeared so significant that he translated instructions into German and suggested the codification of similar rules for the German armies. See Adams: *op. cit.*, p. 16.

[3] In Bluntschli's letter of September 1879, published in *Lieber's Miscellaneous Writings* (ed. D. C. Gilman, Philadelphia, 1881), he spoke of the intimate personal connections in which he stood with Lieber, although only through the interchange of letters. He concluded: 'From 1860 to 1870, Francis Lieber in New York, Edward Laboulaye in Paris, and I in Heidelberg, formed what Lieber used to call a scientific clover leaf.' See also Ernest Nys: 'Francis Lieber—his life and his work', *A.J.I.L.*, vol. 5, 1911, pp. 354–60.

[4] Nys: *op. cit.*, p. 390. See also Elihu Root: 'Francis Lieber', *A.J.I.L.*, vol. 7, 1913, pp. 458 and 462.

[5] Translated into French as *Le Droit International Codifié* by M. C. Lardy, 3rd rev. edn., Paris, 1881. The first translation appeared in 1869, the second in 1873.

E

Thus the horizon of Bluntschli's scientific interest in codification widened gradually from the parochial limits of a Swiss canton, first to the German states, then to Europe, and finally to the law of nations. Bluntschli himself said of his project *Völkerrecht:* 'It is substantially the same kind of work as that which I early attempted with success at Zürich upon the narrow field of a little Swiss Republic with reference to private law. The principles of that work were now only transferred to the broader field of civilized states in general, and were applied to the moving stream of international relations and legal opinions.'[1]

Bluntschli's code consisted of 862 articles preceded by an elaborate introduction dealing with the nature, objects and basis of international law as well as with the general plan of the code. It dealt with the entire law of nations in three general parts: the law of peace (Articles 1–509); the law of war (Articles 510–741); and the law of neutrality (Articles 742–862). Each part was subdivided into books and sections. The Appendix contained Lieber's Instructions, the draft declaration of Laws and Customs of War on Land of Brussels, the Rules of Land Warfare adopted by the Institute of International Law at Oxford in 1880, and the Project of Arbitral Procedure proposed by the Institute of International Law in 1875 at the Hague session.

Bluntschli's project was the first of the comprehensive attempts at codification. He added numerous notes and explanatory commentaries to most of the articles, which showed his clarity of mind, courage and sincerity. He had no pretensions of codifying an ideal law of nations. In general he intended to formulate positive international law as actually practised and applied by states. But the code also included a number of scientific postulates and personal opinions of the author in regard to controversial questions. The result was that, whilst the code on the one hand was animated by the author's inspiration to reform and criticize the existing abuses of the law, supported by examples and historical facts to prove his point of view, on the other hand it caused some confusion, owing to the difficulty in distinguishing between universally accepted rules of law as such and the personal opinions of the author. But the great merit of the code consisted in demonstrating the possibility of scientifically stating the great body of the rules of international law in clear and precise terms. At the same time it set in motion the tendency to include in a code of law explanations, definitions, and doctrinal observations in the form of a commentary following the articles. This served as the pattern and the basis of various subsequent projects on codification. Such was the merit and influence

[1] Adams: *Bluntschli's Life Work*, p. 26.

of Bluntschli's project that it was quoted in French by statesmen throughout Europe and America. It was even translated into Chinese, in the very year of his death.

DAVID DUDLEY FIELD

Like Bluntschli, the American jurist David Dudley Field had much experience of the codification of state law before he published in 1872 his *Draft Outlines of an International Code*. This exceptionally gifted man laboured long and devotedly serving the movement for adopting a comprehensive code of substantive law in New York state, and the nation-wide copying in whole or in part of Field's 'Code of Civil Procedure' (1848) attested the value of the New York example. In the mid-nineteenth century the driving intellectual ambition and energy of this great jurist stirred debate over the movement for codification. It is said that 'intellectual pride and regard for the public welfare entered in imponderable mixture, into the amazing, single-handed battle which David Dudley Field waged for codification of the law from 1840 to 1887'.[1]

Field had the advantage over Bluntschli that he was also engaged in legal practice and was therefore more practical in his method and point of view. Since the passion for codification was almost an obsession with Field, it came about naturally that, while engaged in the struggle for the adoption of his New York codes, he also headed a movement for the codification of the law of nations. His brother's success in laying the Atlantic cable stirred Field's imagination and induced him to believe that a further bond between nations might be forged by the preparation of an international code.

It was at the Manchester meeting of the British Association for the Promotion of Social Sciences on October 5, 1866, that Field drew attention to the most important need to prevent or mitigate that greatest scourge of the human race—war—and to the uncertainty prevailing in many parts of international law.[2] He proposed that, if there were ever to be a uniform system of international regulation for the guidance of men, it must be by means of an international code, suggesting two methods of codification: one by a conference of diplomatists 'to negotiate and sign a series of treaties, forming the titles and chapters of a code'; the other, the preparation by a committee of publicists of a code 'embodying the mature and

---

[1] J. W. Hurst: *The Growth of American Law. The Law Makers*, 1950, p. 353. See also *Dictionary of American Biography*, vol. VI, 1931, pp. 360–2; H. M. Field: *The Life of David Dudley Field*, New York, 1898; Alison Reppy (ed.): *David Dudley Field, Centenary Essays*, N.Y. Univ. School of Law, 1949.

[2] D. D. Field: *Speeches, Arguments and Miscellaneous Papers of David Field*, ed. A. P. Sprague, New York, 1884–90, pp. 384–95.

scientific opinion of the best thinkers and most accomplished jurists', and then procuring the sanction of the different nations. He thought the latter method to be more feasible since, notwithstanding many difficulties in securing the assent of the nations and other obstacles, the governments would finally give way before the mature judgment of reflecting and impartial men. Thus Field conceived of the convention method as well as of the restatement method, and it is a tribute to his vision that, in our times, the United Nations has been following both of these methods.

On Field's suggestion, the British Association for the Promotion of Social Sciences took the initiative in appointing a Committee (of which Field became a member) to prepare the outlines of an international code. Because the widely separated committee members could not readily meet, the work moved very slowly, and Field proceeded in the task alone. With the assistance of some friends he published in 1872 *Draft Outlines of an International Code*, dealing only with the relations between states in time of peace.[1] In the second edition published in 1876, a second part on rules of war was added.

Field's project consisted of 982 articles and was divided into two books—Peace and War. The first book was subdivided into two portions, the first dealing with public, the second with private, international law. The book relating to war dealt with problems of war and neutrality. The author said in the preface to the 1872 edition:

The scheme embraced not only a codification of existing rules of international law, but the suggestion of such modifications and improvements as the more matured civilization of the present age should seem to require. The purpose was to bring together whatever was good in the present body of public law, to leave out what seemed obsolete, unprofitable or hurtful, and then to add such new provisions as seem most desirable.[2]

Unlike earlier draft codes, the *Draft Outlines* was set out in legal language and Field did not lose himself in a maze of theories and reflections. The work had the character of a code: the articles, in legal language, were clear; the comments upon them explained their origin, the authorities supporting them and the reason for their existence. It embraced in a fairly comprehensive manner the whole field of international law and drew attention especially to

---

[1] D. D. Field: *Draft Outlines of an International Code*, New York, 1872—is in the Edward Fry Library of the London School of Economics. An Italian translation appeared in 1874, a French translation of the 2nd edn. in 1881.

[2] It is interesting to note that Article 77 recognized the right of every nation and each of its members to explore and colonize any territory not within the limits of a civilized nation, and that the next article excluded the continents of Europe, America and Asia from colonization or settlement since every part of these areas was under the dominion of some established government.

the law as it was accepted and applied by the United States. This overemphasis on American practice was perhaps its principal defect.[1]

David Dudley Field made Bentham's principles his own, and because of his courage and persistence the actual practical results achieved by him stood, in a way, high above Jeremy Bentham's. The latter's contribution to jurisprudence related to the development of a scheme comprehending the nature and ends of the legal system and its institutions in general, and to the identification of particular defects and of suitable measures to correct them.[2] Field's services were primarily in drafting, publicizing and advocating codified reformative statutes, and in setting in motion an organized international codification movement through the Association for the Reform and Codification of the Laws of Nations (Brussels) and the Institute of International Law (Ghent), organized in 1873, of which he was a founder member.[3]

Field's code, along with Bluntschli's, was criticized by Professor Leone Levi on the ground that it did not include the positive portion of the law resulting from treaties and conventions.[4]

PASQUALE FIORE

A still more elaborate individual project on codification was that of an Italian jurist, Pasquale Fiore, who published his *Il diritto internazionale codificato e la sua sanzione giuridica* in 1890.[5] This work contained 1,985 articles, preceded by an introduction which in five chapters dealt with the organization of international society, the purpose of international law, its formulation, enforcement, etc. According to the author the purpose and scope of his work was 'to set forth international law, taking into account the existing law and such rules as may be capable of becoming law'. In other words, it intended 'systematically to formulate the body of rules which consist in part of those accepted by states in general treaties, in their legislation or in diplomatic documents, and in part of those rules

[1] J. W. Garner: *Recent Developments in International Law*, Calcutta Univ., 1925, pp. 714–15.

[2] Reppy: *David Dudley Field*, pp. 5–6.

[3] See pp. 63–6 below.

[4] Levi published in 1887 *International Law with Materials supplied for a Code of International Law* (2nd edn., London, 1898; Int. Scientific Series, vol. LXII), based heavily on prevailing treaties but giving no reference to sources or authorities.

[5] An English translation by E. M. Borchard was published in New York in 1918 under the title *Fiore's International Law Codified*. Fiore's work went through several editions. The 4th edn. (1909) was re-written, almost new work. The 5th edn., slightly enlarged, was published in 1915 and was the basis of the English translation.

found either in the popular convictions which have manifested themselves in our time, or in the common thought of scholars and the most learned jurists. As a natural consequence, the rules systematically assembled in the present volume represent in part present international law, and in part the international law of the future. As a whole it comprises the system which, in our opinion, is calculated to endow international society with a legal organization'.[1]

Fiore's project, like that of Bluntschli, was really a treatise on international law, as in both projects the articles expressed the views of their authors as to what the law was or should be, followed by notes, references and discussions. It was not intended like Field's project to be a code proposed to governments for adoption by them in its entirety. According to Fiore it was impracticable to codify at once the whole body of international law because the different governments could never be induced to agree upon a complete code.[2]

Fiore pointed out that he had drawn the materials for his proposed code from various sources: international conventions, being the most important source of positive international law; the proceedings of international congresses; the declarations of the representatives of governments participating in such congresses; such bilateral treaties as were concluded between a large number of states and containing common provisions; municipal legislation, such as military and naval codes; diplomatic acts of different states; custom; and the opinions of renowned publicists and text writers of authority.[3] These materials he used to elaborate a body of definite rules based on historical, scientific and rational law,[4] not a code of existing international law, but a body of rules which should govern states in their mutual relations *de lege ferenda*.[5]

The defects of the contemporary international legal system for which Fiore endeavoured to find a feasible remedy were several: the divergent doctrines of the principal schools of international law —the Anglo-American and the Continental; the absence of any recognized method of changing a rule of law or repealing an

---

[1] Borchard: *op. cit.*, p. 78.

[2] Borchard: *Fiore's Int. Law*, pp. 79–80, 725.

[3] *Ibid.*, pp. 91–8.

[4] Fiore substituted 'rational law' for 'natural law' in the new edition from which the English translation was made; he regarded the former as the law of reason and a residuary source from which positive law is derived.

[5] According to Borchard: 'His proposals are founded in part upon positive law, in part upon the accumulated labours of the Institute of International Law in the reform of international law, in which Fiore took so prominent a share, and in part upon his own solutions for the existing defects in the law of nations which matured thought and experience had dictated.' *Op. cit.*, p. vii.

antiquated or obsolete rule; the absence of any method of uniform interpretation of ambiguous rules; the absence of any provision for compulsory arbitration; and the lack of any substitute for force and war. According to him the solution lay in the legal organization of the international society by first determining the 'common law'[1] applicable to it, then ensuring the effective sanction of that law, and, finally, by providing for efficient measures and means to settle international conflicts and differences. To that end he elaborated his plan for the institution of the congress (a legislative body), the conference (a quasi-judicial body to settle political disputes between states) and the court of arbitration.[2]

It is interesting to note that Fiore was opposed to any permanent confederation of states where the Great Powers prevailed; that he believed that as international law could at no period be permanent and definitive but changed and grew with the times, so his proposed congress was not to be a permanent legislature but would meet only at periodic intervals or as exigencies required; that he regarded public opinion with great esteem and believed that the people should be specially represented in the congress since they had international rights distinct from those of the state; and, lastly, that he strongly supported collective action on behalf of the rights of humanity, believing that all measures and institutions established to assure the authority of international law must be considered within the collective protection of all the states.

Fiore's code was subdivided into four books: Book I dealt with persons and things subject to international law; Book II with international obligations arising principally from treaties; Book III with property as an object of international law; Book IV with sanctions of international law, comprising the fundamental principles which must govern the enunciation and legal protection of international law. The last part of the book dealt with war as an extreme measure of legal protection, which largely followed the lines of several Hague Conventions. The second and third Italian editions of the work concluded with the following sentence: 'The Primitive Juridical Society was the Family; the final Society will be the Juridical Union of Civilized Peoples.'[3]

It was for Fiore a matter of justifiable pride that the Hague

---

[1] *Ibid.*, p. 14. Fiore thought it might be better to employ the expression 'Law of Mankind' for his code of the law of humanity, though he clung to the title 'International Law'; *ibid.*, p. 35. Compare C. W. Jenks: *Common Law of Mankind* (1958).

[2] Borchard: *Fiore's Int. Law*, pp. 53–68; see also Fiore's address: 'Some considerations on the past, present and future of international law', *Proc. Amer. Soc. Int. Law*, 1912, pp. 17–33.

[3] Borchard: *op. cit.*, p. 730.

Conferences of 1899 and 1907 not only represented the triumph of his ideas but had also transformed into legislation many of the rules he had advocated. His ideal of *Magna Civitas* and the universalization of international law seemed to him to approach realization with the successful meeting of the Hague Conferences and the recognition of the periodicity of such meetings. In them he witnessed 'the triumph of progressive codification' and concluded 'one thing leads to another; we have made a good beginning and we are fairly convinced that step by step the international society will be given its legal organization and a structure adopted to the needs of civilization'.[1]

As the leading Italian authority on public international law, as a jurist, writer, senator of Italy and legal adviser to the Italian government, and as a teacher of distinction—he was professor of international law at the universities of Urbino, Pisa, Turin and Naples—Fiore performed eminent services in the development of international law. His works were accepted as authoritative outside his country and were marked by originality and an objective scientific point of view. The value of his project on an international code lay not merely in the fact that it gave expression to scientific views as distinct propositions and arranged in a systematic order with great clarity and precision, but also in indicating a course to be followed by others who might improve upon his work. Fiore did not entertain the pretension of legislating for international society and made clear that 'the codification of international law cannot be the work of one person or of a small number of persons. It will be the final outcome of the laborious efforts of a great many scientists and the latest expression of the legal convictions which, with the progress of civilization, will gradually be formed in the conscience of civilized peoples and will undoubtedly modify the function of diplomacy and the most liberal governments.'[2] It was clear to him that eventually a body of rules having the authority of law for all states could be proclaimed only as a result of the initiative of the most liberal governments. The principal merits of Fiore's code consisted in advocating codification of parts of international law step by step, in emphasizing official codification, and in making it clear—in most cases—whether a rule in his proposed code was one already in force or one of 'rational law' which ought to become positive law.

E. DUPLESSIX

Of the several projects of codes on international law published in

---

[1] Borchard: *Fiore's Int. Law*, p. 730.   [2] *Ibid.*, p. 725.

the early twentieth century,[1] the more important were by Duplessix, in 1906, and Internoscia, in 1910. Duplessix's work, *La loi des Nations. Projet d'Institution d'une Autorité internationale législative, administrative et judiciaire. Projet de code de Droit international public*,[2] comprised 786 articles in all. In his introduction, the author, referring to the earlier projects by Bluntschli, Field and Fiore, said that they were welcomed in the scientific world but met with no practical success owing to their failing to be adopted by governments. Moreover, he held, those projects were prepared at times when international law was going through an active period of transition, with the result that any attempt to reduce the law to the form of a code was not regarded with favour; they were not presented in legislative form but were recommendatory; they mixed up private and public international rules, made no proper distinction between a law and a regulation, were timid in regard to improvement of the law, and did not guarantee to the nations the independence and peace to which they so aspired. The author advocated encouragement to the private efforts at codification which would facilitate the work of future legislators. He claimed that the text of his own code was made easier than those of earlier codes by not burdening it with numerous explanatory commentaries and by not interjecting his personal opinions as to what law ought to be but by confining himself to the statement of existing rules of law.[3]

Duplessix's project presented an international treaty for the organization of a union of the civilized states of the world, with legislative, executive and judicial organs, and with guarantees of the reciprocal independence of the member states. It would adopt a code of international public law covering the personality of states, the rights and duties of states, rights and duties of individuals, international protection of individuals and nations, state territory, international obligations, pacific settlement of international disputes, war and neutrality. In such a project, Duplessix visualized a multilateral treaty, of the kind which in due course became the Covenant of the League of Nations and the Charter of the United Nations.

[1] Less well-known codes were: *Projecto de Codigo de Diretto International Publico*, by Epitacio Pessoa, a Brazilian jurist, published in Rio de Janeiro in 1912; and *Codified Manual of International Public and Private Law*, by Klein, published in Sweden in 1911. Copies of these codes not having been available, their quality and nature have not been ascertained here. See *A.J.I.L.*, vol. 41, 1947, suppl. pp. 144, for U.N. Sectt. Note on Private Codification. Mention may also be made of Professor Holland's *Laws of War on Land*, 1908.

[2] Published in Paris under the auspices of the Bureau of International Peace by Librairie de la Société du Recueil (Larose and Tenin), 1906. A copy of this work is in the Edward Fry Library of the London School of Economics.

[3] Duplessix: *Loi de Nations*, pp. 20–3.

He assigned an important place to the law of war and neutrality, for in his view the disappearance of war was impossible, and he stressed the practicability of the code in terms of its acceptability by the nations.

JEROME INTERNOSCIA

By far the most comprehensive code on the law of nations was prepared by Jerome Internoscia, a practising lawyer before the Courts of Quebec, consul-general for Italy in Canada for several years, and president of the International Code Company of New York, which published his *New Code of International Law* in 1910. It was simultaneously published in parallel English, French and Italian texts (Internoscia was Italian by birth, French-Canadian by settlement). His *New Code* embraced the rules of both public and private international law in 5,657 articles, presented in a logical and methodical way. It was divided into three parts. The first part of the code dealt extensively with public international law in 1,518 articles, covering the concept of international law, international community, international persons, states—their fundamental rights, territory, diplomatic agents, and international duties and obligations, quasi-international rights and duties of man and state protection, and international criminal law and extradition. The second part, Articles 1519–3464, dealt with private international law with a view to determining the most reasonable and practicable rules which might solve all possible conflicts of the different laws. The third part, Articles 3465–5657, dealt with international organization —international legislature, magistrature, procedure and execution.

In the introduction to his work, Internoscia fully dwelt upon the justification, object, merits and general plan of his code. In his view contemporary international law lacked clarity, precise form, and scientific basis, and, if it were to be freed from all its infirmities, obscurity, elasticity and its often palpable injustice, a simple patchwork or slight modification would not save it from inevitable discredit and decadence. He was convinced that the triumph of peace would be impossible until the codification of international law was accepted by all states and, by the will of the whole civilized world, a supreme international magistrature was constituted.[1]

Nevertheless, Internoscia was certain that mere codification of international law was not going to be a panacea for all the evils of interstate relations. He conceived of a legal community of mankind, comprising all nations of the world and organized for the juridical protection of international law, in order that all the controversies

---

[1] Internoscia, *New Code*, pp. xiii–xv.

between states must, without exception, 'be solved by juridical means provided for that purpose, namely, an adequate body of laws, magistrates to apply them, punishment for infringers, and a regular force sufficient to inflict the punishment that any state may incur'.[1] By codification he meant not merely systematization of the existing law, nor even simple modification here and there, but an *instauratio ab imis fundamentis*—a complete recasting of the fundamental doctrines, the usages and the law which were found to be obsolete or insufficient for the exigencies of the new life. Codification also did not mean replacement of what was redundant in parts, but entailed presentation of a more or less complete code dealing with all possible relations between states, as well as those between states and individuals. While his concept of codification was that of progressive development of international law, he seems not to have envisaged it as a long-term step-by-step process towards complete codification. He regarded international law as the highest type of law which included all the other laws of mankind, and which reconciled the welfare of the whole of humanity with that of individual units. He sought to reconcile the authority of the community of states with the freedom of states, somewhat analogous to that of Rousseau's General Will theory[2] which reconciled the authority of the state and the liberty of the individual.[3] In his view it was the function of a conference of the representatives of all states to proclaim international law, to carry out that law and to ensure respect for it by resorting to international force.

Internoscia's code was undoubtedly the largest ever written by an individual. Although he did not pretend to have entirely created the whole body of laws therein, and admitted that two-thirds of it was the production of many minds of many generations, to be found in books of international law, he claimed that the work was not mere reproduction and he necessarily created a great part of the doctrines which were woven into his system. However, he failed to cite any of the writers whose ideas he had borrowed, nor did he name the sources upon whom he had drawn so heavily on the plea

[1] *Ibid.*, p. xiv.
[2] According to Rousseau's theory the laws of state embodying the general will (which was nothing but the sum total of real wills of individuals aiming towards the general good of the community) did not encroach upon the liberty of the individual. By obeying such laws the individual was not obeying some external power but his own real will which found objective expression in the laws of state embodying the general will of the community. By being governed by the authority of the general will each individual was being governed by his own real will and thereby retained his freedom even if punished for his acts which follow his actual will aiming towards his selfish good; see Rousseau: *Social Contract*, trans. G. D. H. Cole, 1955, Book II.
[3] See for Internoscia's view of the freedom of nations reconciled with the authority of international community, *New Code*, p. xxviii.

that they were 'so numerous that the mere title of their works would fill a volume'.[1] But Fiore, in his 5th edition of *International Law Codified*, pointed out that Internoscia's code had textually produced forty articles of his own code relating to public law and similarly summed up principles set forth in many other articles dealing with public or private international law.[2] In fact, not only is it impossible to ascertain from Internoscia's code what doctrines were his own, so as to test his contribution, but also no typographical distinction has been observed between what was supposed to be a statement of the prevailing practice and what was claimed by the author to be innovations.

Notwithstanding these defects in Internoscia's code, it is undeniable that it showed evidence of his extensive industry and his high purpose, which was humanitarian to the last degree. His code emphasized not only the need for and usefulness of uniformity in international law, in the interest of universal peace and human welfare, but also the indispensability of a complete renovation or transformation of that law. Many innovations were in fact introduced:

1. Discarding the theory and practice of inequality of states, the New Code extended the domain of international law to all independent states, great or small, constitutional or despotic, monarchical or republican, playing an active part in the international community organized into a juridical and humanitarian association.[3] By equality of states Internoscia meant equality before the law as well as in the matter of rights.[4]

2. The principle of acquisition of territory by conquest was rejected, as the evils of conquest and abuses of protectorates were considered the very antithesis of rights and justice.[5]

3. While states alone were regarded as juridical person in international law, the New Code gave prominence to the quasi-international rights and duties of man, and of such associations or coteries as organized to pursue his intellectual or spiritual advancement.[6]

4. The sovereignty of state was limited to such liberty or independence as was 'compatible with the necessary organization of humanity, with the independence of other states, with the bonds that

---

[1] Internoscia, *New Code*, p. ix.

[2] Borchard, *Fiore's Int. Law.*, p. 76.

[3] Internoscia, *New Code*, Articles 11 and 12, p. 3; also p. xvii, and Articles 65, 71, pp. 12–13.

[4] *Ibid.*, p. xviii. However, to satisfy the ego of the Great Powers, Articles 67 and 68 recognized their importance by conceding to them the natural right to the imperial rank and titles; special representation corresponding tto heir importance was conceded by Articles 66 and 72. See also Articles 3466–3472.

[5] *Ibid.*, p. xix.

[6] Articles 1112–1432 and Articles 1210, 1211, pp. 192–247, 209.

unite the states among themselves, and finally with the welfare of the whole world.[1]

5. Perhaps the most important innovation was that the New Code provided for the abolition of war and its replacement by the forced execution of judgments, and by a complete and eminently practical international procedure having a scientific basis.[2]

6. Last, but not the least important, was the premise of the New Code that law and state were made for man to secure for himself the possibility of attaining prosperity and happiness. The Code pointed out ways and means whereby man's rights could be protected, and the corresponding duties for the protection of the rights of mankind could be imposed upon states.

Internoscia's code may have been regarded as unsound and unpractical at the time it appeared,[3] but many of the principles he enunciated remain absolutely essential for a stable society of nations —the idea of a precise and complete code of international law, adopted by the representatives of states in a conference; the detailed provisions for an international organization entrusted with legislative, judicial and executive functions; the rejection of the principle of 'self-help' in international life and the substitution of collective action or monopoly of force by the international community; the idea of fundamental rights and international duties of men and states; and the goal of the legal organization of the community of mankind. Of course methods and details of codification and of an international organization and its powers have tended to vary with the passage of time in the context of new developments, but, eventually, if the cherished goal of the legal organization of mankind, as advocated by Internoscia and the publicists before him, is ever to be realized the basic principles will be the same as set forth by the author of the New Code.

Such were some of the more important attempts made by individual jurists to codify international law. Although they by no means exhaust the list[4] they demonstrate that there were admirable specimens of codification which in some degree proved the possibilities of the process. At the same time they revealed the nature and the difficulties of the task of codification as well as the advantages of a restatement of the law of nations in the form of written rules. It was because of the interest generated by the individual jurists

---

[1] Article 61, p. 11.   [2] *Ibid.*, p. xvi.

[3] In Fiore's opinion the means recommended by Internoscia for the abolition of war and for providing all mankind with a legal organization made all his work 'a vain and useless labour'. According to him, Internoscia 'planned an unsound and unpractical undertaking'; see Borchard, *Fiore's Int. Law*, pp. 76–7.

[4] Nys: 'Codification of international law', pp. 881–900.

that the various learned societies and organizations were formed for the study of the legal science, the reform of the law of nations and the advancement of peace. It has already been mentioned that the attention of the British Association for the Promotion of Social Science and the Juridical Society of London had been drawn by Field and Katchenovsky respectively to the need for codifying international law. Other groups, such as the American Society for the Judicial Settlement of Disputes,[1] the Inter-Parliamentary Union,[2] the Universal Peace Congress,[3] the International Committee of the Red Cross,[4] and the International Maritime Committee,[5] produced formal statements of principles in the international field and stressed the desirability of codification. The section that follows is confined to the rôle of the principal scientific bodies which have since their inception continually and regularly devoted themselves to the development of international law.

CODIFICATION BY SCIENTIFIC ORGANIZATIONS

Among the unofficial organizations which have supplemented the work of individual jurists since the mid-nineteenth century by their collective statements on international law, four bodies have contributed greatly to the progress of the codification movement, namely the Institute of International Law, the International Law Association, the Harvard Law School and the American Institute of International Law. The American Society of International Law has also indirectly exercised an important influence in the development of international law. These non-governmental organizations have rendered public service by their widespread, continuous and intensely organized private action which has influenced the governmental agencies concerned with the codification of international law.

[1] For the aims and objects of the Society see *A.J.I.L.*, vol. 5, 1911, pp. 193–5.
[2] The Inter-Parliamentary Union, at its Christiania session held in 1899, charged its council with preparing the project of a code determining the rights and duties of states; at its London session in 1906 it favoured the codification of international law through the agency of an international law commission to be appointed by the Second Hague Conference; and at its Berlin session in 1908 it expressed its desire that the Third Hague Conference should carry further the work accomplished by the Second Conference.
[3] The Universal Peace Congress at its Stockholm session in 1910 appointed a committee to examine the project of a code of public international law presented by M. Arnault for submitting a definitive draft to the various governments, which should serve as one of the bases at the work of the commission charged with the preparatory studies for the Third Hague Conference.
[4] See below, pp. 141–3.
[5] The International Maritime Committee, organized in 1898 and with headquarters at Antwerp, had made noteworthy attempts in the direction of the unification of maritime law. A series of diplomatic conferences called at its suggestion drafted several international conventions dealing with maritime law. See L. S. Woolf, *International Government*, 1923, pp. 169–72.

THE INSTITUTE OF INTERNATIONAL LAW

In the formation of the Institute of International Law, founded on September 10, 1873, the celebrated jurists of Europe and America, many of whose names are familiar in connection with their projects on codification, played a prominent part. Among them were Francis Lieber of Columbia, Bluntschli of Heidelberg, Field of New York, Calvo of Buenos Aires, Lorimer of Edinburgh, Mancini of Rome and Rolin-Jaequemyns of Ghent. The original idea of bringing together some of the foremost international jurists in the form of a non-official association at Ghent came from Francis Lieber.[1] Bluntschli set forth the plan of the Institute with a view to creating a permanent and durable institution which should give form and life, alongside diplomatic action and individual scientific action, to a new aspect of international law—scientific collective action. The confidential note issued to the eminent jurists[2] explained that the proposed Institute was to serve as an organ for the legal opinion of the civilized world on the subject of international law; to promote by all means the knowledge, diffusion and development of the law of nations; to facilitate the codification of international law, and to study and elucidate questions of international law as current events demanded.

Originally launched with a membership of thirty-seven distinguished jurists representing different countries, the Institute of International Law has remained an organization of specialists with a limited membership or associateship of those chosen for their contribution within the field of international law. With its motto 'Justice and Peace', this 'exclusively scientific association without official character' has aimed 'to aid the growth of international law' by various means, including 'giving assistance to every serious attempt at the gradual codification of international law'.[3] Since 1873 the Institute has met annually or biennially in nearly a hundred sessions. Its numerous resolutions on public and private international law have not only been accepted as an authority in the diplomatic correspondence of nations, and in the adjustment of controversies by arbitration, but have also furnished the framework of various conventions of the first and second Hague Conferences.[4]

---

[1] J. B. Scott (ed.): *Resolutions of the Institute of International Law*, Carnegie Endowment for Int. Peace, 1916, p. xv, also p. vii.

[2] *Ibid.*, pp. xvi–xvii.

[3] *Ibid.*, p. xx, Article 1 of the Constitution of the Institute.

[4] According to Elihu Root the work of the Institute 'made possible the success of the official conference at The Hague, by preparing their work beforehand and agreeing upon conclusions which the official conferences could accept'. See his presidential address to the American Society of International Law, in *Addresses on International Subjects*, R. Bacon and J. B. Scott (eds.), 1916, p. 102.

In its early days the Institute was much concerned with the law of war and neutrality; but latterly the bulk of its work has dealt with problems of peace and pacific settlement, including such matters as diplomatic and consular immunities, the use of rivers, canals, territorial waters, the high seas and submarine cables, treaties, recognition, responsibility of states for injury to aliens, and many questions which have arisen in recent times, as a result of new technologies and ideologies, in the field of human rights, regulation of aviation and radio, and international organization.[1]

The Institute has provided some of the most careful and scientific specimens of codification, covering many of the most important branches of international law. Among the more comprehensive of these are:

1. The Draft Code of the Laws of War on Land, adopted at Oxford on September 9, 1880, and consisting of 86 articles, which facilitated and influenced the work of the first and second Hague Conferences.[2]

2. The Draft Regulations for International Arbitral Procedure, in 27 articles adopted at the Hague on August 27, 1875.[3]

3. The project on the law, jurisdiction and procedure in the matter of prizes, consisting of 84 articles, adopted in 1882 and 1883 at Turin and Munich respectively.[4]

4. The Draft of Regulations for the Navigation of International Rivers, in 40 articles adopted on September 9, 1887, at Heidelberg.[5]

5. The Draft of Regulations concerning the status of ships and their crews in foreign ports in time of peace and in time of war, in 46 articles adopted at The Hague in 1898.[6]

6. The Draft of a Manual of Naval War governing the relations between the belligerents, in 116 articles adopted at Oxford in 1913.[7]

7. The Declaration of the International Rights of Man adopted at the New York session of the Institute in 1929.[8]

8. The Juridical Nature of the Advisory Opinions of the Perma-

---

[1] Q. Wright: 'Activities of the Institute of International Law', *Proc. Am. Soc. Int. Law.*, 1960, p. 197.
[2] Scott, *Resolutions, op. cit.*, pp. 26–42; see also T. E. Holland: *Studies in International Law*, 1898, pp. 89–95.
[3] Scott: *Resolutions*, pp. 1–7.
[4] *Ibid.*, pp. 46–62. Further articles 85–122 were adopted at Heidelberg on September 8, 1887, *ibid.*, pp. 71–7.
[5] *Ibid.*, pp. 78–83.
[6] Scott: *Resolutions*, pp. 144–56.
[7] *Ibid.*, pp. 174–201. The American government attached much importance to this project and referred to the rules relative to the laying of automatic contact mines in the footnotes of the U.S. Rules of Land Warfare, War Dept., 1914, pp. 149–50.
[8] P. M. Brown: 'The New York Session of the Institut de Droit International', *A.J.I.L.*, vol. 24, 1930, pp. 126–8.

nent Court of International Justice—their value and significance in international law, resolutions adopted in 1937 at Luxembourg.[1]

9. The resolutions on the codification of international law adopted in 1947 at Lausanne.[2]

10. Resolutions on Asylum in Public International Law (excluding neutral asylum) and on Exterritorial Scope of Foreign Penal Judgments adopted at the Bath session in 1950.[3]

11. The resolution on the procedure for the election of judges to the International Court of Justice, 1952.

12. The resolution on Amendments to the Statute of the International Court of Justice, the determination of 'reserved domain' and its effects; and immunity of foreign states from jurisdiction and measure of execution, 1954.[4]

13. Resolutions on the distinction between the Régime of the Territorial Seas and the Régime of Internal Water, and judicial redress against the decisions of international organs, 1957.[5]

14. Resolutions on Legal Régime of Outer Space and on conflict of laws in the Law of the Air.[6]

The work of the Institute on codification (particularly on Territorial Waters and the High Seas) has been of much assistance to the work of the International Law Commission and the U.N. Conference on the Law of the Sea, held in 1958.

Work on the Institute's projects is carried on by committees under rapporteurs. After committee discussion over several years, both by correspondence and in meetings during sessions of the Institute, a draft is prepared which is fully debated in the general meeting of the Institute. A final amended draft is usually adopted after reconsideration by the committee concerned.[7]

However the Institute suffers some major limitations in its procedures. The high costs of meetings of committee members coming from all over the world and the infrequency of meetings combine to slow down the rate of work on projects. Although its members are the most highly qualified international jurists in the world, the Institute remains predominantly European in composition,[8]

---

[1] *Annuaire de l'Institut de Droit International*, vol. 40, 1937, pp. 268–78.

[2] *Ibid.*, vol. 41, 1947, pp. 261–2.

[3] English text of these resolutions reproduced in *A.J.I.L.*, vol. 45, 1951, suppl. pp. 15–20.

[4] *Annuaire de l'Institut*, vol. 45, 1954, p. 554; *A.J.I.L.*, vol. 49, 1955, pp. 82–3.

[5] *Annuaire de l'Institut*, vol. 47, 1957, p. 485.

[6] *A.J.I.L.*, vol. 58, 1964, pp. 118–22.

[7] See Scott: *Resolutions*, pp. xxiii, xxv: Article 17 of the Constitution, and Article of the By-Laws of the Institute. Also Scott: 'The two Institutes of International Law', *A.J.I.L.*, vol. 26, 1932, pp. 94–7.

[8] In 1960, of the 119 members (70 members, 49 associates) 89 were west European, 10 from U.S.A., 8 from Latin American countries, 7 from Asian and African countries and 5 from communist countries.

with the result that non-European legal and cultural concepts are less fully comprehended when projects are framed. However, more recently, more jurists from Asian, African, Latin American and communist countries have been admitted to membership. Lastly the working language of the Institute continues to be French (although English is allowed in the debates) which limits the accessibility of its work, published in *Annuaire de l'Institut de Droit International*, to French-reading scholars. Its projects are usually translated into English, as are its reports, and it has recently started publishing English translations of its resolutions.

As a body of eminent scholars, text writers and authorities on international law, the Institute has given a united expression to the most authoritative opinions on various aspects of that law, which in many cases have formed the basis of definite action by international conferences. The records of the International Law Commission, which has been working on the codification of international law under the auspices of the United Nations, frequently refer to the Institute's projects on related subjects during the preparation of its drafts. A closer association between the Institute and the national and international bodies connected with the codification of international law might be of great value.

INTERNATIONAL LAW ASSOCIATION

On May 15, 1873, an American committee was formed in New York with the title 'The International Code Committee', through the efforts of Elihu Burritt, the Reverend Dr. Miles and David Dudley Field. From this it was extended to form an international association to prepare a code of international law[1] and a conference was held in Brussels in October 1873. The meeting of international lawyers at Ghent in September of that year, which had founded the Institute of International Law, appointed a deputation of eight members to attend this conference, at which the Association for the Reform and Codification of the Law of Nations was established. Amongst the distinguished founder members were M. Frederic Passy, veteran apostle of peace in France, M. Auguste Visscher, eminent Belgian publicist, who presided at the conference, Sir Travers Twiss, Q.C., Thomas Webster, Q.C., Henry Richard, M.P., Dr. Bluntschli, David Dudley Field, Rev. Dr. Miles and M. Rolin-Jaequemyns. The title adopted by the Association expressed the conviction of most of its founders—especially the American

---

[1] For six resolutions passed by the International Code Committee see Reports of the First Conference of the Association (Brussels 1873) and of the Second Conference (Geneva, 1874), London, 1903.

jurists who had played a principal part in its establishment—that a code of international law was an essential prerequisite to any general resort to international arbitration. The subject of international arbitration always remained in the early period at the head of its programme, although it also turned its attention to more practical questions.

The Institute and the Association, though founded at almost the same time, have proceeded on different lines, both in constitution and in objects.[1] In contrast to the Institute, the Association welcomed to its membership not only lawyers, whether or not specialized in international law, but also shipowners, merchants, politicians, economists, philanthropists, and delegates from Chambers of Commerce and Shipping, and from arbitration and peace societies. As might be expected, its composition affected the nature of its work and the Association was less well-equipped than the Institute to undertake the task of codification. Instead of giving purely scientific treatment to the questions of international law, as did the Institute, the Association brought such questions into public discussion, seeking solutions from the suggestions of practical men and formulating recommendations likely to have practical effect.

In 1895 the Association's name was changed to the International Law Association. According to Article 2 of its constitution, its aims included 'the study, elucidation and advancement of international law, public and private, the study of comparative law, the making of proposals for the solution of conflicts of law, and for the unification of law, and the furthering of international understanding and good will'.[2]

The annual reports of the International Law Association give an excellent account of its achievements which have been predominantly in the field of international commercial law, maritime law, monetary law, conflicts of laws and medical law; of comparative legal procedure; and of administrative international law.[3] The

---

[1] For the debate on the mission of the two bodies see First Report of the Association for 1873–4, pp. 17–22, 44–6.

[2] Constitution of the Association, I.L.A. Report, 1962, p. xxxviii.

[3] In the field of public international law the following projects may be mentioned: Rules of Procedure for International Arbitration, and Rules of Jurisdiction in Territorial Waters, 1895; Law of Belligerency and Neutrality, and International Prize Court of Appeal, 1905; Regulations for the Treatment of Prisoners of War, 1921; Statute of an International Penal Court, and Law of Neutrality, 1926; Draft Convention on Extradition, Draft Convention on Maritime Neutrality, and Rules for the Governance of Territory occupied by Hostile Forces, 1928; The Budapest Articles of Interpretation of the Briand Kellogg Pact or Pact of Paris, 1934; the McNair Committee Report on the Development and Formulation of international Law, 1947. Since 1947 its work on the Rights of the Sea-bed and Subsoil Review of the Charter of the United Nations, Uses of the Waters of the International Rivers, Legal Aspects of the Peaceful Uses of Nuclear Energy, and Juridical Aspects of Peaceful Existence, has been noteworthy.

Association seems to have found it easier to bring about agreement among those who largely influenced its work—the merchants, underwiters, average adjusters—than to influence governments and to ask for legislation. Despite the priority and prominence given in its constitution to public international law, the Association has given much of its attention to commercial and mercantile law.

In the field of codification, the Association's achievements have contributed towards improvement rather than mere restatement of existing law. Although its projects have not always immediately resulted in treaties, conventions or laws, they have in some cases exercised an important influence on state legislations. By virtue of its seniority, the size of its membership (nearly 4,000 in 1964), the world-wide spread of its branches and its experience and achievements, the Association has brought a knowledge of the principle of international law to the attention both of the public and of governments.

The selection of topics for scientific investigation from among those which currently engage the study of the International Law Commission could allow both the Institute of International Law and the International Law Association to render more practical services in the field of codification of public international law.

THE HARVARD LAW SCHOOL

Under the auspices of the Harvard Law School the Research in International Law (commonly called the Harvard Research) was organized in 1927–8 in anticipation (but independently) of the preparatory work of the League of Nations for the First Conference on the Codification of International Law. A group of American scholars and lawyers having seen the need to make a scientific study of the three topics for discussion by the proposed conference,[1] the Research in International Law was initiated under the directorship of Professor Manley O. Hudson in November 1927 for the purpose of preparing a draft of an international convention on each of the three conference subjects: Nationality, Responsibility of States for Injuries to Foreigners, and Territorial Waters. Funds for the investigations were made available by the Commonwealth Fund and were further supplemented by a Rockefeller Grant.[2]

Besides the director, the organization of Research in International Law included an advisory committee of 44 (later 60) scholars and jurists, and executive committee of seven (later fourteen) members, and one reporter (in some cases also assistant reporters) on each

---

[1] The League Assembly Resolution of September 27, 1927: see L. of N. Offl. Jnl., 1927, sp. suppl. no. 53, p. 9.   [2] *A.J.I.L.*, vol. 23, 1929, sp. suppl., p. 3.

of the subjects. The reporters were assisted by special advisers. Working procedures were similar to those of the American Law Institute[1] and of the Institute of International Law. A draft prepared by the reporter was submitted to the advisory committee and then discussed and modified at meetings of the reporters and advisers.[2]

The Research, conducted in four phases, covers thirteen subjects relating to the principal aspects of the international law of peace and of neutrality. To the original three subjects new ones had been added after the first conference of 1930. The first phase (1927-9) was devoted to three subjects and draft conventions were prepared as follows: i. Nationality, with R. W. Flournoy Jr. as reporter;[3] ii. Responsibility of States for Injuries to Foreigners, with E. M. Borchard as reporter;[4] iii. Territorial Waters, with G. G. Wilson as reporter.[5] These drafts were circulated by the Secretary General of the League of Nations to the governments invited to the Hague Conference of 1930. A *Collection of Nationality Laws of Various Countries*, edited by R. W. Flournoy Jr. and M. O. Hudson, published by the Harvard Research, was frequently referred to, with appreciation, at the Conference.[6]

The second phase (1929-32) was devoted to four subjects: i. Diplomatic Privileges and Immunities, with J. S. Reeves as reporter;[7] ii. Legal Position and Functions of Consuls, with Q. Wright as reporter;[8] iii. Competence of Courts in regard to Foreign States, with P. C. Jessup as reporter;[9] iv. Piracy, with J. W. Bingham as reporter.[10] Also in 1932, a *Collection of Piracy Laws of Various Countries*, edited by Stanley Morrison, was published and in 1933 *A Collection of the Diplomatic and Consular Laws and Regulations of Various Countries* (2 vols.), edited by A. H. Feller and M. O. Hudson.

---

[1] The American Law Institute, a body of practitioners, law teachers and jurists, was founded in 1923 with the object of reducing the deficiencies of form and substance of the municipal law of the states of the U.S.A. It pursued the two-fold method of the restatement of the common law and the drafting of model statutes in selected fields of the law.

[2] *A.J.I.L.*, vol. 23, 1929, sp. suppl., pp. 4-9. The Advisory Committee met on eight occasions between 1928 and 1935. Although the drafts were made with reference to the 'Schedule of Points' drawn up by the Preparatory Committee of the League of Nations (February 15, 1928), the replies of the various governments to these points could not be made available to the reporters.

[3] *Ibid.*, pp. 13-79. This draft convention contained 22 articles.

[4] *Ibid.*, pp. 133-218. Composed of 18 articles.

[5] *Ibid.*, pp. 243-365. Composed of 23 articles.

[6] See recommendation of the Conference, Final Act, L.N. Doc. C. 228, M.115. 1930, V, p. 18.

[7] *A.J.I.L.*, vol. 26, 1932, sp. suppl. pp. 19-143. Composed of 31 articles.

[8] *Ibid.*, pp. 193-375. Composed of 34 articles.

[9] *Ibid.*, pp. 455-736. Composed of 28 articles.

[10] *Ibid.*, pp. 743-872. Composed of 19 articles.

During the third phase of its activity (1932–5) the Research dealt with three subjects: i. Extradition, with C. K. Burdick as reporter;[1] ii. Jurisdiction with respect to Crime, with E. D. Dickinson as reporter;[2] iii. Law of Treaties, with J. W. Garner as reporter.[3]

During the fourth phase (1935–9) three drafts covering the following subjects were published: i. Judicial Assistance, with J. G. Rogers and A. H. Feller as reporters;[4] ii. Neutrality, with P. C. Jessup as reporter;[5] iii. Rights and Duties of States in Case of Aggression, with P. C. Jessup as reporter.[6] Also, *A Collection of Neutrality Laws, Regulations and Treaties of Various Countries*, edited by Francis Deak and P. C. Jessup, was published in 2 volumes in 1939.

The result of the work of Research was published by the Harvard Law School in separate volumes and was also reproduced, with the same pagination, as supplements to the American Journal of International Law. Its presentation was uniform, in the form of draft conventions on each of the subjects investigated. Articles were accompanied by extensive commentaries of copious notes and references to opinions of writers, decisions of courts, national legislation and governmental practice. Almost all the drafts were accompanied by introductions and by appendices giving extracts from and analysis of municipal laws and treaties, official documents, and the projects prepared in the past by individuals and scientific associations. The addition of exhaustive bibliographies on each subject made the creative as well as the critical work of Research of particular value both to those concerned with the shaping of international law and to students and teachers of the subject.

These drafts, wholly unofficial in character, demonstrated the usefulness of independent co-operative effort directed towards the clarification and improvement of international law.[7] The McNair Committee of the International Law Association on the Development and Formulation of International Law spoke of the Harvard drafts as being 'a production of distinguished scientific merit from the point of view both of analysis and of the material', and recommended them as a basis of study for the formulation of rules on the various branches of international law.[8] The form of the Harvard Restatements set a pattern for future draft projects and the technique

---

[1] *A.J.I.L.*, vol. 29, 1935, suppl. pp. 21–240. Composed of 27 articles.
[2] *Ibid.*, pp. 439–635. Composed of 18 articles.
[3] *Ibid.*, pp. 657–1,204. Composed of 36 articles.
[4] *A.J.I.L.*, vol. 33, 1939, suppl. pp. 15–118. Composed of 14 articles.
[5] *Ibid.*, pp. 175–817. Composed of 114 articles and three annexes.
[6] *Ibid.*, pp. 827–909. Composed of 16 articles.
[7] See *Re Piracy Jure Gentium* (1934), A.C. 586; also *A.J.I.L.*, vol. 29, 1935, p. 148.
[8] I.L.A. Report on 42nd Conference, Prague, 1947, Annex 1, Section ix, 1948, p. 106.

developed in them has influenced subsequent work on codification. They are regarded as the most important contribution to the systematization of international law while at the same time indicating the desirable law in certain cases.

One handicap to the activities of the Harvard Research organization lies in the fact that it has always attempted to codify international law by means of international agreements.[1]

In contrast to the Institute of International Law and the International Law Association, the Harvard Research organization was brought in recent years into closer association (though in a limited sphere) with the International Law Commission, when it produced a new draft on the Responsibility of States for Injuries to Aliens, for the Commission's consideration.[2]

THE AMERICAN INSTITUTE OF INTERNATIONAL LAW

The origin of the American Institute of International Law lay in a proposition made in 1911 by two jurists, Dr. Alejandro Alvarez of Chile and Dr. James Brown Scott of the United States, to establish a scientific organization of an unofficial character, to deal with the international law of the American republics in the same way that the Institute of International Law was concerned with the law of the world at large.[3] The Institute was established at Washington on October 12, 1912. Its objects have been to aid the scientific development of international law by taking the initiative in establishing principles and determining rules that have previously been vague or ill-defined or even non-existent; to strive for unity of thought on international matters among the American nations as a prelude to the general agreement of the states; to aid the work of codifying international law by undertaking preparatory work; and, by becoming the organ of the juridical conscience of the American continent, to form and direct public opinion in American republics.[4] The constitution of the Institute explicitly stipulates that one of its purposes is 'to contribute, by gradual and progressive steps, to the codification of international law'.[5]

[1] Statement by M. O. Hudson as chairman of the International Law Commission at its second meeting, *Y.B.I.L.C.*, 1949, p. 15.
[2] See below, pp. 264–5.
[3] 'Project for the creation of an American Institute of International Law', circular letter issued to the European and American jurists by Dr. Scott and Dr. Alvarez, October 10, 1911: see *A.J.I.L.*, vol. 6, 1912, pp. 952–4. See also pp. 954–7 for Dr. Scott's Confidential Note of July 4, 1912.
[4] Circular letter to the publicists of the American republics by the officers of the Institute, October 12, 1912; *A.J.I.L.*, vol. 7, 1913, pp. 163–7.
[5] Article 2(3) of the Statute: Ruth D. Masters (ed.): *Handbook of International Organizations in the Americas*, 1945, p. 4.

Having active members in all the American republics the American Institute has met irregularly in several plenary sessions as well as in informal meetings. Moreover, the national societies of international law in American countries have been affiliated with the Institute, which co-ordinates their work and investigations in the field of international law and relations. The Institute publishes reports after each session and a quarterly journal, *Revista de Derecho Internacional*.[1]

Almost from the start the Institute has engaged in the codification of international law and the establishment of an American international court of justice. Its first well-known project was the Declaration of the Rights and Duties of Nations, adopted by the Institute in January 1916,[2] which stated, in six articles, the fundamentals of international rights—the right of every nation to continued existence, to independence, to exclusive jurisdiction over its own territory, and to equality with every other nation—and denied the right of every nation to commit, for its own protection or preservation, unlawful acts towards innocent and unoffending states. This project was based upon decisions of American courts and the authority of American publicists.

In 1924, at the request of the governing body of the Pan-American Union, the Institute drew up thirty projects covering major subjects in the field of public international law in time of peace,[3] which were reviewed in 1933 at the Union's Montevideo session, for submission to the Commission of Jurists.[4] It is significant that these projects were restricted to the international law of peace, since the Institute members believed that the law of war should find no place in the relations of the American republics.[5] A number of the projects served as the basic material for certain conventions eventually signed at subsequent international conferences of American states, and today form an integral part of inter-American international law. Further, the intensive study by the Institute for many years of the subject of the establishment of an American international court of justice resulted in several draft proposals which helped in the

[1] Other important Institute publications are: *The American Institute of International Law: Its Declaration of the Rights and Duties of Nations*, by J. B. Scott, 1916; *Le Droit International de l'Avenir*, by A. Alvarez, 1916; and *Codification of American International Law*, 1925.

[2] E. Root: 'The Declaration of Rights and Duties of Nations adopted by the American Institute of International Law', *A.J.I.L.*, vol. 10, 1916, pp. 211–21.

[3] Printed by the Pan-American Union under the title 'Codification of American International Law, 1925; see summary account by J. B. Scott: *A.J.I.L.*, vol. 19, 1925, pp. 333–7 and his address in *Proc. Am. Soc. Int. Law*, 1925, pp. 14–48.

[4] See below, pp. 135–6.

[5] See the statement of the Secretary of the United States at the time of presenting the projects to the governing body of the Pan-American Union: Scott, *A.J.I.L.*, vol. 19, 1925, p. 337.

promotion of both official and unofficial considerations of this project. The Institute's projects have demonstrated private American initiative and collaboration between the Institute and the Pan-American Union (now called the Organization of American States), and they have been an excellent example of co-ordination between private and official efforts for codification at a regional level.

THE AMERICAN SOCIETY OF INTERNATIONAL LAW

This society was organized at New York on January 12, 1906, as the result of a strong desire expressed at the Lake Mohonk Conference on International Arbitration (May 31–June 2, 1905) for the formulation of an association for the advancement of international law and the establishment of a periodical in English devoted to the expression of American thought on international law.[1] It has functioned as a valuable means of communication between jurists and students of international law on the one hand and the scientific and lay public on the other. Apart from its well-known services to the science of international law through its *Proceedings* and the *American Journal of International Law*, the Society has also taken some interest in the codification of international law. At its third annual meeting, April 24, 1909, it appointed a committee of nine members (of which Elihu Root was chairman) for the codification of the principles of justice which should govern the relations of states in time of peace.[2] Though its work was interrupted by the first World War, the committee submitted valuable reports between 1910 and 1918, including papers on the 'Primary Sources of International Obligations', 'Relative Value of Authorities' and the 'Plan of Codification'.[3]

Again, in response to the request of the Secretary General of the League of Nations, the American Society appointed a Committee for the Extension of International Law in 1925 with a view to co-operating with the Committee of Experts appointed by the League, to examine the question of progressive codification of international law.[4] Since then a committee on codification of international law has functioned continuously, and the Proceedings of the Society contain reports on codification submitted from time to time. The Society co-operated actively with the Harvard Research in International Law and the membership of its codifica-

---

[1] For the Society's history see Address by Richard Olney: *Proc. Am. Soc. Int. Law*, 1907, p. 23.

[2] *Ibid.*, 1909, pp. 260–9.

[3] *Ibid.*, 1910, pp. 197–227, and 1911, pp. 257–338, especially 'Outline of a Code of International Law' by P. S. Reinsch, pp. 313–20.

[4] *Ibid.*, 1925, pp. 172–6.

tion committee corresponded in many respects with that of the Advisory Council of the Harvard Research. In 1949 the name of the Committee on Codification of International Law was changed to Committee on Research in International Law.[1]

This committee reports on the progress of codification of international law by private or official bodies and thus the Society avoids duplication of effort by devoting itself to co-operation with other organizations which are doing effective work in this field. After the United Nations' decision to create the International Law Commission (1947), the American Society passed three resolutions: one welcoming that decision; another appealing to the government of the United States to encourage the selection of the persons of recognized competence in international law to serve on the Commission; and a third deciding to continue its committee on codification to improve opportunities of active collaboration with the International Law Commission.[2]

This account of the codification work of some of the more important scientific associations reveals that, unlike the individual publicists, these non-governmental groups have not undertaken any ambitious project of preparing a complete code of the whole body of international law, but have preferred the more modest task of piecemeal codification. They have limited themselves to special fields of international law and have contributed much to research in and the development of the techniques of codification. Their methods of working (appointing committees to study and report on particular topics, extended discussions, reflection and thorough reconsideration of the draft projects submitted by the reporters) have shown how codification may best be achieved. By advising governments, informing the public and sharing information, they have operated as 'pressure groups' across national frontiers to influence the development of international law.

The scientific associations should also be credited with stimulating new proposals, drawing attention to important developments which might require legislation,[3] and developing attitudes and understanding that would emphasize the long-term value of international

---

[1] *Proc. Am. Soc. Int. Law*, 1948, p. 13, and 1949, p. 161.

[2] *Ibid.*, 1948, p. 15.

[3] For example, the serious problem of the Indo-Pakistan dispute over the Indus river system was brought to the notice of the International Law Association by the late Professor Clyde Eagleton in August of 1954. The Association set up, on his motion, a committee to consider and report on the law governing international rivers: Report of the I.L.A. 46th Conference, Edinburgh, 1954, p. vii. The sound principles adopted by the Association in August 1956 at Dubrovnik, Yugoslavia, became the subject of critical study throughout the world: *ibid.*, 47th Conference, Dubrovnik, 1956, pp. 244–8.

co-operation and agreement with international decisions. In view of their significant contribution, continuing collaboration between them and the official national or international agencies dealing with the codification of international law is highly desirable.

CHAPTER THREE

OFFICIAL EFFORTS AT CODIFICATION

Notwithstanding the significant contribution made by individual scholars and scientific societies towards the creation of a world-wide movement and public opinion, and to the indoctrination of en-lightened sovereigns and statesmen in favour of strengthening international law by its codification, all this private activity has not of itself made international law. Though private efforts have promoted the law-making process, in the international community only the nations as such possess law-making power.

Throughout history the expression of public opinion has resulted in a readjustment of the relations between the rulers and the ruled, and in the participation of citizens in the government of their own countries; in a similar way, growing and irresistible international opinion has forced sovereigns and statesmen to formulate some precise rules for the conduct of relations between states. It was not until the nineteenth century, however, that international gatherings became common, for the purpose of devising measures for the settle-ment of the results of a war or for the regulation of interstate relations. The development of conventional international law by means of *ad hoc* conferences of representatives from several states— a system that reached its high watermark in the contribution of the two Hague Conferences of 1899 and 1907—is examined here after a review of the efforts of governments, acting individually or in concert, towards the codification of the rules of international law. For national states, problems connected with war and warfare are of prime interest; the desire to reduce the horrors of war led indivi-dual governments to lay down some fair rules of action for their armies and navies during hostilities.

EFFORTS OF GOVERNMENTS ACTING INDIVIDUALLY OR IN CONCERT

INITIATIVE OF INDIVIDUAL GOVERNMENTS

Russian initiative

What was perhaps the first attempt at codification was made by Catherine II, Empress of Russia, when, by forming the League of Armed Neutrality of 1780, she proposed to declare a new system of maritime law. This strong coalition of Russia and seven other

European powers aimed to secure the rights of neutrality and to put an end to the irregularities of the admiralty courts after England, in her struggle with the Americans in the 1770s, had endeavoured to suppress neutral commerce with her former colonies. The fundamental principles of the armed neutrality which the Empress proposed should be adopted as universal rules for the conduct of naval war[1] were as follows: to permit the seizure of neutral vessels only where the duties of neutrality had been unquestionably violated; to impose upon the belligerents the duty of commencing without delay judicial proceedings against neutrals, in accordance with a uniform, clear and legal system; to compel the belligerents, in case of unjust suffering to neutrals, not only to pay damages, but also to make compensation for the insult offered to the neutral flag; and to adopt these rules as the principle of a future maritime code.[2]

Several countries published their decrees in conformity with this declaration, which led to a diminution in the number of privateers. The principles of the 1780 declaration were later more fully developed 'and having been introduced nearly by all the nations of Europe into their commercial treaties and alliances, found support *even in America*'.[3] The principles of the declaration were incorporated into the conventions of the League of Armed Neutrality of 1780 and were approved by France, Spain, the United States and Austria. In 1800, they were re-affirmed, with some modifications, by the Second League of Armed Neutrality (Russia, Prussia, Sweden and Denmark). According to Lawrence the Armed Neutrality 'did almost as much to clear up the question of neutral rights as the Alabama controversy and the action of Washington in his second administration did to clear up the question of neutral duties'.[4]

American initiative and manuals of land and naval warfare

Land warfare. An event of far-reaching influence was the action taken by the government of the United States in 1863 when it promulgated Francis Lieber's 'Instructions for the Government of the Armies of the United States in the Field'. During the civil war in America, when an urgent need soon became manifest for written rules defining the rights and duties of commanders of large armies as well as those of combatants and non-combatants, President Lincoln charged Professor Francis Lieber of Columbia University,

[1] J. B. Scott (ed.): 'Declaration of the Empress of Russia regarding the principles of Armed Neutrality, addressed to the Courts of London, Versailles and Madrid, February 28, 1780', in *Armed Neutralities of 1780 and 1800: A Collection of Official Documents*, Carnegie Endowment, 1918, pp. 273–4.   [2] *Ibid.*, p. 402.
[3] D. I. Katchenovsky: *Prize Law: particularly with reference to the duties and obligations of Belligerents and Neutrals*, trans. F. T. Pratt, 1867, p. 61; see Scott: *op. cit.*, p. 118.
[4] T. J. Lawrence: *The Principles of International Law*, 1st edn., 1895, p. 104.

78 CODIFICATION OF PUBLIC INTERNATIONAL LAW

a distinguished German–American scholar,[1] with the preparation of rules for the guidance of the military commanders and troops.

The code prepared by Lieber in 1863 was issued by the War Department in revised form as 'Instructions for the Government of Armies in the Field, General Orders No. 100'; it consisted of ten sections subdivided into 157 articles.[2] It contained detailed rules for martial law and military jurisdiction, the rights of non-combatants, the status of enemy property, the treatment of prisoners and hostages, lawful and unlawful methods of war, and various kinds of lawful combatants, spies, traitors, etc. The Instructions represented the first serious attempt on the part of a government at codifying the laws and customs of land warfare—no work of this kind was in existence at that time in any language; it was accepted as standard by international jurists and exerted a profound influence upon the subsequent development of the law of nations as the basis of international understanding on the conduct of war. Moreover, characterized by generous conceptions and human sentiment as it was, it was adopted by several countries.[3] Similar ordinances were promulgated by the governments of the Netherlands in 1871, of France in 1877, of Switzerland in 1878, of Serbia in 1878, of Portugal in 1890, of Spain in 1893, of Italy in 1896 and of England in 1904.[4]

This movement towards framing national manuals or statements of the rules of warfare encouraged the Institute of International Law to adopt a Manual of the Laws of War on Land at the Oxford Session in 1880, and to call the attention of governments to the duty of promulgating authoritative instructions to their armies. The Republic of Argentina adopted the Spanish edition of the Institute's Manual in 1881.[5]

[1] Elihu Root: 'Francis Lieber', *A.J.I.L.*, vol. 7, 1913, pp. 453–69; also E. Nys: 'Francis Lieber—his life and his work', *A.J.I.L.*, vol. 5, 1911, pp. 84–117 and 355–93.
[2] See Root, *op. cit.*, pp. 455–9; for the relation between General Orders No. 100 and the Hague Convention with respect to the laws and customs of war on land, *op. cit.*, pp. 466–9. For text of General Orders No. 100, see Naval War College, International Discussions (1903), U.S. Naval War Code of 1900, 1904, Appendix, pp. 115–39.
[3] T. E. Holland, however, regarded them as unnecessarily long, not well arranged, and more severe than the rules generally enforced in a war between two independent nations: *Studies in International Law*, 1898, p. 85; for the testimony of jurists, such as Bluntschli and Laboulaye, see Nys: *op. cit.*, pp. 358–9.
[4] See Holland, *Studies in International Law*, pp. 85–7, and *Laws of War on Land*, 1908, pp. 72–3. Also H. H. L. Bellot, 'War crimes: their prevention and punishment', in *Problems of the War, Trans. Grotius Soc.*, vol. II, 1917, pp. 40–1. Professor Holland prepared 'The Laws and Customs of War on Land' issued by the British War Office in 1904; he made revisions to the manual after the Geneva Convention of 1906 and the Hague Convention of 1907, after which the work was taken out of his hands.
[5] See Holland, *Studies in International Law*, pp. 87–95, and *Laws of War on Land*, p. 73.

The U.S. Instructions became the basis of the project adopted by the Brussels Conference of 1874 and encouraged a congress of officers representing the armies of Spain, Portugal and various Latin states of South and Central America (held at Madrid in 1892) to adopt a draft on the basis of which the Spanish government in 1893 prescribed the use in its military academies of a *Cartilla de leyes y usos de la guerra*.[1] The American manual also influenced the decisions of the Hague Conferences of 1899 and 1907, which imposed upon the contracting parties to the Convention concerning the laws and customs of war an obligation to issue instructions to their armed forces in conformity with the annexed regulations governing land warfare, in response to which several governments issued manuals or ordinances.[2]

Naval warfare. The starting point in the preparation and issue of codes relating to the conduct of naval forces in maritime warfare should be regarded as the famous Declaration of Paris of 1856 which formulated and reformed certain rules in this field and which received the explicit or tacit consent of all maritime powers.[3]

Following the Declaration of Paris, governments promulgated their own maritime regulations: Norway in 1860, Prussia in 1861, Sweden in 1864, Britain in 1866, Russia in 1895, U.S.A. in 1900, Italy in 1908, Germany in 1909, France in 1912 and Austro-Hungary in 1913.[4] The British *Manual of Naval Prize Law*, for the guidance of Royal Navy officers in maritime war, was prepared by Sir Godfrey Lushington in 1866. It contained 303 articles grouped in 18 chapters and served as the basis of the later manual of naval prize law of 326 articles, prepared by Professor T. E. Holland and issued by the Admiralty in 1888.[5] This was a veritable code of maritime law, containing a systematic exposé of the views of the British government relating to the rights of belligerents in maritime warfare; it was based upon treaties, conventions, usages, and the decisions of British Prize Courts. Although it was a comprehensive code, it did not conform to contemporary developments in the law of maritime warfare. In contrast, the naval code of the United States, prepared by Captain Stockton of the U.S. Navy and President of the Naval War College on the lines of and for purposes similar to those of Lieber's Instructions, was a brief document of 55 articles. Issued in 1900 by the Secretary of the Navy, this code incorporated the principles of the Geneva Convention (1864) and the Hague Con-

---

[1] Holland: *Studies in International Law*, p. 87, n. 1.

[2] Nys: 'Francis Lieber', *op. cit.*, p. 86. J. W. Garner: *Recent Developments in International Law*, Calcutta University, 1925, pp. 726–32.

[3] See pp. 82–3 below.   [4] Garner: *op. cit.*, pp. 726–40.

[5] T. E. Holland: *A Valedictory Retrospect (1874–1910) being a lecture delivered to All Souls College*, June 17, 1910 (monograph), pp. 13–15.

vention (1899). Moreover, it went further than current doctrine and state practice in Europe by narrowly restricting the right of bombardment, forbidding the use of false colours, proclaiming the absolute immunity of innocent coastal fishing vessels, exempting neutral ships under convoy from search, and by speaking in clear terms about the immunity of neutral mail steamers and their mail bags.[1]

The American Naval Code was much commended as worthy of being followed by other governments.[2] Although it was revoked by the U.S. Secretary of the Navy in 1904—not because of any change of views as to the rules but because many of the rules, while binding on U.S. naval forces, would put them at a disadvantage as against the forces of other powers in Europe which did not accept or follow them—the United States delegation at the Hague Conference of 1907 nevertheless urged that it should remain the basis for the formulation of international rules of war. In 1918 the United States adopted a new code, 'Instructions to the Navy of the United States governing Maritime Warfare', which consisted of 113 articles and substantially followed the general line of the code of 1900 while conforming to international treaties and conventions, to which the United States was party, and to the statutes, practice and attitude of the United States as determined by court decisions and pronouncements.

Thus, a movement initiated by the United States of America in 1863 to define and determine with precision the laws and usages of war resulted in the partial codification by many countries of the laws of land and maritime warfare. These manuals, however, were in no sense internationally binding, being only unilateral acts on the part of individual governments. Nevertheless they were valuable in that they were declaratory of precise rules on the part of the governments concerned. They demonstrated the advantages of precise written rules and pointed the way to potential codification in the future. In fact they inaugurated such codification at an international level.

INTERNATIONAL CONFERENCES

The groundwork for the next step in official codification had been laid much earlier in the nineteenth century, starting with the law-

[1] For the history of the preparation of the code, see Naval War College, *International Law Discussions 1903*, 1904, pp. 5–7; for the text see *ibid.*, pp. 103–14; also *Proc. Am. Soc. Int. Law*, 1908, p. 104.
[2] T. E. Holland: 'Letters to *The Times* upon war and neutrality, 1881–1909', 1909, especially April 8, 1901, pp. 29–32.

making treaties signed in 1814–15 after the Napoleonic Wars. The conference of states was summoned after those conflicts primarily because the interests of so many states were involved. At this and later conferences, however, broader questions of general interest arose, and states participating in the conferences discovered in multilateral treaties a means of directing and controlling the conduct of the signatories, by express rules. These public treaties, concluded by numerous powerful states, came to be regarded as so extensively authoritative that they became part of the general law of nations—the statutory part.

Congress of Vienna 1815

No serious attempt had been made in the eighteenth century to realize any of the many projects that had been elaborated by philosophers and jurists for the reorganization of international life on a basis of law. The Napoleonic Wars destroyed the old feudal Europe and sowed the seeds of a new and regenerated Europe whose reconstruction was the task of the four victorious powers, Britain, Russia, Prussia and Austria. They faced this problem at the Congress of Vienna in 1814–15, when a first move was made in the direction of the international control of interstate relations.

The Congress of Vienna designed a programme of peace similar to that of one hundred and thirty years later, envisaging peace with a security system. At Vienna the participating powers, without yielding any right of sovereignty to a higher unit of which the Congress might have become the first parliament, became signatory to the Act of the Congress, which they obeyed for a long period. The special importance of the Congress lay in the facts that it rearranged the map of Europe (in itself an experiment in political science under the auspices of leading nations), established the new German Confederation, and concerned itself with several important aspects of general problems of international law.[1] It proclaimed the principle of free navigation for riparian as well as non-riparian states in regard to international rivers; the rules laid down at the Congress for the freedom of the Rhine and other European rivers served as models for all subsequent international treaties. It recognized and guaranteed the neutrality of Switzerland which had been seriously violated during the Napoleonic Wars. In the field of diplomatic representation it defined several grades which have virtually persisted up to the present day. Yet another important problem dealt with by the Congress was the suppression of the then flourishing slave trade, which action was sponsored principally by

[1] See G. Butler and S. Maccoby: *The Development of International Law*, 1928, pp. 352–6.

G

the British government under the pressure of public opinion in Britain on religious and humanitarian grounds. Although the Congress did not prohibit the slave trade but merely condemned it in general terms, the perseverance and humanitarian efforts of Britain led to the conclusion of a number of bilateral treaties which eventually culminated in the comprehensive and effective General Act of the Anti-Slavery Conference of Brussels in 1890.[1]

Thus the Congress of Vienna constituted the first attempt to establish an international system for Europe and to lay down in international relations the basis for public law which, as the nucleus of an international public code (to which additions were to be made as occasion required), was destined to guide the relations of the Great Powers during the greater part of the nineteenth century.[2]

Declaration of Paris 1856

Following the close of the Crimean War, the Congress of Paris of 1856 was an assembly similar to the Congress of Vienna. It assumed to a limited degree the rôle of an international legislature and formulated four important rules relating to privateering, blockade, the immunity from capture of private property on neutral ships, and the immunity of non-contraband neutral property under an enemy flag. While the rules relating to blockade and the immunity of neutral goods under an enemy flag were in the main merely declaratory of general opinion and practice, those abolishing privateering and exempting enemy goods under a neutral flag from capture were in the nature of a progressive development of law, inasmuch as they had not previously been regarded as obligatory, save where explicitly made so by a treaty stipulation.[3]

The Declaration was a separate instrument issued by the signatory powers of the Paris Treaty at the end of the Crimean War (in which France and England, assisted by Austria, had been opposed to Russia). All the countries of the world were invited to participate and most of the important maritime countries, such as Argentina, Brazil, Japan and Spain, acceded to it. The United States did not accede, since it considered privateering as a necessary tool for countries not possessed of a strong navy.

Thus the Declaration of Paris, which aimed at universality by making provision for the adhesion of states not represented at the Congress, was signed by a great majority, and embodied the explicit consent of a substantial number of states and the tacit

[1] Oppenheim: *International Law*, vol. 1, 1905, p. 347, n. 1.
[2] R. Rie: 'The origins of public law and the Congress of Vienna', *Trans. Grotius Soc.*, vol. XXXVI, 1951, p. 227.
[3] E. A. Whittuck: *International Documents*, 1908, pp. 1–2; A. Pearce Higgins: *The Hague Peace Conferences*, 1909, pp. 1–4.

consent of the remainder.[1] Accepted as a law-making treaty and reserving no right of denunciation, the Declaration constituted a statute book of the law of nations.[2] In the words of Malkin 'the Declaration of Paris was the first and remains the most important international instrument regulating the rights of belligerents and neutrals at sea which received something like universal acceptance'.[3]

The Geneva Convention 1864

The Geneva Convention for the Amelioration of the Condition of the Wounded in War was concluded on the initiative of Switzerland. It sprang from a humanitarian movement promoted by Henri Dunant and Gustav Meynier, both citizens of Switzerland who had witnessed the horrors of the battle of Solferino, and by the private associations formed for the purpose of succouring the sick and wounded in the field.[4] In June 1864 the Swiss government was induced to summon a congress at Geneva which was attended by the representatives of 16 of the states invited. The Convention was signed originally by 12 states and ratified by only nine, but it was rapidly made general in its application by the accession of others. Some states later became bound by its rules by becoming parties to the Hague Convention of 1899, which incorporated this convention.[5]

The general principles of the Convention were intended to provide full security for the sick and wounded in the field with the least possible interference with military operations. It gave, however, no recognition to the Red Cross or other voluntary aid societies and was in a way defective and incomplete in providing a too restricted definition of 'ambulance'.[6] In subsequent years this led to several attempts to modify the Convention,[7] which materialized in 1906 when the Geneva Conference of 35 powers signed a convention as to the care of the sick and wounded that was designated as superseding that of 1864.[8]

The Declaration of St. Petersburg 1868

This was the work of an international military commission of representatives from 18 states, which on the proposition of the

---

[1] Whittuck: *op. cit.*, pp. x–xi, 1–2.
[2] T. J. Lawrence: *The Principles of International Law*, 7th edn. rev. P. H. Winfield, 1923, p. 39.
[3] H. W. Malkin: 'The inner history of the Declaration of Paris', *B.Y.B.I.L.*, vol. 8, 1927, p. 2.
[4] Higgins: *Hague Peace Conferences*, p. 12; Holland: *Laws of War*, pp. 75–7, Appendix II (1); Whittuck: *International Documents*, pp. 3–9.
[5] Article XXI Convention II on the Laws of War; see Whittuck: *International Documents*, pp. xi–xiii, p. 5, n. 1. [6] Higgins: *op. cit.*, pp. 13–14.
[7] Higgins: *op. cit.*, pp. 19–38.
[8] For example, the 'Additional Articles of 1868'; see Whittuck, *op. cit.*, pp. 3–9.

Imperial Cabinet of Russia met to formulate rules for the purpose of prohibiting the use of 'any projectile of less weight than 400 grammes (about 14 ounces) which is either explosive or charged with fulminating or inflammable substance'.[1] The Declaration was based on the principle that the only legitimate object of war 'is to weaken the military forces of the enemy', that for this purpose 'it is sufficient to put *hors de combat* (to disable) as large a number of men as possible', and that this object would be exceeded by the employment of arms which uselessly aggravate the sufferings of disabled men or render their death inevitable. Nearly all the states later bound themselves to observe this declaration by their acceptance of the Hague Regulations of 1899 and 1907.[2]

The Declaration of St. Petersburg was the first formal agreement restricting the use of weapons of war, both in land and maritime warfare. Notwithstanding the fact that the humane principles prompting the Declaration were given only limited application and became practically obsolete, their very adoption constituted an attempt on the part of governments to set a standard.

The Brussels Conference of 1874

The treatment of prisoners of war during the American Civil War had horrified many thinking people. This led to the formation in France, in 1872, of a society for the amelioration of the conditions of prisoners of war, which proposed a conference of the powers of Europe to be held at Paris, to attempt to realize its objective. However, the Czar Alexander II of Russia took the initiative to convene a conference to consider the more general question of the conduct of war. This conference, attended by the delegates of Austria, Belgium, France, Germany, England, Greece, Italy, the Netherlands, Russia, Spain, Switzerland and Sweden, met at Brussels from July 27 to August 27, 1874, to consider the circular of the Czar which contained a draft project as a basis. Dr. Bluntschli, one of the German delegates, acted as the Chairman of the Committee on Codification. In preparing the *Projet de Déclaration*, which was adopted merely as a record of the proceedings without any commitment on the part of governments, considerable use was made of Dr. Lieber's *Instructions*. The Declaration was never ratified since the British government declined to accept it (because it contained many innovations) and Germany saw in some of its rules a condemnation of her recent practices in the conduct of the Franco-

---

[1] Whittuck: *International Documents*, p. 10; see for the reasons for summoning the Conference Higgins: *Hague Peace Conferences*, p. 7, and Holland: *Laws of War*, pp. 77–8, Appendix II(2).
[2] Article XXIII Convention II, 1899, and Article XXIII Convention IV, 1907.

German war.[1] Obviously the Declaration never became part of international law but it did exercise considerable influence on many of the manuals prepared for the use of armies by individual governments. Further, it formed the basis of the 'Regulations concerning the laws and customs of war on land' adopted as the annex to the Second Convention of the Hague Conference of 1899.

The Brussels Conference of 1874 was a landmark in the history of international codification, since it met in response to the increasing feeling that it was not only desirable but also entirely practicable to systematize and codify through international action at least the more important rules relating to the conduct of war on land. It was also regarded as 'epoch-making, since it showed the readiness of the Powers to come to an understanding regarding' a code of laws and customs of war.[2] The Institute of International Law, in 1875, fully approved the Brussels Draft and recognized in its form and content 'the zenith of present-day science', and during the Russo-Turkish war (1877) appealed to both belligerents to observe the rules of the Draft.[3] Russia issued a decree in accordance; Turkey took no action.

These congresses and conferences adopting rules of war were in a way not far removed from an international legislature, whose acts were submitted *ad referendum* to the participating nations.[4] Their importance was two-fold: firstly, they demonstrated the possibility of holding international congresses for the purpose of determining, in advance of war, rules and regulations for its conduct; and secondly, they furnished useful precedents for the codification of international law at the Hague Peace Conferences.

INTERNATIONAL REGULATION OF SOCIAL AND ECONOMIC PROBLEMS

During the nineteenth century, under the impact of the industrial revolution and with increasing international interdependence, governments were impelled to solve international economic and

---

[1] For the text of the Declaration see Higgins, *op. cit.*, pp. 273–80. The British government from the outset was unsympathetic; in its view the time was not ripe for codification; also it considered that the Declaration would give preponderant advantage to the great military powers. See T. A. Walker: *Science of International Law*, 1917, pp. 364–6.

[2] Oppenheim: *International Law*, vol. I, 4th edn., 1928, p. 78.

[3] J. B. Scott (ed.): 'Regulations of the Laws and Customs of War . . .', *Resolutions of the Institute of International Law*. Carnegie Endowment, 1916, pp. 8 and 17–22.

[4] J. B. Scott: *The Hague Peace Conferences of 1899 and 1907*, Carnegie, 1909, vol. I, p. 6. For the differences between a parliament and a diplomatic assembly, *ibid.*, pp. 35–6.

social problems and there was a steady increase and improvement of the law of nations in fields other than those of land and naval warfare. This process covered the growth not only of the written municipal law of foreign relations, but also of the law of treaties, compelled by the need for co-operation among nations. This era of congresses and conferences led to the multiplication of non-political treaties. More particularly, the period after 1850 saw the spread of multipartite conventions in the state practice of the second half of the century.[1] These instruments 'may be said to have contributed to the experience of governments in their search for solutions through international legislation of the manifold problems of international relations. Many instruments were isolated events dealing with particular problems. A substantial number, however, represents the fruit of the sustained efforts of governments to develop conventional international law for certain aspects of international relations at successive international conferences'.[2]

Beginning with the first International Sanitary Conference held in Paris in 1851, official congresses were convened to deal with subjects such as statistics, sugar duties, weights and measures, monetary matters, international postal and telegraphic correspondence, navigation of rivers, submarine cables, private international law, protection of industrial property, railroad transportation, international copyright, custom duties, abolition of the slave trade, repression of epidemic diseases, protection of labour, international arbitration, and suppression of traffic in women and children.[3] These conferences and congresses, which established a great number and variety of international unions, led to the development of a new branch of jurisprudence, namely international administrative law.[4] They may be looked upon as the legislative apparatus, and the commissions and bureau (many of which were located at Berne) established by them as the organs of administration. The international movements in the common interests of the nations and the importance of the exchange of knowledge in experimental and applied sciences led nations to give up certain parts of their sovereign powers to international administrative organs.

In contrast to private international congresses, the official con-

---

[1] M. O. Hudson: *International Legislation*, vol. 1, 1931, pp. xx–xxxvi.

[2] U.N. Doc. A/AC.10/5, 'Historical survey of the development of international law and its codification by international conferences', in *A.J.I.L.*, vol. 41, 1947, suppl. p. 33ff.

[3] See S. E. Baldwin: 'International Congresses and Conferences in the last century . . .', *A.J.I.L.*, vol. 1, 1907, pp. 565–78, 808–29.

[4] For a brief account of the establishment of international unions, see P. S. Reinsch: *Public International Unions, their Work and Organization*, 1911; also J. E. Harley: *Documentary Text Book on International Relations*, Los Angeles, 1934, pp. 287–314.

gresses naturally came under the domination of particular influences. For instance, the four successive conferences at The Hague for the advancement of private international law, held between 1893 and 1904, did not seek to declare the true rules on which all disputes of a private character, between nations and individuals, or between individuals of different nationalities, or concerning foreign transactions, ought to be decided. They only marked out which of several possible rules should be applied in certain particular cases. One finds that international conferences have commonly been called on the initiative of an individual state or group of states, which were prompted by considerations, sometimes commercial, sometimes scientific or philosophic, sometimes altruistic. But quite often these official conferences also resulted from private congresses, as was the case of the Red Cross Conventions, the idea of which was first conceived by an international conference of private individuals at Geneva in 1863.

Prior to the nineteenth century the principles of the balance of power, of nationalities, and of sovereignty played a definite rôle in the interstate relations in the successive stages of European modern history. But in the nineteenth century a new idea of the solidarity of interests as a basis for a corresponding international organization profoundly influenced international relations. The greater interest of states in the regulation of common problems by agreement, the corresponding need of establishing unity by creating appropriate legal institutions and legal obligation upon the states, and the strengthening of this unity by means of a separate and independent organization created by the concurrent wills of states—all these things led to the drawing up of a new programme of international law which gave birth to the work at The Hague. This new programme as envisaged in the work of the Hague Conferences stressed the necessity for an international organization of peace and for the establishment of a system to combat international anarchy.

The Work of the Hague Peace Conferences of 1899 and 1907

These conferences, the lineal descendants of the diplomatic assemblies that preceded them, may be regarded as the natural consummation of the international peace movement.[1] Their distinguishing

[1] An official communication from Russia, explaining the object of the Rescript issued by Count Mouravieff and published in the Journal of St. Petersburg of September 4, 1898, referred directly to the classic precedents of the nineteenth century, particularly the Congress of Vienna and the Congress of Paris. See G. F. W. Holls: *The Peace Conference at The Hague*, 1900, p. 13.

The Carnegie Endowment for International Peace has published, under the

feature was that neither were they held at the end of a period of warfare nor had they as their primary object that of restoring peace between existing belligerents. They were the first international diplomatic assemblies which were called upon, on the initiative of an individual ruler, to discuss guarantees of peace without reference to any particular war. Their designation as 'peace conferences' was unconsciously adopted by the delegates without any formal vote, as the public acclaimed them so, well knowing that a meeting of official delegates to consider the reduction of armament and the means by which peace could be maintained was in fact, if not in theory, a Peace Conference.[1] Encompassing three objects—disarmament, the organization of peace, and codification—they represented a first concrete step in international co-operation for the preservation of law and order and showed that it was no longer a dream to think that international conferences might come to be held periodically, and that they might develop some international organization for the more or less permanent settlement of the affairs of mankind.

Perhaps the chief importance of the Hague Conferences consisted in laying the foundation of the principle of equality of states. This they did by adopting the principle that the congress, which was to enact rules of conduct designed to be followed not only by the signatory states but also by the whole world, would not be effective unless this legislative assembly, unique in the world's history, were so organized that all units, great or small, had equal voting power and that practical unanimity was necessary in order to carry a measure. Historically, the doctrine of equality was not followed in European affairs, and only the Great Powers formed themselves in concert and either compelled respect for their opinions or assumed legislative functions.[2]

---

direction of J. B. Scott, a series of translated proceedings and documents of the Hague Conferences, with an Index volume (1921): *Proceedings of the Hague Conferences, Translations of Official Texts—Conference of 1899* (1920); *Conference of 1907* (3 vols.) (1921). *Reports to the Hague Conferences of 1899 and 1907* (1917). *The Hague Conventions and Declarations of 1899 and 1907*, 2nd edn. (1915). *The Hague Peace Conferences. American Instructions and Reports* (1916). *The International Union of the Hague Conferences*, by W. Schücking, trans. C. G. Fenwick (1918).

The standard works on the Conferences are: J. B. Scott: *The Hague Peace Conferences of 1899 and 1907*, 2 vols., Carnegie, 1909; G. F. W. Holls: *The Peace Conferences at The Hague*, 1900; E. D. Mead: *The Results of the Two Hague Conferences and the Demands upon a Third Conference*, 1911.

[1] Scott (ed.): *Reports to the Hague Conference* (1917), p. xviii.
[2] T. J. Lawrence: *Essays on Some Disputed Questions in Modern International Law* (chapter 'The Primacy of Great Powers'), 1885, pp. 226–30. The author was the chief exponent of the political and legal hegemony of the Great Powers.

THE HAGUE PEACE CONFERENCE OF 1899

The First Conference, which was proposed by the humanitarian and youthful Emperor of Russia, Nicholas II, met at The Hague from May 18 to July 29, 1899, under the presidency of M. de Staal, the first Russian plenipotentiary, and was attended by the representatives of 26 powers, including China, Japan, Persia and Siam. Although it was a fairly representative gathering, the only delegates from the American states were those of the United States of America and of Mexico. No African state was invited although there were at that time six states on that continent that claimed to be sovereign.[1]

As a mark of tribute to his interest in world peace, the Conference opened on the Czar's birthday. The Hague was chosen as the meeting place as the Czar wished to avoid entangling questions that often press upon a great capital. The hundred delegates included diplomatists, professors of law, military and naval experts and others professionally qualified.

Originally the programme of the Conference, as contained in the first circular letter of August 12, 1898, to governments, was limited principally to disarmament, but, in view of the scepticism indicated in the reply of some governments as to the practicability of any scheme proposing universal disarmament or even a substantial reduction of armaments, the Czar, while keeping the original aim of the Conference in the foreground, enlarged it to include other means of attaining the general end for which public opinion seemed ripe.[2] His circular letter of December 30, 1898, furnished an enlarged programme for the Conference. The articles for international discussion were summarized as follows: i. The prohibition for a fixed term of any increase of the armed and naval forces beyond those then maintained; ii. the prohibition of, or limitation on, the employment of new firearms or explosives; iii. the restriction of the formidable explosives already existing, and the prohibition of the discharge of projectiles or explosives of any kind from balloons or by any similar means; iv. the prohibition in naval warfare of submarine torpedo-boats or similar engines of destruction, and the

[1] See *Proceedings of the Hague Peace Conferences, Translation of Official Texts* (J. B. Scott, ed.), *Conferences of 1899* (Carnegie, 1920), hereafter cited as *Proc. H.P.C. 1899*. For Scott's views on the origin of the Conference see his *Hague Peace Conferences of 1899 and 1907*, pp. 33–4 (1909). For the names of delegates see Holls: *Peace Conferences at The Hague*, p. 38.

[2] See Russian Circular Notes of August 12 and December 30, 1898, in Scott: *Reports to the Hague Conferences*, pp. 1–4. The fact that the first note emanated from a power supposed to be the most military government in Europe made it at once the more remarkable and persuasive. The Despatch from the Chargé d'Affaires of the U.S.A., dated November 9, 1898, summarizes the reactions in the Press and the diplomatic circles in different countries: see Holls: *op. cit.*, pp. 16–23.

ultimate abolition of vessels with rams; v. the application to naval warfare of the stipulations of the Geneva Convention of 1864 on the basis of additional Articles of 1868; vi. the neutralization of ships and boats employed in saving those shipwrecked during or after an engagement; vii. the revision of the unratified Brussels Declaration of 1874 concerning the laws and customs of war on land; and vii. the acceptance in principle of the employment of good offices, of mediation and facultative arbitration with the object of preventing armed conflicts between nations, and the establishment of a uniform practice in using them.

No preparatory work for the deliberations of the Conference was done. In order to ensure the progress of the work a method of procedure proposed by the President was approved.[1] The Conference formed three committees or Commissions, each of which was assigned a group of topics. To the First Commission were assigned the matters dealt with in Articles i. to iv. of the programme; to the Second Commission, those in Articles v. to vii.; and to the Third those concerning the peaceful settlement of international differences comprised in Article viii. It was the last which, both from the importance of the subject and from the results achieved, justified the name given to the Conference. Each Commission had the power to subdivide itself into sub-Commissions,[2] and every state was to be represented upon every sub-Commission. The Commissions were free to appoint their own officers and to regulate the order of their labours. The conventions they submitted to the Conference occasioned little discussion and, with rare exceptions, were adopted as proposed, being subjected only to purely formal changes of style by a general drafting committee before signature.

The results of the labours of the Conference were embodied in a Final Act[3] which was signed by all the powers present (which thereby affirmed the authenticity of the record), without binding them to sign each of the Conventions or to adhere to each of the

---

[1] *Proc. H.P.C. 1899*, 2nd meeting, p. 19.

[2] The First Commission divided its work into two sub-Commissions, one military, the other naval; the Second Commission was subdivided into two sub-Commissions, one to examine questions relating to the Red Cross, the other those concerning the Brussels project regarding the laws of war; the Third Commission was not subdivided.

[3] *Proc. H.P.C. 1899*, pp. 228–67. The Final Act is a document prepared by the Conference and formally signed by the delegates. It states the call of the Conference, its place of meeting, the powers represented, the names of the delegates, the dates of assembling and adjournment, a list of Conventions and signed Declarations, and the text of unsigned declarations, resolutions and *voeux*. It is in itself not a treaty but only a complete official statement in summary form of the positive and tangible results of the Conference.

Declarations and wishes contained in the Act. These included the following:

three *Conventions*:[1] i. for the pacific settlement of international disputes; ii. regarding the laws and customs of war on land; iii. for the adaptation to maritime warfare of the principles of the Geneva Convention of 1864.

three *Declarations*:[2] i. prohibiting the discharge of projectiles and explosives from balloons or by other similar new methods; ii. prohibiting the use of projectiles, the only object of which was the diffusion of asphyxiating or deleterious gases; iii. prohibiting the use of bullets which expanded or flattened easily in the human body.

one *Resolution*:[3] affirming 'that the restriction of military budgets which are at present a heavy burden on the world is extremely desirable for the increase of the material and moral welfare of mankind'.

six *voeux* (wishes):[4] i. that a special Conference might be summoned by the Swiss government for the revision of the Geneva Convention; ii. that the question of the rights and duties of neutrals might be included in the programme of a Conference in the near future; iii. that the questions regarding rifles and naval guns, as considered by the Conference, might be studied by the governments in order to come to an agreement concerning the employment of new types and calibres; iv. that the governments might examine the possibility of an agreement on the limitation of armed forces by land and sea and of war budgets, taking into consideration the proposals made at the Conference; v. that the proposal for the exemption of private property from capture in naval warfare might be referred to a subsequent Conference for

[1] The Convention is a document which is a treaty or a contractual agreement, formally signed by the official representatives of the governments approving it after it has been adopted by the Conference. After signature it is transmitted to the governments of the participant countries for formal acceptance and ratification by the treaty-making power of the various countries. After ratification, the Convention becomes binding on the country accepting it and is deposited with the depository. It is the ratification and deposit, not the signature, which makes the Convention legally binding.

[2] The Declaration is a formal statement by the Conference which declares or establishes a principle in so far as the Conference can declare or establish it. A Declaration is of two kinds. One is signed by the official delegates and differs from a Convention only in the sense that its text is confined to a single subject instead of having many provisions, as may be the case with Conventions. The unsigned Declaration on the other hand requires no action on the part of governments to perfect it and constitutes merely an expression of opinion, more or less formal, of the Conference.

[3] The Resolution is also merely the expression of an opinion of the Conference, not necessarily the opinion of participating countries. It is not necessarily the opinion of all the members because all may not have voted for it, or all may not have approved it. The Resolution, therefore, although expressing the opinion of the Conference, and not of governments, as in the case of a Convention or a Declaration, is not the binding expression of opinion controlling the actions of the respective governments. It is not meant to be signed, whereas a Declaration when signed becomes, to all intents and purposes, a Convention.

[4] A *voeu* or wish may mean anything from an expression of opinion or desire to a recommendation. It is not signed. Whereas a Declaration or a Resolution is a positive statement of the Conference laying down a principle, the *voeu* is a solemn utterance of recommendation or wish for something to be done in a future conference which the present one is unable to do.

consideration; vi. that the question of the bombardment of ports, towns and villages by a naval force might be referred to a subsequent Conference for consideration.

The Conference, therefore, failed to achieve the purpose for which it was originally convoked; the question of disarmament or even of the limitation of armaments and military budgets, which was central in the Russian Rescripts, was buried beneath a resolution endorsing in general terms the desirability of the restriction of military budgets. The platonic resolution and the pious wishes expressed in *voeux* iii. and iv. notified to the world the failure on the question of disarmament, and the nations were left free, without any check whatsoever, to increase their military and naval power.

The real achievement of the Conference lay in the three Conventions, two of which, pertaining to the laws of land and naval warfare, in effect completed work which the gatherings of Geneva (1864, 1868) and of Brussels (1874) had failed to accomplish.

The Convention (II) with respect to the laws and customs of war on land itself had five articles and its Annex, which dealt with the regulations on the subject, contained 60 articles which were intended to be promulgated by the signatory states in the form of a manual on land warfare. It was ratified by 25 signatory powers without reservations, and adhered to by 21 nations. The whole spirit and purpose of the Convention was reflected in the preamble which was animated by the humanitarian sentiment and enlightened opinion of the time.[1] Its purpose was to define precisely the laws and general customs of warfare and to lay down certain limits intended to modify its severity as far as possible. It defined in some detail the qualifications of armed forces, militia or voluntary corps which entitled them to the status of lawful belligerents, the duties and obligations of belligerents in respect of the treatment of prisoners of war, the restrictions upon the means employed by a belligerent to injure his enemy, the prohibitions against certain methods and instrumentalities, and the law of military occupation of enemy territory. Some articles also dealt with spies, flags of truce, capitulations, armistices and the sick and wounded. It did not claim to be a complete code of the laws of war and took the precaution of declaring that, in cases not covered by it, populations and belligerents would remain under the protection and empire of the principles of international law resulting from the usages established between civilized nations and from the laws of humanity and the requirements of the public conscience.

In the main, however, the Convention attempted the systematic

---

[1] Scott: *Hague Conventions and Declarations of 1899 and 1907* (1915), pp. 100–2.

codification of the existing customary law of land warfare, but the desire 'to diminish the evils of war so far as military necessities permit' and to serve 'the interests of humanity and the ever-increasing requirements of civilization' led necessarily to a progressive modification and development of the law. It was largely a revision and amplification of the unratified Brussels Draft Declaration of 1874, which in turn grew out of Lieber's 'Instructions'. Although its scope was broadened at the Conference as it seemed to have been made binding upon all the parties attending, it was in practice not observed.[1]

The Convention (III) for the adaptation to maritime warfare of the principles of the Geneva Convention of August 22, 1864, ratified or acceded to by 46 states, contained only 14 articles.[2] It confined itself to the essential principles, with a view to securing for hospital ships, as well as the sick and wounded aboard them and the personnel in charge of them, immunities similar to those enjoyed under the Convention of 1864 by hospitals, ambulances, the wounded and medical staffs in land warfare. It did not enter into details of organization and of regulations which were left to be fixed by each state according to its interests and customs, but determined the international legal status of hospital ships.[3]

Thus, for the first time, the assembled nations accepted the Red Cross treaty for times of naval warfare—the culmination of several years of effort since 1868 when the extension of the beneficent influence of the Geneva Convention was attempted by means of the 'Additional Articles'. The assembly also unanimously decided that the Swiss government which enjoyed the well-merited honour of leadership in all matters pertaining to the Red Cross Convention should take further initiative in calling a conference to revise the Geneva Convention.

These two Conventions, notwithstanding the fact that their purpose and result were humanitarian, presupposed in their provisions the existence of a state of war. The conference originally convened for the maintenance of general peace had therefore devoted the greater part of its labours to the elaboration of the rules of war. It is noteworthy that its work of humanizing the laws of war, both on land and sea, was subsequently put to the test when war broke

---

[1] Article 1 of the Convention was an important provision which imposed upon the contracting parties an obligation to issue 'instructions' to their armed forces, although this obligation was not complied with by several governments which ratified the Convention; Scott: *Hague Conventions and Declarations*, p. 102.

[2] For text, *ibid.*, pp. 163–79.

[3] See Articles 1–7, *ibid.*, pp. 164–9. The delegates of Persia, Turkey and Siam objected, on religious grounds, to the adoption of the Red Cross as the distinctive flag of hospital ships.

out between the South African Republics and Britain (only Britain was a signatory), and also between Russia and Japan in the Far East (both were signatory powers); and that in these conflicts the terms of the two Conventions were well observed.[1]

The crowning work of the First Hague Conference and the one which probably produced the most beneficial results was the Convention (I) for the pacific settlement of international disputes, dealing with arbitration as a substitute for war. Consisting of 61 articles and arranged under three chapters, it was, subject to certain reservations, ratified and adhered to by 43 states.[2] Under it the powers expressly agreed 'to use their best efforts to insure the pacific settlement of international differences', in order 'to obviate as far as possible, recourse to force in the relations between states'.[3]

The Convention dealt specifically with a number of methods for the peaceable settlement of differences. One such means consisted of an agreement to resort, before appealing to arms and so far as circumstances permit, in case of serious disagreement or conflict, to the good offices or mediation of one or more friendly powers (Articles 2–8). Independently of this, strangers to the dispute were given the right to offer their good offices or mediation to the states at variances; that an offer of mediation was not to be regarded as an unfriendly act was an original contribution made to international law. The good offices or mediation, whether offered at the request of the disputing parties or upon the initiative of powers who were strangers to the dispute, had exclusively the character of advice and without any binding force or any effect on measures of preparation for war, or on actual military operations in progress unless otherwise agreed. In case of serious differences endangering the peace, the provision was made for special mediation by powers chosen by the states at variance, with the object of preventing the rupture of pacific relations. The provisions relating to mediation were based on the previous experience of many cases in which it had averted war.[4]

A newer and less frequently used means of adjusting state differences not involving the honour or the vital interests of the parties

[1] In accordance with Article 13 of the Regulations for the laws of war, bureaux for information about prisoners of war were established by Japan and confirmed by Russia; see S. Takahashi: *International Law applied to the Russo-Japanese War*, 1908, p. 114.
[2] Scott: *Hague Conventions and Declarations*, pp. 41–82 Holls, in an assessment of its historical value, compared it to the Magna Carta of England, see *Peace Conferences at The Hague*, pp. 354–6.
[3] See Article 1, Scott: *Hague Conventions and Declarations*, pp. 42–3.
[4] For the mediation of Pope Leo XIII between Germany and Spain concerning the Caroline Islands in 1885, see Moore: *International Arbitrations*, vol. V, pp. 5043–6; on joint mediation by Britain and France in a dispute between Spain and Morocco in 1844 see *Encyclopaedia Britannica*, vol. XVIII, 11th edn., p. 22.

was by recourse to international commissions of inquiry (Articles 9–14). The function of such commissions consisted in 'elucidating the facts by means of an impartial and conscientious investigation' and in making a report of findings to the parties in dispute.

The report of a commission of inquiry was limited to a statement of facts and was explicitly declared not in any way to be regarded as an arbitral award. It left the conflicting parties entirely free to act—or not—on the findings of the commission. The institution of a commission of inquiry for ascertaining and reporting to the conflicting parties was an important contribution towards the solution of differences by correct understanding of the facts in question.

A third and most important amicable means of settling international disputes dealt with by the Conference was international arbitration (Articles 15–57). Although there was nothing novel or unprecedented in this mode of settlement, since from time immemorial arbitrations have been successfully resorted to as the vehicle of compromise, it was important that, in the discussions at The Hague, for the first time an obligation to resort to arbitration was assumed by the powers and the necessary machinery and procedure were provided. It was declared that 'in questions of a legal nature and especially in the interpretation or application of international conventions, arbitration is recognized by the signatory powers as the most effective, and at the same time the most equitable, means of settling disputes which diplomacy has failed to settle'. Moreover, it was declared that agreement to arbitration implied the obligation to submit loyally to the decision of the arbitral tribunal.

Unfortunately the proposals looking to obligatory arbitration were defeated owing to the opposition of the U.S.A. and Germany[1] and, consequently, the Convention left the parties free to resort to arbitration as they might choose. It created no obligation to resort to arbitration in all cases but only expressed the pious wish in the preamble that the empire of law might be extended and the appreciation of international justice be strengthened by the permanent institution of a Court of Arbitration, accessible to all, in the midst of the independent powers.

Nevertheless, the creation of a so-called permanent court at The Hague and the formulation of a body of rules for its procedure was probably the most significant accomplishment because not only did it give expression in a palpable way to the community of states under the rule of international law, but it also opened the way to the development of a legal and pacific organization in the international

[1] See Holls: *Peace Conferences at The Hague,* pp. 228–32; also A. D. White: *The First Hague Conference,* 1912, pp. 52–69.

community.[1] The Convention established a Permanent Court of Arbitration which was neither 'permanent' nor a 'court', but only a panel of judges available to the conflicting parties which could create a court whenever they had occasion to resort to arbitration. There was also established a Permanent International Bureau at The Hague to serve as the record office for the Court, as the medium of all communications, and to have the custody of its archives and the conduct of all administrative business.[2] Each of the signatory powers was to select not more than four persons of recognized competence in questions of international law, enjoying the highest moral reputation, and disposed to accept the duties of arbitrators. The arbitrators so selected were to be enrolled as members of the Court for a term of six years, to be succeeded by other appointments in case of death or resignation. The Arbitration Court was to hold its sessions at The Hague or at other places with the assent of the parties in case of necessity. Its jurisdiction extended to all cases of arbitration, unless there should be an agreement between the parties for the establishment of a special tribunal. The Convention provided for elaborate rules of arbitral procedure for the proceedings in the Court.

The establishment of the Permanent Court of Arbitration with the Administrative Council of the International Bureau, supported by the signatory states as a body, unquestionably laid the basis of an international organization. It was the very embodiment of the international idea of law, and it made the beginning towards strengthening in the world the sense for law in interstate relations. It heard and settled between 1899 and 1907 important cases such as the Pious Fund Case of the Californias—a claim between the U.S.A. and the Republic of Mexico (1902); the Venezuela Preferential Payment Case concerning the claims of Britain, Germany and Italy against Venezuela (1904); the Case of the Japanese House Tax between Great Britain, France and Germany on the one side, and Japan on the other (1905); and the Muscat Dhows case between Great Britain and France.[3] The provision for the Court and for separate arbitration treaties accelerated the cause of arbitration. Until the Second Hague Conference met in 1907, a great number of arbitration treaties stipulating that disputes be referred to the Permanent Court of Arbitration were concluded between different

[1] Three countries, Britain, Russia and the U.S.A. presented plans for a court; that proposed by Sir Julian Pauncefote of Britain formed the basis of the institution adopted. See *Proc. H.P.C. 1899*, Annexes 2(A)(B), 3(A)(B), 7, pp. 813–16, 833–4.

[2] The Bureau was under the control of an Administrative Council to be composed of the diplomatic representatives of the signatory powers accredited at The Hague.

[3] J. B. Scott: *The Hague Court Reports*, Carnegie, 1916, pp. 1–109; also J. H. Ralston: *International Arbitration from Athens to Locarno*, 1929, pp. 263–86.

states and most of them reflected the influence of the First Hague Conference.[1] Another evidence of influence was found in the matter of reservations. The drafts proposed to the First Hague Conference strongly influenced the trend of the presence of such classic reservations as 'vital interests', 'national honour' and 'independence', which came to be taken for granted in the arbitration treaties.[2]

A review of these three Conventions gives some idea of the practical progress made since the Peace Movement of the mid-nineteenth century aroused the conscience of the world. Three propositions of the movement—a Congress of Nations, a Court of Nations, and a Code of International Law—were *in part* realized in practical form at the First Hague Conference. It is interesting to notice how the peace movement, passing through distinct stages of development (the ethico-religious period of combating war, the phase of the campaign for arbitration as a substitute for war, and lately that of organized efforts to eliminate international anarchy by seeking establishment of an international legal system), has influenced the progress of international law.[3] Moreover all three Conventions emanating from the 1899 Conference were shortly put to the test of meeting practical situations, and the experience thus gained helped towards the adoption of amendments at the Second Hague Peace Conference. In considering the substance and value of the accomplishments of the Conventions, one should bear in mind that they were adopted by the Conference *unanimously*—a marvel of achievement.

The three Declarations, on the other hand, were not adopted unanimously.[4] Like the Conventions they were in the nature of contracts which when ratified became binding on the ratifying governments. The first Declaration prohibited the launching of projectiles and explosives from balloons for a term of five years; thereafter it lapsed. But the Declarations were all observed during the war in South Africa and also during the Russo-Japanese War. The first *voeu* was realized in 1906 when the Geneva Convention was adopted. Other wishes were discussed at the Second Hague Conference, and the second, regarding the rights and duties of neutrals, and the sixth, on the bombardment of unfortified towns by naval forces, both resulted in Conventions in 1907.

In some quarters considerable disappointment and even criticism followed the adjournment of the Conference; in others, high tributes and appreciation were expressed regarding its accomplishments.[5]

[1] Scott: *Report to Hague Conferences*, p. 198; also *A.J.I.L.*, vol. 2, 1908, pp. 823–30.
[2] See H. M. Cory: *Compulsory Arbitration of International Disputes*, 1932, p. 49.
[3] Schücking: *International Union of the Hague Conferences*, vol. 1, pp. 29–30.
[4] Scott: *Hague Conventions and Declarations*, pp. 221–8, 230–4.
[5] See Schücking: *International Union of the Hague Conferences*, pp. 22–42.

H

With regard to its bearing on the codification of international law, those who had done practical work at The Hague, as well as the international scholars, have acknowledged that the Hague Conference was epoch-making in the following respects. Firstly, the Hague Conference laid the foundations of international codification by the convention method, which has become the most acceptable and practical method of effectively codifying and developing international law. Secondly, it set the pattern for future international conferences which were no longer to be confined to the European powers. The subsequent participation of an increasing number of non-European powers has tended to give a truly international character to what was in fact the European interstate customary law. Thirdly, the Hague Conference introduced the system of international assembly, a quasi-legislative organ for the international community,[1] from which developed a judicial organ in the shape of the Court of Arbitration and a rudimentary executive organ in the form of the International Bureau. These rudimentary legislative, judicial and executive organs were the forerunners of the Assembly, the International Court of Justice and the Secretariat later established under the Covenant of the League of Nations and the Charter of the United Nations. Holls, an eminent delegate from the United States of America to the First Conference, thought that 'the federation of the world—for Justice and for Universal civilized interests—that is the idea which found its best, if not its first, illustration in the Peace Conference'.[2] Professor Walther Schücking of Marburg University went further, to the extent of establishing his thesis (which appeared in German in 1912) that the organs like the Permanent Court of Arbitration were not merely the agency of two or more parties constituting the special or temporary tribunal for the trial of an individual case, but were in fact the organs of the union formed by the states. 'In the year 1899 the Hague Conference, although not *expressis verbis*, yet *implicite* and *ipso facto*, created a world federation.'[3]

The First Conference made the work of the Second Hague Conference (1907) possible. Having been unable to consider various matters on its programme or having failed to reach agreement on them, the First Conference created a widespread feeling that the work of international legislation which it had begun—the result of a century of agitation—ought to be carried forward to completion by a series of conferences. Peace societies soon began to urge the calling of another conference.

---

[1] T. J. Lawrence: *The Principles of International Law*, 7th edn., 1923, p. 43.
[2] Holls: *Peace Conferences at The Hague*, p. 364.
[3] Schücking: *International Union of the Hague Conference*, p. 86.

THE HAGUE CONFERENCE OF 1907

The Second Hague Peace Conference, convoked by the Czar of Russia, was a larger and more representative body than its predecessor. It was attended by 44 of the 47 states then recognized as members of the family of nations. On the insistence of the United States of America, the delegates of the Latin American states were also invited and all except Costa Rica and Honduras were represented. The Conference met at The Hague from June 15 to October 18, 1907 and was attended by 256 delegates, many of whom had participated in the First Conference. Europe was represented by 21 states, the Americas by 21 states and Asia by 4 states, and the Conference is sometimes called the First Parliament of Man or the first World Conference that had ever been held. It was presided over by His Excellency M. de Nelidov, the Russian Ambassador at Paris, a privilege reserved for Russia as the initiator of the Conference.[1]

The programme of the Conference had been prearranged by the Russian government with the assistance of the Russian jurist Dr. Frederic de Martens, who had consulted the Foreign Offices of the leading powers and obtained from them an understanding on the subjects for discussion. It included consideration of unfinished business from the First Conference, revision and improvements of the Conventions of 1899, and the formulation and adoption of new conventions relating to matters not regulated at that time.

The subjects dealt with by the Second Hague Conference were: i. measures for the prevention of war; ii. measures for the regulation of war; and iii. measures relating to neutrality. The work was mainly done in four Commissions dealing respectively with arbitration and cognate topics, improvement in the system of laws and customs of land warfare, maritime warfare, and the law of prize. In addition to these four Commissions which were subdivided into sub-Committees and Examining Committees, a Drafting Committee and a Committee to examine and report on the numerous addresses presented to the Conference were also appointed. The average number of the membership of each committee was 93 since, in accordance with the principle of equality of states, all states zealously asserted their claim to be represented on each one.

Four months of deliberations resulted in more legislation than did the work of the First Conference. The Final Act contained 13 Conventions, one Declaration, two Resolutions, one Recommendation and four *voeux*. Of the 13 Conventions, ten were entirely new; the

[1] For the correspondence leading up to the Conference see Scott: *Reports to the Hague Conferences*, pp. 180–91.

remaining three revised and improved the Conventions of 1899 in the light of the working experience gained between the two Conferences.[1]

The first Convention, on the pacific settlement of international disputes, rewrote and improved that of 1899 in 97 articles. The provisions for commission of inquiry were modified in the light of experience in the Dogger Bank Case,[2] a code of procedure was framed and the system of arbitral procedure was developed. A nation was enabled to arbitrate a case with its opponent through the International Bureau without approaching the opposite party directly.

The second Convention, which restricted the use of force for the recovery of contract debts and applied arbitration to them, was largely the outcome of the experience of Latin American countries and was founded primarily on the Drago Doctrine.[3] While it required that, before war was resorted to, arbitration must first be tried for the recovery of contract debts claimed from the government of one country by that of another, it also left nations free to use force in cases of obstinacy or irregularity. If on the one hand it protected Latin American states from European aggression for the collection of debts, on the other hand it minimized the application of the Monroe Doctrine by the United States of America by excluding from American waters European fleets intending to blockade debtors. Thus the Monroe Doctrine made its first and formal entry into the public law of Europe. The value of this Convention was weakened by the abstention from signature and the reservations of many of the powers in whose interest it was enacted.

The third Convention, on the opening of hostilities, was intended to protect belligerents from surprise attack and bad faith. By providing for a prior notification or declaration of war, it marked a radical change in the historic practice of nations.[4] Neutrals also were not to be subjected to the burdens of war until they were fully notified.

The fourth Convention, relating to the laws and customs of war on land, was a slight revision of the Convention of 1899 on the same subject.

[1] For the Final Act of the Second Hague Conference and for the text of the Conventions and other legislation, see Scott: *Hague Conventions and Declarations*.

[2] For the Protocol of submission and the findings of the International Commission of Inquiry between Great Britain and Russia arising out of the North Sea incident, see *A.J.I.L.*, vol. 2, 1908, pp. 929–36. Also A. S. Hershey: 'Convention for the pacific adjustment of international differences', *A.J.I.L.*, vol. 2, 1908, pp. 29–49.

[3] A. S. Hershey: 'Calvo and Drago Doctrine', *A.J.I.L.*, vol. 1, 1907, pp. 26–45. See also G. W. Scott: 'Hague Conventions restricting the use of force to recover on contract claims', *A.J.I.L.*, vol. 2, 1908, pp. 78–94.

[4] E. C. Stowell: 'Convention relative to the opening of hostilities', *A.J.I.L.*, vol. 2, 1908, pp. 50–7; also *op. cit.*, pp. 57–62.

The fifth Convention attempted to define neutrality and to regulate the rights and duties of neutral powers and persons in case of land warfare. It imposed upon belligerents obligations to respect the inviolability of neutral territory, and upon neutrals the duty of impartiality. Although it cleared up certain difficulties and produced written law out of certain recognized principles, the articles adopted had no transcendent value from the point of view of complete codification.[1]

The sixth Convention related to the status, upon the outbreak of war, of enemy merchant ships in an opposing enemy port or on the high seas and unaware that war had started. It did not affirm the growing custom of allowing enemy vessels in the opponent's port to get away without molestation after unloading and discharging their cargoes but only declared the customary practice desirable. This Convention was considered retrogressive because it did not categorically affirm an incompletely established customary law.[2]

The seventh Convention dealt with the transformation of merchant vessels into warships in time of war. It provided for the responsible control of such transformed vessels and for the abolition of the evils of privateering. Although a series of regulations was made on the subject, the vital questions connected with the place and duration of the transformation were left unsolved because of the impossibility of any agreement. Hence the Convention's practical value was not very great.[3]

The eighth Convention related to restrictions on the laying of automatic contact submarine mines, and was intended for the protection of commercial shipping. The regulation of the use of mines was made in such a way as not to deprive belligerents of a recognized and legitimate means of warfare, and also to restrict, as far as possible, damage to the immediate belligerents. The Convention failed to prohibit the use of these weapons under circumstances which would render their employment disastrous to innocent neutrals.[4]

The ninth Convention, which was declaratory of existing practices, forbade the naval bombardment of undefended harbours, coast towns or buildings. It prescribed conditions when bombardments

[1] For the internal history of the Convention see A. S. de Bustamente: 'The Hague Conventions concerning the rights and duties of neutral powers and persons in land warfare', *A.J.I.L.*, vol. 2, 1908, pp. 95–120.

[2] J. B. Scott: 'Status of enemy merchant ships', *A.J.I.L.*, vol. 2, 1908, pp. 259–70.

[3] G. G. Wilson: 'Conversion of merchant ships into warships', *A.J.I.L.*, vol. 2, 1908, pp. 271–5.

[4] C. H. Stockton: 'The use of submarine mines and torpedoes in time of war', *A.J.I.L.*, vol. 2, 1908, pp. 276–84.

were allowable and was in conformity with the practice and custom of enlightened nations.[1]

The tenth Convention adapted to maritime warfare the principles of the new Geneva Convention on the Red Cross (1906) and marked a step forward in humane regulations in succouring the sick and wounded and mitigating the evils necessarily incidental to war.[2]

The eleventh Convention codified rules as to the rights of capture of private property at sea in time of war, exempting from capture postal correspondence of neutrals and belligerents, fishing vessels, small coasting vessels, and vessels employed in scientific or philanthropic missions. It also regulated the legal conditions of the crew of an enemy merchant vessel by providing that subjects of neutral states were exempt from capture, as were also the subjects of the enemy state provided they undertook on oath not to serve during the continuance of war. By contracting the range of war on some points covered by it, it extended the bounds of peace.[3]

The twelfth Convention sought to establish an International Court of Prize to adjudicate cases of the capture of neutral merchant ships and cargoes and of such belligerent ships and cargoes as may be captured in violation of treaties, national declarations or other rules of international law. There was no agreement on rules for contraband of war, and there were difficulties of a constitutional nature preventing its acceptance (though some of these were removed by the Declaration of London of 1909). The Convention was repudiated by the Great Powers on the ground that there was no law for the guidance of a Court of Prize, and by many of the minor powers, mainly Latin American states and Siam and Persia, because the graduated representation in constituting the Prize Court was regarded by them as against the principle of equality of sovereign states. It remained unratified.[4]

The thirteenth Convention regulated the rights and duties of neutral powers as well as of belligerents in case of maritime war. It forbade hostile acts in neutral waters and the use of neutral territory as the base of operations. It likewise forbade enemy vessels to remain longer than a certain period in neutral harbours and prescribed certain order for their leaving so that hostilities might not begin within neutral jurisdiction. It harmonized divergent views in some

[1] J. B. Scott: 'Bombardment by naval forces', *A.J.I.L.*, vol. 2, 1908, pp. 285–94.
[2] L. Renault: 'Convention for the adaptation of the principles of the Geneva Convention to maritime warfare', *A.J.I.L.*, vol. 2, 1908, pp. 295–306.
[3] S. E. Baldwin: 'The eleventh Convention proposed by the Hague Conference of 1907', *A.J.I.L.*, vol. 2, 1908, pp. 307–12.
[4] C. N. Gregory: 'The proposed International Prize Court and some of its difficulties', *A.J.I.L.*, vol. 2, 1908, pp. 459–75; H. B. Brown: 'Proposed International Prize Court', *ibid.*, pp. 476–89; T. R. White: 'Constitutionality of the proposed International Prize Court', *ibid.*, pp. 490–506.

degree and introduced more certainty into the law of maritime neutrality.[1]

The Declaration, forbidding the throwing of projectiles and explosives from balloons, re-enacted the (limited) Declaration on the same subject of the First Conference, which had expired in 1905. The Second Conference, being unwilling to make the prohibition permanent, limited it to a period ending with the close of the Third Peace Conference. Since only half the states present at the Conference signed the Declaration it could hardly be recognized as a rule of international law.[2]

Like its predecessor the Second Hague Conference did not legislate for abolishing war but only for humanizing the conduct of war and to substitute for resort to arms a pacific settlement of international disputes. The question of limitation of armaments was again made the subject of a Resolution only, referring the matter to the nations for further serious study.[3] What was achieved in the form of Conventions represented to a great extent undesirable compromises and, in some cases, even retrogression. The obligations imposed by the Conventions exhibited lamentable timidity and their value was considerably diminished by attenuating clauses which allowed belligerents to evade them on grounds of military exigencies, military necessity, or exceptional circumstances and the like. This was an inevitable consequence of some 40 to 50 sovereign states attempting to make or harmonize laws on large questions without loss to themselves; in the event they found themselves able to agree only on those of less importance or on solutions not affecting their own interests.

Hence, where agreement could not be reached, the Conference, instead of adopting a Convention, contented itself by formal utterances or *voeux*, two of which related to the commercial and industrial relations between belligerent governments and neutral residents of belligerent or occupied territory, and a third to the preparation by the next conference of a code of laws governing maritime warfare. These important questions, such as the immunity of the private property of neutral residents in belligerent or occupied territory, the seizure of private property of enemy subjects at sea, contraband of war, blockade, the destruction of neutral ships at sea, and the

---

[1] C. C. Hyde: 'The Hague Convention respecting the rights and duties of neutral powers in naval war', *A.J.I.L.*, vol. 2, 1908, pp. 507–27.

[2] G. B. Davis: 'The launching of projectiles from balloons', *A.J.I.L.*, vol. 2, 1908, pp. 528–9.

[3] See R. P. Hobson: 'Disarmament', *A.J.I.L.*, vol. 2, 1908, pp. 743–57; he points out the harmful effects of agitation for national disarmament on the Hague Conferences and on peace in general. For an opposite view see B. F. Trueblood: 'The case for limitation of armaments', *ibid.*, pp. 758–71.

general application to sea warfare of the rules already established for land warfare, involved special interests of the leading powers, and the Conference was able to produce nothing except expressions of opinion.

Such vital improvements as the use of obligatory arbitration and the provision for the automatic and periodic assembly of nations for codifying international law were merely mentioned and passed on for future consideration. Having failed to make a universal treaty of obligatory arbitration, even of limited scope and only for specified cases, the Conference adopted a colourless resolution endorsing the principle that disputes relating to the interpretation of treaties were susceptible of compulsory arbitration and that there were subjects that ought always to be referred to arbitration. This left the matter of the negotiation of arbitration treaties to the nations acting in pairs.[1] Although it endorsed the proposal of the creation of an Arbitration Court, the Conference was unable to agree on the precise method of appointing judges of the Court. The Central and South American states insisted that there should be nothing short of an absolute equality in their appointment, a claim unacceptable to the Great Powers.[2]

The results of the First Hague Conference and the achievement of assembling the Second had so much impressed American public opinion as to the value of international conferences that the Secretary of State, Elihu Root, had instructed the American delegation to advocate the holding of further conferences within fixed periods, a proposal that was met in *voeu* 5, where the Conference recommended the holding of a third conference within a period corresponding to that which had elapsed since the First Conference.[3]

APPRAISAL OF THE HAGUE CONFERENCES

Tested by the quantity and quality of its output, the Second Conference more fully justified its existence than did the First, but to many it was disappointing and its failures, in not accomplishing and safeguarding the general peace by prohibiting war and by imposing effective sanctions, were the object of much criticism. The success of the Conferences should be assessed rather by the

[1] W. I. Hull: 'Obligatory arbitration and the Hague Conferences', *A.J.I.L.* vol. 2, 1908, pp. 731–42; see also J. L. Tryon, 'A world treaty of arbitration', *Yale L.J.*, vol. 20, 1910–11, pp. 163–75.
[2] J. B. Scott: 'The proposed Court of Arbitral Justice', *A.J.I.L.*, vol. 2, 1908, pp. 772–810; J. H. Choate: *The Two Hague Conferences*, Princeton, 1913, pp. 78–9.
[3] Scott: *Hague Peace Conferences, American Instructions and Reports* (1916), p. 72; also Scott: 'Recommendation for a Third Peace Conference', *A.J.I.L.*, vol. 2, 1908, pp. 815–22, and Choate: *op. cit.*, pp. 83–5.

progress they set in motion than by what they failed to accomplish, but the reasons for the failures are worthy of examination. The matters that gave rise to adverse criticism lay chiefly in faulty methods of organization and procedure and in the limitations inherent in the nature of international conferences assembled as these were.

The calling of the Conferences, the determination of their programmes, the division into Commissions and the organization and procedure were in the hands of Russia, the inviting power, through its chief representative who, according to international custom, acted as president of the assembly. Also, the appointment of the officers of the Conferences and of the Commissions, and of the necessary personnel of the Secretariat were made in accordance with the desires of the inviting power.[1] At the First Conference, in accordance with the practice of diplomatic gatherings, no rules of procedure were adopted save what was proposed by the President regarding the formation of committees and the allotment of projects. As a result, the procedure remained confusing and inconsistent: for instance, it was not clear whether the deliberations were governed by the ordinary rules of parliamentary practice. To avoid repeating this confusion, a set of rules of procedure was adopted at the Second Conference. In fact, however, the organizers did not perceive that, because of the very legislative character of these assemblies, which contemplated the drafting of rules of conduct for the whole international community, they were more in the nature of parliamentary bodies than diplomatic conferences for the negotiation of political bargains, and therefore required a different method of procedure. Consequently, the code of rules, or *réglement*, consisting of 12 rules,[2] was merely a fragmentary compromise between the procedures for a diplomatic gathering and a parliamentary assembly. The procedure was practically the same for the Conference as for the Commissions, which were too large (in deference to the doctrine of equality), each power being entitled to a place on as many committees as it chose) for the expeditious handling of business. Each delegation had a right to one vote, of equal weight with that of all other states, and the vote was taken by roll-call of the states in alphabetical order (in French, the official language of the Conference). The practice of voting not on the amendment but on the original proposal was corrected in the Second Conference.

The chief target of criticism, however, was the principle of the

[1] Scott: *Hague Peace Conferences of 1899 and 1907*, vol. I, pp. 114–16. For Scott's criticism of the working method at the Conferences see *Reports to the Hague Conferences*, p. xxxi.

[2] For the text of the *réglement* see Scott: *Hague Peace Conferences, American Instructions and Reports*, pp. 89–91; for commentary see his *Hague Peace Conferences of 1899 and 1907*, vol. I, pp. 112–24.

equal voting powers of the states, which was arbitrarily adopted by the Czar of Russia in the belief that unless the legal equality of states was thus recognized a conference of any except the Great Powers could not have been assembled. Moreover, it seems to have been assumed by him from the outset that the rule of unanimity in voting, which prevailed in the negotiations of diplomatic conferences, would have to be applied to the larger gatherings at The Hague, even though they would be of the nature of an international legislative assembly. Once the smaller powers had participated in the deliberations of the Great Powers on an equal footing, they consciously asserted their right of equality, and were unwilling to admit in principle that anything less than a unanimous vote could bind the Conference. However, it soon became evident that a strict adherence to the rule of unanimity would inevitably militate against the practical results that were expected of the Hague Conferences. The strict application of the rule was not in fact enforced and the fiction of 'quasi-unanimity' was developed, which recognized as unanimously accepted a proposal receiving a substantial majority of the votes cast; this led either to undesirable compromises and retrogressive solutions on many of the important matters, or else to merely platonic resolutions.

Another aspect, the insistence on complete equality in the distribution of judges for the proposed Court of Arbitral Justice, although waived in case of the Prize Court, produced great difficulties as it was deemed impracticable to give to all the powers equal representation on an international tribunal; the most that could be achieved was the adoption of a *voeu* recommending a draft convention for the creation of such a court.

The unanimity rule and the principle of equality of states should not, however, be treated equally. While the former was an unnecessary obstacle the latter was an essential condition for the success of an international conference. The unanimity rule may serve a useful purpose in a diplomatic conference in negotiations leading to the striking of a bargain between independent nations, but in conference of the legislative type it effectively gives every participating state an absolute power of veto over every action. On the other hand, the principle of equality of states, by ensuring the admission of all states to full participation, representation on all committees as well as in plenary sessions, one vote to each regardless of its size, and equal rights of signature, ratification, reservation, denunciation and adhesion, is conducive to results which are both effective and widely influential.[1] Hence, if the principle of equality of states is a *sine qua*

[1] F. S. Dunn: *The Practice and Procedure on International Conferences*, 1929, pp. 123–31.

non of the codification conferences, the rule of unanimity is both unnecessary and impracticable in an assembly representing the whole international community and seeking to lay down rules of international conduct.[1] After 1907, however, the critics strongly denounced both principles and stressed that, if a third Peace Conference should ever be called, it ought to be organized with different principles.[2] Ultimately, the experience of the first two Conferences greatly influenced the organization of subsequent international conferences.

Yet another organizational fault of the Hague Conferences was the lack of preparatory work, for which reason the Commissions had to consider a large number of imperfectly elaborated proposals, involving much loss of time in the planning of meetings and in preparing preliminary studies.[3] The President of the Second Conference referred to the wearisome and laborious discussions on much of the Conference business and stressed the desirability of some preparatory work.[4] For a Third Conference, it was suggested that, some two years before the probable date of the meetings, a preparatory committee should be charged by the various governments with the duty of collecting the propositions to be brought before them; of ascertaining which matters were susceptible of international regulation; of preparing a programme and proposing a mode of organization and procedure which might be seriously considered in advance by each government intending to participate.[5] The important implication of this recommendation was that in future the arrangement of a conference and its methods and procedures would not be determined by a single power. A programme prepared and communicated to the participants in advance would allow them to formulate their views; these views would be collected and printed in advance of the opening session for communication to the delegations, a system which came to be followed by subsequent international conferences.

Apart from the failings in the organization and procedures of the Hague Conferences, there were limitations inherent in the nature of these assemblies, for they did not form an international legislature in the real sense of the term; they were not the product of the

---

[1] For Professor Dickinson's doubts on the proper application of the principle of complete political equality in international organization see E. D. Dickinson: *The Equality of States in International Law*, 1920, p. 336.

[2] The London *Times* condemned the principle of equality of states under the editorial 'The Hague Fiasco' on October 19, 1907. See also F. C. Hicks: 'The equality of states and the Hague Conferences', *A.J.I.L.*, vol. 2, 1908, pp. 530–61.

[3] See J. Westlake: *The Collected Papers of John Westlake on Public International Law*, ed. L. Oppenheim, 1914, p. 534.

[4] Scott: *Hague Conferences of 1899 and 1907*, vol. I, pp. 735–6.

[5] Scott: *Hague Conventions and Declarations*, Final Act of 1907, pp. 29–30.

fundamental law of an integrated political community but evolved more or less haphazardly to meet the needs of relationships between nations. They were composed of official representatives of the participant states who were not free to act in accordance with their own judgment but were under instructions from their respective governments. That these Conferences were regarded purely as gatherings of negotiators rather than as legislative bodies was clear from the remarks of M. de Nelidov, President of the Second Conference, in his closing speech:

When strangers to our labours pass judgment on the activity of the Conference, they too often lose sight of the fact that we are not called upon to elaborate abstract theories, to seek, by means of mental speculation, ideal solutions for the problems submitted to us. We are the agents of our Governments and act by virtue of special instructions, based before all other considerations upon the interest of our respective countries. The higher considerations of the good of mankind in general should no doubt guide us, but in applying them we must have uppermost in our minds the intentions of those who direct our Governments. But the direct interests of different states are often diametrically opposed.[1]

In assemblies of this kind, where the participating states did not consider themselves bound by 'majority decisions', the Conferences were able to pass but few important or complex measures. Unless the right of national veto of international legislation could be qualified or replaced by some form of majority rule binding upon all—unless the international conference became a truly legislative body—the hoped-for production of a codified body of international law could not be expected.

Over and above this, the acts of the Hague Conferences could not bind any state without its consent, manifested in the form of signature, ratification, adhesion or accession.[2] The 'open-door' system was adopted with regard to the powers not represented, save in relation to the Convention concerning the pacific settlement of international disputes. Furthermore, reservations in the instrument of ratification could be made by a nation before or after signing. International conventions were thus often compromises, and the price of a compromise to a nation could be the very article which another nation excluded from that convention or interpreted in a special sense in its act of ratification.

[1] Closing Address, October 18, 1907: Scott, *Reports to the Hague Conferences*, p. 200.
[2] The Conventions of 1899 were ratified by all the powers represented at the Conference and were adhered to by a considerable number of others not represented. But those of 1907 were not ratified at all by 15 out of 44 nations represented at the Second Conference. Many of the Conventions were ratified by certain states with reservations. See Scott: *Hague Conventions and Declarations*, pp. 230–59.

Those who did not appreciate the limitations of an international conference as compared with a legislative body like a parliament tended to belittle what the Hague Conferences had with great difficulty attained. The reputation of the Conferences suffered because too much was expected from them, and even more because they were unfortunately designated as Peace Conferences, which accentuated popular hopes for perpetual peace; they should more properly have been called Conferences on International Law. It must be admitted that they accomplished much for international law. They represented a climax in the codification movement; no comparable progress has since been recorded in the formulation of international law by general state consent until recently, under the auspices of the United Nations.

OTHER EFFORTS BEFORE WORLD WAR I

The Third Conference recommended by the Hague Conference of 1907 could not be called because of the outbreak of war in 1914. But one task mapped out for it was undertaken by a different conference—the International Naval Conference held at London in 1908–9.

The London Conference of 1908–9

The Hague Convention of 1907 relating to the establishment of an International Prize Court caused great concern because of the uncertainty of the law that the Court would apply in its interpretation of the phrase 'the general principles of Justice and Equity' (Article 7). In order to fix certain rules for the Court, the British government invited the principal naval powers (Germany, Spain, France, Italy, Russia, Japan, Austro-Hungary, the United States of America and the Netherlands) to a conference in London between December 4, 1908, and February 26, 1909, the outcome of which was the Declaration of London concerning the Laws of Naval Warfare, comprised of 71 articles. Although intended merely as an attempt to codify the existing law, the Declaration was in fact largely of a legislative character in vital matters, such as the application of the doctrine of continuous voyage to conditional and absolute contraband, in which it created new law by way of a compromise. The Declaration stated that it corresponded in substance with the generally recognized principles of international law, and Great Britain had really invited the other powers to the Conference not 'to deliberate *de lege ferenda*' but 'to crystallize, in the shape of a few simple propositions, the questions on which it seems possible to lay down a guiding principle generally accepted'. Since it created new law, however, Article 65 provided that the Declaration must be accepted as a whole or not at all. As the Declaration was never ratified it never came into force; in 1916 the British and French governments declared that they would revert to the rules of customary international law existing prior to the Declaration. It deserves mention, however, because it represented the first effort of the maritime powers to codify the law of prize.[1] Moreover, the notable and exemplary work which took place in connection with the Declaration was said to constitute 'a model never yet surpassed in the annals of diplomacy'.[2] The represented powers were requested to communicate in advance a statement of their views concerning different subjects on the programme; summaries of these memoranda, accompanied by observations and draft proposals, were prepared under the direction of the British government as bases of discussion; and finally, in a spirit of co-operation, and desiring to reach an agreement on a 'declaration' of the generally recognized rules dealing only with the relations between belligerents and neutrals, the Conference adopted a Declaration rather than a Convention.[3]

The Declaration represented the *media sententia* of the views and practices prevailing in the different countries, and was accompanied by a General Report which contained a most lucid, explanatory and critical commentary on the provisions of the Declaration.[4] It was first applied in World War I by the belligerents on the initiative of the United States of America, though with diverse modifications and reservations, a state of affairs that soon ended when Britain and France formally withdrew from the Declaration in 1916. Notwithstanding its abrogation by the allied governments, it must be said that as regards those of its rules which were already a part of the established customary law of nations and did not embody innovations, the Declaration was claimed by some as binding upon belligerents and neutrals alike, independently of its status as an international instrument.[5]

[1] For a review of the origin and nature of the Declaration see Elihu Root: 'The real significance of the Declaration of London', in *Addresses on International Subjects*, ed. R. Bacon and J. B. Scott, Harvard Univ. Press, 1916, pp. 73–87.
[2] Records of the 8th Ordinary Session of the Assembly of the League of Nations, L. of N. Offl. Jnl., sp. supp. no. 54, 22nd Pl. mtg., 1927, p. 204. The First Committee of the Assembly of the League recommended the same method in drawing up of schedules in preparation for the Hague Codification Conference in 1930. See also C. H. Stockton: 'The International Naval Conference on London', *A.J.I.L.*, vol. 3, 1909, pp. 596–618.
[3] For a collection of official papers and documents relating to the Conference see J. B. Scott (ed.): *The Declaration of London of February 26, 1909*, 1919. Also U.N. Doc. A/AC.10/5, 'Historical survey of development of international law . . .', in *A.J.I.L.*, vol. 41, 1947, suppl. pp. 45–6.
[4] Report by M. Renault, quoted by Elihu Root, *op. cit.*, p. 81.
[5] Garner: *Developments in International Law*, pp. 138–40. Idem: 'Violation of maritime law by the allied powers during the World War', *A.J.I.L.*, vol. 25, 1931, p. 27.

Appraisal of Codification before World War I

Reviewing the work on the codification of public international law through official action up to 1914, we can see that such progress as had been made was confined almost entirely to the domain of the law of war; that this work of codification was gradual and piecemeal, covering one particular part after another of the general field; that by co-ordinating and formulating rules which were finally adopted by states, the process transformed the larger and more important part of international law governing the conduct of war, especially of war on land, into codified form. This suggests that it seemed impracticable to attempt, at one time, to codify the entire body of international law, that codification must proceed in parts until the whole body of law becomes codified, and that, using the methods adopted at the Hague Conferences, the law relating to particular subjects must from time to time be formulated into conventions by agreement. Judging by these early practical and fruitful efforts at codification, it must also have seemed that the codes prepared individually by such eminent jurists as Bluntschli, David Dudley Field and Fiore, notwithstanding their juridical value, had scant hope of being accepted or seriously considered by governments; so it was apparent that, if concrete results were to be accomplished, the initiative must necessarily be taken by governments themselves. However, it was also true that the progress of the international conferences had certainly been greatly facilitated by the labours and discussions of the most learned international lawyers of the time, as well as of the technical experts and diplomatists representing various foreign offices.

At the same time, a parallel movement for the codification of private international law was also active, as a result of which a considerable part of continental European private international law was unified, and a common procedure for the application of foreign law agreed upon.[1] Similarly, through the initiative of the International Maritime Committee established in 1898 to bring about the unification of maritime law, international conferences of leading maritime states were held, leading to the signing and ratification of important conventions.[2] Somewhat analogous to this work may be mentioned the Convention dealing with the safety of life at sea adopted at the London International Conference in 1914 and ratified by a number of signatory powers.[3] Certain governments

---

[1] The unification of private international law was promoted by six governmental conferences held in 1893, 1894, 1900, 1904, 1935 and 1928. See U.N. Doc. A/AC.10/5 'Historical survey . . .', *A.J.I.L.*, vol. 41, 1947, suppl., pp. 38–9.
[2] *Ibid.*, pp. 39–41.   [3] Woolf, *International Government*, p. 266.

displayed a marked continuity of interest in some of these fields: e.g. the government of the Netherlands took the initiative in convening conferences on the unification of private international law, the Belgian government on the unification of maritime law, and the British government on the safety of life at sea.

The very fact that a considerable part of international law had been codified in the form of conventions at international conferences proved the practicability as well as the desirability of codification and increased optimism that further progress could be made by a continuation of the methods and procedures already employed. The outbreak of war in 1914, however, was a great setback to the progress of codification. Yet it revealed that codification meant that the standard of judgment was shifted from a moral to a legal basis, with the result that any obscurities and ambiguities in the codified law provided any power with a plausible justification for almost everything that was done. It was frequently alleged that the Hague Rules had been openly flouted by belligerents, but the truth is, as Professor H. A. Smith rightly observed, that in the Hague Texts ambiguous phrases such as 'so far as possible' or 'except when absolutely necessary' were deliberately scattered throughout the Conventions.[1]

Moreover, the general practice of signing or ratifying the Conventions with reservations, many of these touching matters of fundamental principle, further whittled down the actual effect of the Hague Rules.[2] These defects and weaknesses of conventional law were revealed by the war in a more striking degree than ever before. The period of lawlessness in the war, however, was followed by a greater appreciation of the value of law, and it aroused determination not only to rehabilitate but also to strengthen the law of nations in order that it may better subserve the common interests of states and the welfare of mankind.

CODIFICATION EFFORTS UNDER THE AEGIS OF THE LEAGUE OF NATIONS

The Covenant of the League of Nations was a solemn treaty between independent nations, which established for the first time an association of sovereign states. In it were embodied, in part, ideals and

---

[1] H. A. Smith: 'International law making', *Trans. Grotius Soc.*, vol. XVI, 1930, pp. 96–7.
[2] J. W. Garner: *International Law and the World War*, 1920, 2 vols. In vol. 1, pp. 18–27, the author explained that throughout the greater part of the war the Hague Conventions were not in force. See also M.O. Hudson: 'Present status of the Hague Conventions', *A.J.I.L.*, vol. 25, 1931, pp. 114–17, where the author gives a short account of the position of ratifications or adhesions to the Conventions before and after the war.

principles that had been advocated for centuries by many thinkers, including those who would codify international law. Its scope and significance as a purposeful instrument in the political integration of mankind, and its comprehensiveness which sought to delimit the right of resorting to war and to impose most far-reaching obligations on the member states, gave to the Covenant the character of the 'Higher Law'.[1]

The Covenant can be understood better in the light of the progressive pattern of thought which culminated in the League concept.[2] Sir Alfred Zimmern spoke of five strands being intertwined in the Covenant, four of them being part of the pre-war system and the fifth a product of wartime thinking:

1. An improved and enlarged Concert of the Powers, using the method of regular Conference.

2. A reformed and universalized Monroe Doctrine, using the method of all-round mutual guarantees of territorial integrity and independence.

3. An improved Hague Conference system of Mediation, Conciliation and Inquiry, using the political organ of the Conference for this purpose.

4. An improvement and co-ordination of the Universal Postal Union and other similar arrangements for carrying on of world services and the administration of world public utilities, by the establishment of a Secretariat of Secretariats.

5. An agency for the mobilization of the Hue and Cry against war as a matter of universal concern and a crime against the world community, the political Conference being employed for that purpose.[3]

Zimmern further classified 26 articles of the Covenant within these five categories in order to explain how, as a result of various influences acting and reacting upon one another under the impact of experience, the process of dovetailing or codification or synthesis, carried through in the letter of the Covenant, assumed new spirit in the whole field of international politics.[4] Through the ratification of the Peace Treaty to which it was attached, the Covenant became part of the Treaty Law of the world and the League of Nations part of governmental machinery. In its content, form and method, the Covenant may be described as codification.[5] It was the statute of the new world organization, for which all the earlier

[1] H. Lauterpacht: 'The Covenant as the Higher Law', *B.Y.B.I.L.*, vol. 17, 1936, pp. 54–65.
[2] See W. Schiffer: *The Legal Community of Mankind*, 1954, pp. 189–277, where the author analyses the concept which made a scheme of international organization along the lines of the League plausible.
[3] Alfred Zimmern: *The League of Nations and the Rule of Law 1918–1935*, 1936, pp. 264–5. [4] *Ibid.*, pp. 266–74.
[5] Dr. Max Huber, looking backward to Sully, Penn, Crucé, the Abbé, St. Pierre and Kant, in relation to the establishment of the League of Nations, said that 'Its method can be described as that of codification of practical politics. It is a systematic dovetailing (*Zusammenfassung*) of all the elements in the politics of the

I

private codes on international law had, in one form or another, provided. It was a multilateral treaty which created a loose association of states with the two-fold object of preserving international peace and security and promoting international co-operation. It sought to strengthen and expand those international practices, many rudimentary in nature, which lacked the sanction of a world organization.

A tremendous advance embodied in the Covenant was the creation of the Permanent Court of International Justice, for the signatories to the organic conventions committed themselves to the standing policy that justice should be the controlling principle in all relations between nations, and that its application to concrete cases by an impartial tribunal ought to supersede the barbarous method of trial by combat. A corollary of this was that the adoption of an international code of the principles of the law of nations, for the guidance of an international court, became as essential as the creation of the Court itself.

It is remarkable, however, that law was not mentioned at all in the Covenant, except in the preamble, where its principles were characterized as 'understanding' that required firmer establishment. This feeble reference to international law indicated its subsidiary place in the great scheme for a 'Covenant of the League of Nations'. The call for firmer establishment was made because not only had few of the general international conventions of the preceding decades survived the war, but also some of those that survived no longer corresponded with the changed conditions and needs of the international community.

In the history of international legislation, the first World War seems to have marked the close of an era of some fifty years of activity which strove to build a legal basis for international relations by means of multilateral law-making treaties. The end of the war inaugurated a new era of international co-operation in new fields. The establishment of the League of Nations, including the International Labour Organization, quickened the legislative process. The frequent assembling of international conferences contributed to the conclusion of numerous multipartite instruments, which not only revised much of the pre-war legislation but also brought within the range of legislative control many subjects to which it had formerly never been extended.[1] The document prepared by the

---

last hundred years which are either themselves safeguards of peace or which having originally formed part of the system of power politics, can now be made to serve the cause of general peace'. Quoted by Zimmern: *op. cit.*, pp. 284–5.

[1] M. O. Hudson: 'The post-war development of international law and some contributions by the United States of America', *Int. Con.*, no. 301, 1934, pp. 177–95, and 'The development of international law since the war', *A.J.I.L.*, vol. 22, 1928, pp. 330–50.

United Nations Secretariat in 1947, entitled 'Historical Survey of Development of International Law and its Codification by International Conferences', classified the legislative work of the League of Nations, comprising a wide range of subjects affecting relations between states, under 25 headings.[1] The majority of the 120 international conventions, concluded under the auspices of the League of Nations between 1920 and 1939, had as their object the general regulation of relations between states. All of them promoted the progressive development of international law in many fields of international relations. Moreover, the International Labour Conference of the I.L.O., created as part of the League of Nations organization in 1919, adopted 80 international labour conventions and the same number of recommendations in the course of 29 sessions held from 1919 to 1946. These covered a wide field, and the *International Labour Code 1939*, published by the I.L.O. Office in 1941, arranged the subject matter covered by the conventions under twelve main headings.[2]

It is sufficient to emphasize here that before the League undertook a systematic study of codification of international law in 1924, it had already contributed to the formation of a body of law in other ways. The activities of the League and of the I.L.O. in connection with the conclusion of technical conventions were only a continuation, through a specially convenient and world-wide organization, of activities which had been carried on since early in the nineteenth century, through the formation of international unions.[3] The enormous services of the League and the I.L.O. in what the League Assembly's Resolution of September 22, 1924, described as 'meeting the legislative needs of international relations'[4] were in the nature of a piecemeal codification confined to special, rather technical subjects. This work considerably stimulated interest in the method by which international law may be vivified and extended.

[1] These were: International law; Arbitration and security; Economic and financial; Unification of commercial law; Settlement of commercial disputes; Agricultural credit; Treatment of foreigners; Counterfeiting currency; Customs; Bones, hides and skins; Veterinary questions; Economic statistics; Whaling; Model conventions; Communications and transit; Unification of river law; Maritime questions; Railways; Road traffic; Emigrants; Electricity; Intellectual co-operation; Social and humanitarian questions; and Narcotics. See U.N. Doc. A/AC.10/5, in *A.J.I.L.*, vol. 41, 1947, suppl. pp. 53–61.

[2] *Ibid.*, pp. 61–5.

[3] Report of the League Council on the work of the Committee of Experts, L. of N. Offl. Jnl., 8th yr., no. 7, 45th sess., p. 750.

[4] Resolution of the Assembly of the League of Nations, September 22, 1924, L. of N. Offl. Jnl. sp. suppl. no. 21, 1924, p. 10. Also in *A.J.I.L.*, vol. 41, 1947, sp. suppl. p. 103, Appendix 6.

APPOINTMENT OF THE COMMITTEE OF EXPERTS, 1924

Under Article 14 of the Covenant of the League of Nations the Council of the League was directed to submit a plan for a Permanent Court of International Justice, for the preparation of which it appointed a Committee of Jurists. On July 24, 1920, on the suggestion of Elihu Root, the American member, the Council adopted a Resolution which recommended the continuation of the work begun by the First and Second Hague Conferences so that the nations should agree upon the law to be interpreted and applied by the Permanent Court of International Justice.[1] A conference was proposed for the advancement of international law which would re-establish the laws which had been damaged by the events of World War I, would make the revisions that the changed conditions of international life demanded, would reconcile divergent opinions on controversial rules, and would give special consideration to those points which were not adequately provided for and on which a definite settlement was required in the interest of international justice. The terms of this Resolution seemed to view codification in the wider sense of progressive development of international law, and favoured collaboration with scientific organizations in the preparation of draft plans for submission to the various governments, and subsequently to the Conference for the realization of the codification work.

The First Assembly of the League was not disposed to take immediate action, believing that public opinion had not yet recovered sufficient stability for codification to be undertaken without serious risks with regard to the future.[2] It was not until 1924 that the Assembly adopted a Swedish proposal to study those subjects of international law which might usefully be examined with a view to their incorporation in international conventions or in other instruments established by a conference under the League's auspices.[3] The Assembly and the Council of the League established a Committee of Experts for the systematic study of the progressive codification of international law.[4]

---

[1] Procés-Verbaux of the Proceedings of the Committee, 1920, p. 747. The Resolution is reproduced in *A.J.I.L.*, vol. 41, 1947, sp. suppl. pp. 102–3, Appendix 5; also *Proc. Am. Soc. Int. Law.*, 1920, pp. 79–81.

[2] See L. of N. Offl. Jnl., Records of the 1st Assembly, 1920, pp. 745–7.

[3] L. of N. Offl. Jnl. sp. suppl. no. 23, 1924, Records of the 5th Assembly, 12th Pl. mtg., pp. 82–3.

[4] The Assembly's Resolution of September 22, 1924, L. of N. Offl. Jnl. sp. suppl. no. 21, 1924, p. 10 and Council's Resolution of December 12, 1924, L. of N. Offl. Jnl., February 1925, pp. 274–5, Annex 719, are reproduced in *A.J.I.L.*, vol. 41, 1947, suppl. pp. 103–5. The members of the Committee were: Hammarskjöld, Chairman (Sweden), Brierly (U.K.), Fromageot (France), Guer-

The Assembly Resolution of September 22, 1924, concerning the development of international law, instead of calling upon governments to indicate appropriate subjects as was proposed by the delegate for Sweden and endorsed by the First Committee of the Assembly, entrusted the initiative to the Committee of Experts. This Committee, which was proposed to represent 'the main forms of civilization and the principal legal systems of the world', was assigned the following tasks: i. to draw up a provisional list of the subjects of international law, the regulation of which by international agreement appeared most desirable and realizable; ii. to communicate the list to governments of states, whether members of the League or not, for their opinion; iii. to examine the replies from governments; iv. to report to the Council of the League on the questions which appeared sufficiently ripe for progressive codification of international law; and v. to submit a report to the Council on the procedure which might be followed to prepare those questions eventually for conferences.

The Committee of Experts selected 11 subjects for preliminary examination[1] by sub-committees: nationality; territorial waters; diplomatic privileges and immunities; the legal status of ships owned by states and used for trade; extradition; the criminal jurisdiction of states with regard to crimes perpetrated outside their territories; the responsibility of states for damage suffered within their territories by foreigners; the procedure of international conferences and the conclusion and drafting of treaties; the suppression of piracy; the application in international law of the concept of prescription; and the rules regarding the exploitation of the products of the sea. The Committee adjourned the consideration of problems concerning war and neutrality, and, with regard to problems of private international law, appointed a sub-committee to draw up a list of such problems.[2]

At its next session in 1926 the Committee of Experts drew up

---

rero (Salvador), Loder (Netherlands), Barbozade Magalhaes (Portugal), Mastny (Czechoslovakia), Matsuda (Japan), Rundstein (Poland), Schücking (Germany), Suarez (Argentina), Visscher (Belgium), Chung Hui Wang (China), Wickersham (U.S.A.), a Spanish legal adviser, and a legal expert in Moslem law (Sir Muhammad Rafique).

[1] The Committee originally agreed on a list of 21 subjects as suitable for consideration, comprising subjects of private as well as public international law. Among the scientific bodies consulted by this Committee were the American Society of International Law (which suggested an alternative list of five subjects), the International Law Association, Institute of International Law, Society of Comparative Legislation, Institut ibérique de droit comparé, American Institute of International Law, Union Jurisdique Internationale, and Comité Maritime International. See L. of N. Offl. Jnl., 1925, sp. suppl. no. 33, pp. 176-7.

[2] *Ibid.*, pp. 842-4.

questionnaires on the following seven topics: nationality; territorial waters; diplomatic privileges and immunities; responsibility of states in respect to injury to persons or property of foreigners; procedure of international conferences and procedure for the conclusion and drafting of treaties; piracy; and exploitation of the products of the sea.[1] In 1927 the Committee reported to the Council of the League on the basis of the replies of various governments, observing that in selecting the seven topics 'the Committee was at special pains to confine its inquiry to problems which it thought could be solved by means of conventions without encountering any obstacles of a political nature'.[2] These subjects were considered by the Committee to be 'sufficiently ripe', since favourable replies, although by no means uniform, were received from governments, only a small number of them adopting a frankly negative attitude. However, an analysis of the actual views of several governments clearly indicates that even at this early stage of the preparatory work the range of variation in the reservations expressed in the governments' replies was bound to influence the result of the proposed codification conference.

The Committee submitted a general report on procedure which could be followed in the preparation for an international conference, and two special reports on procedure for two particular subjects, namely, the question of the exploitation of the products of the sea, and that of procedure for the conduct of international conferences and the conclusion and drafting of treaties. It emphasized the need for additional and thorough preparation in order to facilitate and shorten the work of conferences; in its opinion the most desirable method was the preparation of complete drafts which might serve as bases for discussion. It also stressed the desirability of collecting and classifying, as part of conference preparation, all the historical, legislative and scientific data on the subjects chosen for codification. Moreover, it preferred that a single conference should be held to discuss all subjects deemed ripe for codification, although the decision was left to the Council of the League.

In its subsequent report to the Assembly, adopted on June 13, 1927,[3] the Council observed: that most of the governments in their replies to the questionnaires had avoided detailed expression of their views as to the provision which might be inserted in an international convention to solve the various questions raised by the

[1] L.N.Doc. C.43.M.18, 1926, V; L.N.Doc. C.45.M.22, 1926, V; L.N.Doc. C.49.M.26, 1926, V. The documents relating to the Committee of Experts are reproduced in *A.J.I.L.*, sp. suppl. January 1928, pp. 1–233.
[2] L.N.Doc. C.196.M.70, 1927, V, p. 7; also *A.J.I.L.*, vol. 41, 1947, suppl. p. 70.
[3] L. of N. Offl. Jnl. 8th yr. no. 7, 45th sess. of Council 1927, pp. 749–57.

Committee of Experts; that the Committee itself had abstained from adding the weight of its authority to any of its own detailed suggestions; and that, since all the subjects proposed for codification were not of equal importance, two of them—piracy and diplomatic privileges—should be excluded. It maintained that the method of the preparatory work used by the Committee of Experts did not enable governments to state their views fully on the existing state of law, but that, if the conference had before it draft conventions embodying the views and practices of governments, it had more likelihood of success. Then it drew attention to the nature of the codification work as enunciated by the Assembly Resolution of September 22, 1924, which furnished 'no justification for thinking that that body considered that any single initiative, or the work of any single body of experts, could be expected to result in the formulation of a *corpus* of written law governing the more important relations between the members of the international family. On the contrary, the resolution recognizes that the establishment of positive rules of law in international relations must be a gradual process, to which contribution is made from every side as the need is felt and the possibility of action presents itself.'

The League Assembly considered this report at its 8th session. The First Committee of the Assembly[1] agreed to limit the programme of codification to three subjects: nationality; territorial waters; and responsibility of states for damage done in their territory to the person or property of foreigners. It favoured a single conference for discussion of all subjects, convened by the League of Nations rather than by a particular government. In its view, 'the convocation and preparation of the First Codification Conference should be left entirely to the League of Nations' as 'any other course would be interpreted by a section of public opinion as a real blow to the prestige of the League'—evidence of its sensitivity to public opinion. It also recommended that a Preparatory Committee, composed of five persons appointed by the Council, be entrusted with the preparatory work of the conference, and that detailed reports be drawn up on every question under study, on the basis of information received from governments relating to the state of the positive law, national and international, their existing practice, and their opinions regarding possible modifications or additions to the existing rules. These reports, showing the points of agreement and divergency, were recommended to serve as bases of discussion for the conference.[2] Finally, discussing the form of codification, whether it

---

[1] See for its Report L. of N. Offl. Jnl., sp. suppl. no. 54, Records of the 8th ordinary sess. of the Assembly, Pl. mtgs. pp. 484–8, Annex 35.

[2] The Committee defined in detail the functions of the preparatory committee

involved mere registration of the law in force or adaptation to practical needs, the Committee stated that 'while, in order to lead to useful results, the Conference must refrain from making too many innovations, it cannot limit itself to the mere registration of the existing law'.

PREPARATORY COMMITTEE FOR THE CODIFICATION
CONFERENCE

Three months later, on the basis of these recommendations, the Assembly adopted a resolution to the effect that, considering that it was material for the progress of justice and the maintenance of peace to define, improve and develop international law, it was the duty of the League to make every effort to contribute to the progress of codification of international law, to which end systematic preparation should be made for the first Codification Conference to be held at The Hague in 1929.[1] It asked the Council to transmit to the invited governments draft regulations for governing the deliberations in the Conference and indicating

(a) the possibility, if occasion should arise, of adopting amongst themselves rules accepted by a majority vote; (b) the possibility of drawing up, in respect of such subjects as may lend themselves thereto, a comprehensive convention and, within the framework of that convention, other more restricted conventions; (c) the organization of a system for the subsequent revision of the agreements entered into; and (d) the spirit of codification, which should not confine itself to the mere registration of the existing rules, but should aim at adapting them as far as possible to contemporary conditions of international life.

This shows that the Assembly had in mind a combination of codification and legislation and the adoption on a limited scale of a parliamentary method of enacting laws passed by the majority for the states constituting that majority. At the same time, by calling upon a single conference to work on three major problems of international relations, the Assembly unduly enlarged the programme of the forthcoming conference.

The Preparatory Committee for the Codification Conference,

---

and the method of preparation, which were adopted in the Assembly's resolution. It may be noted that the proposal for the formation of a permanent organization for codification in the form of a permanent legal committee and enlarging the Legal Section of the Secretariat was considered by the Committee as somewhat premature; *ibid.*, p. 487.

[1] Resolution adopted by the Assembly September 27, 1927, L. of N. Offl. Jnl. sp. suppl. no. 53, October 1927, pp. 9–10; also in *A.J.I.L.*, vol. 41, 1942, suppl., pp. 105–7.

appointed by the President of the Council,[1] issued lengthy question-naires on the three subjects selected for codification and drew up bases of discussion for the Conference. In some cases these merely stated existing law, in others they included new law which appeared acceptable to some governments. Hence they were neither mere summaries of views of governments nor simply statements of the Preparatory Committee about what the law might be.[2] The Com-mittee also drafted the rules of procedure for the Conference.[3]

Thus, in contrast to the Hague Peace Conferences of 1899 and 1907, the preparatory work for the first Hague Conference called under the auspices of the League of Nations extended over a period of approximately six years, since the decision of the Assembly in 1924 to appoint the Committee of Experts. In addition to the pains-taking work done by the Preparatory Committee, the Harvard Law School had also prepared draft conventions on the same three topics with copious comments which were made available to the Conference. Last but not least, the services of the excellent staff from the Secretariat of the League, well-trained in the mechanics of international conferences, greatly eased the working of the codification conference. But considering all this preparation and the facilities provided by the League, the results achieved by the Hague Conference of 1930 were disappointing.[4] Officially designated as the First International Conference for the Codification of Inter-national Law, it was in fact, if not in form, the third of a series. In a sense it was *over*-prepared, as the participants had taken up positions, which, having been made public, seemed to be fixed, with little scope left for subsequent changes of attitude.

THE HAGUE CONFERENCE OF 1930

Acting on the request of the Assembly Resolution of September 24, 1929, the Council invited all members of the League and twelve non-member governments, including the Union of Soviet Socialist Republics and the United States of America, to the Codification Conference, and appointed as president M. Heemskerke, Minister of State and former Prime Minister of the Netherlands.[5]

[1] L. of N. Offl. Jnl. 8th yr. no. 10, 47th sess. of Council, 1927, pp. 1452–3. The documents referring to its meetings and reports are reproduced in *A.J.I.L.*, vol. 24, 1930, suppl. pp. 1–8.

[2] See *A.J.I.L.*, *op. cit.*, pp. 9–74.

[3] *Ibid.*, pp. 74–9.

[4] See Sir Cecil Hurst: 'A plea for the codification of international law on new lines', *Trans. Grotius Soc.*, vol. XXXII, 1947, pp. 139–40.

[5] Resolution of Assembly, L. of N. Offl. Jnl. sp. suppl. no. 74, October 1929, p. 9; Report of Rapporteur of the First Committee, *ibid.*, sp. suppl. no. 75, pp. 169–71; Council Resolution, L. of N. Offl. Jnl. 10th yr. no. 11, 56th and 57th sess. of Council, November 1929, pp. 1700–1.

The Conference met at The Hague from March 13 to April 12, 1930 and was attended by 47 states including nine countries which were not members of the League. The delegations included chiefly government officials and diplomats as well as several members of the legal profession. The work of the Conference was done primarily in three committees, one for each of the three subjects on the agenda.[1]

Nationality

On the subject of nationality the Conference was, relatively, most successful and adopted the following instruments:

1. The Convention on Certain Questions relating to the Conflict of Nationality Laws, signed by 30 governments, contained 31 articles of which the first 17 set forth substantive rules concerning nationality.[2] It aimed to remove certain consequences of statelessness and double nationality. Notwithstanding almost insurmountable obstacles due to divergencies in the laws of different states, it attempted to regulate the problem of nationality and was 'imbued with a general idea which the legislatures of every country must regard as expressing the feeling of the Conference'. This idea was that 'every individual has a right to a nationality and that it is most important for all countries to prevent any person from possessing multiple nationality'.[3] However, it failed to deal adequately with the conflicts arising from the applications of the *ius soli*, *ius sanguinis*, and naturalization Law. Its main defect consisted in its liberal provision for reservations (Article 20) according to which it was permissible for any party to the Convention to append an express reservation excluding any one or more of the provisions.[4] The Convention came into force on July 1, 1937.

[1] For the composition of the committees see Final Act of the Conference, *A.J.I.L.*, vol. 24, 1930, p. 181.
The Proceedings of the Conference are printed in *Acts of the Conference for the Codification of International Law* (hereafter cited as Acts of Hague Conf. 1930) in 4 vols.: Vol. I, L.N.Doc. C.351.M.145, 1930, V, Plenary mtgs.; Vol. II, L.N.Doc. C.351(a).M.145, 1930, V, Minutes of the First Committee on Nationality; Vol. III, L.N.Doc. C.351(b).M.145(b), 1930, V, Minutes of the Second Committee on Territorial Waters; Vol. IV, L.N.Doc. C.351(c).M.145(c), 1930, V, Minutes of the Third Committee on Responsibility of States.
[2] The Convention consisted of six chapters of which five dealt with the general principles, expatriation permits, nationality of married women, nationality of children, and adoption. For text of Convention, see *A.J.I.L.*, vol. 24, 1930, suppl. pp. 192–200. On the nationality of married women the Conference heard delegates from the Women's International Organizations, see Acts of Hague Conf. 1930, vol. II, pp. 178–83; see also *ibid.*, Annex VI, pp. 318–21.
[3] Report of the First Committee submitted by the Rapporteur, Acts of Hague Conf. 1930, vol. II, Annex V, p. 315.
[4] For criticism of the Convention see J. B. Scott's editorial in *A.J.I.L.*, vol. 24, 1930, pp. 556–61; also R. W. Flournoy Jr.: 'Nationality Convention, Protocols and Recommendations adopted by the First Conference on Codification of International Law', *A.J.I.L.*, vol. 24, 1930, pp. 467–85.

2. Three Protocols were adopted by the Conference by a majority, the First and Second being approved by a majority of more than two-thirds of the delegations present. The First Protocol, relating to Military Obligations in certain cases of Double Nationality, aimed at relieving persons having dual nationality of one of the chief inconveniences of their status by exempting them from military service in one of the countries of which they were nationals.[1] The two other Protocols dealt with the problems of statelessness. That relating to a certain case of statelessness provided that, where the *ius soli* was not applied, a person on the territory of a state born of a mother who had the nationality of that state and of a father who had no nationality, or whose nationality was not known, shall have the nationality of that state. The other special Protocol concerning statelessness laid down the conditions under which a state was bound to receive into its territory a former national who had lost his status without acquiring another, at the request of the state in whose territory such a person was. Although it failed to receive the approval of two-thirds of the delegates voting in the First Committee, it became the Act of the Conference.

The texts of these instruments were drafted with the caution necessitated by the wide divergencies between various systems of municipal law. They did not attempt to achieve complete uniformity, nor did they remove all the difficulties attendant upon dual nationality or entirely eliminate statelessness. But, considering the constant clash between different legal systems, the achievement of the Conference in this field marked a noteworthy advance in that it represented a first attempt to transfer this subject, which hitherto depended on municipal law, into the domain of international law.[2]

Furthermore the Conference formulated eight recommendations on various aspects of nationality which may be grouped under four headings: the regulation of statelessness in general; the regulation of the problem of dual nationality; the introduction into the laws of the various states of the principle of sex equality in the matter of nationality, with particular consideration for the interests of children and the granting of greater liberty to a woman marrying a foreigner, in respect of retention of her original nationality; the proof of nationality.[3]

[1] For text of Protocols, see *A.J.I.L.*, vol. 24, 1930, suppl. pp. 201–15.
[2] Report of the First Committee, Acts of Hague Conf. 1930, vol. II, p. 315; *A.J.I.L.*, vol. 24, 1930, suppl., p. 216.
[3] Final Act of the Conference of 1930; *A.J.I.L.*, vol. 24, 1930, suppl., pp. 182–3.

Territorial waters

On this subject, although the Conference failed to produce a convention, unanimous agreement was reached on two principles: freedom of navigation and the sovereignty of coastal states over the maritime belt.[1] Since it was impossible to reach agreement on the breadth of the territorial sea and the rules governing the exercise of sovereignty within and about this area, the Conference only adopted a Resolution including as an annex 13 articles on the legal status of the territorial sea, which defined and regulated the right of passage for warships and other vessels. These were provisionally approved and were intended by the Conference to form part of a convention determining the breadth of the territorial sea, or to serve as constituent elements of a special convention on the legal status of the territorial sea.[2]

In addition to the Resolution two recommendations were adopted, the first on the legal status of foreign vessels in inland waters,[3] and the second on the protection of fisheries which called attention to the desirability of assisting in scientific research on marine fauna and the means of protecting fry in local areas of the sea.

In this Conference the rule of three miles of territorial waters was challenged, and the bases of discussion recorded lack of unanimity on this rule.[4] However, a general resolution expressed the desire of the Conference to continue the work of codification on this subject, and the Council was requested to invite governments to study the question and to convene a new conference, 'either for the conclusion of a general convention on all questions connected with the Territorial Sea, or even—if that course should seem desirable—of a convention limited' to the legal status of the territorial sea.[5]

While the Conference failed to deal with the extent of the territorial sea and the problem of the contiguous zone, it had made a

---

[1] Report of the Second Committee on Territorial Waters, by M. François, Rapporteur, Acts of Hague Conf. 1930, vol. III, ap. 209–12; *A.J.I.L.*, vol. 24, 1930, suppl., pp. 234–58.

[2] Final Act of Hague Conf. 1930, Part B; *A.J.I.L.*, vol. 24, 1930, suppl., pp. 183–7.

[3] *Ibid.*, p. 187. It suggested that the Convention on the International Régime of Maritime Ports (Geneva, December 9, 1923) should be supplemented by provisions regulating the scope of the judicial powers of states regarding vessels in their inland waters.

[4] Report of the Second Committee on Territorial Waters, *A.J.I.L.*, vol. 24, 1930, suppl., pp. 234–7; also J. S. Reeves: 'The codification of the law of territorial waters', *A.J.I.L.*, vol. 24, 1930, suppl., pp. 486–99. The author summarizes the position taken by different countries regarding the three-mile limit, contiguous zone and six-mile limit. Also R. W. Hale: 'Territorial waters as a test of codification', *ibid.*, pp. 65–8.

[5] *A.J.I.L.*, vol. 24, 1930, suppl., pp. 183–7.

useful exploration of the divergent points of view. The excellent report by M. François has been of great value in paving the way for far more fruitful efforts under the United Nations Organization.[1]

Responsibility of states

The work of the Conference on this subject was the least successful. The Third Committee was unable to complete its study and submitted no conclusions to the Conference.[2] During their discussions the delegations seemed to agree on certain fundamental ideas. In particular, they accepted the principle of the responsibility of states for the actions of their legislative, executive and judicial authorities. One of the principal reasons for the failure of achievement lay in the mistake of attempting to regulate these questions in detail, but the shortage of time and the intrinsic nature of the subject were more responsible for the failure to produce any conclusion than that international law could not be submitted to the principle of codification.[3]

Finally, certain *desiderata* of far-reaching importance relating to the future work of codification were adopted by the 1930 Conference.[4] The first, recognizing the necessity of resorting to scientific labours for codification in general, stressed the idea that all the scientific national and international associations should apply themselves to the study of the fundamental questions of international law, particularly the principles and rules and their application, in order that their work might be placed at the disposal of future codification conferences. The second stressed the desirability of the widest possible co-ordination of all efforts made for the codification of international law, and recommended the establishment of an harmonious link between the codification undertaken by the League of Nations and that effected by the Conferences of American States. The third contained suggestions on the organization of the preparatory work for future conferences, including some improvements in the technique already adopted by the League and implying thereby

---

[1] See below, pp. 300–1.
[2] In fact the Committee adopted a preliminary proposal of a Convention but this could not be passed because of the lack of a two-thirds vote in the Committee; Acts of Hague Conf. 1930, vol. IV, pp. 236–7. See G. H. Hackworth: 'Responsibility of states for damages . . .', *A.J.I.L.*, vol. 24, 1930, pp. 500–16. Also E. M. Borchard, *ibid.*, pp. 517–40. These authors represented the U.S.A. on the Committee.
[3] Hackworth, *op. cit.*, pp. 515–16. Also Report of M. de Visscher, Rapporteur of the Committee, Acts of Hague Conf. 1930, vol. IV, pp. 237–8, Annex V.
[4] Final Act of Hague Conf. 1930, Part D, General Recommendations with a view to the progressive codification of International Law, *A.J.I.L.*, vol. 24, 1930, pp. 188–90; Acts of Hague Conf. 1930, vol. I, pp. 171–2.

both that the methods hitherto adopted were defective and that it was intended that further conferences would be held.

APPRAISAL OF THE WORK OF THE 1930 CONFERENCE

In the history of the Hague Conference of 1930 all the facets of the task of codifying international law were demonstrated: the selection of subjects, the extent of the preparation, the organization of the Conference, the conflict of interests between participating states, the differences in the systems of domestic jurisprudence and in political attitudes, and the harmonizing of conflicting concepts in the international sphere. Appreciation of the results of the Conference may be made from two standpoints: the degree of its success in realizing the object for which it was called; and the facts established and the lessons left for the future. If it failed according to the first criterion, it was very fruitful according to the second.

The achievements of the Conference were disappointing in the context of the high hopes in which it had been convened for the avowed codification of international law. Its results were meagre— they embodied only four signed instruments, all subject to ratification and open for accession, and to come into force on the 90th day after the Secretary General of the League had drawn the *procés-verbal* when ratifications or accessions on behalf of ten states had been deposited.[1] The formal clauses of these instruments left to the states a wide liberty of making reservations, which were limited, however, to the exclusion of one or more of the provisions of certain articles. The freedom was further increased by the privilege of denouncing the instruments at any time; the only limitation was that denunciation was to become effective only after one year. The identical formal provisions of the instruments constituted one of the contributions of the Conference which influenced the shaping of such provisions in future conventions.

These instruments covered between them only a small section of the field of nationality and provided law only as between contracting parties. They made it clear that their formulation was not exhaustive and in no way to be deemed to prejudge the question whether they did or did not already form part of international law. The provision was also made for a possible revision in the future. Although the direct and immediate influence of these agreements was not great, their indirect significance has been considerable inasmuch

[1] The Convention came into force on July 1, 1937; the First Protocol (relating to Military Obligations) on May 25, 1937; the Second Protocol (relating to a certain case of statelessness) on July 1, 1937; the Third Protocol (concerning statelessness) has not come into force. See L. of N. Offl. Jnl., sp. suppl. no. 193, pp. 61–4; also L.N.Doc. A.6.1939. Annex 1.V, Legal, 1939, V.2; Section XXIII, pp. 72–5.

as the subsequent nationality legislation of a number of states, including states which did not become parties to them, has been influenced by the principles set forth at the Conference.[1] However, the practical results were certainly not conspicuous. Active nationalism, the conflicts between the attitudes of states of large emigration on the one hand and those of large immigration on the other, the fundamental dichotomy between allegiance to *ius soli* and *ius sanguinis*,[2] and the rigid attitude of the various delegations and their efforts to secure consecration of their own national law—all these factors militated against a common agreement on many questions.

The fact that the Conference achieved limited results on nationality and failed to produce any agreement or concrete results on the other two subjects on its agenda led many enthusiasts for codification to declare the Conference a dismal failure in comparison with the previous two Hague Conferences. Their disappointment was the greater since the Conference was avowedly convoked for the codification of international law.

Why was the Conference a failure? Four points may be considered in this connection: the highly ambitious programme; defective preparatory work; confused ideas about the purpose of codification; and entire reliance on the convention method.

Ambitious programme. It was most unfortunate that the agenda of the Conference was too extensive. Charged with the duty of codifying three particular and mutually independent sections of the field of international law, the Conference was in fact undertaking the work of three conferences simultaneously.[3] It was a mistake to attempt consideration of three subjects, which were of great importance nationally and internationally, in a single conference, and that too in a limited period of just one month. The result was not only a hurried business through the Committees,[4] but also that the personnel of some of the delegations was insufficient to be represented on the three committees formed by the Conference, so that the meetings could not be held simultaneously. This experience has probably helped to determine the practice of the United Nations,

---

[1] P. Weis: *Nationality and Statelessness*, 1956, p. 31.

[2] J. B. Scott: 'Nationality: *Ius soli* or *Ius sanguinis*', *A.J.I.L.*, vol. 24, 1930, pp. 58–64.

[3] M. O. Hudson: 'The First Conference for Codification of International Law', *A.J.I.L.*, vol. 24, 1930, pp. 449–50. See also observations of Hunter Miller in his address to the American Society of International Law, Proceedings, 1930, p. 214; and the observations of the President of the Conference, April 12, 1930, Acts of Hague Conf. 1930, vol. I, p. 57, and Visscher's Report (Third Committee), *ibid.*, vol. IV, p. 238.

[4] Flournoy, 'National Convention . . .', *A.J.I.L.*, vol. 24, 1930, pp. 483–4.

which has been convening codification conferences only on one subject at a time.

Preparatory work. The experience at the Conference demonstrated that even the most thorough preparations by an international agency was no guarantee of success unless preparations were supplemented by active association of governments at all stages of codification. The recommendations of the Conference itself, suggesting improvements in the preparatory work for future codification conferences, seem to draw attention to the following defects: the initiative for the selection of subjects for codification lay with the Committee of Experts, which approached the problem solely from the technical point of view; the governments had no responsibility for the initial selection of subjects, nor any opportunity of sending their observations in the light of the comments made by other governments; and finally, the bases of discussion presented by the Preparatory Committee were not put before the Conference in the form of draft conventions.[1]

The Conference suggested improvements in the technique of preparation which stressed the desirability of engaging the responsibility of governments by procuring their formal approval even prior to the meeting of a Conference. The important features of the suggested technique were: the actual selection of subjects for codification by a political body composed of governments, rather than by a technical body of experts; the formulation of draft conventions by an appropriate body taking into account the observations of governments on the subjects proposed for codification; the transmission of such drafts to governments for their comments; and the final selection of the subjects by the League Council for the agenda of the Codification Conference, as formally approved by a very large majority of powers.[2]

The importance of the preparation by an international agency, by governments, and by jurists and scholars, and the need to associate the governments were recognized by the Assembly Resolution of September 25, 1931, which formulated for the future a new procedure for the codification of international law.[3] This provided for consultation with governments at least three times and again for their collective decision in the Assembly at least three times in

---

[1] M. O. Hudson: *Proc. Am. Soc. Int. Law*, 1930, pp. 231–2. The recommendations of the Committee of Experts and the League Council in this regard were ignored; see pp. 112–19 above.

[2] Recommendation IV, Act of the Hague Conf. 1930; *A.J.I.L.*, vol. 24, 1930, suppl. p. 189.

[3] L. of N. Offl. Jnl., Records of the 12th ordinary session of the Assembly, 1931, sp. suppl. no. 93, 14th Pl. mtg. pp. 135–7. Also in *A.J.I.L.*, vol. 41, 1947, sp. suppl. pp. 110–11.

the following way: governments, members or not, should have the initiative of proposing subjects for codification, and, prior to the Assembly meeting, ample opportunity to study the proposals of other governments; the Committee of Experts would then prepare for transmission to the Assembly drafts of conventions, which after approval would be communicated to the governments for their comments; and finally in the light of these comments the Committee of Experts would revise the draft conventions if necessary, resubmit them to the governments for comments, and eventually place them before the Assembly along with the comments of the governments, for such action as the Assembly may wish to take. Thus the emphasis placed upon the co-operation of governments at different stages of the preparatory work aimed to correct the defects from which the preparation for the 1930 Conference suffered. This emphasis later seems to have become a guiding principle of the United Nations' efforts in codification.

Confused ideas about the purpose of codification. Whether the purpose of codification was to arrive at an agreed statement of the existing rules of international law or whether the object was to revise the rules of international law in the light of modern requirements has been a controversial question. But these two tasks, codifying and legislating—different in purpose and technique—became confused at the Codification Conference of 1930.[1] Sir Cecil Hurst drew attention to the confusion of ideas as indicated by the terms of resolution by the Committee of Jurists and by the League Assembly, and those of the communications which emanated from the Secretariat.[2] These resolutions and communications showed that the League was never clear as to the purpose of codification and the method it wanted to adopt.

An essential condition of success for any organized effort aimed at reforming a system of law is a clear conception of the specific reforms desired to be introduced.[3] The very selection of topics for codification depends to a large extent upon the purpose and meaning of the term 'codification'. The facile use of the term and the lack of clarity of its purpose at the Conference overlooked this elementary condition of effective legislation. The Committee of Experts at the very outset of its activity confronted this question of the purpose of

---

[1] M. O. Hudson, addressing the American Society of International Law, said: 'I think not all of us were quite clear in our minds in the beginning as to just what the term [codification] is to be taken to mean, but it was soon decided that this was not to be an attempt to study merely the pre-existing law', *Proceedings*, 1930, p. 230.

[2] Hurst, *op. cit.*, *Trans. Grotius Soc.*, vol. XXXII, 1947, pp. 135–53.

[3] See Professor Brierly: 'The future of codification', in *The Bases of Obligation in International Law and other papers by James Leslie Brierly*, ed. H. Lauterpacht, 1958, p. 200.

K

codification and most of its members insisted that its task went
beyond that of registering the existing law.[1]

Insofar as the positive results of the Conference, in particular
in the field of nationality, are concerned, it is not easy to determine
whether some of the provisions of the Convention are only declaratory of existing customary international law or whether they make
new law. Whereas the Convention expressly declared that it did
not derogate from customary international law,[2] the two principal
protocols on nationality were distinctly legislative in character.
Considering the evils of the existing law there should have been no
uncertainty about the goal of reform in this branch of the law; it was
simply the elimination or reduction of the two unfortunate conditions of double nationality and statelessness. Some governments,
apprehending the possibility of written codification being interpreted as laying down the existing law and no more, were led to suggest that codification should refrain from registering international
law and should 'lay down rules which it would appear desirable to
introduce into international relations in regard to subjects dealt
with.[3] The experience of the 1930 Conference and of the entire
work of codification under the auspices of the League of Nations was
instructive in clarifying the true goal of codification in international
law. It showed that there were only a few branches of international
law in regard to which there existed such a pronounced measure
of agreement in the practice of states as to demand no more than
what has been called consolidating codification. It taught the
lesson that the legislative element in the attempt to codify any part
of international law was not merely subordinate or incidental, but
far outweighed the codifying element. Señor Alejandro Alvarez, in
a paper read before the Grotius Society, acknowledged the enormous
contribution of the Conference in drawing attention to the need to
reconstruct and renew international law 'by basing it on elements
which are essentially positive, and notably by taking note of international life as at the present time and in its actual world it exists'.[4]
The experience of the Conference also emphasized the fact that the
decisive criterion for the selection of a subject for codification must
be not the 'ripeness' or the ease with which the task could be
accomplished, but the *need* for codifying it. These lessons have been

[1] See the views expressed by Dr. Suarez, Professor Diena, Dr. Rundstein,
Professor Brierly and Professor Visscher, Minutes of the First Session of the Committee of Experts, April 1–8, 1925, pp. 7, 8, 14, 17 and 25.

[2] Article 18 of the Convention.

[3] Statement of the delegates of the Swiss government in 1931 in connection with
the discussion of the future work of codification. L.N. Doc. A.12(b), 1931, V, p. 3;
of the French government, L.N. Doc. A.12(a), 1931, V, p. 2.

[4] 'Impressions left by the First Hague Conference . . .', *Trans. Grotius Soc.*,
vol. XVI, 1931, p. 121.

very helpful to the United Nations in determining its goal of codification.

Entire reliance on the convention method. Although the great volume of international legislation and many successes of the Inter-American Conferences provide evidence of the successful application of the convention method, this system has many drawbacks. No state would be bound by a convention unless satisfied with its contents; diverse interests make it difficult for the governments to arrive at an international agreement binding in the definite future and covering unforeseen situations; states may make reservations on one or more articles of a convention, and may even denounce that convention. Because of these inherent characteristics, several multilateral conventions, not having been ratified by some states, or having been denounced by others, remain in a state of uncertainty since it is difficult to know whether they are in force or not, or which states are bound by them.

The League, however, did much useful work to improve its legislative method by appointing, in 1930, a committee to consider the ratification and signature of conventions concluded under its auspices. This committee examined the causes of delay in ratification and made valuable suggestions, some of which were given effect by certain resolutions of the Assembly.[1] The important feature of the new procedure, adopted to the League Conventions from that of the International Labour Organization, was to secure a larger degree of consultation in advance with the various governments in order to ascertain whether there was a probability that a proposed convention would receive their approval; to obtain their collaboration throughout the preparatory stage; and to aviod submitting to them definitive projects which after the consultations seemed unlikely to be ratified generally.

The problem of the place that should be accorded to the conclusion of conventions that conferred the character of international law on the rules they enacted, and to the signature of declarations designed to recognize existing law, was found by the Preparatory Committee for the 1930 Conference to be an exceedingly delicate matter. It was left to the Conference to take such line as it might decide.[2] The Committee, however, suggested in its draft rules of procedure a distinction between declarations establishing agreed principles of existing law and conventions dealing with matters not clearly covered by previously existing law, and also a distinction

[1] Report of the Committee submitted on May 9, 1930, L.N. Doc. A.10, 1930, V, p. 11. Five Resolutions were adopted by the Assembly on October 3, 1930, L. of N. Offl. Jnl., Records of 11th ordinary sess., 22nd Pl. mtg., 1930, pp. 512–17.
[2] Second Report of Preparatory Committee, L.N. Doc. C.73, M.38, 1929; also in *A.J.I.L.*, vol. 24, 1930, suppl. pp. 7–8.

between declarations or conventions agreed to unanimously and those agreed to only by a majority of the delegates at the Conference.[1]

The delegates at the Conference showed a determination to avoid anything like a declaration of the existing law[2] and were prepared to accept only a convention requiring acceptance by the parties.[3] The Conference was reluctant to commit itself to the distinctions suggested by the Preparatory Committee. The rules of procedure adopted by it laid down that each provision of a draft approved by a two-thirds majority of the delegates voting in the committees should be followed by a definitive voting of the text in the Conference by a simple majority. It was further added that when a provision had failed to receive a two-thirds vote in a committee, the committee might, upon a majority vote, report it to the Conference for inclusion in a special provision which would be an act of the Conference if five delegations requested a vote to that effect.[4] This system of adopting formal instruments—conventions or protocols— by majority vote in conferences acting *ad referendum* was a departure from the traditional rule of unanimous consent, and became acceptable because participant states could not only withhold their signatures but also not consider themselves bound until their consent was given through ratification of the instruments.

The fundamental difficulty in connection with any effort to secure an agreement on conventions stating fundamental rules of international law has been that if a particular government refused to recognize a rule as being the expression of existing law, another government, whilst recognizing that provision as existing law, might not desire to see it included in a convention, apprehending that the authority of that provision would be weakened by the replacement of customary international law by what in effect is a treaty. Moreover, another problem revealed by the 1930 Conference was that, from the moment states met in conference to determine the rules of international law on a given subject, the tendency was for them to devote their energies to the shaping of rules of international law to suit their own interests, although it is undeniable that international law cannot be made or altered to suit the convenience of one or a few states. It appeared then that the formulation of the

---

[1] Draft Rules of Procedure, L.N. Doc. C.190(1).M.93, 1929, V; also *A.J.I.L.*, *op. cit.*, pp. 74–9. See rules XXIV and XXV.

[2] Hudson remarked 'that sentiment grew quite rapidly against any attempt to state what was existing law as distinguished from new legislation, and after two weeks it became clear that even the use of the term *declaration* was strongly opposed'; 'The First Conference of Codification . . .', *A.J.I.L.*, vol. 24, 1930, p. 449.

[3] Hudson, *Proc. Am. Soc. Int. Law*, 1930, p. 230.

[4] Acts of Hague Conf. 1930, vol. I, pp. 20–5, 62–5. See Rules XVIII–XXIII.

rules of international law could not be undertaken by the states themselves because to do so seemed to make them judges in their own cause.

The experience of codification under the League brought out the utility of the preparation of scientific restatements of international law drawn by an international body functioning under mandate from an organization like the League. Such restatements should serve as an alternative to international conventions as a method of codification, and also as useful preliminary groundwork for eventual codification by international agreement.[1]

The Hague Conferences of 1899, 1907 and 1930 were examples of co-operation on the part of the members of the growing international community, but attention should also be given to the efforts of governments coming together at the regional level, in an attempt to codify and develop international law in order to regulate interstate relations in their region. Perhaps the leading rôle in this respect has been played by the states in the American hemisphere. The study of the codification of international law in the inter-American system deserves particular attention because the codification movement there was from the very beginning sponsored by governments rather than by private bodies. This unique feature, and the fruitful experience of the American states, earned a special reference in the League of Nations Resolution of September 25, 1931, as well as in the Statute of the International Law Commission adopted by the United Nations General Assembly in 1947.[2]

CODIFICATION OF INTERNATIONAL LAW IN THE INTER-AMERICAN SYSTEM

History

No sooner had the Latin American states renounced their connection with Europe than they sought to connect themselves with each other and with North America in some form of inter-American union. These states formed part of western civilization because of the strong Spanish, French and European influences within them; readily accepting the idea of international law, they were unusually active in broadly conceived and ambitious projects, conferences and agreements relating to it.[3]

[1] Hurst, 'A plea for codification . . .', *Trans. Grotius Soc.*, vol. XXXII, 1947. pp. 135–53.
[2] Respectively Recommendation (2) of the Resolution, L. of N. Offl. Jnl., sp. suppl. no. 92, 1931, p. 9; and Article 26 of the Statute of the ILC. See pp. 159–160, below.
[3] For brief synopses of Inter-American congresses, commissions and other agencies, see J. B. Scott (ed.): *The International Conferences of American States 1889–*

The earliest suggestion of a union of American nations manifested itself in the Congress of Panama convened in 1826 by Simon Bolívar, President of Peru and a statesman of vision. This congress, attended by the representatives of Colombia, Central America, Mexico and Peru, was the first of the series of the conferences of the American states which sought a close alliance, and harmonization of legal rules and remedies in their systems of jurisprudence, which were derived from different sources. It served as a two-fold precedent —for the Hague Conferences and for an American model of the League of Nations at Geneva. Although its Pact of Perpetual Union, League and Confederation signed in 1826 was never ratified, one of its articles suggested that the ratifying nations should lay down rules and principles to govern their conduct in times of peace and war.[1] This congress planted the seeds of the movement which led to the formation of the Pan-American Union.

The Inter-American conferences fall into two periods—those held before 1889, and those held subsequently to that year. The conferences before 1889 were inter-American in character but not continental in scope. Moreover, they were mainly concerned with the codification of private international law.[2] But, beginning with the First International Conference of American States of 1890, which met at Washington, the conferences of the second period included all the American nations, inspired the Pan-American movement and led to the formation of the Pan-American Union. It was the Second Conference, held at Mexico City from October 22, 1901, to January 31, 1902, which first attempted to set up a joint agency for the codification of international law. A Convention for the 'Formation of Codes on Public and Private International Law' provided for the appointment of a committee of five American and two European jurists of acknowledged reputation to be entrusted with the drafting of a Code of Public International Law and another, Code of Private International Law, which would govern the relations between the American nations.[3] This Committee could not be appointed because the Convention did not receive the requisite number of ratifications.

1928, 1931; R. D. Masters (ed.): *Handbook of International Organizations in the Americas, First Supplement, 1933–40*, 1945; and U.N. Doc. A/AC./10/8, 'Outline of Codification of International Law in the Inter-American System . . .', also reproduced in *A.J.I.L.*, vol. 41, 1947, suppl. pp. 116–38.

[1] Scott, *Int. Conf. Amer. States*, pp. xii and xxix.

[2] The Lima Conference of 1877 approved a treaty on rules to co-ordinate conflict of laws, and a convention on extradition. The Montevideo Conference of 1888 adopted five conventions covering nearly all subjects pertaining to private international law. Besides these juridical conferences, five inter-American political conferences were held between 1826 and 1877 and their principal object was the common defence and mutual protection of the participating states. Few of the treaties signed in these conferences were ratified.

[3] Scott: *op. cit.*, pp. 69–70.

The first agency for codification was not established until the Third International Conference of American States met at Rio de Janeiro in 1906 and adopted a convention forming an International Commission of Jurists[1] which comprised one representative from each of the signatory states. The Commission of Jurists divided itself into six working committees, four to work on public international law and two on private international law; they were to prepare projects for submission to the Commission which, after approving all projects by a two-thirds majority, was to place them before the Inter-American Conference. The work of this Commission and its committees was suspended because of the first World War. The Fifth International Conference of American States met at Santiago in 1923. Accepting as the basis the project presented by Dr. Alejandro Alvarez, entitled 'The Codification of American International Law', the Conference agreed on the advisability of a gradual and progressive codification. It resolved to re-establish the International Commission of Jurists whose recommendations, if approved by the Conference, were to be communicated to the governments for incorporation in conventions.[2]

The reorganized Commission of Jurists met at Rio de Janeiro from April 18 to May 20, 1927, and considered 30 projects of conventions on public international law which were prepared by the American Institute of International Law at the request of the Governing Board of the Pan-American Union. These projects had presented a tentative plan for the total codification of international law, but the Jurists favoured the theory of gradual codification and adopted 12 projects on public international law and one on private.[3] On the basis of these 12 projects the Sixth Inter-American Conference, which met at Habana in 1928, formulated seven conventions, covering the following subjects: status of aliens; rights and duties of states in the event of civil strife; treaties; diplomatic officers; consular agents; maritime neutrality; and asylum. They tended to create purely American international law, but they were so drafted as to leave open the possible adherence of states outside the system. They were ratified by a large number of American states.

The Habana Conference also adopted a resolution on Future Codification of International Law which established a new procedure. Besides the Commission of Jurists, it created three permanent committees: one on public international law at Rio de

---

[1] Scott: *op. cit.*, pp. 144–6.
[2] Resolution on Codification of American International Law, Scott: *Int. Conf. Amer. States*, pp. 245–7.
[3] This code, originally drafted by the Cuban jurist Antonio S. de Bustamente, was officially designated the 'Bustamente Code'; Scott: *op. cit.*, pp. 325–70, 415–41.

Janeiro, another on private international law at Montevideo, and a third on comparative legislation and uniformity of legislation at Habana. These committees were to be national bodies being 'constituted by governments with members of the respective National Societies of International Law'. They were to communicate with the American governments and with the Executive Council of the American Institute of International Law through the Pan-American Union. The governments, having received from the three committees the final draft proposals, 'may agree upon the advisability of convening the Commission of Jurists, or else have them incorporated into the program of a forthcoming International Conference'.[1]

Since this method of codification adopted at Habana proved ineffective, the Seventh International Conference of American States, Montevideo, 1933, changed the procedure by deciding to create a Committee of Experts with power to initiate questionnaires and drafts of proposed codes; this was probably influenced by the Hague Codification Conference of 1930. The Montevideo Conference also provided for the establishment of a National Commission on the Codification of International Law in each American state. Its Resolution LXX on Methods of Codification of International Law stated that the national commissions were to act through their respective foreign offices, and were to deal with the questionnaires and drafts communicated by the Committee of Experts which was to be entrusted with the whole of the preparatory work for the Commission of Jurists.[2] These recommendations were duly put into effect by the Pan-American Union. Besides this important resolution, the Montevideo Conference adopted a Convention on the Rights and Duties of States, and three additional conventions on Nationality of Women, Extradition, and Political Asylum.[3]

The Inter-American Conference for the Maintenance of Peace, held at Buenos Aires in 1936, by its Resolution VI on the Codification of International Law, re-established the Permanent Committees created by the Sixth Conference (Habana, 1928) to undertake the preliminary studies for codification. The National Commissions were to transmit the results of their studies of the doctrine on various subjects to be codified, to three Permanent Committees who were to prepare draft conventions and resolutions for submission to the Committee of Experts. This Committee in turn was to revise and co-ordinate the preparatory studies for a detailed report to the Pan-American Union, for transmission to the governments of American

[1] Scott: *Int. Conf. Amer. States*, pp. 439-40.
[2] Resolution LXX, Final Act of Seventh Inter. Conf. Amer. States, Appendix I, p. 108; also in *A.J.I.L.*, vol. 28, 1934, suppl. pp. 55-8.
[3] Masters: *Int. Conf. Amer. States, First Suppl. 1929-1933*, p. 502.

republics and ultimate submission to the International Commission of Jurists.[1]

The Committee of Experts held two sessions, one in Washington in 1937 and another in Lima in 1938, and submitted for the consideration of the Eighth International Conference of Inter-American States held at Lima in 1938 the following projects: definition of the aggressor and sanctions; investigation, conciliation and arbitration; nationality; code of peace; immunity of government vessels; pecuniary claims.[2] But the main contribution of the Lima Conference was to revise the existing system of carrying out the work of codification and to provide a more elaborate machinery in its comprehensive Resolution XVII. This resolution attempted to co-ordinate the codification of international law in America by classifying the successive stages of the work, and by establishing the precise duties of each of the agencies. The Permanent Committees of Habana, Rio de Janeiro and Montevideo were enlarged by the addition of six non-national members, thus losing their purely national character. They were to consider the studies of the National Commissions submitted in the form of preliminary drafts, and forward them to the Committee of Experts which was enlarged by two additional members. The drafts prepared by the Committee of Experts were then to be forwarded to the Pan-American Union, and thence to the American state governments. The resolution also changed the name of the International Commission of Jurists to International Conference of American Jurists, which was to be composed of the delegates with plenipotentiary powers. Its function was 'the revision, co-ordination, approval, modification or rejection of the draft prepared by the Committee of Experts'. The instruments adopted by it were to be transmitted to the American governments for ratification.[3]

A further addition to the existing agencies for codification was made to meet urgent problems, created by the outbreak of the second World War, in the field of neutrality. The foreign ministers meeting at Panama in 1939 created the Inter-American Neutrality Committee—an *ad hoc* body composed of seven experts in the field of international law and appointed by the Governing Board of the Pan-American Union—to deal with these problems and to draft a

---

[1] C. G. Fenwick: 'The Inter-American Conference for the Maintenance of Peace', *A.J.I.L.*, vol. 31, 1937, pp. 201–25; E. Borchard: 'Committee of Experts, Pan-American Codification of International Law', *ibid.*, pp. 471–3.

[2] E. Borchard: 'The Committee of Experts at the Lima Conference', *A.J.I.L.*, vol. 33, 1939, pp. 269–82.

[3] Borchard: *op. cit.*, pp. 271–2. For details of resolutions on method of codification of international law adopted at Inter-American Conferences of 1933, 1936, 1938, see Masters: *Int. Conf. Amer. States, First Suppl. 1933–1940*, pp. 84, 145 and 246.

project of Inter-American Convention.[1] However, in 1942, following the attack on Pearl Harbour, the Third Meeting of Ministers of Foreign Affairs, Rio de Janeiro, 1942, transformed the Inter-American Neutrality Committee into the Inter-American Juridical Committee of seven jurists, to which was entrusted the duty 'to develop and co-ordinate the work of codifying international law, without prejudice to the duties entrusted to other existing organizations'.[2]

Codifying agencies

By the time the United Nations sponsored the codification of international law there were in existence the following agencies created by the American governments:[3]

> nineteen National Committees (The United States of America and Haiti did not establish such committees);
> three Permanent Committees of Habana, Rio de Janeiro and Montevideo, although not fully organized;
> the Committee of Experts with headquarters at Washington;
> the International Conference of American Jurists;
> the Inter-American Juridical Committee.

The functions of these agencies of codification appear to have been assigned without any general plan of codification. Whereas National Committees and Permanent Committees made no significant contribution, the Committee of Experts submitted a number of valuable reports. But on the whole the experience gained by inter-American codification efforts showed that i. no effective codification was possible unless a small committee of technical experts representing the whole inter-American community and permanent in character were created as a central agency for the co-ordination of activities relating to codification; ii. the task of codifying international law was inextricably bound up with the progressive development of international law. These were the conclusions of the Inter-American Juridical Committee itself which recommended that a permanent central codification committee should maintain a close

---

[1] C. G. Fenwick: 'The Inter-American Neutrality Committee', *A.J.I.L.*, vol. 35, 1941, pp. 12–40; see Text of 'General Declaration of Neutrality of the American Republics', *A.J.I.L.*, vol. 34, 1940, suppl. p. 12, para. 5.

[2] C. G. Fenwick: 'The Inter-American Juridical Committee', *A.J.I.L.*, vol. 37, 1943, pp. 5–29. For summary of projects prepared by or in the Inter-American Juridical Committee from 1943 to 1950 see M. M. Whitman: *Digest of International Law*, vol. 1, 1963, pp. 143–4.

[3] See Report of the Inter-American Juridical Committee accompanying the Recommendation on the Reorganization of the Agencies engaged in the Codification of International Law, October 17, 1944, *A.J.I.L.*, vol. 39, 1945, suppl. pp. 232–42.

contact with the Secretariat of any international organization to be established after the war. In its words: 'The task of codifying international law is in large part a work of *de lege ferenda*, the formulation of new rules to meet the changing conditions of the time.' Hence in its view the members of a codification committee 'should be jurists who are in touch with the political, economic and social factors involved in the maintenance of law and order, and who are guided by a high sense of their obligations to promote international justice'. It also stressed the need of creating a special secretariat for the work of codification, and of properly co-ordinating the work of inter-American agencies, national or otherwise.[1]

These recommendations were given effect by the Charter of the Organization of American States, signed at Bogota in 1948.[2] Under it the existing inter-American agencies of codification ceased to exist, and were replaced by the Inter-American Council of Jurists (Article 57) and the Inter-American Juridical Committee (Article 68). The former is an advisory body on juridical matters 'to promote the development of codification of public and private international law; and to study the possibility of attaining uniformity in the legislation of the various American countries, insofar as it may appear desirable' (Article 67). The latter body is a permanent committee of nine jurists representing all member states of the Organization of American States, which undertakes such studies and preparatory works as are assigned to it, or those studies and projects initiated by it (Articles 68–70).[3]

This brief account of codification in the inter-American system is sufficient to draw attention to the rich practical experience already gained by American states in this field before the United Nations took up the initiative after the second World War. The Pan-American efforts at codification undoubtedly achieved a great success inasmuch as their results were embodied in treaties which have been binding on the American states irrespective of any formal act of consent, although the position has remained obscure as to the extent to which the participating states in the Pan-American Codification Conferences have been bound by the conclusions in cases where they have refused to accept the treaties, or have annexed reserves. However, a century or more of their experience had shown that, even with the best of good will, there remain certain obstacles—principally in the co-ordination of the systems of jurisprudence and

---

[1] Report of the Inter-American Juridical Committee of October 17, 1944, *A.J.I.L.*, vol. 39, 1945, suppl. pp. 242–5.
[2] J. L. Kunz: 'The Bogota Charter of the Organization of American States', *A.J.I.L.*, vol. 42, 1948, pp. 568–89.
[3] For a summary account of the work of these bodies, see Whitman: *Digest of International Law*, vol. 1, pp. 144–76.

of the differences between legal institutions of the civil law and those of common law—which only time and constructive effort could remove. Codification at international level could learn much by this experience which led to the special reference to the advisability of consultation by the International Law Commission with the Pan-American Union.[1]

CODIFICATION OF THE LAWS OF WAR AS A RESULT OF TWO WORLD WARS

It was noted earlier that from the middle of the nineteenth to the first decade of the twentieth century, the law of war was the first to be partially codified by government efforts. These codifications had been preceded and were followed, up to the first World War, by municipal regulations helped by various international conferences. But it is not surprising that they proved inadequate during the two World Wars, when the belligerents used all arguments apt to up-root the whole law of war.[2] Nevertheless the movement for the codification and revision of the laws of war did not disappear altogether during the inter-war period, although there had been a general trend not only to neglect but also even to discourage any attempt to codify the laws of war.[3] For instance, the scientific organizations like the Institute of International Law, the International Law Association, the Hague Academy of International Law and the Inter-Parliamentary Union, in contrast to the pre-1920 period, paid no attention to the problem of laws of war, and the League of Nations and in our times the United Nations would have nothing to do with the laws of war.[4]

Notwithstanding the fact that since 1914, and particularly since 1939, there has been a disastrous decline in the conduct of war, new techniques of warfare have lent themselves to increasingly inhuman practices and to wholesale devastation, and have fostered the adoption of unlimited war aims, limited efforts to codify some aspects of the laws of war have been made ever since the end of World War I. The increased destruction of total war, first demon-

[1] Article 26(4) of the Statute of the International Law Commission.

[2] See H. A. Smith: *The Law and Customs of the Sea*, 1948, p. 67; J. W. Garner: *International Law and the World War*, 1920; E. G. Trimble: 'Violation of maritime law by the allied powers during the World War', *A.J.I.L.*, vol. 24, 1930, pp. 79–99.

[3] See for a very sharp criticism of this trend J. L. Kunz: 'The chaotic status of the laws of war and the urgent necessity for their revision', *A.J.I.L.*, vol. 45, 1951, pp. 37–61.

[4] Although the Committee of Jurists which elaborated the plan for the Permanent Court of International Justice adopted a *voeu* recommending the revision of the laws of war and a new Hague Conference, the League did nothing about it. Similarly the International Law Commission established by the United Nations has expressly declined to deal with the laws of war.

strated by that war, generated through multilateral treaties new efforts intended to limit the right of states to make war[1] and also led to treaties of a codificatory nature regulating the use of weapons. The instruments of the latter category were as follows:

i. The Geneva Gas Protocol of 1925 for the prohibition of the use in war of asphyxiating, poisonous or other gases, and of bacteriological methods of warfare was ratified or acceded to by 40 states, including all the Great Powers of Europe, and China.[2] The Council of the League of Nations by resolutions of May 14, 1938, and September 30, 1938, stated that 'the use of toxic gases is a method of war condemned by international law, which cannot fail, should resort be had to it, to meet with the reprobation of the civilized world'.[3] The general prohibition of gas and bacteriological warfare was infringed by Italy against Ethiopia during 1935–6.

ii. The Geneva Conventions concerning the treatment of the sick and wounded, and of prisoners of war, signed on July 27, 1929, came into force on June 19, 1931.[4] They replaced those of 1864 and 1906, revising them in the light of the experience of the first World War. Both were based on the projects prepared by the International Conference of the Red Cross.

iii. The London Protocol relating to the rules of Submarine Warfare, incorporating verbatim the provisions of Part IV of the Treaty of London of April 22, 1930 (which was allowed to expire on December 31, 1936), signed on November 6, 1936, by the United States of America, Great Britain (including Dominions and India), France, Italy and Japan and open for accession by other states,[5] provided that merchant vessels may not be sunk without regard for the safety of their crews. But the observance of the Protocol during the second World War was the exception rather than the rule.

iv. Geneva Conference of 1949: At the conclusion of the second World War, on the initiative of the International Committee of the Red Cross, the complex and vital task of completing and amending the rules of international law for the protection of the victims of

---

[1] *Viz.* the general limitations imposed by the Covenant, the Treaty of Renunciation of War (popularly known as the Kellogg-Briand Pact of 1928, signed by 65 nations), and the Charter. See I. Brownlie: *International Law and the Use of Force by States*, 1963, pp. 55–65, 74–92; E. M. Borchard: 'The Multilateral Treaty for Renunciation of War', *A.J.I.L.*, vol. 23, 1929, pp. 116–20; and M. Greenspan: *The Modern Law of Land Warfare*, 1959, pp. 23–32.

[2] The People's Republic of China announced its adherence to the Geneva Protocol on July 16, 1952. The United States of America and Japan signed but did not ratify the Protocol.

[3] L. of N. Offl. Jnl., 19th year, 1938, pt. I, p. 378, pt. II, p. 881.

[4] *A.J.I.L.*, vol. 27, 1933, suppl., pp. 43–91.

[5] For the text see *A.J.I.L.*, vol. 31, 1937, suppl. pp. 137–9. The Protocol was acceded to by 11 other states, including Germany.

armed hostilities was undertaken in 1945. First assembling the fullest possible data and settling upon those aspects of international law that required confirmation, completion or amendment, then co-operating with experts of various countries,[1] the texts of revised and new conventions were drafted by the Committee for submission to the International Red Cross Conference of 1948[2] and finally, to the Diplomatic Conference convened by the Swiss government as trustee of the Geneva Conventions, and which met in Geneva from April 21 to August 12, 1949. It was attended by 63 governments and established four Conventions:

1. Geneva Convention for the Amelioration of the Condition of the wounded and sick in the armed forces in the field, comprised of 64 articles, and a revision of the Convention of 1929 on the same subject.

2. Geneva Convention for the Amelioration of the Condition of the wounded, sick and shipwrecked members of armed forces at sea, containing 63 articles and revising the 10th Hague Convention of 1907.

3. Geneva Convention relative to the Treatment of Prisoners of War, consisting of 143 articles, and revising the Convention of the same name of 1929.

4. Geneva Convention relative to the Protection of Civilian Persons in time of war, a new code of 159 articles which took account of the urgency and capital importance of international rules in this particular field in the context of the bitter experiences of World War II.[3]

One of the most noteworthy achievements of these Conventions is Article 2 of each of them, which makes them applicable to all cases of declared war or any other armed conflict, even if not recognized as war by the parties, and to all cases of partial or total

---

[1] For a brief account of the series of processes involved in this see J. S. Pictet: 'The New Geneva Conventions for the Protection of War Victims', *A.J.I.L.*, vol. 45, 1951, pp. 464–7.

[2] The Seventeenth International Red Cross Conference met in Stockholm from August 20 to 30, 1948, and was attended by the representatives of 50 governments and 52 Red Cross Societies. The International Red Cross Conference is the supreme legislative authority of the Red Cross and is convened every four years. For background and the work of the Geneva Conventions of 1949 see J. A. C. Gutteridge: 'The Geneva Conventions of 1949', *B.Y.B.I.L.*, vol. 26, 1949, pp. 294–326.

[3] For the text of the Conventions see G. I. A. D. Draper: *The Red Cross Conventions*, London, 1958, pp. 125–216. Gutteridge: *op. cit.*, pp. 307–26, gives an excellent critical appreciation of the new conventions. See also J. L. Kunz: 'The Geneva Conventions of August 12, 1949' in *Law and Politics in the World Community*, ed. G. A. Lipsky, 1953, pp. 279–316.

occupation of the territory of a contracting party, even if the said occupation meets with no armed resistance.

These Conventions, containing in all 429 articles and forming the 'Geneva legal code', form more than one half of the total written law of war. Having produced a *corpus juris* as imposing as the Hague Conventions,[1] they are regarded as a noteworthy contribution to the volume and appearance of the modern laws of war. Establishing a balance between humanitarian considerations and the realities of war, extending the law of war for the protection of civilians and their property to a remarkable degree, and rejecting in a large measure the principle of reciprocity and the general participation clauses from the central law of war, they represent a high-water mark of humanitarian achievement. They came into force in 1950 and now form part of the law of war.[2]

[1] According to Professor Lauterpacht, the Conventions 'revising, developing and codifying a very substantial part of the law of war . . . [represent] a historic and in many ways almost a revolutionary piece of international legislation transcending in some respects the achievements of the two Hague Conferences'; 'Problem of the revision of the law of war', *B.Y.B.I.L.*, vol. 29, 1952, p. 380.

[2] See Draper: *op. cit.*; also Gutteridge: *op. cit.*, p. 326. For a comprehensive commentary see J. S. Pictet (ed.): *Commentary on the Geneva Conventions*, 4 vols., 1952–8, published by the International Committee of the Red Cross.

PART THREE

CODIFICATION SPONSORED
BY THE
UNITED NATIONS ORGANIZATION

CHAPTER FOUR

THE INTERNATIONAL LAW COMMISSION AND ITS ORGANIZATION

The second World War stimulated world public opinion to search for peace and for methods and organizations to attain the ideal of the reign of law in the international community. As the war went on and the victory of the allied powers approached, increasing attention was paid in many quarters to the questions of post-war reconstruction, both national and international.[1] We have seen that two events in particular retarded the progress of the codification movement—the failure of the Hague Codification Conference of 1930, and the outbreak of war in 1939. Renewed efforts after that war were assisted, however, by the experience gained at the 1930 Conference with regard to preparatory work and the assessment of the need for the prospects of the codification of international law.

PRELUDES TO THE ESTABLISHMENT OF THE INTERNATIONAL LAW COMMISSION

The Dumbarton Oaks Conference 1944

The Dumbarton Oaks Conference of delegates of the United States of America, Great Britain, the U.S.S.R. and China, which met in August–September 1944 to prepare a plan for a general international organization, made proposals emphasizing international peace, security and welfare, but showed an evident lack of concern for legal principles.[2] Disappointingly, the delegates stressed the political aspect of international organization at the expense of law and justice: international law was mentioned at only one point—in a paragraph which purported to prevent the application of international law in the case of 'domestic questions'.[3] The cause of their

---

[1] See W. E. Rappard: *The Quest for Peace since the World War*, 1940; 'Typical plans for post-war world peace', *Int. Con.*, no. 384, 1942, pp. 431–52; 'The Universities Committee on Post-War International Problems', *A.J.I.L.*, vol. 38, 1944, pp. 112–14; P. E. Corbett: 'World Order—an agenda for lawyers', *A.J.I.L.*, vol. 37, 1943, pp. 207–21; 'The future of international law', *Trans. Grotius Soc.*, vol. XXVII, 1942, pp. 289–312. For Atlantic Charter Declaration, Moscow Declaration, and the developments between 1941 and 1944 see W. Chamberlin and T. Hove , Jr.: *A Chronology of Fact Book of the United Nations 1941–1961*, New York, 1961, p. 11.

[2] See UNCIO (Docs.) Doc. 1 G/1, 1945, vol. 3, pp. 1–23.

[3] *Ibid.*, p. 13, para. 7.

omission lay in their concentration upon matters of security, which led the framers of the draft to apprehend that the introduction of legal principles might hamper those preventive and enforcement measures which the proposed international organization might apply in the event of a threat to international peace and security.

Numerous comments from both official and unofficial sources called attention to this omission.[1] These comments and a large number of amendments[2] proposed by governments to make the new system more of a legal order were indicative of an increasing realization that the new United Nations Organization, as a genuine instrument for the maintenance of international peace and security, would have to be founded upon recognized principles of law and justice. The Chinese delegation took the initiative by submitting at the second phase of the Dumbarton Oaks Conference two proposals which laid emphasis on the place and the importance of the rule of law in international relations. One of these emphasized the requirement that the settlement of disputes should be achieved with due regard for 'principles of justice and international law', and the other suggested that 'the Assembly should be responsible for initiating studies and making recommendations with respect to the development and revision of the rules and principles of international law'.[3] These proposals were subsequently accepted in the form of joint amendments at the San Francisco Conference.[4]

The San Francisco Conference and Article 13 of the UN Charter

The first proposal regarding the settlement of disputes with due regard for 'principles of justice and international law' was adopted by the San Francisco Conference (April 25 to June 25, 1945) as part of the Article 1 of the Charter of the United Nations.[5] The second proposal as 'to the development and revision of the rules and principles of international law' was the subject of a very lengthy discussion in the Committee II/2 of the Conference. This Committee had to deal with the measures to be taken for revitalizing and strengthening international law, after the upheaval of two major

---

[1] See H. Kelsen: 'The Old and the New League: the Covenant and the Dumbarton Oaks Proposals', *A.J.I.L.*, vol. 39, 1945, p. 46; P. B. Potter: 'The Dumbarton Oaks Proposals viewed against recent experience in international organization', *ibid.*, pp. 103–7.

[2] See UNCIO (Docs.), 1945, vol. 3; also vol. 13, pp. 752–4.

[3] See UNCIO (Docs.) Doc. 1 G/1(a), 1945, vol. 3, p. 25.

[4] UNCIO (Docs.) Doc. 2 G/29, 1945, vol. 3, pp. 622–3.

[5] Article 1 of the Charter dealing with the purposes of the United Nations speaks of bringing about 'by peaceful means, and in conformity with the principles of justice and international law, adjustment or settlement of international disputes or situations which might lead to a breach of peace'; see critical comments of H. Kelsen in *The Law of the United Nations*, 1950, pp. 15–18.

wars.[1] There was a great deal of debate in its 21st meeting on the question whether the phrase 'development' included also 'revision'.[2] Those favouring mention of the phrase 'revision' insisted on the distinction between 'development' and 'revision'—the former being interpreted as adding to existing rules, the latter as modifying those rules. Others, supporting the use of the words 'progressive development' in the second alternative draft, insisted that the phrase implied 'modifications of, as well as addition to, existing rules', and that it struck 'a nice balance between stability and change'.[3] Since the latter view prevailed, there emerged the draft embodied in Article 13, paragraph I(a) of the Charter.

Article 13, paragraph I(a) of the Charter empowers the General Assembly of the United Nations to initiate studies and make recommendations for the purpose of 'promoting international co-operation in the political field, and encouraging the progressive development of international law and its codification'. The article is very carefully worded. In framing it, the delegates at the San Francisco Conference had in mind two important considerations: (a) that the contemporary international law was inadequate as a standard for the settlement of international conflicts (because of the uncertainty of many of its precepts, and the divergence in its interpretation and application in practice by many states); and (b) that the rules of international law could not be readily amended or revised to meet the rapidly changing needs of international society, because of the conspicuous absence of an international legislature.[4] The new organization therefore was not intended 'merely to pick up the threads of international action where the League of Nations left off. Rather it was hoped that, with the new powers vested in the organization, a fresh and bolder approach could be made which would stress the progressive development of the law and its codification'.[5]

It is noteworthy that the drafters of Article 13 did not limit the function of the General Assembly to a mere static concept of codification, but clearly indicated their emphasis on the progressive

[1] See UNCIO (Docs.), vol. 9, 1945, pp. 69–70, 346–7, 419–20.
[2] For the proposals of the sub-Committee B see UNCIO (Docs.), vol. 9, 1945, pp. 423–4.
[3] *Ibid.*, pp. 177–8.
[4] See Yuen Li-Liang: 'The United Nations and the development and codification of international law', I.L.A. Report, 43rd Conf., Brussels, 1948, pp. 159–60.
[5] Memorandum of the Secretariat, U.N. Doc. A/122 and add. 1 of October 17, 1946, gives the historical background of the provision in Article 13 and surveys previous efforts in the field of codification of international law: UNGAOR 1st sess. 1946, pt. II, 6th Committee, Annex 13, pp. 227–36. Article 67 of the Charter of the Organization of American States, 1948, also makes a similar mention, as one of the functions assigned to the Inter-American Council of Jurists is to promote the development and codification of public and private international law.

development of the rules of international law by giving 'progressive development' a precedence over 'codification' in the order of statement in the provision.[1] Although the language of the article is simple, it has provided a starting point for the United Nations to clarify and improve the content of international law, notwithstanding the vicissitudes of world affairs. It embodies the idea that a conscious and concerted effort is essential in order to expand and consolidate the rule of law among nations, and that the new international organization must be equipped with the power to take measures for developing international law and rendering its precepts more certain. In fact, it is not fully realized that the idea of a code for the world, which has long stirred men's minds in the search for the rule of law in world society, has crystallized itself into the explicit provision in the Charter to impose, for the first time, a definite responsibility on the United Nations Organization.[2]

The implementation of Article 13 (1)(a) of the UN Charter

After the United Nations came into existence, the task of implementing the provisions of Article 13 regarding the progressive development and codification of international law was entrusted by the General Assembly to the Sixth Committee.[3] A sub-committee of the Sixth Committee recommended that a governmental committee be set up to study the methods which the General Assembly might adopt to carry out its obligations in the matter, and to submit a comprehensive report to the General Assembly before the adoption of any definite plan.[4] The Sixth Committee favoured the appointment of the proposed Committee of sixteen members by the General Assembly on the recommendation of its President. It adopted the sub-committee's report and draft resolution as a whole, save that

[1] For the speech of the Chinese delegate stressing the significance of the power of the General Assembly under this article, in regard to promoting respect for international law and its development, see U.N. Doc. 1151 (Eng.) II/17, fourth meeting of the Commission II, June 22, 1945, UNCIO (Docs.), vol. 8, p. 204.
[2] Underlining the revolutionary idea of the progressive development of international law and its codification contained in Article 13 (1)(a), Rosenne observes: 'It stresses the *political intent* [author's italics] of the organized international community in what had hitherto been a community regarded as little more than the special preserve of lawyers'; 'The International Law Commission 1949–59', *B.Y.B.I.L.*, vol. 36, 1960, p. 111. For the history of Article 13, see Y. Li-Liang: 'The General Assembly and the progressive development and codification of international law', *A.J.I.L.*, vol. 42, 1948, pp. 66–9.
[3] Of the seven main committees of the General Assembly, the Sixth Committee, also known as the Legal Committee, is empowered to deal with the legal matters and questions relating to the International Court of Justice and the development of international law; Rules of Procedure of the General Assembly, U.N. Doc. A/520 and A/3660 and corr. 1. As to the Assembly's decision see U.N. Doc. A/222, UNGAOR 1st sess. 1946, pt. II, 46th pl. mtg., annex 58, p. 1516, para. 1.
[4] See U.N. Doc. A/C. 6/114, UNGAOR *ibid.*, 6th Com. Annex 13d, pp. 239–40.

relating to the number of members of the proposed committee. Here mention may be made of the committee's recommendations concerning a fresh approach to the problem of codification. In the Committee's view, a study of existing projects and the methods followed by official and unofficial bodies engaged in promoting the development and formulation of public and private international law was also necessary to the work of the proposed codification committee.[1]

The General Assembly, at its 55th plenary meeting on December 11, 1946, adopted unanimously Resolution 94(1):[2]

The General Assembly
Recognizes the obligation laid upon it by Article 13, paragraph 1, subparagraph a, of the Charter to initiate studies and make recommendations for the purpose of encouraging the progressive development of international law and its codification;
Realizes the need for a careful and thorough study of what has already been accomplished in this field as well as of the projects and activities of official and unofficial bodies engaged in efforts to promote the progressive development and formulation of public and private international law, and the need for a report on the methods whereby the General Assembly may most effectively discharge its obligations under the above mentioned provisions: Therefore
Resolves to establish a Committee of seventeen [3] members of the United Nations to be appointed by the General Assembly on the recommendation of the President, each of these members to have one representative on the Committee;
Directs the Committee to study:
(a) the methods by which the General Assembly should encourage the progressive development of international law and its eventual codification;[4]
(b) methods securing the co-operation of several organs of the United Nations to this end;
(c) methods of enlisting the assistance of such national or international bodies as might aid in the attainment of this objective;
and to report to the General Assembly at its next regular session;

[1] U.N. Doc. A/222, UNGAOR *ibid.*, Annex 58, pp. 1516–18, paras. 5–8.
[2] For the text of this resolution, which retained the theme of the sub-committee's and the Sixth Committee's reports, see Resolutions adopted by the General Assembly, 1st sess., part II, U.N. Doc. A/64/Add. 1, pp. 187–8.
[3] The number of sixteen committee members in the original proposed resolution was increased to seventeen at the request of the President of the Assembly (P. H. Spaak of Belgium), who said that he 'had great difficulty in choosing among the States of South America; they all have legal traditions, and are all interested in the question. . . . being limited by the number of sixteen, I was unable to include Brazil . . . moreover it is the only Portuguese-speaking state of Latin America'. Since there was no opposition to increasing the number Brazil was added to his recommendations. See UNGAOR 1st sess. 1946, pt. II, pl. mtgs. 55th, p. 1131.
[4] It may be noted that the General Assembly had added the adjective 'eventual' before 'codification' which had the significance of recognizing the fact that codification was a long-term task and required to be undertaken in stages.

Requests the Secretary General to provide such assistance as the Committee may require for its work.

The Committee on Progressive Development of International Law and its Codification

Known as the Committee of Seventeen, this Committee came into existence with the adoption of the above-mentioned Resolution 94(1) by the General Assembly,[1] whose first positive step it was in launching a body of experts to undertake a detailed and comprehensive study of the methods by which it might fulfil its obligation under Article 13 of the Charter. The establishment of the Committee of Seventeen inaugurated a new era in the history of the world in which institutionalized and concerted efforts were to be made to bring about the codification and development of international law.

The General Assembly entrusted additional functions to the new codification committee over and above its primary task, by directing it: i. to report on the rights and duties of states at the Assembly's second regular session;[2] ii. to draft a report and resolution affirming the principles of international law recognized by the Charter of Nuremberg Tribunal, in the context of a general codification of offences against the peace and security of mankind, or of an international code;[3] and iii. at the request of the Economic and Social Council (ECOSOC), to prepare a draft convention on the crime of genocide.[4] These additional assignments differed in kind from the Committee's primary task as envisaged by the General Assembly, but they offered new scope for revitalizing and strengthening international law. In the words of Rosenne, they illustrated 'a somewhat broad approach to the substantive context of the work, which was not restricted to matters comprised within the scope of classic international law'.[5] They also set the trend that the initiative for the additional assignments to the codification committee

[1] The Committee was composed of the following member states: Argentina, Australia, Brazil, China, Colombia, Egypt, France, India, Netherlands, Panama, Poland, Sweden, U.S.S.R., United Kingdom, U.S.A., Venezuela, Yugoslavia. Sir Dalip Singh of India was the Chairman, Prof. Brierly of the United Kingdom the Rapporteur. For the names of representatives see U.N. Jrnl. no. 58, suppl. A.A/PY/55, pp. 470–3.
[2] A matter that originated in a draft declaration submitted by the delegation of Panama. See Res. 38(1) of December 11, 1946, Resolutions adopted by GA, U.N. Doc. A/64/Add.1, pp. 62–3.
[3] Arising from a proposal by the U.S.A. delegation to the Sixth Committee. Res. 95(1) of December 11, 1946, ibid., p. 188.
[4] ECOSOC Res. 47(IV) of March 28, 1947, U.N. Doc. E/325, p. 5. Also Res. 96(1) of December 11, 1946, Resolutions adopted by GA, U.N. Doc. A/64/Add. 1, pp. 188–9.
[5] See S. Rosenne: 'The International Law Commission 1949–59', *B.Y.B.I.L.* vol. 36, 1960, p. 114.

was not confined solely to the Sixth Committee or the General Assembly.

Under Resolution 94(1) of the General Assembly, the Secretary General was directed 'to provide such assistance as the Committee [of Seventeen] may require for its work'. Accordingly, the Division of Development and Codification of the Secretariat of the United Nations undertook preliminary studies on various subjects before the first meeting of the Committee on May 12, 1947. These studies constituted a very valuable and copious documentation for the Committee's reference purposes and aided the discussion of its problems.[1]

The Report of the Committee of Seventeen

The Committee of Seventeen met from May 12 to June 17, 1947, in New York. Its reports on its additional assignments were not elaborate[2] but its report on its primary task relating to codification and progressive development of international law was substantial.

The report on the methods and machinery that might be set up for the purpose of codifying and developing international law was submitted to the General Assembly on June 17, 1947.[3] The Com-

[1] The documents made available by the Secretariat were:
Historical Survey of the Development of International Law and its Codification by International Conferences, U.N. Doc. A/AC/.10/5;
Memorandum on the Methods of Encouraging the Progressive Development of International Law and its eventual Codification, U.N. Doc. A/AC.10/7 with corr. 1 and 2;
Outline of Codification of International Law in the Inter-American System, U.N. Doc. A/AC.10/8 with corr. 1;
Note on the Private Codification of Public International Law, U.N. Doc. A/AC.10/25;
(All the above are reprinted in *A.J.I.L.*, vol. 41, 1947, suppl. pp. 29–147.)
Bibliography on the Codification of International Law, U.N. Doc. A/AC.10/6;
Memorandum on the Methods for Enlisting the co-operation of other bodies, national and international, concerned with International Law, U.N. Doc. A/AC.10/22 and Add. 1–4.
[2] For the report on the rights and duties of states see U.N. Doc. A/AC.10/53, June 16, 1947 (reprinted in *A.J.I.L.*, *op. cit.*, pp. 27–8).
For the report on the question of formulating the principles of the Charter of the Nuremberg Tribunal, see U.N. Doc. A/AC.10/52, June 17, 1947 (*A.J.I.L.*, *op. cit.*, pp. 26–7); also U.N. Doc. A/332, UNGAOR 2nd sess. 1947, 6th Com., Annex 2, pp. 164–5 and 212, para. 3.
On the question of a convention on genocide, the Committee of Seventeen failed to give its views since it received no government comments; see U.N. Doc. A/510, UNGAOR 2nd sess. 1947, pl. mtg., Annex 32, pp. 1625–8.
[3] The Committee concluded its consideration of its primary task at its 15th meeting, May 29, 1947. See for its report U.N. Doc. A/AC.10/51 (reprinted in *A.J.I.L.*, vol. 41, 1947, suppl. pp. 18–26). U.N. Doc. A/331 contains the report of the Committee, July 18, 1947. See UNGAOR 2nd sess. 1947, 6th Com., Annex 1, pp. 173–82.
See also for a comparative study the Report of the McNair Committee on the Development and Formulation of International Law, May 3, 1947, which made

mittee had examined several problems which may be conveniently grouped under the following main headings:

1. whether any distinction between codification and progressive development of international law was appropriate, and if so, whether a division between the methods and procedures of the two tasks was also indispensable;
2. whether the codification or development of international law should take place through the means of international conventions or through scientific restatements undertaken by independent legal experts;
3. what appropriate machinery should be set up by the General Assembly of the United Nations for carrying out the task assigned by the Charter for codifying and developing international law;
4. how the proposed machinery should proceed in its work, and what should be its relation with the General Assembly and the other bodies;
5. how the codifying agency should seek the assistance of such national and international bodies as might aid it in the attainment of its objective.

1. On the first question, although the Committee recognized a distinction between the two tasks of 'progressive development' and 'codification', it did not make it very clear, and wisely avoided committing itself to any narrow definition of 'codification'. According to the Committee, the task involving 'the drafting of a convention on a subject which has not yet been regulated by international law, or in regard to which the law has not yet been highly developed or formulated in the practice of states' was referred to as 'progressive development', in contrast to another type of task which involved 'the more precise formulation and systematization of the law in areas where there has been extensive state practice, precedent and doctrine' described as 'codification'.[1] At the same time, the Committee recommended two alternative procedures for 'progressive development' and 'codification' of international law.[2] In fact, it felt it necessary to distinguish between the two tasks for the convenience of reference only and for the sake of a division between the methods and procedures which it regarded as most appropriate for the accomplishment of the general objective. It acknowledged

---

similar recommendations as to the need for the appointment by the UN of a Commission for undertaking codification: I.L.A. Rep. of 42nd Conf. Prague 1948, Annex I, pp. 82–111.
[1] U.N. Doc. A/AC.10/51, para. 7.
[2] *Ibid.*, paras. 8–15.

the fact that the two terms were 'not mutually exclusive, as for example, in cases where the formulation and systematization of the existing laws may lead to the conclusion that some new rule should be suggested for adoption by states'. In view of the contradictory views expressed as regards the relative importance of two fundamental aspects of the problem (the legislative and the codification aspects) and the methods to be followed, the Committee tried to combine the two aspects and did not commit itself to any decision on the theoretical exactness of the distinction made.[1]

2. On the second question, i.e. the means of codification or development of international law, whether through the traditional method of making a general convention or treaty for its purpose, or through scientific restatement by expert lawyers, the Committee of Seventeen made provision for the use of both methods.[2] Both approaches were suggested in the Memorandum presented by the Secretariat for the assistance of the Committee, prompted by the necessity emphasized in the report of the Sixth Committee recommending a 'fresh approach to the problem' in view of the 'difficulties encountered in past efforts to promote the progressive development of international law and its codification'.[3] The Committee of Seventeen had no doubt that in the development of international law in new fields the concluding of multipartite conventions was the only possible method. On the other hand, in the field of codification it recommended that the proposed codifying agency of the United Nations might frame its conclusions in the form of draft articles of multipartite conventions, which should be given the widest possible publicity and be submitted to the General Assembly together with its own recommendations.[4] Although the term 'restatement' was not used in the report, the Committee recommended a detailed procedure which included essential elements of the restatement process, namely, thorough examination of all precedents, treaties and relevant data and views of leading publicists; study of the practice of states and of the areas of disagreement or agreement in practice and doctrine, and consultation with scientific institutions and even

[1] U.N. Doc. A/AC./10/51, para. 10. Paragraphs 7 and 10 were approved by the Sub-Committee 2 of the Sixth Committee: see its report U.N. Doc. A/C.6/193, para. 15, UNGAOR 2nd sess. 1947, 6th Com., pp. 188–204, Annex 1. The report was approved by the Sixth Committee.
[2] U.N. Doc. A/AC.10/51, para. 7. Compare with the recommendations of the McNair Committee (1947): I.L.A. Rep. of 42nd Conf., Prague, 1948, Annex 1, p. 110ff. The Committee of Seventeen seems to have been guided by the Secretariat's Memorandum on 'Methods for Encouraging the Progressive Development . . .', U.N. Doc. A/AC.10/7.
[3] U.N. Doc. A/AC.10/7; and U.N. Doc. A/222, Report of the 6th Com., UNGAOR 1st sess. 1946, pt. II, pl. mtgs. Annex 58, pp. 1516–18.
[4] U.N. Doc. A/AC.10/51, paras. 8–14; para. 15 dealt with the recommendations that might be made.

with individual experts.[1] With regard to the task of codification the Committee obviously recognized the scientific value of the restatement process.

3. On the question of an appropriate machinery for carrying out the task of codifying and developing international law, the Committee concluded that the best means would be the establishment of a special committee or commission of a more or less permanent nature as a subsidiary organ of the General Assembly[2]—a single commission for all branches of the task, it was unanimously agreed, to be called the International Law Commission.[3] The Committee felt that the proposed International Law Commission should not do anything which might detract from the valuable work being done in the field of the development and codification of private international law by the Hague Conferences on Private International Law, and when dealing with questions within that field the Commission might, therefore consider the appropriateness of consultation with the Netherlands government.[4]

In the Committee of Seventeen, different views were expressed on the question of the composition of the International Law Commission.[5] As regards its strength, the numbers nine, eleven, thirteen and fifteen were suggested. But, by a majority of nine votes to five, the Committee recommended that the ILC should consist of 15 members.[6] As to the question of the method of appointment of members of the Commission, two distinct points of view were expressed in the Committee. Some members of the Committee felt strongly that the ILC should be a purely scientific body comprised

---

[1] U.N. Doc. A/AC.10/51, para. 13. The substance of this was adopted in Article 20 of the Statute of the I.L.C. which reflects a compromise between the convention method and the restatement technique.

[2] For the various suggestions considered see U.N. Doc. A/AC.10/SR.7, p. 2. Compare similar conclusion reached by the Inter-American Juridical Committee set up by the Foreign Ministers' meeting at Rio de Janeiro in 1942: Report of Inter-American Juridical Committee, *A.J.I.L.*, vol. 39, 1945, suppl. p. 231.

[3] U.N. Doc. A/AC.10/51, para. 3. See also the recommendation of the McNair Committee (1947), I.L.A. Rep. of 42nd Conf., Prague, 1948, p. 108. The Committee of Seventeen referred to the proposed codifying authority as the Commission of Jurists or the Commission of Experts on International Law during the early stages of its deliberations. It was Brierly (U.K.) who suggested the name International Law Commission at the 15th Meeting of the Committee; it was adopted unanimously: U.N. Doc. A/AC.10/SR.15, pp. 14–15.

[4] U.N. Doc. A/AC.10/51, para. 3. See also ECOSOC Resolution 678(XXVI) of July 3, 1958, regarding co-operation between U.N.O. and the Hague Conferences on Private International Law and the International Institute for the Unification of Private Law.

[5] See U.N. Docs. A/AC.10/14 (for plans presented by U.S.A.); A/AC.10/16 (U.K.); A/AC.10/18 (Netherlands); A/AC.10/20 (Poland); A/AC.10/SR.4 (U.S.S.R.).

[6] U.N. Doc. A/AC.10/51, para. 4; for minority views see U.N. Doc. A/AC.10/SR.23, pp. 10–14; for similar views, expressed by the McNair Committee, I.L.A. Report, *op. cit.*, p. 108.

of jurists of highest standing and widest international repute, free from the risk of political appointments, and divorced from political considerations. Others laid more emphasis on having the representatives of governments in the Commission. But there was a consensus of opinion that whilst the task of codification could not be left to a body of government representatives, it could hardly be effectively undertaken in a wholly academic way. The Committee therefore discussed two main methods for the selection of the members of the ILC: i. appointments to be made by the judges of the International Court of Justice; ii. a system of nomination and election of candidates as prescribed for the election of judges of the International Court of Justice, but with slight modifications. By a large majority, the latter proposal was accepted.[1] The procedure modified the system of indirect nomination by national groups, as provided for the International Court, in that it prescribed direct nomination of candidates for the ILC by governments. Thereafter, in the election of the 15 members of the ILC, the Security Council and the General Assembly were to follow Articles 3 and 8–12 of the Statute of the Court. Casual vacancies in the ILC were to be filled by the election out of the nominees of the Commission by the Security Council, pending the regularization of the election at the next annual session of the General Assembly. The Committee of Seventeen unanimously recommended that the members of the ILC be given 'a salary proportionate to the dignity and importance of their office'. By a majority of nine votes to five the Committee favoured the idea that the ILC might be a permanent body and, in fact, thought that this would be both desirable and necessary. However, it agreed that initially the Commission be appointed for an experimental period of three years.

4. As to the question of how the ILC should proceed in its work, the Committee favoured the questionnaire technique. For both progressive development and codification there was to be a Rapporteur[2] working with a sub-committee by circulating a questionnaire and making extensive consultation with governments at various stages of preparation of its draft articles.[3] For the purpose of

---

[1] U.N. Doc. A/AC.10/51, paras. 5 and 6. The Committee adopted the joint proposal by the United States and China, U.N. Doc. A/AC.10/33 of 23 May, 1947.

[2] A special Rapporteur was to be appointed for each topic under study by the Commission which was left free to go outside its ranks in the choice of the Rapporteur. Articles 16–17 and 18–23 of the Statute of ILC substantially incorporated the procedures recommended by the Committee save with the modification that the appointment of a special Rapporteur for codification was not made obligatory although, in practice, the appointment is always made.

[3] There was considerable discussion on the question of the stage of the codification procedure at which the comments from governments should be sought: U.N.

progressive development the Committee assumed that the General Assembly would normally take the initiative in referring the projects to the Commission. But at the same time, it did not exclude any initiative from governments, from other United Nations organs, specialized agencies, and other official bodies established by inter-government agreement.[1] As regards codification, both the General Assembly and the ILC were recommended to share the right of initiative, the former instructing the latter 'to survey the whole field of customary international law together with any relevant treaties, with a view to selecting topics for codification, having in mind previous governmental and non-governmental projects'.[2] If the ILC should find codification of a particular topic desirable or necessary, it was to present its recommendations to the General Assembly in the form of a multipartite convention. It was required to give precedence to any request from the General Assembly to prepare a draft convention on any subject or to explore the necessity or desirability of preparing such a draft convention.[3]

As regards the final disposal of the items, the procedure for progressive development was conceived to stop short at the point where the report of the Rapporteur and his sub-committee was submitted to the General Assembly in the form of a final draft, along with the explanatory comments and the recommendations.[4] On the other hand, in the case of codification, the report of the ILC to the General Assembly, in the form of a final draft and accompanied by the explanatory notes, was required to carry definite recommendations ranging from a 'no action' proposal to the convening of a special conference for the consideration of the conclusion of a convention.[5] But the Committee's report, strangely enough, did not specify any procedure to be adopted by the General Assembly in

---

Docs. A/AC.10/SR.15 and SR.27. The Committee decided by a narrow majority that government comments be sought only after completion of the drafts: U.N. Doc. A/AC.10/51 paras. 8(c)(g), 9(a)(ii)(v), 9(b)(ii), 12(c) and 13(e).

[1] For instance, the competence of the ECOSOC to take initiative in proposing conventions was unanimously recognized: U.N. Doc. A/AC.10/51, para. 9. See also U.N. Doc. A/331, UNGAOR 2nd sess. 1947, 6th Com., pp. 176–7, 177, n. 1; and U.N. Docs. A/AC.10/SR.25, pp. 5–8, A/AC.10/SR.51, pp. 5–6.

[2] U.N. Doc. A/AC.10/51, para. 11. Article 18(1) of the Statute of the ILC adopted this recommendation. The members from the U.S.S.R., Poland and Yugoslavia asserted that only governments should have a right of initiative in matters involving systematization of custom and the practice of states. The American member thought that for codification which was mere formulation of existing rules the initiative of governments was not required: U.N. Doc. A/AC.10/SR.14, pp. 5–6.

[3] U.N. Doc. A/AC.10/51, para. 11; adopted in Article 18(2) and (3) of the Statute of the ILC.

[4] Ibid., paras. 8(h) and 9; adopted in Articles 16(j) and 17(c) and (d) of the Statute of the ILC.

[5] Ibid., para. 15; adopted in Article 23 of the Statute of the ILC.

dealing with the ILC's reports, nor did it prescribe the manner in which the General Assembly was to carry out its responsibilities in regard to the reports submitted by the ILC. Neither did it consider it necessary to make any specific mention about the obligation of the ILC about any regular submission or the frequency of its reports to the General Assembly.

5. Specially charged by the General Assembly to investigate the question of enlisting the assistance of national and international bodies in the task of codification, [1] the Committee recognized the importance of not only securing the co-operation of the several organs of the United Nations,[2] but also of enlisting the assistance of such national and international organizations as might aid in the attainment of the objective, recommending consultation not only with scientific institutions but also, if necessary, with individual experts.[3] Its recommendations were: (a) that the ILC be authorized to consult such organizations; (b) that the documents of the ILC circulated to the governments be also distributed to such bodies, and (c) that the Secretary General draw up a list of the organizations, national or international, official or unofficial, dealing with questions of international law, in consultation with the ILC.[4] The last recommendation (c) of the Committee was apparently affected by the political bias when it went on record to exclude some organizations from the list to be drawn by the Secretary General.[5] Also, at the same time, the Committee insisted on referring specially to the necessity and importance of frequent consultation between the ILC and the organs of the Pan-American Union 'without, however, disregarding the claims of other systems of law'.[6] Even though it may be recognized that the Pan-American Union possessed

[1] It is relevant to note here the recommendation in the Final Act of the Hague Conference, 1930, in this regard. L.N. Doc. C.228, M.115, 1930, V, p. 18. Also note the recommendation of the Assembly of the League of Nations, Resolution of September 25, 1931. L. of N. Offl. Rec., sp. suppl. no. 92, 1931, p. 9.

[2] U.N. Doc. A/AC.10/51, para. 19. Compare the recommendation of the McNair Committee, I.L.A. Report, *op. cit.*, pp. 108-9.

[3] U.N. Doc. A/AC.10/51, paras. 8(e) and 13(c).

[4] *Ibid.*, paras. 19(a) and (c), and 20(a) and (b); adopted in Articles 25(1) and (2) and 26(1) and (2) of the Statute of the ILC.

[5] In sub-para. (c) of para. 20, *ibid.*, the Committee desired the Secretary General to exclude from the list the organizations which collaborated with the Nazis and Fascists, and to take into account the resolutions of the General Assembly and of the ECOSOC concerning relations with Franco-Spain. According to Professor Jennings such recommendation 'can only be considered as an unfortunate and gratuitous interposition of politics into an activity which should be kept as far as possible on a strictly scientific and objective basis.' See R. Y. Jennings: 'The Progressive Development of International Law and its Codification' *B.Y.B.I.L.*, vol. 24, 1947, p. 318, Article 26(3) of the Statute incorporated this recommendation.

[6] U.N. Doc. A/AC.10/51, para. 20(d); see Article 26(4) of the Statute of the ILC.

the greatest practical experience in the field of codification of international law for the union of American states, special mention would
seem to have been unnecessary.[1]

The Committee of Seventeen also made other recommendations
for encouraging the progressive development of international law,
such as: the consideration by the ILC of improvements in the
technique of multipartite instruments by bringing about uniformity
in the drafting of their formal clauses; of the utility and importance
of encouraging the ratification of and accession to multipartite
conventions already concluded; of the development of customary
international law and the development of law through the judicial
process; of the ways and means for making the evidences of customary international law more readily available by the compilation
of digests of state practice, and by the collection and publication of
the decisions of national and international courts on international
law questions.[2]

The work of the Committee is acclaimed by Rosenne as 'a mile-
stone in the history of the codification of international law, the first
step to place this important process squarely in its proper context
combining the requirements of sound learning with the realities
of political life, a "proper and legitimate object of endeavour on the
part of the organized international community"'.[3] Many of the
Committee's suggestions were later substantially incorporated in the
Statute of the International Law Commission.

THE ADOPTION OF THE STATUTE OF THE INTERNATIONAL LAW COMMISSION

When the Report of the Committee of Seventeen was discussed by
the Sixth Committee, there was no difference of opinion as regards
the establishment of an international law commission in principle,[4]
but the differences in the debate centred round the following principal questions: i. whether the Commission be established on a
whole-time or a part-time basis; (ii) whether in the election of the

---

[1] Jennings, *op. cit.*, p. 318. Three members of the Committee objected to the
special mention of the Pan-American Union although they paid tribute to its
work. In their view it was in violation of 'the principle of equality between states
and systems of law': see U.N. Doc. A/AC.10/SR. 18. Article 26 of the Statute of the
ILC incorporates the recommendations of the Committee.

[2] U.N. Doc. A/AC.10/51, paras. 16, 17 and 18. Article 24 of the Statute of the
ILC incorporates these recommendations, which were based upon the Memor-
andum presented by the Secretariat: U.N. Doc. A/AC.10/7 with corr. 1 and 2
(*A.J.I.L.*, vol. 41, 1947, suppl., particularly pp. 112–15.)

[3] 'International Law Commission', *B.Y.B.I.L.*, vol. 36, 1960, p. 120.

[4] UNGAOR, 2nd sess., 1947, 6th Com., pp. 4–16.

Commission only the General Assembly should participate or also the Security Council; (iii) whether the Commission be established immediately along with the approval of its Statute, or in the following session of the General Assembly; (iv) whether or not a distinction between codification and progressive development was necessary and practicable.[1] Since these questions required a thorough examination, a sub-committee was set up to draft a resolution and to report back to the Sixth Committee.

As the recommendations made by the Sub-Committee (particularly on the Commission's part-time basis and its election by the General Assembly alone, which were incorporated in the Statute of the ILC) changed the character of the Commission and its work, it is relevant to examine them. The Sub-Committee pronounced itself unanimously in favour of the establishment of an international law commission as recommended by the Committee of Seventeen and accepted by the Sixth Committee, but it was divided on the question of whether the Commission be elected during the current session of the General Assembly or postponed until the next session.[2] Since it was only by a narrow majority of 8 to 7 that the Sub-Committee favoured the Commission's election during the current session, it was thought advisable to consult the whole Sixth committee in view of the importance of the matter. The whole Committee, however, decided that the election be postponed until the next session of the General Assembly.[3] On other questions such as the structure of the Commission, the method of its election and its work, the Sub-Committee submitted its report and a draft resolution after fifteen meetings. Although it largely agreed with the viewpoint of the Committee of Seventeen, the Sub-Committee put forward the following modifications:[4]

i. Whilst recognizing the advantages of a permanent and full-time commission, that proposal was unanimously rejected on the grounds of a. 'the imperative necessity for the greatest possible reduction in the United Nations budget', and b. the difficulty of making outstanding jurists accept the membership of the proposed commission on a full-time basis.[5]

[1] See for views expressed against the distinction between codification and progressive development, UNGAOR, 2nd sess., 1947, 6th Com., pp. 4–16.

[2] Ibid., pp. 188–8, Annex J, f; also U.N. Doc. A/C6/150, Sub-Committee's Interim Report.

[3] UNGAOR, 2nd sess. 1947, 6th Com., pp. 24–7.

[4] U.N. Doc. A/C6/193, UNGAOR 2nd sess. 1947, 6th Com., pp. 188–204, Annex I, g. The Sub-Committee only reviewed the Report of the Committee of Seventeen paragraph by paragraph from para. 7 onwards and generally endorsed it subject to certain minor modifications.

[5] Ibid., p. 189. But it is submitted that, considering the imperative need of the world community for a system of codified international law, and the fact that the task of codification is very laborious, extremely difficult and a long-term process,

M

ii. In regard to the method of constituting the International Law Commission, the Sub-Committee suggested only a few minor changes: a. in the proposal that each government should nominate as candidates not more than two of its own nationals and not more than eight persons of other nationalities, the latter number was considered by the Sub-Committee so large that the difficulties of governments both as to the nomination of the candidates as well as their selection would be increased. It reduced the number of nominees from other nationalities from eight to two;[1] b. The proposed system of election of fifteen members of the Commission, both by the Security Council and the General Assembly, was modified by dissociating the Security Council from the election. In the opinion of the Sub-Committee, under Article 13 of the Charter, only the General Assembly was entrusted with the work of codifying international law, and so, it alone should elect the Commission's members by a simple majority;[2] c. The proposal of filling casual vacancies in the Commission was changed and the commission itself was authorized to fill its casual vacancies, having due regard to the provisions contained in Articles 2 and 8 of the proposed statute, namely the requirements of nationality and professional qualifications;[3] d. As regards the nationality of the Commission's members, the Sub-Committee decided against the participation of nationals of states which were not members of the United Nations for the reason that their participation in the Commission, which was concerned primarily with the codification and development of international law among the members of the United Nations, would complicate matters since non-members might uphold ideas contrary to the principles and purposes of the Charter.[4]

iii. As to the functions of the Commission the Sub-Committee did not agree with the Committee of Seventeen that its task extended to the sphere of private international law. In its view the Commission should concern itself primarily with public international law although it was not precluded from entering the field of private

---

the arguments against a full-time codification commission did not carry enough weight to justify the rejection of the proposal by the Committee of Seventeen for a commission on a full-time basis.

[1] *Ibid.*, p. 189, Annex I, g, para. 4.

[2] *Ibid.*, pp. 190-1, para. 7. It had considered three solutions: i. of a simple majority of members present and voting, i.e. half of the votes plus one; ii. a two-thirds majority of members present and voting; iii. an absolute majority, i.e. half of the votes plus one of the total number of members of the UN.

[3] *Ibid.*, pp. 191-3, para. 8.

[4] This recommendation did not find its place in the Statute. But during the first decade of its existence the UN followed in practice the principle, even excluding important countries from its ranks. However, with the increasing admission of more and more new members in the UN the question has lost its political significance.

international law.[1] Besides, it omitted paragraphs 16 and 17 of the report of the Committee of Seventeen which required the Commission to suggest ways and means of encouraging the progressive development of international law by improving the technique of multipartite instruments in relation to such matters as uniform treaty clauses, and encouraging the ratification of, and accession to, multipartite conventions.[2]

iv. The Sub-Committee did not think it advisable to re-open the controversy about the distinction between codification and progressive development enunciated in paragraph 7 of the report of the Committee of Seventeen.[3] The only material modification suggested in the system proposed was that the Commission was required to appoint one of its own members as Rapporteur rather than a person from outside. It saw no reason in departing from the generally followed practice of international commissions and other organs of the United Nations in this regard.

Save the above-mentioned points, the Sub-Committee introduced only textual modifications in the Report of the Committee of Seventeen, and substantially endorsed its recommendations. A draft statute of the International Law Commission based on the report and on discussions in the Sub-Committee was approved by the Sixth Committee at its 58th meeting on November 20, 1947.[4] In view of the Sixth Committee's prior decision to defer the election

[1] In the view of several members, most jurists who had specialized in private international law were little interested in public international law, and so, the system of having representatives of the principal legal systems of the world on the Commission would be 'seriously compromised if some systems of law are represented by experts in public international law and others by jurists who have specialized in private international law'. Also, if the Commission was composed of experts in public law alone, it would be inadmissible for such a committee to direct its work on private law. Some members thought that the borderline between public and private international law was not sharp and there was a good number of jurists engaged in both fields. See para. 16, U.N. Doc. A/C6/193, UNGAOR 2nd sess. 1947, 6th Com., pp. 203–4. The Sub-Committee's recommendation was unanimously adopted with one abstention.

[2] See para. 15 of Sub-Committee's report dealing with paras. 16 and 17 of the report of the Committee of Seventeen, *ibid.*, p. 201.

[3] In the Sub-Committee W. E. Beckett (U.K.) drew attention to the resolution adopted by the Institute of International Law at its Lausanne meeting of August 22, 1947, and to that adopted by the International Law Association at its 42nd Conference at Prague in September 1947. Both resolutions, which were circulated as documents of the Sixth Committee, gave general approval to the method of scientific restatement as a basis for obviating the imperfections and filling the gaps in international law.

[4] UNGAOR 2nd sess. 1947, 6th Com., pp. 147–57. All 10 amendments moved by the U.S.S.R. representative, which related to the citizenship of the members of the ILC, the system of filling casual vacancies between sessions of the GA, and the limiting of the functions of the ILC to the drawing up of conventions, were rejected. For the report of the Sixth Committee, see U.N. Doc. A/504, November 20, 1947, UNGAOR 2nd sess. 1947, pl. mtgs., Annex 31, p. 1624.

of members of the International Law Commission to the next session
of the General Assembly, controversy had arisen as to whether it was
necessary to establish an interim committee entrusted with the task
which would have devolved upon the Commission had it been able
to begin its work immediately.[1] The Sub-Committee's draft resolution had considered it desirable to have such an interim body function until the establishment of the International Law Commission
and proposed the continuance of the Committee of Seventeen as an
interim organ; this was rejected by the Sixth Committee. Instead,
the Sixth Committee requested the Secretary General to prepare
the work for the International Law Commission and to pursue
the study of questions such as that of a draft declaration of the rights
and duties of states and the codification of the Nuremberg principles.

The recommendations of the Sixth Committee were adopted
by the General Assembly in the form of resolutions 174(II) and
175(II) of November 21, 1947, and the Statute of the International
Law Commission.[2] The Statute adopted by the General Assembly
in 1947, as amended several times since then,[3] provides the basic
law for the constitution and working of the International Law
Commission, which came into existence as a result of elections in
1948. Thus was born the International Law Commission to codify
and develop international law—a dream of mankind throughout
the ages—to carry out a task similar to Justinian's, but on a world-
wide scale, to establish the rule of law in international life. The
Statute represents an act of faith in the assumption that, to replace
the reign of power politics by the rule of law, international jurisprudence must be expressed in a codified system of laws binding on
all nations. The establishment of the Commission marks an important date in the history of international law, and, as the Commission's work proceeds to accomplish its delicate and continuous
task, appreciation of its importance will grow.

[1] UNGAOR 2nd sess. 1947, 6th Com., 40th mtg., pp. 24–7.
[2] The text of the Statute is printed in Resolutions adopted by the GA, UNGAOR
2nd sess. 1947, 123rd pl. mtg., pp. 105–10. See also *ibid.*, pp. 1272–9. Gromyko, the
U.S.S.R. representative, declared that his delegation would abstain from voting
in view of the rejection of important amendments put forward by him, p. 1278.
[3] Mainly with regard to its strength and the tenure of its members, by:
GA Res. 485(v) of December 12, 1950
GA Res. 984(x) and 985(x) of December 3, 1955
GA Res. 1103(xi) of December 18, 1956
GA Res. 1647 (xvi) of November 6, 1961.
See Statute of ILC amended, U.N. Doc. A/CN4/4, rev. 1, New York, 1962 (UN
Publ. Sales no. 62.V.2.)

The Working Machinery of the International Law Commission

THE COMPOSITION OF THE COMMISSION

Number of Members

Originally, under Article 2 of the Statute the Commission was composed of 15 members, but the number was increased in 1956 to 21, and in 1961 to 25.[1] The enlargement of the membership of the International Law Commission in 1956 was brought about in view of the increased membership of the principal organs of the United Nations, viz. General Assembly, ECOSOC, and International Court of Justice, and because of the General Assembly's decision to increase the number of its vice presidents to eight. There was no difference of opinion as to the two main points: i. that in view of the increase in the membership of the United Nations, the composition of the International Law Commission no longer fully satisfied the terms of Article 8 of the Commission's Statute which required the International Law Commission as a whole to be representative of 'the main forms of civilization and of the principal legal systems of the world', and ii. that in order to cure that defect it was desirable not to lose the services of the Commission's existing members but to increase its membership.[2] The further enlargement of the Commission in 1961 to 25 members was brought about in consequence of a significant change in the size of the composition of the United Nations by the admission of 21 new members.[3]

Qualifications of Members

Articles 2 and 8 of the Statute embody directions to the nominators and electors (i.e. states) that members of the Commission 'shall be persons of recognized competence in international law' (Article 2(1)), and that 'the electors shall bear in mind that the persons to be elected to the Commission should individually possess the qualifications required and that in the Commission as a whole representation of the main forms of civilization and of the principal legal

---

[1] GA Res. 1103(XI), December 18, 1956, UNGAOR 11th sess. 1956, pl. mtg. 623rd, p. 728; see also UN Doc. A/3427 and corr. 1, UNGAOR *ibid.*, Annexes, Ag. it. 59.
    GA Res. 1647(XVI), November 6, 1961, U.N. Doc. A/4939, UNGAOR 16th sess. 1961, Annexes Ag. it. 77.
[2] See for debate in the Sixth Committee, UNGAOR 11th sess. 1956, 6th Com., 483–5th mtgs., pp. 11–25.
[3] For debate see UNGAOR 16th sess. 1961, 6th Com. 689th–699th mtgs., pp. 7–61. UN Doc A/C6/L481, *ibid.*, Annexes, Ag. it. 77.

systems of the world should be assured' (Article 8(1)).[1] These provisions do not impose any enforceable bar or disqualification against persons once duly elected. But, in addition, the requirement of nationality is made enforceable under Article 2, sub-sections (2) and (3), and Article 9, sub-section (2), of the Statute. According to Article 2, sub-section (2), 'no two members of the Commission shall be nationals of the same state',[2] and sub-section (3) provides that 'in case of dual nationality a candidate shall be deemed to be a national of the state in which he ordinarily exercises civil and political rights'. In the words of Article 9(2), 'In the event of more than one national of the same state obtaining a sufficient number of votes for election the one who obtains the greatest number of votes shall be elected and if the votes are equally divided the elder or eldest candidate shall be elected.' These provisions were intended to assure a balanced representation in the composition of the International Law Commission. But, notwithstanding the consideration of nationality, the members of the Commission are not deemed to be representatives of governments, and are to participate in the Commission in their individual capacity.[3]

These provisions of the Statute laid down three important principles regarding the composition of the International Law Commission: i. recognized competence of the members in international law; ii. representation of the main forms of civilization and of the principal legal systems; and iii. exclusion from the membership of more than one person of the same nationality. Excepting the objective principle of nationality, the other two principles are ambiguous and involve an abstract statement of criteria for membership. Because of the ambiguity of the phrasing of the first two provisions, much flexible interpretation has been possible in the distribution of seats in the International Law Commission, and this has been reinforced through the system of election of the members of the

---

[1] Article 8 of the Statute of the ILC is reproduced from Article 9 of the Statute of the International Court of Justice. But Article 2 of the Statute of ILC differs from Article 2 of the Statute of the ICJ, which lays emphasis on independence of judges and their election, 'regardless of their nationality'.

[2] As in the procedure followed in the Year Book of the International Court of Justice, the Commission also decided to indicate the nationality of its members in its reports: *Y.B.I.L.C.*, 1949, pp. 221–2, paras. 4–9. See *Y.B.I.L.C.*, vol. II, Doc. A/3859, para. 4 for the case of the resignation of the Egyptian member upon the amalgamation of Egypt and Syria in the United Arab Republic. Also U.N. Doc. A/4799 Memorandum of the Secretary General transmitting a list of candidates for election to the ILC, UNGAOR 16th sess. 1961, Annexes Ag. it. 17.

[3] See, for a reiteration of this principle, the ruling given by the Chairman, Hudson, in a discussion over a member's objection to a nomination, to the effect that members did not represent states or governments, instead they served in a personal capacity. 'Being a creation of the General Assembly, the Commission is not competent to challenge the latter's application of Article 8 of the Statute': *Y.B.I.L.C.*, 1950, vol. I, 39th mtg., pp. 1–2.

Commission[1] by the General Assembly, being itself an exclusively political body.

There exists no absolute measurement to determine 'recognized competence in international law'.[2] Moreover, western Europe and lately America, have played a dominant and vital rôle in international life and in the development of international law—one which is quite out of proportion in relation to Asian and African countries with a prolonged subservient rôle in this respect. This is undeniable historical reality in the context of which it is difficult to find many persons of 'recognized competence in international law' in Asian and African countries, or even in the so-called socialist countries whose interest in international law is a much more recent phenomenon. Since the original languages of the non-western legal systems are relatively little known to western international lawyers, very few of them can reasonably be expected to possess any substantial familiarity with legal works in Slavonic and Oriental languages. Consequently, major legal works and important articles appearing in these languages are far too little known. Also, in comparison with the Hague *Recueil*, or American Journal of International Law, or British Year Book of International Law, the non-western periodicals such as the Japanese Journal of International Law, the Soviet Year Book of International Law and the Indian Journal of International Law first appeared much more recently and are much less known. So, the scholars of the non-western world are at a marked disadvantage as compared with their colleagues in other parts of the world as their competence has lesser opportunities of being recognized unless their significant writings on international law and related legal matters appear in western languages and periodicals.

Turning to the ambiguity of 'main forms of civilization' and 'principal legal systems',[3] 'civilization' and 'legal system' are not

---

[1] See below, pp. 173–7.

[2] The wording 'recognized competence in international law' owes its origin to Article 2 of the Statute of the Permanent Court of International Justice. It was the subject of some debate in the Committee of Jurists (1920) which was set up to draft a plan for a court (L. of N. Offl. Rec., June 1920, pp. 71–2, 123), a similar debate having taken place at the Hague Conference of 1907. The Hague Convention of Pacific Settlement (Article 2) required the selection of persons 'of recognized competence in questions of international law'. It was on the suggestion of Lord Phillimore and Mr. Root that the 1920 Committee of Jurists had adopted the wordings of the Hague project. See M. O. Hudson: *The Permanent Court of International Justice, 1920–1942. A Treatise*, 1943, pp. 145–7, §138.

[3] In regard to these phrases in Article 8 of the Statute of the ILC, which reproduces Article 9 of the Statute of the ICJ which, in turn, adopted the same article of the Statute of the PCIJ, see Minutes of the 1920 Committee of Jurists. The Committee had stated that the reference to 'main forms of civilization' was an essential condition 'if the Permanent Court of International Justice is to be a real World Court for the Society of all Nations'. It pointed out that it did not refer 'to

rigidly geographical concepts. For instance, western civilization covers a large part of the world extending far beyond Europe to America, South Africa, Australia and New Zealand and linking their fairly homogeneous legal systems as well as social and political institutions. On the other hand, Asia and Africa have a large number of countries with very diverse and ancient civilizations and different legal, political and social traditions. A civilization and a legal system may be shared by various nations, or groups of nations, or even by parts of a nation. For instance, Islamic civilization is shared not only by a group of Arab nations and by countries in Africa and Asia, but also by millions of Muslims living in India, Indonesia, Malaysia, Turkey and U.S.S.R. Similarly, Common Law and Roman Law systems have extended their ramifications to the most diverse and distant regions of the world.[1]

It may also be noted that differences between various legal systems had been most apparent in private law. But, considering the fact that, in modern times, with the assumption of responsibilities by the state, mainly in the interests of economic and social welfare that have found expression in the admixture of public and private law, a strict distinction between the two (public and private law) tends to vanish within the national legal systems.[2] As a result of this, using comparative law as a guide, it is possible in many cases to find substantially the same principle, though in different form, in different legal systems.[3] On the basis of considerable uniformity on a broad basis existing in the public law of different countries of the world, it might be possible to group them only under Civil Law, Common Law and Communist Law systems. Evidently, 'civilization' and 'legal system' are the terms which are, in practice, insufficiently precise to be interpreted and applied appropriately for the composition of the International Law Commission.[4]

---

the various systems of international law', but referred to 'principal legal systems' in order to ensure that 'no matter what points of national law may be involved in an international suit, all shall be equally comprehended'. See Minutes of the 1920 Committee of Jurists, pp. 363–5, 709. Also, Hudson, *op. cit.*, p. 157, §148.

[1] See P. D. Edmunds: *Law and Civilization*, 1959, Part III, 'Rome's Great Legacy', and Part VI, 'Civilization Under the Common Law', pp. 120–90, 324–473; W. A. Robson: *Civilization and the Growth of Law*, 1935.

[2] B. A. Wortley: 'The interaction of public and private international law today', Hague Academy, *Recueil des Cours*, vol. I, 1954, pp. 245–338, illustrating the process of intermingling of public and private law at international level.

[3] H. C. Gutteridge: *Comparative Law*, 1949, 2nd ed., pp. 65, 70–1. See for international discussion envisaged by the International Committee of Comparative Law on General Principles of Law recognized by Civilizations, *International Social Science Bulletin*, vol. 5, 1953, p. 850.

[4] Schwarzenberger observes: 'The nexus between civilization and international law is a basic question of international law. At the same time, it may claim to be a current legal problem of the first order': 'The standard of civilization in international law', *C.L.P.*, vol. 8, 1955, p. 212.

Since the criteria laid down in the Statute to assure representative character or balanced composition of the International Law Commission were too vague and difficult to be followed in practice, we find that they were abandoned, and, instead, a more objective political criterion of geographical distribution has gradually developed as a result of repeated pressure from countries in Asia, Africa and eastern Europe. These countries drew attention to the predominant representation of western civilization and western legal systems in the International Law Commission, pointing out that in consequence, the Commission could hardly be said to reflect the image of the present-day world.[1] An appraisal of the data regarding the composition of the International Law Commission as given in Tables I and II shows that between 1948 and 1966, representation of western civilization and western legal systems has always been strong although the representation of Asian, Islamic and African countries has recently improved.

In 1956, at the time of increase in the membership of the International Law Commission from 15 to 21, a 'gentlemen's agreement' was arrived at in the Sixth Committee for the distribution of additional seats of the Commission.[2] According to it, the distribution of additional seats was as follows:

three to nationals from African and Asian members of the United Nations; one to a national of eastern Europe; and one, in alternation, to a national from Latin America and a national from the British Commonwealth countries not otherwise included in any recognized regional grouping. It was also understood that the distribution as between different forms of civilization and legal systems would be maintained in respect of the existing fifteen seats.[3]

This agreement gave an explicit recognition to the principle of 'equitable geographical distribution' as a guide to the composition

[1] See the discussion in the Sixth Committee over the distribution of seats in the ILC at the time of the proposed enlargement in the membership of the Commission, first in 1956 and later in 1961. UNGAOR 11th sess. 1956, 6th Com., 482nd–485th mtgs., pp. 11–25; *ibid.*, 16th sess. 1961, 6th Com., 689th–699th mtgs., pp. 7–63.

[2] It was based on the proposal of the delegate from Cuba, Garcia Amador, in 483rd mtg. of the Sixth Committee, see UNGAOR 11th sess. 1956, 6th Com., 483rd mtg., p. 15, para. 6.

[3] U.N. Doc. A/3427, Sixth Committee Report, UNGAOR 11th sess. 1956, 6th Com. Annexes, Agenda item No. 59, para. 13; see U.N. Doc. A/4799, Memorandum of the Secretary General giving an account of distribution of seats in accordance with the 'gentlemen's agreement' of 1956, UNGAOR 16th sess. 1961 Annexes, Agenda item 17. This agreement was in the nature of mutual understanding between states and could hardly be made effective in view of the secrecy of ballots in the election of the members of the Commission. In the following election it was not adhered to in regard to the sharing of seats between the South American states.

TABLE I *Representation on the International Law Commission*[1]

Election years	1948	1953	1956	1961	1966
1 CIVILIZATIONS					
European (Christian)	12	12	14	15	15
Arabic (Islamic)	1	1	3	3	3
Indo-Chinese (Hindu–Buddhist)	2	2	4	3	2
African (Tribal)	nil	nil	nil	3	4
Hebrew	nil	nil	nil	1	1
Total	15	15	21	25	25
2 LEGAL SYSTEMS					
Roman or Civil Law	8	8	9	9 ⎫+1*	10 ⎫+1*
Anglo-Saxon or Common Law	2	2	2	3 ⎭	2 ⎭
Islamic	1	1	3	3	3
Hindu–Buddhist–Confucianist	2	2	4	3	2
Communist	2	2	3	3	3
African (Tribal)	nil	nil	nil	3	4
Total	15	15	21	25	25
3 GEOGRAPHICAL REGIONS					
Europe	7	7	10	9	9
America	5	5	4	6	6
Asia	3	3	6	6 ⎫+1†	5 ⎫+1†
Africa	nil	nil	1	3 ⎭	4 ⎭
Total	15	15	21	25	25

* Dr. Rosenne, of Israel, has been a member of the Commission since 1962. The legal system of Israel is an admixture of English civil law, and Muslim and Jewish law. But it is largely influenced by the West. See N. Bentwich: 'The legal system of Israel', *I. & C.L.Q.*, vol. 13, pt. 1, 1964, p. 236.

† U.A.R. is classified geographically as jointly Afro-Asian and U.S.S.R. classified as European.

[1] The idea of these tables is owed to Shabtai Rosenne's article in *Y.B.I.L.C.*, *op. cit.*, pp. 128–9. Tables I, II, III. The tables have been reassembled in a revised form and brought up-to-date.

TABLE II   *Distribution of seats in the ILC by nationality, 1949–68*

Countries	Period of representation	Countries	Period of Representation
Afghanistan*	1962–	Israel*	1962–
Algeria*	1965–	Italy*	1957–
Argentina*	1964–	Japan*	1957–
Austria	1957–66	Madagascar*	1967–
Bolivia	1954–56	Mexico*	1949–63, 1967–
*Brazil**	1949–	Netherlands*	1949–61, 1967–
Canada	1962–66	Nigeria*	1962–
Cameroon	1962–65	Panama	1949–53, 1958–59
Chile*	1967–	Poland	1962–66
China	1949–66	Senegal	1965–66
Colombia	1949–53	Spain	1962–66
Cuba	1953–61	Syria (UAR) and Syrian Arabic Republic	1949–61
Czechoslovakia	1949–61		
Dahomey*	1962–64, 1967–	Sweden	1949–61
Egypt	1957–58	Thailand	1957
Ecuador	1962–66	Turkey	1959
Finland*	1962–	UAR*	1962–
*France**	1949–	*U.K.**	1949–
Greece*	1949–57, 1967–	*USA**	1949–
Hungary*	1967–	*USSR**	1949–
*India**	1949–	Uruguay*	1960–
Iran	1957–61	Yugoslavia*	1957–
Iraq*	1960–		

Note: 1. Countries marked with an asterisk (*) are those whose nationals have been elected in 1966 by the General Assembly for the term 1 January 1967 to December 1971.

2. Countries in italic have continuously had a national serving on the ILC since 1948.

of the International Law Commission in relation to at least the additional seats.

But the gentlemen's agreement had not assured balanced representation in the Commission, and so, again in 1961, when the Commission was enlarged from 21 to 25 members,[1] the debates in the Sixth Committee demonstrated dissatisfaction with the composition of the Commission. The delegates of east European and of several countries of Asia and Africa linked the question of the

[1] On the admission of 21 new states to the UN, including 19 from the central and southern part of Africa. Until Nov. 1961, there was no member from the African area in the ILC. See U.N. Docs. A/C6/L481 and Add. 1, and A/C6/L483 and Add. 1, UNGAOR 16th sess. 1961, Annexes agenda item 77.

enlargement of the International Law Commission with general redistribution of seats, and did not consider themselves bound by the gentlemen's agreement of 1956.[1] Not much is left, therefore, of the agreement as shown by the elections of 1961 and 1966.

The question of the representative character of the International Law Commission is of considerable importance. The codification and progressive development of international law in new domains depends to a great extent upon a maximum degree of consensus of opinion, among the constituent members of the world society whose actively law-making members are expanding from being a small group of western nations to include the whole of mankind and a variety of civilizations with diverse political and economic systems.[2] For psychological reasons, the Commission should not be monopolized by a group with a particular legal system. Also, in order to bring about the progressive development of international law a body like the Commission would have to turn increasingly to 'the general principles of law recognized by civilized nations', enumerated in Article 38(c) of the Statute of the International Court of Justice, as one of the most potential material sources of international law but the practical use of which has been rather limited.[3] The use and adaptation of general principles of law in the development of international law,[4] would involve comparative study of legal principles of different legal systems of the world. For the Commission's successful working it is very necessary that it commands universal confidence and respect. For that, not only should it fairly represent the present-day world community but it should also be composed of jurists independent of governmental influence. The Commission has tended, however, to be filled excessively with foreign office lawyers, i.e. official or unofficial governmental legal advisers. Though these members of the Commission are there in their own right on purely scientific grounds, the very fact that their membership depends upon straight governmental nomination makes them conscious of confrontation on the scientific plane by the national interests of their own states. It is important that the Commission should have a balance of foreign office lawyers and academic

[1] See UNGAOR 16th sess. 1961, 6th Com., 689th–699th mtgs., pp. 7–63. See U.N. Doc. A/4939, *ibid.*, Annexes to item 77.

[2] See C. W. Jenks: *Common Law of Mankind*, 1958, pp. 62–92; Schwarzenberger: Standard of civilization and international law', *C.L.P.*, vol. 8, 1955, pp. 212–34.

[3] See W. Friedmann, 'The uses of "General Principles" in the development of international law', *A.J.I.L.*, vol. 57, 1963, p. 280; C. W. Jenks: 'The challenge of universality', in *Law, Freedom and Welfare*, 1963, pp. 144–6.

[4] See for uses of general principles of law in international law, B. Cheng: *General Principles of Law as Applied by International Courts and Tribunals*, 1953; Wortley: 'Interaction of public and private international law today', Hague Academy, *Recueil des Cours*, vol. I, 1954, chap. IV; Friedmann: *op. cit.*, pp. 286–99.

lawyers. In fact, the Commission's composition has tended to be influenced by an unconcealed political approach which is an inevitable result of the present system of the Commission's election by the General Assembly.

Method of election

The governments of member states of the United Nations nominate for election to the Commission 'not more than four candidates, of whom two may be nationals of the nominating state and two nationals of other states' (Articles 3 and 4).[1] A list of such candidates nominated by states, bearing in mind the direction of Article 2 of the Statute (i.e. recognized competence in international law), has to be submitted in writing by the governments to the Secretary General by June 1 of the year in which an election is held (Article 5). The Secretary General is required to communicate to the governments of member states of the United Nations the names of all candidates along with a statement of their qualifications as supplied by the nominating governments (Article 6), and to prepare a list of the candidates in alphabetical order to be submitted to the General Assembly for the purposes of the election (Article 7). The General Assembly thereafter elects, keeping in mind the direction given by Articles 2 and 8 of the Statute, 25 candidates obtaining 'the greatest number of votes and not less than a majority of the votes of the members present and voting' by secret ballot.[2] If candidates are not elected by first ballot, additional ballots are taken to fill the places remaining vacant, the voting being restricted to the candidates obtaining the greatest number of votes in the previous ballot, to a number not more than twice the places remaining to be filled, provided that, after the third inconclusive ballot, votes may be cast for any eligible person. Should three such restricted ballots remain inconclusive, the next three ballots are restricted to the candidates obtaining the greatest number of votes in the third of the unrestricted ballots, to a number not more than twice that of the place still remaining vacant, and the following three ballots thereafter are unrestricted, and so on until all 25 places are filled.[3] The persons so

[1] The sub-committee report U.N. Doc. A/C6/193, in para. 9 recommended against the participation of non-member states of the U.N. in the Commission. The Statute has no explicit provision to that effect, but no national of non-member states like Germany or Switzerland has ever been elected to the Commission.

[2] See Article 9, as amended by GA Resolution 1647(XVI) of November 6, 1961. Under Rule 94 of the Rules of Procedure of the GA all elections are held by secret ballot.

[3] See U.N. Doc. A/697 Memo of the Secretariat dealing with the procedure of the election of the ILC, UNGAOR 3rd sess. 1948, pt. II, pl. mtgs, Annex Ag. it. 50. For the elections in 1961 see U.N. Doc. A/4799, UNGAOR 16th sess. 1961, Annex. Ag. it. 17.

elected are notified and asked by the Secretary General whether they are prepared to accept membership of the International Law Commission.[1]

As regards casual vacancies occurring in the Commission in the event of the resignation or death of a member, the Statute authorizes the Commission itself to fill the vacancies, having due regard to the directions set forth in Articles 2 and 8 of the Commission's Statute (Article 11). During the first two periods—1948 to 1953, and 1953 to 1956—the Commission followed the practice of electing persons of the same nationality as the outgoing members so as to retain the distribution of seats determined by the General Assembly in the first election, but this practice was not followed from 1956 onwards.[2] In 1961, however, three vacancies were filled by persons of the same nationality as the outgoing members (British, French and Japanese).

The Commission has always discharged its responsibility of filling the casual vacancies with care and competence, always discussing the matter at a private meeting of the members prior to a formal election. In 1955, when the question was raised in the General Assembly of amending Article 11 of the Commission's Statute so that the casual vacancies would be filled by the General Assembly instead of by the Commission itself,[3] and the Assembly sought the opinion of the Commission on the matter, the Commission was not favourably inclined to any amendment, mainly on the ground of practical convenience.[4] Hence Article 11 of the Statute remained unchanged. Had this not been done even the filling of casual vacancies in the Commission would have allowed political factors to creep in.

The establishment of the International Law Commission is an important institutional development. If the International Law Commission were to accomplish the consolidation of the formal authority on international law on a universal basis, it is vitally important that, in its composition, the Commission should represent a wide range of legal systems and should ensure that no particular

[1] See U.N. Doc. A/C6/193, para. 7 of the Sub-Committee Report which modified the recommendation of the Committee of Seventeen in regard to the election of the Commission above, 162.

[2] See *Y.B.I.L.C.*, 1952, vol. I, mtgs. 136th, 182nd and 183rd, pp. 3, 245, 251; and U.N. Doc. A/4779, UNGAOR 16th sess. 1961; Annexes, Ag. it. 17.

[3] UNGAOR 10th sess. 1955, 6th Com., 452nd–454th mtgs. and Annexes Ag. it. 50, pp. 47, 50–4; see Doc. A/CN4/L6 to 5, *Y.B.I.L.C.*, 1956, vol. II, p. 233.

[4] *Y.B.I.L.C.*, 1956, vol. I, 333rd and 336th mtgs., pp. 2–17; *ibid.*, vol. II, p. 301. In the words of Sir Gerald Fitzmaurice: 'The result of leaving the decision with the General Assembly would be that the persons elected would have to miss at least one session before being able to take an active part in the Commission. The only possible advantage would be that the Commission would be relieved of a certain responsibility', *ibid.*, vol. I, p. 17.

legal system or family of legal systems is predominant.[1] At the same time, it must ensure the independence and professional competence of its members. That perfection may not be attained under the current system of nomination and election with its tendency towards undue emphasis on political factors.

The General Assembly which has sole responsibility of electing the Commission's members is not a body of jurists, scientists or philosophers engaged in an academic search for ultimate truth, but exclusively a political body where coalitions, groups and blocs operate in the form of an embryonic party system at an international level. All elections in the Assembly are influenced by the crystalliza-tion of such groupings, rendering the possibility of reaching an unbiased and objective judgment difficult. Besides, in all its elections, it is the representative principle which, explicitly or implicitly, operates as a predominant factor.[2] Considering the variegated complexion of the United Nations as a whole, it becomes extremely difficult for bodies of limited membership to be so constituted as to be an exact representation in miniature of the whole United Nations. A learned body like the International Law Commission, which is required to undertake a highly specialized and difficult task of codifying and developing international law, should be kept as compact as possible and not expanded *ad infinitum*. It must have persons with a profound knowledge of international law and a world perspective, who should also possess legal scholarship, drafting ability, and a capacity for co-ordinating codified rules into a coherent system.[3] And yet, to be successful, they must enjoy a high degree of confidence of the whole United Nations so as to give concrete expression in terms of jurisprudence to the changing con-

[1] Wilfred Jenks, addressing the American Society of International Law, appealed for the need of a fundamental rethinking of international law: 'The pro-found transformation in the distribution of political power and influence has changed significantly, though much less decisively the relative weight in world affairs of the different legal traditions which must be taken into account in deter-mining what the Statute of the International Court describes as "the general principles of law recognized by civilized nations". The civil and common law traditions no longer enjoy a virtual monopoly of recognition of this status; Islamic law and Soviet law now claim, and are widely accorded, a similar recognition. Jewish law has attracted renewed attention, and Chinese, Japanese, Hindu, Buddhist and African law, profoundly affected as they have been by Western influence, can no longer be disregarded', 'The Challenge of Universality.' in *Law, Freedom and Welfare*, 1963, p. 138.
[2] See D. Bailey: *The General Assembly of the United Nations*, Chap. on 'Coalitions, Groups and Blocs in the Assembly', Carnegie, 1960, pp. 26–47; M. M. Ball: 'Bloc voting in the General Assembly', *International Organization*, vol. 5, 1951, no. 1, pp. 3–31; A. Lijdphart: 'The analysis of bloc voting in the General Assembly; a critique and a proposal', *Am. Pol. Sc. Rev.*, vol. LVII, 1963, no. 4, Dec., pp. 902–17.
[3] See for an excellent analysis of what constitutes legal scholarship, Max Radim: 'On legal scholarship', *Yale L.J.*, vol. 46, 1936–7, pp. 1124–41.

cepts of the world community. It is difficult in the Commission to attain a measure of universality comparable to that of the United nations itself.

The system of nomination by member states and election by the General Assembly was not necessarily the best one because it does not guarantee the Commission's efficiency, nor its independence of governments. Under the present system, by filling the Commission with official or unofficial governmental legal advisers, states are in fact sending 'committed lawyers' who are likely to be under instructions. And it is of the essence of the impartial accomplishment of the task of the codifying agency, that governments should respect its independence, and should not require it merely to register the existing municipal legislation and practice of states. The Commission should also preserve its independence of governments in regard to the character of its proposals as well as its methods and procedure.[1] Perhaps better results to that effect could be attained if the list of candidates for the Commission were drawn up by the International Court of Justice keeping in mind the principles of balanced distribution on the basis set forth in the Commission's Statute, thereby, accommodating principal legal systems and civilizations of the world and reflecting broadly the character of the United Nations. A list so drawn by the consensus of the judges of the International Court of Justice might be either voted upon by the General Assembly or be treated as a list of appointments subject to the approval of the General Assembly.[2] This system might well have reconciled legal perfectionism with political realism, thus freeing the Commission from official propaganda and competitive politics. Whereas the criteria set forth by the Statute for the membership of the International Law Commission might have been more appropriately and competently interpreted by the International Court at the time of nomination, it has in fact been politically interpreted by the General Assembly. While some states are permanently represented on the Commission others get representation by rotation and as a result of political adjustments.

The Commission, however, has much improved in its composition and, with its enlargement, an attempt has been made to make it fairly representative. The apprehension that the enlargement of the Commission would seriously impair its efficiency and output of work, has been belied; the association of a large number of jurists from different parts of the world in the Commission has been a valuable asset rather than a handicap. After the latest increment in the number of the Commission's members, delegates in the Sixth

[1] H. Lauterpacht: 'Codification and development of international law', *A.J.I.L.* vol. 49, 1955, p. 37.   [2] See pp. 157 and 160, above.

Committee expressed the conviction that the quality of its work showed that the increase in the Commission's membership had benefited the codification and progressive development of international law by making it possible for the various existing legal systems to be better represented.[1] Some writers have also emphasized the desirability of enlarging the Commission so as to include a number of technical experts to advise the lawyer members on what is technically feasible in regard to subjects which have very technical implications and which are not comprehended by the lawyer members.[2] Drafting can best be done by a small compact body, and so the ILC has evolved the method of working through committees and sub-committees.[3]

The balanced and equitable representation in the Commission is a *sine qua non* for its useful working and enables it to give expression to the will of the world community. This principle has much importance in the light of Professor Jennings's observation: 'The predominance of European states in the relatively small world community of the last century, during what we have already seen was at the commencement of the most formative era of international law, has *not unnaturally*[4] aroused some suspicion, amongst newly emerged nation states in the Americas, in Africa and in Asia; and has led them to ask whether they can reasonably be said to be bound in all respects by a law in the formation of which they had no part and which in fact is the characteristic product of what is to them an alien civilization.'[5] What is worth attaining in the composition of the Commission is reconciliation of the principle of representation with that of professional merit. It would not be difficult to obtain it if governments, actuated by international interest, were to send persons of highest competence and legal acumen to serve on the Commission, or if the International Court were to accept responsibility for their selection.

Tenure and emoluments of the Commission's members

Tenure. Members of the Commission are elected for five years and are eligible for re-election (Article 10).[6] They are not required to work for the Commission on a full-time basis and, therefore, they receive a special allowance and travel expenses, as determined by the

---

[1] U.N. Doc. A/5287, Sixth Com. Rept., UNGAOR 17th sess. 1962, Annexes Ag. it. 76, para. 16.

[2] See F. Honig: 'Progress in the codification of international law', *International Affairs*, vol. 36, 1960, p. 72.

[3] On the committee system, see pp. 253–55, below.

[4] Author's italics.

[5] 'The progress of international law', *B.Y.B.I.L.*, vol. 34, 1958, p. 350.

[6] See GA Resolution 985(X) December 3, 1955, which amended the text of Article 10 of the Statute of the ILC.

General Assembly (Article 13).[1] Originally, when the proposal was made to establish the Commission, it was recommended that the International Law Commission be a permanent body.[2] The Committee of Seventeen had also pronounced in favour of full-time service, but the Sub-Committee, to which the Sixth Committee had referred the report of the Committee of Seventeen, had unanimously rejected the idea of a full-time Commission.[3] Hence the International Law Commission was eventually established as a body meeting for a short time every year. Its Statute is silent on the length of its sessions although in practice they have lasted for some ten or eleven weeks every year. There is no formal provision in the Statute regarding the date of commencement and termination of the tenure of the members. The General Assembly had taken no final decision regarding the term of office of the Commission's members, and kept on extending their term of office by stages. First, by its Resolution 486(V) of December 12, 1950, the General Assembly extended the term of the Commission's members by two years, making a total of five years, from their election in 1948. Then in 1953, the General Assembly again elected the necessary fifteen members for a term of three years at its eighth session. Finally, it was in 1955 that the General Assembly made a final decision, by accepting the Commission's formal proposal of the amendment of Article 10 of the Statute,[4] recommending a five-year term to take effect from January 1, 1957.[5]

The extension in the term of office of the Commission's members in an apparently hesitant manner, and the reluctance to establish the Commission on a full-time basis appeared to show the General Assembly's tendency to proceed very cautiously and gradually, with regard to its responsibility of bringing about the codification of international law. For that reason, the Statute of the International Law Commission was, at the outset, intended to be provisional and its revision had been envisaged ever since it was drawn up. The General Assembly, therefore, invited the Commission by its Resolution 484(V) of December 1950, to review the Statute with the object of recommending its revision on the basis of its experience.

[1] Text amended by GA Resolution 485(V) of December 12, 1950.
[2] See UN Doc. A/AC. 10/11 and UN Doc. A/AC. 10/33.
[3] See pp. 156 and 161, above.
[4] See *Y.B.I.L.C.*, 1955, vol. I, 315th mtg., p. 190, *ibid.*, vol. II, pp. 41–2, paras. 27–28. In the opinion of the Commission 'The change of the term of office from three to five years would be beneficial to the continuity of the work of the Commission, in particular, with respect to the preparation and consideration of reports of the special rapporteurs.'
[5] This article originally provided for a three-year term which was extended to five years, first on an *ad hoc* basis by GA Resolution 486(V) of 12 December 1950 and later on a permanent basis by Resolution 985(X) of 3 December 1955. Accordingly elections have taken place in 1948, 1953, 1956, 1961 and 1966.

During its discussion of several questions of substance relating to the Statute,[1] the Commission considered the importance of establishing the Commission on a full-time basis on the following grounds: i. that under the arrangement of a part-time commission, with two months session every year, no rapid results could be produced, since the study of important and complicated issues demanded a great deal of time; ii. that a working session of nine to ten months a year might produce excellent results, but it would cause very great difficulty because it would involve the Commission's members absenting themselves for a long time from their countries and their normal professional activities; iii. that no member could devote a substantial amount of time to the Commission, unless he received emoluments of such magnitude that would attract him to forego his professional activities, or his public office or university chair in exchange for a fixed-term appointment on the International Law Commission; iv. that the codification work was a long-term project and the Statute laid down a complex procedure (the main stages of which were the drawing up of a preliminary report, its communication to the governments for comments, and providing a final report) which necessarily required continuity in the Commission's work.[2] Similar views in favour of its full-time character were reiterated in the Commission in 1961, and, recently in 1968 sessions although it realized that the factor of additional expenses entailing the proposal would prove a difficult obstacle to surmount.[3]

The view favouring the transformation of the International Law Commission into a full-time body was certainly justified considering the obligation of the United Nations to present to the world a comprehensive code of international law within a definite period of time. If that task were intended to be accomplished rapidly then the better course would be to spread the work of the Commission over the whole year. However, the Commission's consensus of opinion in favour of a full-time Commission was rejected in 1951 for the following reasons: i. that the slow work of codification work could not entirely be attributed to the fact that the International Law Commission had given only a limited time to the work assigned

[1] See *Y.B.I.L.C.*, 1951, vol. I, mtgs. 83rd, 96th and 97th, pp. 6–11, 122, 132.

[2] *Y.B.I.L.C.*, 1951, vol. I, 83rd mtg., paras. 34–41, 64–73, 75–78; 96th mtg., para. 115; 97th mtg., paras. 3–6. Hudson and Spiropoulos were the principal protagonists of a full-time Commission. Although most of the Commission's members favoured this view positive decision to that effect was not taken because of the apprehension that the GA would not approve the proposal. The Commission, however, recommended a full-time Commission in general terms only. See *Y.B.I.L.C.*, 1951, vol. II, Report of the Commission, Doc. A/1858, Chap. V, pp. 138–9, para. 70.

[3] For general discussion on planning future work of the Commission, see *Y.B.I.L C.*, 1961, vol. I, 614th–616th mtgs., pp. 206–23; *ibid.*, 1968, vol. I, 979th mtg., pp. 206–10.

to it. The decisive factor was either the cleavage of opinion between experts in the Commission and governments, or the extent to which the Commission's conclusions were acceptable to United Nations members; ii. that in view of the contemporary period of international tensions, which was not conducive to the process of crystallization and stabilization of international law, the time was not yet appropriate to establish a full-time commission; iii. that, in order to accelerate the efficiency of the ILC, it might be possible to set up within the Secretariat a group of specialists to carry out the preparatory work under the Commission's supervision, and also, rapporteurs might be appointed with special honoraria to work for the progressive development of international law; iv. that appointment of a full-time commission would involve heavy financial commitments; v. that it would be hard to find eminent jurists willing to devote their full-time to the Commission; vi. that a full-time commission would reduce itself to a body of officials comparable in its nature to the Secretariat of the United Nations, with a consequent risk of overlapping in the work done by the latter; vii. that a full-time commission would need its own Secretariat like the Registry of the International Court of Justice, which would involve additional financial commitments; viii. that a full-time commission would have to provide for a sufficient security of tenure and emoluments similar to, or even better than, the International Court of Justice; and ix. that the full-time members of the Commission would lose contact with the outside world and its legal and political realities.[1]

It is submitted that none of the arguments in opposition to a full-time commission are weighty enough to postpone indefinitely the question of establishing the International Law Commission on a permanent and full-time basis. Undoubtedly, additional expense ought to be no reason for the much-needed reform: the work of transforming international law into a generally acceptable common law of mankind, in order to establish a universal legal order, ought to be worth any necessary financial support. Nor can it be denied that the jurists, devoting themselves to an extremely complex and difficult work of codification and development of international law, require continuous and dedicated attention to the International Law Commission's work. They ought to be accorded equal status, facilities, emoluments and attractive conditions in comparison with the judges of the International Court of Justice. Several members of the Commission such as Rau, Lauterpacht, Spiropoulos and Fitzmaurice, in order to join the International Court of Justice,

[1] UNGAOR 6th sess. 1951, 6th Com., mtgs. 295th–297th, pp. 261–76; also Doc. A/2088, UNGAOR 6th sess. 1951, Annexes, Ag. it. 49.

resigned from the International Law Commission.[1] If the process could be reversed to attract the judges of the International Court to the International Law Commission, it would demonstrate unequivocally the value and importance attached by the world community to the task of codification. A system of conditions of service, if suitable for the International Court of Justice, should not be unacceptable for the International Law Commission. Also, the value and record of the International Law Commission cannot be gauged statistically. A full-time International Law Commission would certainly have been a most valuable subsidiary United Nations organ. Radhabinod Pal, Indian member of the Commission, has observed: 'Under the existing conditions in the international community, especially in view of the present effort to bring it within a constitutional framework, it would have been proper and wise to provide the community organizations with a permanent institutionalized or organized legislative unit of will. Law having to do with life would have to face continuous change and would thus require continuous adaptation to changing circumstances through the help of a *constantly watchful, discerning and active body*.'[2] He further suggested that 'the International Law Commission itself [be] placed on a permanent footing at least like the Court, with the provision that a certain fraction only of the membership would retire at intervals and that the Commission itself could withdraw from routine retirement those of its members appointed as Special Rapporteurs, who had already submitted their reports the acceptance of which had not been completed by the Commission'.[3]

But the question of a full-time International Law Commission is undoubtedly linked with several interrelated questions, such as the number of members, their term of office, emoluments, incompatability, method of appointment, special secretariat and the relationship with the General Assembly.[4] Most of these questions involve financial implications. But the crux of the matter is whether the International Law Commission is believed to be a useful body by the nations of

[1] It may be noted that neither the Statute of ILC nor the Statute of ICJ, stipulates that the simultaneous membership of both the bodies is incompatible. Consequently, a member of the ICJ can continue to remain a member of the ILC. In the past, under the League system, the members of the PCIJ were allowed to serve on the Committee of Experts for the Progressive Codification of International Law: see L. of N. Offl. Rec., 1924, pp. 143, 274. The PCIJ also did not consider it incompatible for judges to take part in international conferences concerned with development of international law: PCIJ, series E, no. 1, 1922, p. 247. No similar decision regarding the principle of incompatibility seems to have been taken by the present bodies but, in practice, the members of the ILC have resigned from the Commission on their appointment as judges of the ICJ.

[2] Author's italics.

[3] *Y.B.I.L.C.*, 1961, vol. I, 615th mtg., p. 213, paras. 20–21.

[4] See *Y.B.I.L.C.*, vol. I, 97th mtg., pp. 125–35.

the world. In fact there did exist considerable doubts regarding any rapid and positive results of the Commission's work possibly because a large part of it had not been utilized by the General Assembly.[1] However, the General Assembly, as an alternative to a full-time basis, accepted the International Law Commission's recommendation of a simple five-year term for the Commission's members,[2] and amended for this purpose Article 10 of the International Law Commission's Statute by Resolution 985(X) of December 3, 1955,[3] which ensured a certain continuity and greater stability to the Commission's work. But the International Law Commission could still hardly be expected to achieve spectacular results under the present arrangement of a part-time commission with a two-month session every year.[4]

Emoluments. The members of the Commission, being only part-time, receive travel expenses and daily allowance along with an honorarium as approved by the General Assembly (Article 13).[5] The present arrangement of their emoluments has passed through several difficulties at various stages since 1949, and its history throws much light on what was a complete lack of appreciation on the part of the Fifth Committee, which deals with budgetary and financial matters of the United Nations, of the special importance of the Commission

---

[1] See UNGAOR 6th sess. 1951, 6th Com. 295th–296th mtgs., pp. 261–71. Many delegates expressed the view that no report of ILC had been accepted in full by the GA, and questioned whether it would be of any value to maintain a group whose conclusions were not adopted by the GA and were re-examined by it. Sir Gerald Fitzmaurice (U.K.) said that there existed no agreement on legal principles and the very bases of international law were put in issue: *ibid.*, pp. 267–8.

[2] See *Y.B.I.L.C.*, 1955, vol. I, 315th mtg. During the Sixth Committee's debate on the ILC's report on the 2nd sess. (U.N. Doc. A/1316, UNGAOR 5th sess., supp. no. 12) the U.K. representative suggested the introduction of a full-time service for a part only of the Commission's members. This did not find favour as it would create an invidious distinction between the members and would also present insuperable difficulties in the nomination of the candidates for the election. In its 3rd sess. the ILC, while reviewing its Statute on invitation from the GA, favoured not less than seven years' term for its members. See *Y.B.I.L.C.*, 1951, vol. I, p. 128, para. 50. In 1955, at its 7th sess., the ILC formally proposed an amendment of Art. 10 of the Commission's Statute stipulating a five-year term which was adopted by the GA. See *Y.B.I.L.C.* 1955, vol. II, chap. IV, Rept. of the Commission (U.N. Doc. A/2934), pp. 41–2, paras. 27, 28.

[3] For debate in the Sixth Committee see UNGAOR 10th sess. 1955, 6th Com., mtgs. 443rd–446th, pp. 10–23. U.N. Doc. A/C6/L351, the draft resolution of Gt. Britain and N. Ireland. UNGAOR, *ibid.*, Annexes, Ag. it. 50.

[4] It becomes difficult for the members to be well prepared, briefed and documented on all and each subject to be discussed when they assemble each summer for only two months in Geneva. As Mr. Córdova was compelled to say: 'Under the present system, a few days before the beginning of each session the members of the Commission received a report they had never set eyes on before': *Y.B.I.L.C.*, 1951, vol. I, 129th mtg., para. 67.

[5] The text of the Article was amended by GA Res. 485(V) of December 12, 1950.

and the nature of its work. If the financial position of the members of the International Law Commission is regrettably unattractive it should be attributed to the Fifth Committee which, by rigidly applying the principle of uniform system of subsistence allowance for all eligible bodies of the United Nations, found it difficult to admit any exception, even in the case of International Law Commission for the special nature and scope of its work.[1]

On the basis of the recommendation of the Fifth Committee,[2] the General Assembly, by Resolution 1106(XI) of February 21, 1957, decided to distinguish between a subsistence allowance and payments additional to it. The subsistence allowance was to be paid on an uniform basis to members of all eligible bodies at the rates approved by General Assembly's Resolution 1075(XI) of December 1956. The rates approved were: $25 per diem for meetings at Headquarters, $20 per diem for meetings elsewhere; $8 per diem during periods of travel abroad. But additional payments were to be paid to the Chairman and Special Rapporteurs, and to the other members of the International Law Commission as honoraria at the rate of $2,500 and $1,000 respectively.[3] Final revision of rates of payment was made by the General Assembly at its 15th Session 1960, when by Resolution 1588(XV) of December 20, it authorized an increase of subsistence allowance to $30 per diem at Headquarters and $23 per diem elsewhere so as to adjust with the requisite standards of accommodation and subsistence.[4] Accordingly, the subsistence allowance of the members of the International Law Commission who were receiving it at a special rate of $35 per diem ($20 subsistence allowance and $15 additional allowance) has come down to $23 per diem as they invariably hold meetings at Geneva and not at New York. It seems illogical that members of the International Law Commission should be placed in the same category as other Commissions or expert bodies.[5] Perhaps the most suit-

---

[1] See U.N. Doc. A/C5/713, Annex. The report of the Secretary General of September 20, 1957, gives an excellent history of the system of honoraria and special allowances to the members of the Commission, Committees and other subsidiary bodies of the GA or other organs of the UN. See UNGAOR 12th sess. 1957, Annexes, Ag. it. 41.

[2] See U.N. Doc. A/3766, para. 6, UNGAOR 12th sess. 1957, Annexes, Ag. it. 41, pp. 60–1.

[3] In the case of the Chairman and rapporteurs the payment of higher sum was subject to the preparation of specific reports or studies between sessions of the Commission, *ibid.*, p. 61.

[4] See UNGAOR 15th sess. 1960, pl. mtgs. 960th; also U.N. Doc. A/C5/813, for the Report of the Secretary General.

[5] According to the Commission 'the case of each technical commission and committee must be decided on its merits . . . The work of the Commission makes heavy demands on the members . . . Even if no direct money consideration should arise, a serious burden of additional work is subsequently imposed on all members of the Commission, without exception, by reason of such a long absence from

able category for them would be that of the judges or the *ad hoc* judges of the International Court of Justice, from the point of view of fixing their emoluments and standing. The Commission deserves a status and conditions of service, if not higher and better than, at least equal to that of the International Court of Justice. The success of its work would be due largely to its high reputation and the personal qualifications of its members commanding universal respect in the legal world. The exodus of its members intermittently to the International Court of Justice adversely affects the continuity of its work, and this fact underlines the comparative importance attached to the two institutions. The periodic filling of casual vacancies as well as re-election of the Commission's members under the existing system tends to disrepute the codification work, and an improvement in this respect is definitely required. Addressing the American Society of International Law, Professor Milton Katz has emphasized the need for a sustained and systematic effort to strengthen the International Law Commission, lubricate its machinery and facilitate and accelerate its work. Among other measures, he favoured a progressive evolution of the Commission towards a full-time status, extension of its sessions to the point where it would meet twice a year for at least three months duration. He suggested that 'the evolution should also entail a corresponding enhancement of the status, compensation and pension arrangements of the members. These should be established on terms, and on a level, appropriate to the importance of the work to be done and to our constant concern to attract personnel of the highest quality'.[1]

THE ORGANIZATION OF THE COMMISSION'S WORK

Sessions

The Commission is not enjoined by the Statute to hold any particular number of meetings every year. It holds its regular session at the end of April every year. Originally, under Article 12 of the Statute, the Commission was required to meet at New York, although it could also hold its meeting at other places after consultation with the Secretary General. But the Commission's members were unanimously in favour of meeting at Geneva in preference to New York since in their view general conditions at Geneva were

---

their normal activities or duties. In addition, if adequate progress is to be made with the work at the Commission's sessions, it is necessary for all its members to devote a considerable amount of time to personal research and preparation between the sessions': *Y.B.I.L.C.*, 1957, vol. II, Report of the Commission, U.N. Doc. A/3623, chap. IV, p. 145, para. 31.

[1] *Proc. Am. Soc. Int. Law*, 1960, pp. 257–8. Also, U.N. Doc. A/7209/Rev 1, 1968, *op. cit.*, p. 32, para 98(b).

more conducive to efficiency in the kind of work it had to perform.[1]
It decided to recommend to the General Assembly an amendment of
Article 12 of the Statute, at its seventh session in 1955, in order to
settle once and for all that its sessions should be held in Geneva.[2]
The reasons put forward in support of the preference for Geneva
were as follows: i. the library facilities at Geneva were exceptionally
well planned and, since the days of the League of Nations, proved to
be unsurpassed in the field of international law; ii. favourable
working conditions existed during summer when the Commission's
sessions were held, since several of its members who were university
professors were normally free only in summer vacations, a time
when the New York climate was hardly conducive to satisfactory
work; iii. the amendment no more than confirmed a regular practice
of the International Law Commission and was designed to bring
Article 12 into line with that practice of meeting at Geneva where
most of the sessions except only a few had been held; iv. the atmosphere of Geneva was more favourable, because of Switzerland's
neutrality, than that of New York for the studies of a body of technical experts like the International Law Commission which was
called upon to solve legal problems setting aside the political
contingencies of the moment as far as possible.[3] The amendment
was adopted by the General Assembly Resolution 984(X) of
December 3, 1955, which authorized and confirmed the continuation of the practice of meetings of the International Law Commission at Geneva. Where the International Law Commission met
was purely an administrative matter but it was a wise step to make
the seat of the International Law Commission at Geneva, which
may be considered to be a more accessible place.

The sessions of the Commission have varied between eight and
eleven weeks. The experience of the Commission has been that a

[1] Report of the Commission, U.N. Doc. A/2456, *Y.B.I.L.C.*, 1953, vol. II,
p. 232, paras. 173–174.
[2] Garcia Amador proposed the amendment of Article 12 of the Statute at
311th mtg. of the Commission with the object of avoiding a repetition of the
difficulties which had frequently arisen in the Fifth Committee of the GA whenever
the Commission decided to meet at Geneva. For meetings at Geneva additional
budgetary provision was to be made. This was opposed by the Advisory Committee
on Administrative and Budgetary Matters, which based itself on the principle that
Headquarters-based bodies should meet at Headquarters—a principle later
formalized by GA Res. 694(VII) of December 20, 1952. See U.N. Doc. A/3037
UNGAOR 10th sess. 1955, Annexes, Ag. it. 50, pp. 17. paras, 4–6.
[3] All but three sessions of the ILC have been held at Geneva. The GA Res.
2116(XX) of 21 December 1965, para. 2(a), has given further recognition to the
holding of ILC sessions at Geneva. Besides, according to para. 2(h) of the Resolution, sessions of the ILC may also be held at other places than Geneva after consultation with the Secretary General when a government extends an invitation
for a meeting to be held within its territory and agrees to defray the additional
costs.

ten-week session appeared to be the minimum required to deal with all the items on its agenda. The study of questions, drafting of preliminary reports, communication with governments, and production of final draft on the basis of extensive research and thorough preparation, are essential and prolonged stages for the codification on any topic to mature and be fruitful. Manley O. Hudson who had a great experience in regard to the codification work in connection with the Harvard Research Drafts, pointed out at the time of Commission's review of the Statute in 1951: 'A working session of nine to ten months a year might produce excellent results.'[1] The Commission itself has felt that 'within the confines of a ten-week session, no serious increase in the speed or quantity of the work could be achieved except by the adoption of methods that would be detrimental to its quality'[2] which it believed must always remain the primary consideration. Nor has it favoured the proposal of increasing the length of its sessions, or of holding two preliminary meetings a day. The Commission has made it unequivocally clear whenever occasion has demanded that, in view of the conditions in which it has to work, it is absolutely necessary to adhere to the policy of taking enough time in producing drafts of good quality rather than taking a risk of introducing an element of insecurity by formulating too rapidly a law which is not yet ready for codification, and thinks it preferable that the tenure of its members be prolonged.[3]

As to the alternative of prolonging the Commission's sessions or holding a supplementary session, one factor complicated the scheduling of its sessions since 1958. The General Assembly Resolution 1202(XII) of December 13, 1957 authorized the Commission to meet at Geneva subject to the limitation that its sessions did not overlap with the summer session of the Economic and Social Council, since the conference facilities at Geneva would be limited, particularly owing to the resurgence of Geneva as a major conference centre under the five-year 'pattern of conferences' established by the Resolution. The Commission found itself faced with a dilemma as it had to begin in mid-April in order to complete its work before the beginning of the summer session of the Economic and Social Coun-

---

[1] *Y.B.I.L.C.*, 1951, vol. I, p. 122, para. 115; see also observations made by Spiropoulos at the 83rd mtg. of the ILC, *ibid.*, pp. 6–7, paras. 34–37, suggesting a major permanent legal commission with powers in the legal field comparable to those of ECOSOC in the economic field, in order to meet all the year round for codification work. He regarded the shortness of the Commission's sessions as one of the reasons for the slow progress made in its work.

[2] *Y.B.I.L.C.*, 1957, vol. II, Report of the Commission, Doc. A/3623, p. 145, paras. 27–28; *ibid.*, 1958, vol. II, pp. 74–6 and 108, paras. 66–67.

[3] *Ibid.*, pp. 107–10. See also debate in the Commission on 'Planning of future work of the Commission', U.N. Doc. A/CN.4/138, *Y.B.I.L.C.*, 1961, vol. I, 597th and 614th–616th mtgs., also, *ibid.*, 1968, vol. I, 979th mtg., pp. 206–10.

cil, and to accommodate its members who were academicians. If it chose to defer the beginning of its session until after the close of the ECOSOC session, its report would be received too late to be considered at the next session of the General Assembly. However, since the five-year pattern of conferences expired in 1962 (although extended by GA Resolution 1851(XVII) until December 1963) this was no longer a hindrance for the Commission to consider an extension in the duration of its proceedings each year, either by prolonging a single session, or by holding a second one. When the Commission's proposal of holding winter sessions was approved by by GA. Res. 2045 (XX) of 8 December 1965, the second part of the seventeenth session was held in Monaco from 3 to 28 January 1966.[1]

Rules of procedure at meetings

The Commission, a subsidiary organ of the General Assembly, was governed by the provisions of Rule 150 of the Rules of Procedure of the General Assembly, that 'the rules relating to the procedure of committees of the General Assembly, as well as rules 38 and 55, shall apply to the procedure of any subsidiary organ unless the General Assembly or the subsidiary organ decides otherwise'. Accordingly, the International Law Commission had an option to draw up its own rules of procedure for the whole of its work or for specific items, or to adopt the rules referred to above. It decided at its first session that the provisions of the rules of procedure laid down in rule 150, namely rules 88 to 122 and rules 38 and 55, would be provisionally applicable to the Commission.[2] Although the question of adopting the Commission's own rules of procedure was raised by Sir H. Lauterpacht at the sixth session of the Commission in 1954, the matter was dropped after he had resigned from the Commission to join the International Court.[3] Consequently, the International Law Commission abides by Rule 162 of the amended Rules of Procedure of the General Assembly, and the rules relating to the procedure of committees, namely rules 98 to 134 and rules 45 and 62, are applicable to the Commission's conduct of meetings.[4]

One third of the members of the Commission constitute a quorum, but for a question to be put to the vote the presence of the majority of the members is required. Decisions are made by a majority of the

[1] U.N. Doc. A/5509, *Y.B.I.L.C.* 1963, vol. II, paras. 72–74; and U.N. Doc. A/5809, *ibid.*, 1964, vol. II, paras. 36–38; *ibid* 1966, vol. II, pt. I, paras 1–3.
[2] *Y.B.I.L.C.*, 1949, 1st mtg., pp. 10–11.
[3] See *Y.B.I.L.C.*, 1954, vol. I, p. 204, para. 47; also Lauterpacht, 'Codification and development of international law', *A.J.I.L.*, vol. 49, 1955, p. 37.
[4] See *UN Rules of Procedure of the GA*, N.Y., Feb. 1961, p. 29.

members and by voting, and each member has one vote. In case of equal division on matters, the proposal is treated as rejected.[1]

Officers

Rules 105 to 109 of the UN Rules of Procedure govern the appointment and duties of officers. The Commission elects its own Chairman, first and second Vice-Chairmen and a General Rapporteur. In order that all members of the Commission may share the honours and responsibilities, officers are changed every year. Special Rapporteurs for individual topics are also appointed by the Commission from amongst its members.[2] The election of officers is invariably by general acclamation after being settled at a private meeting.

The Chairman of the Commission, apart from presiding and conducting the business of meetings, represents the Commission in the immediately following session of the General Assembly,[3] and is also entitled to take part in the debates of the Sixth Committee on the Commission's report.[4] In his absence the first Vice-Chairman (or failing him the second Vice-Chairman) takes his place and exercises the same powers and duties as the Chairman of the meetings.

The General Rapporteur is also elected for every session by general acclamation. Whereas the Chairman of the Commission has a primary responsibility to give leadership in matters of procedure, the Rapporteur does not have the same responsibility, though nowhere are the functions or duties of the Rapporteur defined in the Rules of Procedure. The principal task of the Rapporteur is to

---

[1] See amended UN Rules of Procedure, U.N. Doc. A/4700, U.N. Pubn. Ser. February 1961. Also S. D. Bailey: *General Assembly of the United Nations.* 1960.

[2] Article 16(a) of the Statute of the ILC.

[3] The Commission had decided at its first session to be represented, for the purposes of consultation, by its Chairman; see *Y.B.I.L.C.*, 1949, p. 284, para. 41. During 1950 and 1951 the Chairman did not attend the sessions of the GA, nor did the Commission expressly make any formal decision to that effect. When this was pointed out by Liang, the Secretary of the ILC, it was again decided that the ILC be represented by its Chairman; *ibid.*, 1952, vol. I, pp. 227–8. Since then a similar formal decision was repeated every year except when the Commission decided that it should be represented in the GA by its Special Rapporteurs on the Law of the Sea and on the Law of Treaties in order to furnish such information on the Commission's draft as might be required for the GA's consideration.

[4] It may be noted that several members of the ILC sat on the Sixth Committee as representative of their governments, who found it difficult to defend the Commission's decisions there if their governments disagreed with them. Córdova raised the question in 179th mtg. of the Commission and proposed that the Commission should recommend that none of its members be asked to sit on the Sixth Committee as representatives of Governments. But it was argued by Spiropoulos that in the Sixth Committee the members of the Commission expressed their governments' point of view, not their own, and also, there was no reason why their own views should coincide with those of the Commission where decisions were taken not unanimously but by a majority vote, see *Y.B.I.L.C.*, 1952, vol. I, p. 227, paras. 13, 17 and 18.

submit to the Commission an objective report of the current session before it is approved for presentation to the General Assembly. He may elucidate the issues involved in a debate for clarification, guide the discussion, and accumulate information formally communicated to the Rapporteur or seek additional information deemed necessary for the Commission's work. In addition to a General Rapporteur, special Rapporteurs are also appointed by the Commission for each major subject or group of subjects under its study. Under Article 16 of the Statute it is obligatory for the Commission to appoint a rapporteur entrusted with the task of submitting to the Commission the draft-proposals on any question to serve as the basis of discussion. The preparation of draft reports requires enormous time, extensive study and research on the part of a rapporteur who, between the sessions of the Commission, carries on work to facilitate the Commission's task to produce a draft for submission to the General Assembly. Although a rapporteur is assisted by the members appointed for the purpose by the Commission, and by the Secretariat, the reports bear the distinctive mark of the personal contribution of the Rapporteurs. For example, this is best illustrated by several reports submitted by successive special rapporteurs on the law of treaties: three reports by Brierly, two by Lauterpacht, a series of five reports by Sir Gerald Fitzmaurice and six reports by Sir Humphrey Waldock.[1] Brierly's reports contained only general outlines since he appeared to believe in attaining practical results more readily by circumscribing the area of controversy and decision. Lauterpacht dealt comprehensively with all aspects of treaties—the definition and nature, the conclusion, and the conditions of validity of treaties—embracing a wide range of contemporary developments. By his comments on each article of his draft, Lauterpacht seems to have followed the pattern of the Harvard Research in International Law. Sir Gerald Fitzmaurice's later reports also followed the same pattern which now seems to be regarded as a model for the future. Sir Humphrey Waldock, on the other hand, received precise directions to prepare his draft articles which should serve as a basis for multilateral convention.[2]

[1] See below, p. 321 n 1 Without specific directions from the Commission the Special Rapporteurs had to exercise their own initiative in formulating a report. If the draft reports on Law of Treaties, Régime of the High Seas, and Arbitral Procedure are compared, the difference between them becomes obvious. Brierly's reports on Law of Treaties dealt with only a portion of the subject and contained precise draft texts; François' reports on the Régime of the High Seas contained a general survey of the subject and no conclusions. Scelle's reports on Arbitral Procedure covered the whole range of the subject and gave general conclusions rather than a draft code on the subject.

[2] See *Y.B.I.L.C.*, 1961, vol. II, Report of the Commission, U.N. Doc. A/4843, chap. III, p. 128, para. 39.

Secretariat of the Commission

Article 14 of the Statute of the International Law Commission directs the Secretary General to make available the staff and facilities required by the Commission to fulfil its task. Since the Commission is not in full-time session it is not provided with its own secretariat and therefore makes heavy demands on the Legal Department and, in particular, on the Division for the Development and Codification of International Law.

The Legal Department of the United Nations Secretariat[1] has the general responsibility to advise the Secretariat and other organs of the United Nations on legal and constitutional questions and to encourage the progressive development of international law and its codification. Its Division for the Development and Codification of International Law is entirely at the disposal of the Commission. The Director of the Division has acted as the *ex officio* secretary to the Commission since the very beginning. The Division bears the primary responsibility, insofar as it concerns the Secretariat, in regard to the following: i. to prepare studies and recommendations aimed at encouraging the development of international law and its codification; ii. to compile and edit documents in this general field; iii. to provide secretariat services for the International Law Commission; iv. to assist the organs of the United Nations in the field of development of international law and its codification, and to provide secretariat services for conferences of experts in this field; v. to prepare collections of international judicial decisions and national laws of importance for the development and codification of international law; vi. to prepare legal opinions on the interpretation and application of the Charter and study the interpretations made by the principal and subsidiary organs of the United Nations; and vii. to maintain liaison with non-governmental organizations engaged in the study or promotion of international law.

The Division for the Development and Codification of International Law of the Secretariat designates a group of staff members for the purpose of ensuring the smooth and efficient working of the International Law Commission. They are assigned all duties pertaining to the preparation of the provisional agenda of the Commission, the preparation of such substantive studies and working papers as may be required; the assistance to the Assistant Secretary General in his capacity as the representative of the Secretary General in meetings of the Commission;[2] the maintenance of liaison

---

[1] Organization of the Secretariat, U.N. Doc. ST/AFS/2, U.N. Pub., June 1951, pp. 31–2, Section II.

[2] The Assistant Secretary General, heading the Legal Department of the Secretariat, or, failing him, any officer is designated and the Director of the

with the Chairman of the Commission and undertaking for him the work connected with the meetings, with conferences, and general services with regard to physical arrangements for the meetings, such as, the interpretation, verbatim reporting, summary recording, translation reproduction, and distribution of material. In addition, other duties undertaken are connected with the Legal Department regarding credentials of representatives, the preparation of summary records and draft reports on the work of the International Law Commission for its approval, and the furnishing of technical advice concerning rules of procedure and appropriateness of expenditures arising from the Commission's meetings.

The Secretariat has also, from time to time, in accordance with the directions of the General Assembly, submitted to the Commission preparatory work, memoranda and documents which have received high appreciation from all quarters. Sometimes, however, the Commission has had to discuss important questions on its agenda without the help of relevant documentation,[1] and to draft articles without sufficient material or information.[2] There is no doubt that non-availability of required documentation has caused some dissatisfaction.[3] Nevertheless, even with regard to the material and documents that are available, it seems difficult for the Commission's members to study and digest them fully, as long as they retain their present part-time positions. However, there is no denying the fact that the Commission's efficiency would be considerably

---

Codification Division of International Law attend the Commission's meetings as the representatives of the Secretary General. They participate in the debates of the Commission but have no vote.

[1] For instance, a complete set of documents compiled by the Secretariat, Laws and Regulations on the Régime of the High Seas, 2 vols., 1951, U.N. Leg. Ser., was not available to the members of the Commission until 1952 whereas the Commission dealt with the Second Report (A/CN4/142) on the régime of the high seas beginning with the chapter on the continental shelf at its 3rd session, 1951, at 113th mtg. (see *Y.B.I.L.C.*, 1951, vol. I, p. 267). Hudson regretted that they had been compelled to discuss this important question without the help of all the relevant documentations (*Y.B.I.L.C.*, 1951, vol. I, 117th mtg, p. 295, para. 1). Moreover, the Commission produced texts and draft articles on the subject (continental shelf and related subjects) in its second report (A/1316, para. 20) without the assistance of the documentation compiled by the Secretariat.

[2] During discussions on the draft articles on sedentary fisheries at the third session, Cordova as well as Keno (Asst. Secty. Gen.) agreed that 'the Commission had insufficient information': see *Y.B.I.L.C.*, 1951, vol. I, 120th mtg., p. 321, paras. 35, 40.

[3] The Commission expressed its dissatisfaction at the inadequate facilities relating to the production of documents, summary records and draft texts in the working languages of the Commission, which created serious inconvenience and considerably delayed its work. See Report of the Commission, U.N. Doc. A/5209, *Y.B.I.L.C.*, 1962, vol. II, chap. V, p. 193, paras. 84–85; also Report of the Commission, U.N. Doc. A/5509, UNGAOR 18th sess. Suppl. No. 9 (reproduced in *A.J.I.L.*, vol. 58, 1964, p. 323, paras. 76–78).

increased if it were provided with a well-equipped permanent secretariat comparable to that of the Hague Conference on Private International Law which might do very useful work for the Commission by thoroughly preparing the work of codification and by rendering services valuable to the Rapporteur's activities and to the Commission's discussions.[1]

Reports of the Commission

The Statute of the International Law Commission requires the Commission to submit specific reports, recommendations or drafts to the General Assembly on various phases of its work connected with the progressive development of international law and its codification.[2] But it does not stipulate that any regular periodical reports be submitted by the International Law Commission to the General Assembly. However, since its inception, the Commission has customarily submitted regular annual reports to the General Assembly which give a summary account of its work and its important decisions or recommendations during every session. These reports are thoroughly discussed by the Sixth Committee before the General Assembly adopts them either in the form of a substantive resolution, or merely in a formal resolution taking note of the report, as deemed necessary by the Assembly.[3]

The Annual Reports of the International Law Commission have, since 1951, followed the practice of primarily setting forth the majority decisions of the Commission. While providing for the inclusion of the various divergent views of the members in the general report, the provision of ways and means of recording dissenting votes and expressing the dissenting opinions in the Commission's report has been a very controversial issue. After much discussion the Commission, at its seventh session in 1955, reaffirmed the rule adopted in 1951 at the third session, that detailed explanations of dissenting opinions should not be inserted in the report, but merely a statement to the effect that, for reasons given in the summary records, a member was opposed to the adoption of a certain article or a particular passage of the record.[4]

The controversy concerning the provision for the expression of dissenting opinions in the Commission's final report on the work of

---

[1] See for such a proposal by the Netherlands government its *note verbale* of September 7, 1961: U.N. Doc. A/4796/Add. 7, UNGAOR 16th sess. 1961–2, Annexes, vol. 3, Ag. it. 70. Also UN Doc. A/7209/Rev. 1, 1968, para. 98(c).

[2] See Articles 16(j), 17(c), 18(2), 20, 22, 23(1), and 24, of the Statute of the ILC.

[3] These reports are published every year in the Year Book of International Law Commission, vol. II, and are also found in the UNGAOR, 6th Committee Report.

[4] For the discussions, see *Y.B.I.L.C.*, 1951, vol. I, 128th mtg., pp. 385–8; *ibid.*, 1953, vol. I, 195th mtg., pp. 66–72; *ibid.*, 1955, vol. I, 322nd and 323rd mtgs., pp. 240–6; also vol. II, p. 43, para. 37.

each session had arisen because of a disastrous precedent established during the first session of the Commission. Then Koretsky was allowed a long reservation inserted in the report relating to the Draft Declaration on Rights and Duties of States.[1] In fact, in the First Report of the Commission (1949), certain dissenting views formed part of the main body of the report as well as of the footnotes. But in the next two Reports (1950 and 1951) the footnote system for stating dissenting opinions was adhered to. However, during the preparation of the Third Report (1951), when Yepes submitted a long explanation of dissent following the precedent established by Koretsky, it was decided that in future a member would be permitted only to express his dissent by means of a reference to the summary records.[2]

Some members of the Commission challenged the decision at the fifth session (1953) and asserted the need to express dissenting opinions in the final report of the Commission submitted annually to the General Assembly.[3] The arguments put forward may be summarized as follows: i. The views of all members of the Commission, elected by the General Assembly with regard to their personal qualifications and representing the main forms of civilization and principal legal systems of the world, should find expression in any proposed rules of international law. The special nature and purpose of the work of the Commission made it necessary to give a complete account of the opinions expressed and the arguments put forward in the Commission; ii. The Commission's method of work required publication of its drafts as Commission documents for submission to governments (Article 16(g) (h) and Article 21 of the Statute), reconsideration in the light of the comments of governments (Article 16(i) and Article 22), and decision by the General Assembly (Article 16(j) and Article 18, para. 2, Article 20 and Article 22 of the Statute). It was of utmost importance that governments, the General Assembly and all parties concerned should have at their disposal reports giving a complete and faithful account of the opinions

---

[1] *Y.B.I.L.C.*, 1949, Report of the Commission U.N. Doc. A/925, pt. II, p. 287, n. 21. Hudson's note following Koretsky's whole column ran into only four lines. See summary records, *ibid.*, 36th and 37th mtgs. for discussion on the question of footnotes, pp. 256–69. See for dissenting views of Alfaro, Hudson and Scelle, *Y.B.I.L.C.*, 1950, vol. II, p. 374, pt. III, n. 3.

[2] See *Y.B.I.L.C.*, 1951, vol. I, 128th and 129th mtgs., pp. 385–8 and 394, paras. 9–10; *ibid.*, vol. II, Report of the Commission U.N. Doc. A/1858, chap. II, p. 128, n. 15.

[3] U.N. Doc. A/CN4/L42, Zourek's proposal; U.N. Doc. A/CN4/L43, Lauterpacht's proposal; and U.N. Doc. A/CN4/L44, Pal's proposal. Zourek's proposal was the most comprehensive document giving reasons justifying the expression of dissenting opinions in the Commission's Final Report, its advantages and disadvantages following from the present practice. See *Y.B.I.L.C.*, 1953, vol. I, 195th mtg., pp. 66–8, n. 1, 3 and 4.

expressed in the Commission; iii. Article 20 of the Statute required the Commission to express dissenting opinions along with its draft articles, and with conclusions relevant to 'the extent of agreement on each point in the practice of States and in doctrine' and 'divergencies and disagreements which exist, as well as arguments invoked in favour of one or another solution'; iv. the right of expressing dissenting opinion has been fully recognized in international law in the arbitral procedure as well as in the International Court of Justice;[1] v. the proposed system of attaching a statement of dissenting opinions had the following five advantages: *a.* the dissenting opinions would commit only their authors and could be annexed to the final report; *b.* the reports would be more consistent with the object and functions of the Commission and with the scientific nature of its work; *c.* they would greatly facilitate the examination of drafts by governments as well as by the General Assembly; *d.* they would obviate the need for useless and sometimes laborious discussions in future; and *e.* they would enhance the scientific value of the Commission's reports on the development of international law.[2]

It is argued that the present system of allowing the members to express their dissent in a footnote (in which reference is made to the opinions expressed by dissenting members, as recorded in the summary records), impels them to make lengthy statements during meetings purely for the purpose of putting their opinions on record. Since many items are usually discussed by the Commission at several sessions, members have to repeat the process at each of the Commission's sessions, thereby delaying progress. Besides, it is said that the present system tends to create the false impression that a decision of the Commission represents the unanimous opinion of its members, thus associating dissenting members with decisions which their scientific convictions would compel them to reject.[3]

---

[1] Examples given were: Article 52, para. 2 of the Convention of 1899 on the Pacific Settlement of International Disputes; Article 57 of the Statute of the ICJ; and Articles 74, para. 2 and 84, para. 2, of the Rules of the Court which recognized the importance of dissenting opinions in the development of international law.

[2] See U.N. Doc. A/CN4/L42, Zourek's proposal: *Y.B.I.L.C.*, 1953, vol. I, pp. 66–8, n. 1 and his arguments, paras. 1–17, in the summary records, pp. 66–9. Also U.N. Doc. A/CN4/L61; *Y.B.I.L.C.*, 1955, vol. II, p. 43, para. 37, *ibid.,* vol. I, pp. 240–1, paras. 45–55 and pp. 244–5, paras. 20–29.

[3] The solution of the problem suggested by Zourek was that the dissenting member 'shall have a right to add a short statement of his dissenting views to any decision taken by the Commission on draft rules of international law, if the said decision does not in whole or in part express the unanimous opinion of the members of the Commission'. See U.N. Doc. A/CN4/L61, *op. cit.,* p. 43, para. 37. See also U.N. Doc. A/CN4/L42, *op. cit.,* p. 67.

Lauterpacht also held the view that it was desirable, contrary to the existing practice, that the Reports of the ILC gave as full a publicity as was practicable to opposing or supplementary views of the minority or of individual members. His

Last but not the least it is argued that numerous dissenting opinions finding no place in the Commission's final report (which embodies only majority views) cause inequality among members. The summary records of the Commission which contain a statement of different members' arguments are not available to general readers, neither do governments pay the same attention to them as to the final report of the Commission. So the dissenting views as a matter of form are not thought to receive the same kind of prominence as the views of the majority do in the Commission's reports.

But are not these arguments, emphasizing the need of adequate expression of dissenting opinions in the Commission's final reports to the General Assembly, based on a misconceived notion of the nature of the Commission's work? Do they not rely on a false analogy between the Commission and the International Court of Justice or an arbitral tribunal? Lauterpacht argued that 'the reasons which have prompted the recognition of the right of the judges of the International Court of Justice to append dissenting or separate judgments or opinions apply with no less cogency to the work of the International Law Commission'.[1] Surely any comparison between the Commission and the International Court of Justice is not valid because the work, the functions and the procedure of the former are entirely different from those of the latter. The Court or an arbitral tribunal is a judicial body required to settle grave matters, in accordance with the rules of international law. Deliberations of judges take place in private, and there are no records of these. Therefore, it is fitting to provide for dissenting as well as separate opinions of the judges to let the general public understand the relative character of justice.[2] The Commission, on the other hand, is in a quite different

---

proposal was that 'Members of the Commission are entitled to record, in footnote, their dissent from any report adopted by the Commission or any part thereof. They are also entitled to append to their dissent a brief statement of reasons at a length agreed to by the President of the Commission. They may appeal from the decision of the President to the Bureau whose decision shall be final': U.N. Doc. A/CN4/L43, *Y.B.I.L.C.*, 1953, vol. I, p. 68, n. 3.

Radhabinod Pal's proposal said: 'Members of the Commission are entitled to append to the report adopted by the Commission their dissent, if any, with a brief statement of reasons therefor': U.N. Doc. A/CN4/L44, *ibid.*, p. 68, n. 4.

[1] See Lauterpacht, 'Codification and development of international law', *A.J.I.L.*, vol. 49, 1955, pp. 37–8. He added 'Any diminution of that right, for reasons of possible abuse, is not in keeping with the scientific character of the Commission and is, on more general grounds, indefensible. The authority of the decisions and drafts of the majority of the Commission is grounded in their intrinsic merit as distinguished from the formal fact of their being the result of a majority vote.'

[2] Even the practice of the ICJ in regard to dissident opinions is considered to be of doubtful value. As pointed out by François, Rapporteur of the Commission, during the discussions on the issue that dissenting opinions of the judges had led in practice to their almost monopolizing public attention. Whereas the Court's

position. It is a technical body—an assembly of jurists—required to prepare texts or drafts in the form of recommendations to the General Assembly. These are intended for incorporation in a Convention with a view to codifying international law. Its deliberations are public, and its members have thorough discussions to enlighten and convince each other in an attempt to reach agreement. These discussions are published in summary records of its sessions. Only the results are recorded in the Commission's reports which are not intended to embody the personal views of individual members. Since the success of codification depends on gathering as much support as possible within the General Assembly, in the Commission itself the majority view has to prevail so that the Commission's recommendations can have maximum authority. The inclusion of extensive dissenting opinions in the Commission's reports or recommendations is bound to constitute a destructive element and thereby undermine its efforts, since in a political body like the General Assembly the dissident views of experts are likely to damage the possibilities of agreement between governments.[1]

The Commission's reports should not be assumed to give full expression to various conflicting views within the Commission. In fact no report can possibly claim to do justice to all the dissenting views. If members were allowed to explain their reasons of dissent in the report then it would open the floodgates for the expression of dissenting views, and some provision would have to be made for separate opinions too, as others supporting the majority view would be entitled to explain why for different reasons they voted with the majority. The result would be that the homogeneity, balance and economy of the Commission's reports would be upset. Besides, as it was claimed, Article 20 of the Statute did not refer to the divergence of views within the Commission, nor did it refer to the general report of the Commission to give therein any 'prominence to the dissenting opinions. The reference in that article was clearly to any commentary the Commission attached to its drafts.

However, the practical importance of various opinions expressed during discussions, which result in a text of the Commission's drafts embodying the whole of the agreement thereafter reached, is doubt-

---

judgments, in an effort to obtain a broad measure of agreement, were bound to keep their reasoning extremely brief leaving out many arguments, the dissident opinions were expressed in great detail and without restraint. The result was that somewhat incompletely motivated judgments of the Court received less attention from learned circles in contrast to the dissenting opinions which had a distinct advantage: *Y.B.I.L.C.*, 1955, vol. I, p. 241, para. 58.

[1] At the national level, a drafting body, similar to the ILC, entrusted with the task of the presentation of draft articles of Acts or Statutes to the parliaments or legislatures, is not entitled to incorporate dissenting views in its draft proposals.

less in regard to the ascertainment of the precise meaning, or the interpretation of the construction of a text in its proper setting. On many occasions the use of *travaux préparatoires*[1] as an element of interpretation of treaties has been recognized by international courts for the purpose of resolving doubt as to a disputed provision or for confirming constructions as to which no doubts existed.[2] While the Permanent Court of International Justice as well as the International Court of Justice showed an attitude of hesitation in regard to recourse to *travaux préparatoires*,[3] a number of cases later decided by the International Court of Justice[4] have indicated the use of preparatory work without qualifications and almost as a matter of course.[5] In the Advisory Opinion on the question of Reservations to the Convention on the Prevention and Punishment of the Crime of Genocide, the International Court of Justice considered it necessary to examine the debates in the Sixth Committee of the General Assembly as well as other preparatory work.[6] Thus,

[1] The term *travaux préparatoires* is applied to the materials of preparatory work. In special circumstances research into the preparatory work and the circumstances in which the treaty was negotiated and concluded may assist in the elucidation of its meaning. The interpretation of a treaty with reference to the preparatory work (*travaux préparatoires*) before its conclusion is called historical interpretation.

[2] The view that the recourse to preparatory work is a constant feature of interpretation of treaties by international tribunals, is held by practically all writers who have devoted detailed study to the matter. See for the list Oppenheim, *International Law*, 1948, vol. I, 7th ed., p. 862. See, for Lauterpacht's opinion: 'Some observations on preparatory work in the interpretation of treaties', *H.L.R.*, vol. 48, 1935, pp. 549–91, also, Art. 32, Vienna Convention on the Law of Treaties, U.N. Doc. A/Conf. 39/27 1969.

[3] The PCIJ went into the details of *travaux préparatoires* in: The Advisory Opinion on the Treatment of Polish Nationals in Danzig, PCIJ, ser. A/B No. 44 (1932); The Minority Schools in Albania, PCIJ, ser. A/B No. 64 (1935); The Lighthouses cases, PCIJ, ser. A/B No. 62 (1934); The Lotus case, PCIJ, ser. A. No. 10 (1927). The ICJ followed the practice of its predecessor as to the use of the preparatory work, invoking the rule that it was not permissible to resort to *travaux préparatoires* when the meaning of the treaty was clear. See, Advisory Opinion on Conditions of Admission of a State to Membership in the United Nations (Article 4 of the Charter), ICJ Reports 1947–8, p. 63; Advisory Opinion on the Competence of the General Assembly for the Admission of a State to the United Nations, ICJ Reports, 1950, p. 8.

[4] See Advisory Opinion on the question of Reservations to the Convention on the Prevention and Punishment of the Crime of Genocide, ICJ Reports 1951, pp. 22, 25; Rights of Nationals of the United States of America in Morocco, ICJ Reports 1952, p. 198. Advisory Opinion on Effects of Awards of the United Nations Administrative Tribunal, ICJ Reports 1954, pp. 54–5.

[5] See Hudson: *Permanent Court of International Justice, 1920–1942*, pp. 652–5, § 572; Lauterpacht: *Development of International Law by the International Court*, 1958: Chapter 7 gives an excellent and detailed account, as well as a critical examination, of the use of recourse to *travaux préparatoires* by the two courts.

[6] See ICJ Reports 1951, p. 22. The Court said, 'The character of a multilateral convention, its purpose, provisions, mode of preparation and adoption, are factors which must be considered in determining, in the absence of any express provision on the subject, the possibility of making reservations, as well as their validity and effect.'

full justification of the relevance and the authority of *travaux pré-paratoires* leading to the conclusion of treaties, especially of multi-lateral and law-making character, is recognized as a legitimate element in their interpretation. Similarly, it is submitted that to attempt an interpretation of the drafts and reports of the Commission without reference to the vast resources of preparatory work which preceded their adoption, is to adopt the method of 'jurisprudence of concepts' in its most questionable connotation.

Publication of summary records and reports

In view of the importance of *travaux préparatoires* leading to the adoption of the Commission's projects, it is heartening to note that the General Assembly decided, on the recommendation of the Commission,[1] in favour of regular publication of the documents and records of the Commission by Resolution 987(X) of December 3, 1955.[2] It answered a long-felt need as, owing to the lack of publicity of the Commission's work and non-availability of its documents and records of its meetings, there existed complete ignorance of the work it undertook.[3] The Year Book of the International Law Commission is now annually published in two volumes, the first containing the summary records of the session, and the second the documents—reports and memoranda, etc. —presented to the Commission as well as its reports to the General Assembly.[4] The publication of these documents and especially of the summary records is a useful contribution to the development of international law and to the

[1] See U.N. Doc. A/CN4/L62 proposal by Krylov concerning the publication of the documents of the ILC and incorporated in Doc. A/2934. The document was later issued in revised form as U.N. Doc. A/CN4/L62/Rev. 1: see *Y.B.I.L.C.*, 1955, vol. II, p. 42, para. 35. On the basis of Krylov's proposal, the Commission unanimously adopted a resolution, see *Y.B.I.L.C.*, vol. I, pp. 238–40, 246.

[2] See Res. 987(X), U.N. Doc. A/RES/344, UNGAOR 10th sess. 1955, Annexes, Ag. it. 50, p. 21.

[3] The Institute of International Law and the American Society of International Law both stressed the need for the publication of the Commission's Documents, U.N. Doc. A/2170, annex III, para. 2, referred to in U.N. Doc. A/C6/348, a study made available to the Sixth Committee by the Secretary General on the Report of the ILC covering the seventh session. UNGAOR 10th sess. 1955, Annexes, Ag. it. 50, para. 33.

[4] Except the Year Book for the 1st session (1949), which contains both records and documents in one volume. The issues of the Year Book from 1949 to 1955 contain documents in original languages (English, French or Spanish) without translation, and summary records of the discussions in English only. From 1956 onwards, the Year Book has appeared in separate English, French and Spanish editions. The Year Books, however, do not contain all the documents of the Commission's session. Many of the L (limited circulation) documents of A/CN4/- series as well as papers originally issued in mimeographed form are omitted. Non-availability of many mimeographed documents as well as of the translation of the documents incorporated in original language only (French, Spanish and Russian) presents perpetual difficulties.

enhancement of the Commission's prestige.[1] But summary records of the Commission do not transcribe in full the views of the members since, according to the regulations, only the principal organs of the United Nations are entitled to verbatim records. It would be much more useful if fuller treatment than usual were given to the Commission's deliberations in the summary records.

Moreover, inadequate facilities at the disposal of the Commission for the production of documents, summary records and translations create serious inconvenience and delay in its work, and have been the subject of some criticism.[2] The delay in the publication of the Commission's documents, which are not available until a very short time before the opening of the session of the General Assembly, usually causes difficulties for the General Assembly in reaching its procedural decision. A prevalence of such situations is likely to disrepute the codification effort as a whole. It is submitted that if the Commission's annual sessions were so arranged that its reports were available at least three months prior to the opening of the sessions of the General Assembly, and the summary records of the Commission were available before the Sixth Committee commenced its discussion on the Commission's reports, such difficulties might be solved.[3]

The Commission did very useful service by recommending publication of a Juridical Yearbook of the United Nations in 1950.[4] The matter remained in abeyance until 1958 when the General Assembly undertook[5] a detailed examination of various aspects of the question relating to the form, contents and budgetary implications of the publication.[6] The General Assembly decided in 1962 to publish the

---

[1] Hudson and Brierly were opposed to the printing of summary records of the Commission's meetings. Hudson thought that it would deprive the discussions of one essential feature, namely, free exchange of views. In Brierly's opinion, 'It would make it possible for anyone on the lookout for such things to find in statements taken out of their context or outstripped by new developments, remarks which would make the speakers appear to contradict themselves': *T.B.I.L.C.*, 1950. vol. I, p. 319, para. 83; *ibid.*, 1951, vol. I, p. 125, paras. 146 and 147.

[2] *T.B.I.L.C.*, 1962, vol. II, Report of the Commission, U.N. Doc. A/5209, chap. V, p. 193, para. 84.

[3] See U.N. Doc. A/CN4/L110, Report of the Committee appointed by the Commission to study the exchanges and distribution of ILC documents.

[4] *T.B.I.L.C.*, 1950, vol. II, Report of the Commission, U.N. Doc. A/1316, para. 91. GA Res. 686(VII) requested the Secretary General to report on the extent to which developments in international law justified such a publication, see Secretary General's Report, U.N. Doc. A/C6/L348, UNGAOR 10th sess. 1955, Annexes, Ag. it. 50.

[5] UNGAOR 13th sess. 1958, 6th Com. 553rd mtg. para. 29, 554th mtg. para. 22, U.N. Doc. A/4007. Sixth Committee Report, *ibid.*, 13th sess. 1958, Annexes, Ag. it. 56, paras. 59–61.

[6] See Doc. A/C6/L428, a working paper prepared as a basis of discussion in the Sixth Committee which proposed that the United Nations Juridical Yearbook of apparently 225 pages be divided into four parts. It could be either the third

Yearbook from 1964 as a separate United Nations publication, and not as a third volume of the Yearbook of the Commission as was originally the idea, in the three working languages of the Assembly.[1] The Yearbook is useful not only because of the unprecedented release of selected legal opinions of the United Nations Secretariat, UN legal documents, index and bibliography, but also because of the gathering together as in a case book of materials already available but widely dispersed, such as decisions, reports and treaties.[2]

---

volume of the *Y.B.I.L.C.*, or a separate publication by itself. See UNGAOR 13th sess. 1958, Annexes, Ag. it. 56. The GA Res. 1451(XIV) of December 7, 1959, decided on the publication of the Yearbook and requested the Secretary General to report about the details of the Yearbook. See Doc. A/4406, Report of the Secretary General, UNGAOR 15th sess. 1960, Annexes, Ag. it. 66.

[1] GA Res. 1814(XVII) of December 18, 1962, provides for the publication of the Yearbook in three parts and not exceeding 256 pages in length. The Annex of the Resolution gives an outline of the Yearbook: UNGAOR 17th sess. 1962, Annexes, Ag. it. 73.

[2] For review see *Bulletin* of American Bar Association, section of International and Comparative Law, December 1964, p. 43. The first issue of the Yearbook for 1963 appeared in 1965, and for 1964 in 1966.

CHAPTER FIVE

THE FUNCTIONS OF THE COMMISSION AND ITS METHODOLOGY

FUNCTIONS OF THE ILC

The Statute of the International Law Commission has provided for specific functions for the Commission to give effect to Article 13, para. 1(a) of the UN Charter, and accordingly 'the promotion of the progressive development of international law and its codification' constitutes the object of the Commission (Article 1 of the Statute of the ILC).

Chapter II of the Statute defines the functions of the Commission which are of three kinds:

1. To formulate rules of international law in the form of draft convention, on subjects 'which have not yet been regulated by international law or in regard to which the law has not yet been sufficiently developed in the practice of states' (Article 15). In other words, this function implies the framing of rules of international law *de lege ferenda* at the request of the General Assembly (Article 16) or on proposals transmitted by the Secretary General, emanating from members of the United Nations, the principal organs of the United Nations other than the General Assembly, specialized agencies, or official bodies established by intergovernmental agreements to encourage the development of international law and its codification. However, the Commission is authorized to proceed to act definitively on the proposals not emanating from the GA only after the GA invites it to do so on the basis of a preliminary report submitted by the Commission (Article 17).

2. To codify existing international law in order to give a 'more precise formulation and systematization' in fields where there has been extensive state practice, precedent and doctrine (Article 15). Whereas for progressive development the Commission has no power itself to initiate a project, it is authorized to initiate projects of codification although it must give priority to requests of the GA (Article 18).[1] This however, does not preclude the Commission from introducing elements of progressive development in the course of its work of codification.

3. To consider ways and means for making the evidence of

---

[1] See below for further discussion, pp. 233–6.

customary international law more readily available, for instance collecting and publishing documents concerning state practice and the decisions of national and international courts on questions of international law, and to submit reports to the GA on them (Article 24). This function of the Commission is distinct from the other two functions mentioned above. While the codification process requires the Commission to seek information from governments furnishing 'the texts of laws, decrees, judicial decisions, treaties, diplomatic correspondence, and other documents relevant to the topic being studied and which the Commission deems necessary (Article 19(2)), this task of the Commission is much broader and, at the same time, restricted. It is broader in the sense that it is concerned not with any particular topic but with the whole range of customary international law. It is restricted because it relates exclusively to evidence of customary international law. This function of the Commission charges it with exploring ways and means of remedying the present unsatisfactory state of documentation relating to the customary practice of states and of decisions of national and international courts on questions of international law in order that the evidences of customary international law become more readily available in the form of the compilation of digests of state practice and the collection and publication of the decisions of national and international courts.

In addition to the three functions enumerated above, the scope of the Commission's activity is much more widely conceived under Article 2 of its Statute, which says that, although the ILC shall concern itself primarily with public international law it is not precluded from entering the field of private international law. So, if the Commission in times to come is also required to codify the rules of private international law on problems which remain difficult to be coped with by private efforts, there would be no obstruction to official initiative in the matter under the auspices of the UN. But the primary task of the Commission—the development and codification of public international law—may extend over a generation, or even more, in order to accomplish what might be called 'The Law of Nations Codified'. This however, does not mean that the Commission is intended by the Statute to codify the entire body of public international law at once in one code, as attempted by earlier private efforts at the hands of Bluntschli, David Dudley Field, Fiore, Internoscia and others. The eventual codification of international law might properly be regarded as the ultimate object of the International Law Commission, but this law is developing so rapidly in practice and doctrine that it can now only be codified subject by subject in stages, in various forms, and with varying degrees of authority.

The Commission as a subsidiary organ of the GA may, from time to time, be assigned special problems by the GA for opinion, report or proposals rather than for codification as such. The GA has, at different times, made categorical requests to the Commission, for instance, to report on the definition of 'aggression', on reservations to multilateral conventions, and on questions of international criminal jurisdiction.[1] The Commission's work pertaining to these special tasks did not consist of a set of articles in the nature of codification but of reports. On the other hand, other special assignments carried out in regard to the Draft Declaration on Rights and Duties of States, Formulation of the Nuremberg Principles, and the Draft Code of Offences against the Peace and Security of Mankind, were submitted by the Commission in the form of a set of articles.[2]

The character and the status of the ILC, and the functions envisaged by its Statute or assigned by the GA, have been simplified by the deliberate elasticity of the Commission's Statute. There is nothing in the Statute to preclude it from interpreting the scope of the ILC's functions by reference to a wide and comprehensive task in keeping with the place which codification of international law occupies in the Charter of the United Nations.

DISTINCTION BETWEEN CODIFICATION AND PROGRESSIVE DEVELOPMENT OF INTERNATIONAL LAW

Since the first and basic function of the ILC is the codification of international law—which could be interpreted in a narrow or a broad sense—the Statute distinguished between the two terms—the 'codification of international law' and 'the progressive development of international law'. In the language of Article 15 of the Statute, 'the expression "codification of international law" is used for convenience as meaning the more precise formulation and systematization of rules of international law in fields where there already has been extensive State practice, precedent and doctrine'. The Statute then goes on to prescribe two distinct procedures, one for progressive development and the other for codification (Articles 16 to 23).

From a legal standpoint, it has always been very difficult to differentiate between these two principal tasks conferred on the Commission—codification and progressive development—since the task of codification itself represents a step forward by means of which existing law during the process of systematization may in fact be amended.[3] For instance, a glance at the history of codification shows that when the French Civil Code, or the Hindu Code were

[1] See below, pp. 270, 282, 284, and 289.   [2] See below, chap. VI, pp. 272–81.
[3] A certain amount of confusion in relation to the term 'codification' existed ever since the Hague Conference of 1930. The replies of the governments of Great

drawn up, some existing norms were retained but many of them were also rearranged and amended. Indeed, if codification did not constitute a legislative advance no useful purpose would be served;[1] and experience seems to have established that it has been difficult in the Commission's own work in practice to follow the distinction envisaged by the Statute.

On the exact relationship between codification and the progressive development of international law there had been much discussion in the Committee of Seventeen concerned with the study of the methods most suitable for attaining the object of the ILC.[2] Dr. Brierly, the Rapporteur of the Committee, fully supported the Committee's view[3] that even codification could not be limited to declaring existing law. In his words:

As soon as you set out to do this, you discover that the existing law is often uncertain, that for one reason or another there are gaps in it which are not covered. If you were to disregard these uncertainties and these gaps and simply include in your code rules of existing law which are absolutely certain and clear, the work would have little value. Hence, the codifier, if he is competent for his work, will make suggestions of his own; where the rule is uncertain, he will suggest how it can best be filled. If he makes it clear what he is doing, tabulates the existing authorities, fairly examines the arguments *pro* and *con*, he will be doing his work properly. But it is true that in this aspect of his work he will be suggesting legislation—he will be working on *lex ferenda*, not the *lex lata*—he will be extending the law and not merely stating the law that exists.[4]

But he added that codification did not necessarily involve developing the law by legislation, and that legislation and codification were merely two names for the same process. He also favoured different methods for codification which is primarily, though not exclusively, concerned with stating the existing law, and legislation which aimed to create law in future as it ought to be.[5]

Britain, Irish Free State and the Netherlands to the Note of the Secretary General of the League of Nations dated May 30, 1931, acknowledged the fact that the same codification might be considered by some states as the creation of new law and by others, for which the rules in question were already part of existing law, as a consolidation of customary into conventional law. See L. of N. Official Journal, pp. 1590–2, 1768.

[1] Professor Jennings maintains that too strict a definition of the codification process would defeat the very end for which the machinery is to be employed: 'The progressive development of international law and its codification', *B.Y.B.I.L.*, vol. 24, 1947, p. 302. See also T. S. Woolsey; 'Practical codification on international law', *A.J.I.L.*, vol. 16, 1922, pp. 423–5; and P. J. Noel Baker: 'The codification of international law', *B.Y.B.I.L.*, vol. 5, 1924, pp. 38–65.

[2] See above, chap. IV, pp. 154–60.

[3] U.N. Doc. A/AC.10/50, p. 7.

[4] See UN Doc. A/AC.10/30, pp. 2–3.

[5] The records of the San Francisco Conference also reveal that since there was controversy among international lawyers as to the meaning of the term 'codifica-

The view of Dr. Brierly about codification, quoted above, received more prominence than what he said about legislation in the Memorandum submitted by the Secretary General of the UN in 1949, entitled *Survey of International Law in relation to the work of codification of International Law Commission*.[1] This document also strongly emphasized the legislative aspect of codification and, after forcible arguments, concluded that the function of the Commission was not limited to a statement of the existing law by way of ascertaining the exact measure of existing agreement or disagreement.[2] The insistence of the Secretariat's document on the legislative aspect of the work of the codification Commission was based mainly on the following grounds:

1. Codification interpreted in a narrow sense, meaning 'mere recording in a systematized form of the existing law as it was and as to which there existed a pronounced agreement in practice of States', was no more than what should properly be called 'consolidation'.[3] If codification were to be limited to the ascertainment of the existing legal position, it would amount to the mere registration of existing disagreements since in most branches of international law although there was a common basis of agreement on principle, there existed a wide divergence of practice in the matter of its detailed application.[4] Besides, a mere restatement of existing rules whether obsolete or unsatisfactory, by the legal experts would constitute a purely static function, rather than a creative use of the existing legal

---

tion' according to the school of thought to which they belonged, the drafters of the Charter employed the terms 'progressive development' and 'codification' in order to avoid the dichotomy inherent in the term 'codification'. The term 'progressive development' was intended to imply modification of, as well as additions to, existing rules. Article 13 of the Charter used the terms in the sense of completing and amending international law as well as systematizing and consolidating it. See Summary Records of 10th mtg. of Com. II/2, May 23, 1945, Doc. 507. Eng. II/2/22, UNCIO Docs.

[1] U.N. Doc. A/CN.4/1, p. 3, para. 3. Dr. Brierly's view was also referred to in the discussion of the Commission in its first session, *Y.B.I.L.C.*, 1949, 2nd mtg., p. 19, para. 39.

[2] *Ibid.*, pp. 3–18.

[3] The British Government's communication addressed in 1931 to the Council of the League of Nations in connection with the future work of codification, did point out a distinction between 'consolidation' and 'codification'. It used the term 'codification' in the sense in which 'development' is used in the Statute of the ILC, describing it as 'free acceptance, by means of law-making conventions, of certain rules by which the parties to such conventions agree to abide in their mutual relations'. On the other hand, it described 'consolidation' as 'the ascertainment and establishment in precise and accurate legal phraseology of rules of international law which have already come into existence'—a process which is defined in the Statute of the Commission as 'codification'. See L. of N. Official Journal 1931, Sp. Supp. No. 94, p. 102.

[4] *Survey of Int. Law, op. cit.*, surveyed in its Part II the whole field of international law in relation to codification to arrive at the above conclusion, pp. 19–58.

and other materials for the purpose of regulating the life of the community.[1]

2. If the Commission's task were assumed to be confined to the codification of rules of international law in fields in which there existed a full measure of agreement among states, the scope of its task would be reduced to a bare minimum—to matters of narrow compass, the exclusive preoccupation which would impair from the very beginning the stature and the authority of the ILC.[2] And, indeed, in any instance where the existing rules were clear beyond all doubt, the codification entailed only a work of supererogation.

3. Codification, conceived of as a mere registration, in a systematized form, of the existing law, would crystallize and perpetuate unsatisfactory and obsolete rules of international law. The danger of such a codification was that it would freeze international law in the existing form and stop its progress in a manner to be compatible with requirements of international society.[3]

4. The drawbacks of codification conceived of as mere registration or systematization of existing customary international law were often voiced by governments. According to them, codifying international law by conventions would be interpreted as a replacement of customary international law by what was in effect a treaty. It would imply exposing what had hitherto enjoyed the unchallenged and secure authority of a customary rule to the uncertainties and vicissitudes of treaties in all phases of their creation and operation.[4] The suggestions emphasizing the drawbacks of considering merely the registration or systematization of existing international law as the only task of the ILC, or as the only main criterion for the selection of topics for codification, militated against the adoption of any narrow meaning of codification.

5. Lastly, the experience of the Hague Codification Conference of 1930 and of the entire work of codification undertaken by the League of Nations led most governments to reject the view that codification ought to be confined only to those branches of international law which connoted a full and clear agreement as ascertained by a uniform governmental practice, judicial precedent and doctrine.[5] Even the resolution of the League of Nations Assembly of September 27, 1927, had declared that codification 'should not confine itself to mere registration of the existing rules, but should aim at adapting them as far as possible to the contemporary conditions of international life.'[6] Indeed, in the Committee of Experts

---

[1] *Survey of Int. Law*, p. 7, para. 10.
[2] *Ibid.*, p. 8, para. 11. [3] *Ibid.*, p. 9, para. 13.
[4] *Ibid.*, pp. 9–10, para. 14.
[5] *Ibid.*, pp. 6–7, paras. 8–9.
[6] *Ibid.*, p. 6, para. 7.

of the League of Nations, most of its members emphasized that its task went beyond that of registration of existing law.[1]

The *Survey of International Law* interpreting the task of the ILC emphasized that the Statute did not intend the Commission to limit itself in the matter of codification to mere recording of the agreed body of existing law. Accordingly, urgent and novel questions demanding international regulation were to be covered by that aspect of the function of the Commission which related to 'development of international law', whereas 'codification' embraced in principle the entire field of international law.[2] The function of the Commission was not then limited to a statement of existing law by way of ascertaining the exact measure of existing agreement or disagreement. Indeed, Article 20 of the Statute, on the face of it, deliberately avoided a limited conception of codification since it laid down that:

The Commission shall prepare its drafts in the form of articles and shall submit them to the General Assembly together with a commentary containing:

    (a) Adequate presentation of precedents and other relevant data, including treaties, judicial decisions and doctrine.

    (b) Conclusions relevant to:

        (i) The extent of agreement on each point in the practice of States and in doctrine.

        (ii) Divergencies and disagreements which exist, as well as arguments invoked in favour of one or another solution.

According to the terms of Article 20, the Commission was required in the commentary to its draft to present its conclusions relevant to the extent of agreement or divergencies, which entailed a critical task of appreciation and weighing the causes of the existing discrepancies. Moreover, the Commission was instructed by the Statute to present its conclusions 'relevant to . . . arguments invoked in favour of one or another solution' and to prepare drafts in the form of articles, which implied the expression of a decisive judgment on the part of the Commission as to what was the proper rule of law. Accordingly, the *Survey of International Law* concluded that 'much of the product of its [the Commission's] work may follow the lines of some of the past great achievements of codification in the municipal sphere. They will not only be acts of international law finding, but also, if necessary, acts of international legislation and of international statesmanship'.[3]

---

[1] See for the views of Suarez, Diena, Rundstein, Brierly and Visscher, Minutes of the First Session, 1925, pp. 7, 8, 14, 17 and 25.

[2] *Survey of Int. Law*, p. 17, para. 23.

[3] *Ibid.*, pp. 63–4, para. 107.

This Memorandum expressed the view that, in order to find what the law was and to present it in a form which was precise, systematic and as detailed as the overriding principle of the necessary generality of the law allowed, the Commission must go beyond its primary task of ascertaining the existing law in two respects: i. it 'must either choose among conflicting contentions, or, more reasonably, formulate a solution which is in the nature of a compromise not of diplomatic character but one reached by reference to requirements of justice, of general interest of the international community, of international progress, and of neighbourly adjustment of international relations, as well as to such established rules of international law in other spheres as are not inconsistent with these factors';[1] ii. in regard to cases in which the practice of states revealed no marked divergencies, the Commission's independent creative function, after laying down what was an indisputable rule of law, was 'to examine that rule in the light of modern developments and requirements, and to suggest such improvements in the law and such modifications of the existing law as may be required in the interest of justice and of international social progress'. That duty of the Commission was probably in terms both of the provisions of the Statute of the ILC and of the task of codification in general, so long as it contrived to preserve a clear distinction between what it found to be the law and what it considered to constitute the necessary improvement of the law.[2] Thus, the Memorandum of the Secretariat interpreted the task of the Commission as giving expression to a constructive and what is currently known as the sociological approach to international law.[3] It underlined four of the principal aspects of the task of the Commission: i. the ascertainment in a systematic form of the existing law; ii. the development of the law, in the wider sense 'in the fields where there has been extensive State practice precedent and doctrine' (Article 15), by filling gaps, reconciling divergencies to their legitimate proportions and the formulation of improvements in cases where a situation called for a combination of the consolidating and legislative aspects of codification; iii. the combining with these tasks of another function which was largely political in nature, namely that of initiation and active assistance in the transformation

---

[1] *Survey of Int. Law*, pp. 64–5, para. 108.   [3] Ibid., p. 66, para. 110.
[2] For evidence of this trend see works such as M. S. McDougal and Associates: *Studies in World Public Order*, 1960; J. Stone: *Legal Controls of International Conflict*, 1954; Charles de Visscher: *Theory and Reality in Public International Law* (tr. by P. E. Corbett), 1957; G. Schwarzenberger: *The Frontiers of International Law*, 1962; W. Friedmann: *The Changing Structure of International Law*, 1965. These works have challenged the appropriateness of the traditional emphases upon the rôle and content of legal doctrine posited by formal law-making sources. According to them, an understanding of legal rules depends heavily upon an awareness of the social context within which these rules are expected to function.

of the products of its work into international conventions proper; and finally, iv. the making of an indirect contribution in the development of international law by way of rendering available abundant material to accumulate in the course of time as a result of the unprecedented centralized direction and resources of the UN as a whole. Such material 'when woven into the fabric of the drafts and commentaries of the Commission will represent a most valuable scientific result covering in the fullness of time, the entire *corpus juris gentium*'.[1]

The viewpoint of the Secretariat's Memorandum has been treated here with what may appear to be excessive detail. But the explanation of this lies in the fact that this document in fact poses the question of what is meant by the codification of international law, and puts forward cogent reasons for not limiting codification to those branches of international law in which there exists a full measure of agreement supported by uniform state practice, judicial precedent and doctrine. Lauterpacht's authorship of this memorandum, apparent from internal evidence, is widely acknowledged.[2] Furthermore, the document was extensively referred to by the Commission in its first sessions. It is difficult to determine to what extent it directly influenced the members of the Commission, but there is no doubt that most of them have repeatedly suggested that the distinction between the codification and the development of international law should be attenuated.[3] Moreover, in practice, the Commission has not maintained this distinction and has applied a single consolidated procedure to both types of work. The Sixth Committee of the GA has also observed while discussing the reports of the Commission, that the formal differentiation envisaged by the Statute has been blurred in the working of the Commission.

To illustrate this some of the Commission's reports may be cited. During its very first session the Commission felt some difficulty in connection with the Draft Declaration on the Rights and Duties of States[4] and concluded that its function fell within neither of the two

[1] *Survey of Int. Law*, pp. 67–8, paras. 112–13.

[2] This fact was acknowledged by Dr. Liang, the Secretary of the ILC, when the Commission was paying tributes to the memory of Lauterpacht on his death in 1960: *Y.B.I.L.C.*, 1960, vol. I, p. 52, para. 33. See also C. Wilfred Jenks: 'Hersch Lauterpacht—The Scholar as Prophet', *B.Y.B.I.L.*, vol. 36, 1960, pp. 85–8.

[3] When the Commission was reviewing at its third session its statute in response to the GA Resolution 484(V) in 97th mtg. it discussed the question of distinction between the progressive development and codification. Most of its members, excepting François and Spiropoulos as well as Kerno (Asst. Secty. Gen. of UN) and Dr. Liang (Secretary of the ILC) agreed that the work of legislation and codification overlapped. They desired that the Statute be improved to make the procedure laid down for two tasks more flexible: *Y.B.I.L.C.*, 1951, vol. I, pp. 132–5, paras. 133–183.

[4] *Y.B.I.L.C.*, 1949, pp. 179–83, paras. 29–57.

P

principal duties laid upon it by the Statute, but constituted a special assignment from the GA. It transmitted the Draft Declaration to the GA immediately to decide what course of action was subsequently to be taken.[1] Similarly, in preparing the Draft on Arbitral Procedure the Commission 'realized that the draft as a whole could not be based on the exclusive adoption of either' the method of codification or that of progressive development, while in some respects the draft gave expression to the practice of governments and arbitral tribunals, in other respects, it 'took into account both the lessons of experience and the requirements of international justice as a basis for provisions which are *de lege ferenda*'.[2]

The Commission also observed in 1953 that, although the Statute clearly envisages, and regulates separately the two functions, 'this does not mean that these two functions can be invariably—or even normally—kept apart in the drafts prepared by the Commission'.[3] In its recommendations to the GA on the final draft Convention on Arbitral Procedure, the Commission recognized that the same cumulation of functions applied and so it seemed 'to matter little whether a final draft falls within the category of development or that of codification'. It found no justification for any differentiation between the two kinds of recommendation envisaged by Article 16(j) and Article 23 para. 1 of the Statute.[4] Again, in 1956, in preparing its rules on the law of the sea, the Commission found it difficult to maintain the distinction established by the Statute and had to abandon its efforts of specifying the articles falling into one or the other category.[5] The Commission came to similar conclusions in connection with its work on Consular Intercourse and Immunities.[6] Furthermore, in regard to the special assignments[7] from the GA,

[1] *Y.B.I.L.C.*, 1949, p. 290, para. 53. GA Resolution 375(IV) of December 6, 1949, declared the draft 'a notable and substantial contribution towards the progressive development of international law and its codification'.

[2] *Y.B.I.L.C.*, 1952, vol. II, U.N. Doc. A/2163, Report of the Commission, p. 59, para. 16.

[3] *Y.B.I.L.C.*, 1953, vol. II, U.N. Doc. A/2456 Report of the Commission, p. 202, para. 15. The Commission added further: 'In the case of some topics it may be possible to limit the function of the Commission to one or the other of these two fields of its activity. In the case of the other topics these two functions must be combined if the Commission is to fulfil its dual task of, in the language of Article 13 of the Charter of the United Nations, "progressive development of international law and its codification". At the same time the Commission considers it of utmost importance that the difference between these two aspects of its activity should be constantly borne in mind.'

[4] *Ibid.*, pp. 207–8, paras. 53–54.

[5] *Y.B.I.L.C.*, 1956, vol. II, U.N. Doc. A/3159, Report of the Commission, pp. 255–6, paras. 26–66; for discussion in the Commission, see *ibid.*, vol. I, pp. 256, 277.

[6] *Y.B.I.L.C.*, 1960, vol. II, Doc. A/4425, Report of the Commission, pp. 145–6, paras. 20, 23; *ibid.*, 1961, vol. II, p. 91, paras. 29, 32.

[7] See below, pp. 270–81, and 284–6.

namely the Draft Declaration of Rights and Duties of States, Principles of International Law recognized in the Charter of Nuremberg Tribunal and in its Judgment, the Draft Code of offences against the peace and security of mankind, and the question of an International Criminal Jurisdiction, the Commission's work was on the borderline between codification and progressive development. The Commission was asked by the GA to study the question of reservations to multilateral conventions both from the point of view of codification and from that of progressive development of international law. Thus, much of the Commission's work has got out of the rut of mere codification[1] and has resulted in a series of declarations *de lege ferenda.*

The Commission's approach as reflected in its reports to the GA has tended to blur the formal differentiation between codification and development. A thorough debate on this issue took place in the Legal Committee of the GA in 1961 on the item entitled 'Future Work in the field of the codification and progressive development of international law'.[2] In the course of this debate some members thought that it was not desirable that the ILC should at the present time undertake progressive development as a separate activity, but should rather codify the rules applied daily in international relations. But the consensus of opinion in the Sixth Committee seemed to confirm the Commission's approach,[3] that successful results can be obtained only through coupling the two elements—codification and progressive development—into a harmonious whole. In any field of international law, being confined to codification only in the sense of mere arithmetical addition and systematization with no regard for the transformation and progressive development of law would mean ignoring the needs and requirements of rapidly changing international society. Equally, seeking new solutions without any consideration for the existing experience, customs and rules of the written law would mean heading for a complete fiasco.

This point of view is supported by outstanding scholars[4] and by the Commission itself. Some writers, who have not welcomed the Commission's plunging into developing international law and are doubtful whether it would thereby be enhancing its prestige,[5] seem

---

[1] See *Y.B.I.L.C.*, 1950, vol. I, p. 203, para. 89.

[2] UNGAOR 16th sess. 1961, 6th Com., pp. 119–220.

[3] U.N. Doc. A/5036, Report of 6th Com., UNGAOR 16th sess. 1961, Annexes, vol. 3, Ag. it. 90, paras. 22–25.

[4] For an interesting discussion on Dr. Liang's address 'Development and Codification of Int. Law' to American Society of Int. Law at 41st Annual Mtg., 1947, see *Proceedings*, 1947, pp. 40–64.

[5] See B. Cheng: 'International Law Commission', C.L.P., vol. 5, 1952, pp. 251–273. Dr. Cheng, finding that the ILC tends to be more concerned with improving existing international law than with its codification and not feeling much more at

to forget that this result was inevitable since codification in international law, unlike codification in other fields, must be substantially legislative in nature. The reason for this is that codification in the limited sense of consolidation, however useful it may be in systematizing the already developed rules in a mature system, can have little place in a comparatively underdeveloped system like international law. Even in mature legal systems most of the great historical codes have included legislation and, whenever attempts have been made in the past at codification, it has almost invariably been found necessary to make new law and to modify existing law. The whole purpose of codification is to induce governments to accept new law where their practices and views are in articulate conflict and also where their views and practices agree, but a progressive change in the law is considered desirable in the international interest.

Sir Hersch Lauterpacht, a member of the ILC for five years, wrote his celebrated article 'Codification and Development of International Law' in the light of his own participation in its work.[1] He comprehended the true nature of codification work in the field of international law and so was not surprised to find that Article 15 of the Statute of the ILC, laying down the artificial distinction between 'codification' and 'development', had been disregarded in practice.[2] He found little substantial meaning or practical purpose in the narrow definition of codification given in Article 15 of the Statute, namely, 'precise formulation and systematization of existing rules of international law in fields where there already has been extensive State practice, precedent and doctrine'. According to him, not only did that definition ignore the fact that there existed no semblance of agreement in relation to specific rules and problems in practically any branch of international law,[3] but also it wrongly assumed that the existence of a rule of international law necessarily followed from the existence of 'extensive State practice, precedent and doctrine'.

The main drawback of Article 15 of the Statute as pointed out by Lauterpacht is that it provides for codification in the sense of introducing precision and systematization in cases where there exists

ease in doing so, remarked, 'it is submitted with deep respect that the work of the Commission would only gain by greater distinction being made than hitherto between its functions of codification and progressive development of international law, and by more attention being devoted to the former' (p. 261).

[1] *A.J.I.L.*, vol. 49, 1955, pp. 16–43; the article was written prior to his election as a member of the ICJ.

[2] *Op. cit.*, pp. 29–31. Professor Jennings also agrees with Lauterpacht: 'Progress of int. law', *B.T.B.I.L.*, vol. 34, 1958, pp. 344–5.

[3] He illustrates this by giving examples covering virtually the entirety of the Law of Treaties: for his brief survey of the absence of agreed law and reasons for it, *op. cit.*, pp. 17–27.

essential agreement evidenced by practice, precedent and doctrine, but does not allow for codification where there exists practice but no agreement. Nor does it provide development where the established practice calls for a change.[1] These defects led Lauterpacht to maintain that the Statute of the ILC conceived of a very narrowly-drawn competence of the ILC and ignored the generally acknowledged and most conspicuous feature of international legislation, which consists of setting in motion and promoting the law-making process for the international community.[2]

Article 15 of the Statute recognizing the distinction between codification and progressive development is neither a result of oversight in drafting[3] nor an expression just for theoretical convenience. It represents a compromise resulting from two factors: first, at the time of the drafting of the Statute in 1947, the main preoccupation having been to avoid holding a codification conference like that of 1930 which had ended in a dismal failure, or having necessarily to prepare conventions for the adoption of drafts proposed, the Committee of Seventeen as well as the Sixth Committee of the GA provided for the distinction between 'progressive development' and 'codification' with the method of concluding conventions for the former and other possible procedures for the latter.[4] Secondly, the system adopted was the only means of obtaining the support of the representative of the U.S.S.R. on the Committee of Seventeen, Professor Koretsky, who advocated the method of preparation of conventions in all cases because, according to him, mere publication of scientific restatements could lead to no practical results. His views on the matter were accommodated in the provision for progressive development, and, as regards codification, he had been induced to give way to the extent of agreeing to the adoption of the scientific procedure among others, as codification pure and simple was not deemed to be a legislative task.[5]

Although the Commission has, in practice, been able to minimize the formal differentiation of its functions contemplated by the Statute, its debates about what the law is, and what it ought to be, have in fact tended to draw attention to new controversies arising from doubts expressed even on such branches of international law

[1] Lauterpacht, *op. cit.*, p. 29.
[2] *Ibid.*, p. 22; pp. 22–3, n. 14.
[3] Lauterpacht said that 'it is probable that the result thus achieved is due to an oversight in drafting; it is so drastically out of keeping with experience and with the views persistently expressed on the subject that it cannot be regarded as intentional': *op. cit.*, pp. 29–30.
[4] See *Y.B.I.L.C.*, 1951, vol. I, p. 132, para. 138, for Dr. Liang's statement giving the background of the provision in Article 15 of the Statute.
[5] *Ibid.*, p. 34, para. 156. See also U.N. Doc. A/AC.10/32; and A/AC.10/SR.9.

as had hitherto seemed well settled.[1] Those who are unwilling to accept the classical system of international law in its entirety regard codification as an opportunity to reject contradictory and outdated norms and remedy the deficiencies of the system so as to adapt it to the rapidly changing world witnessing political, economic and social transformations. For them, customary rules of international law possess no absolute value, as they were the outcome of circumstances, and must change as the circumstances change, allowing for the inevitable time-lag. On the other hand, the protagonists of classical international law allege that those who find existing established norms of international law inconvenient tend to utilize the opportunity offered by the Commission to challenge and weaken the international law under cover of a scientific analysis of legal principles. However the Commission offers an opportunity of discussion by legal experts representing different legal systems and civilizations and thereby may be credited with enabling the juristic imagination to evolve a universal international law by helping the various trends to merge and to move towards synthesis. Moreover, what is more important, as Professor Jennings put it, 'it must also be remembered that in providing an opportunity for change and growth of the law, the Commission is in fact providing just those procedures of legislation of which the international community is so much in need, and which are implicit in the notion of the "development" of the law referred to in Article 13 of the Charter'. He added further that a great value of the debates in the ILC lay in the fact that they gave ventilation to the rival interests of states expressed in a scientific framework and spoken in the language of law.[2]

The codification of international law has presented the Commission with a difficult question of resolving the eternal dilemma between maintaining the stability of the rules of law and the need to allow for their evolution. Generally speaking, any legal rule tends to lose its pertinence in time, and, instead of producing order and harmonizing relations, might become a source of friction. Hence, if law is not to be a rigid imposition it must never be fixed or crystallized but must remain in a constant state of evolution. This is borne out by the experience even of those legal systems which relied primarily on customary law and accorded only a secondary rôle to statute law. In the international field, there being no machinery for bringing about continuous adjustment of law to the requirements of

---

[1] Sir Gerald Fitzmaurice was so upset by 'extravagant notions' submitted and adopted as a result of the Commission's recommendations, that he was compelled to remark that 'absence of any code was preferable to the adoption of codes enshrining the legal monstrosities': UNGAOR 6th sess. 1951, 6th Com., 269th mtg., p. 268, para. 29.

[2] Jennings: 'Progress of int. law', *B.T.B.I.L.*, vol. 34, 1958, p. 345.

momentous political, economic and social developments affecting international life, such as are found in a domestic system, international law is faced with a difficulty, namely, that the discrepancy between law and reality has remained unattended to. The GA Resolution 1505(XV) of December 12, 1960, on the Future Work in the field of the Codification and Progressive Development of International Law, recognized a close interrelationship between the codification and progressive development of international law on the one hand, and the realities of international relations on the other.[1] The text of the resolution by recognizing that 'many new trends in the field of international relations have an impact on the development of international law', and that it is necessary 'to reconsider the Commission's programme of work in the light of recent developments in international law and with due regard to the need for promoting friendly relations and co-operation among States', implicitly acknowledged that, conversely, the codification and progressive development of international law might affect international relations and be conducive to fostering international co-operation. This resolution emphasized two important principles: i. that the general purpose of codification consisted 'in strengthening international peace, developing friendly relations among the nations, settling disputes by peaceful means and advancing economic and social progress throughout the world'; and ii. that the codification and progressive development were suitable means of promoting such beneficial trends in international relations. It visualizes the possibility that codification of international law can contribute to the search for a solution of the problems of mankind, contrary to the view held by some for whom codification was mainly the embodiment of customary law and the existing practice into a systematized form. Thus, the new vistas opened by the GA Resolution 1505(XV) and the impossiblity in practice of distinguishing between codification of existing law on the one hand, and the development of new law on the other, have led the Commission to develop legislative or quasi-legislative procedures for the development of international law. The existence of good international legislation may persuade states to accede to the compulsory jurisdiction of the International Court of Justice.

But the law-making or law-developing process is affected by many factors. For instance, in the case of the progressive development of international law, the willingness of states to accept the final formulations is very necessary. And to bring about agreement where so far there exists only conflict of views and practice, or where fundamental

---

[1] See UNGAOR 15th sess. 1960, Annexes, vol. 2, Ag. it. 65. The Resolution was adopted at 943rd Plenary mtg. of the General Assembly.

notions of law differ owing to political and ideological considerations, is indeed a difficult task. Codification is not purely a work of academic nature but also of statesmanship in harmonizing conflicting claims. The proper task of the Commission in the case of mere doctrinal controversies is to find their solution by bringing authoritatively 'to light the modest dimensions of the issue involved and the absence of any national interest militating against the adoption of an agreed uniform solution'.[1] Where disagreement is marked by conflicting interests and claims in political, economic and other spheres, the Commission should reveal fully the extent of the divergence in all its implications, and take account of these factors as a legitimate component of an eventual legal rule.[2] As Lauterpacht rightly concluded, the 'evaluation of national interest and their reduction to a common denominator of national and international interests is of the essence of codification'.[3]

In fact, the difference between the conservative approach emphasizing codification in the narrow sense and the progressive and practical approach stressing the inevitable development of law, is nevertheless not fundamental, if acceptable and worthwhile draft codes are produced by the Commission. The Commission's extensive experience indicates that a conciliation of the two approaches is indispensable.

The Commission cannot make a purely legal and technical approach to its work. Whether it is performing the task of ascertaining and systematizing existing law, or of filling the gaps and reconciling the divergencies for formulating improvements, or whether it is preparing for international conventions proper, every aspect of its work involves constant consultation with, if not the active co-operation of, governments and of national and international scientific bodies. It would be a mistake to consider the ILC to be comparable to a national codification commission whose work is often divided into well-defined branches of the law, and whose members have the advantage of working on the basis of a close common legal tradition. The Commission's task is a long-range programme of codification of international law as a whole, over a period. The work is undertaken by men of widely different cultural, linguistic and legal backgrounds. This programme may take a generation or more, and it necessarily involves special problems of method and technique. To the methods and technique of codification we must now turn.

---

[1] See Lauterpacht, *op. cit.*, *A.J.I.L.*, vol. 49, 1955, p. 24.

[2] *Ibid.*, p. 25; see also *Survey of Int. Law, op. cit.*, pp. 66–7, paras. 111–112.

[3] Lauterpacht: *op. cit.*, p. 27.

METHODS, PROCEDURES AND TECHNIQUE OF THE COMMISSION'S WORK

The Commission's task of codifying and developing international law involves the selection of suitable topics, long-range planning for eventual codification of the entirety of international law, active collaboration with governments, and co-operation with national and international scientific bodies as well as intergovernmental organizations.

Codification involves an activity concerned with the sources of law,[1] and the difficulties of a codifier vary with the nature of materials on which he has to work.[2] The development of most historically recorded systems of law has taken place by a combination of three processes: (*a*) habitual adherence of the members of the community to certain lines of conduct—known as custom; (*b*) express enactment of norms of conduct binding on all the members of the community to whom the enacted rules apply regardless of their consent—known as legislation; (*c*) repetition and generalization of decisions given by courts of law with binding effect—known as precedent, or case law. If the state of existing law is on the whole well settled in any form, the task of the codifying agency is easy, since it is then mainly concerned with the form of its presentation and orderly arrangement. Any creative part, incidental to the main task, comes into play only in eliminating minor inconsistencies and in filling up the gaps.

On the other hand, if the state of existing law is unsettled in regard to the substance of the rules which are to be embodied in a code, the codifying agency will be required to settle the substance of the law, as a preliminary to its formulation in the code. It has to choose between the competing and conflicting rules. It is called upon to fill in the gaps on matters where the law is doubtful or altogether silent, and to give precision to the abstract principles of unsettled practical application. A preliminary decision as to the substance of rules to be embodied in a code leads the codifying agency to make an examinaton of the sources of the law.

[1] In the words of Dr. Liang: 'The consideration of the methods for encouraging the progressive development of international law might be looked upon as the study of processes by which the growth of international law can be stimulated. The methods to be used will vary with each of the principal sources of international law, whether it be international custom, international convention, or judicial decision': 'Methods for the encouragement of the progressive development of international law and its codification', in *Year Book of World Affairs*, 1948, pp. 239-40.

[2] According to Professor Jennings 'the task of codifying an existing and consistent body of law is very different from the task of creating a code where the existing law is fragmentary and requires the devising of new rules to fill the gaps or resolve discrepancies or even where the draftsman starts with a *tabula rasa*': 'Progressive development of int. law', *B.T.B.I.L.*, vol. 24, 1947, pp. 302-3.

The methods, procedures and the technique of codification work must therefore be determined by the state of the existing law and its sources.

METHODS

The rules of international law are far from being well settled since they have developed in a community of independent states. The decentralized creation, application and interpretation of the rules of international law is the result of several factors: the absence of a world legislature, the slow growth of customary law and the sporadic judicial settlement of disputes because of the lack of authority of international tribunals of adjudicating with binding effect the clashes arising between states. The process of development of international law has taken place by the gradual establishment of rules of international law, by crystallization of principles resulting from the accumulation of the general practice of states[1] and by the development of jurisprudence resulting from the decisions of tribunals.[2] Furthermore, international treaties have functioned as the substitute for legislation in supplementing the rules of general international law.[3] Consequently the present-day international law recognizes the following sources: international custom as evidence of the practice of states; international treaties, general or particular; and general principles of law recognized by civilized nations, judicial decisions and the teachings of publicists of various nations as subsidiary means for the determination of the rules of law.

The two principal sources of rules of international law—slow-growing customs and law-making treaties—have not been entirely adequate substitutes for a true process of legislation in the international community.[4] And so, codification of international law

---

[1] See Lasare Kopelmanas: 'Custom as a means of creation of international law', *B.Y.B.I.L.*, vol. 18, 1937, pp. 126–51; Hudson: *Permanent Court of International Justice*, 2nd edn., 1944, p. 609; McNair Committee Report, ILA, 1947, *op. cit.*, Section II, pp. 84–7.

[2] Sir John Fisher Williams: *Current International Law and the League of Nations*, 1929, p. 84; Sir Arnold McNair: *The Development of International Justice*, 1954, pp. 15–19; McNair Committee Report, *op. cit.*, Section III, pp. 87–9.

[3] See Oppenheim, *International Law*, 8th edn., 1955, vol. I, pp. 27–8. He distinguished between universal, general and particular international law with reference to number of parties to a treaty. Brierly regarded only generally accepted treaties as law-making and proper sources of international law: *Law of Nations*, 2nd edn., 1936, pp. 46–9. M. O. Hudson called such treaties 'multipartite' and their law-making function 'international legislation': *International Legislation*, vol. I, pp. xiii–xiv. See also J. G. Starke: 'Treaties as a source of international law', *B.Y.B.I.L.*, vol. 23, 1942, pp. 341–6.

[4] On the metaphorical use of the term 'international legislation' see Oppenheim, *op. cit.*, p. 27, n. 4. For arguments in favour of the gradual expansion of the legislative functions see R. A. Falk and S. H. Mendlovitz: 'Towards a warless world: one legal formula to achieve transition', *Yale L.J.*, vol. 73, January 1964, pp. 399–424.

represents an organized effort to eliminate the obstacles to and to accelerate the growth of international law in order to meet the new needs of the rapidly changing international society. But so long as there exists no machinery of legislation[1] competent to impose upon all members of the international community the law, as formulated by a majority of states after due consideration of the national and international interests, the scope of codification at international level must differ from that at national level. The task of the codifying agency in relation to international law goes beyond the formal process of systematization and arrangement. In addition to choosing between competitive and conflicting rules, filling up of gaps and modifying the obsolete and outdated rules, it involves decisions of governments as to the law which the code is to embody. And universal codification although desirable is impossible to achieve unless the codifier is actively aided by the co-operation of governments at every stage.

Experience has shown that there are two methods by means of which conscious codification and development of international law are possible: convention and restatement.

Convention method

International conventions, establishing rules expressly recognized by the participant states, have been a potent vehicle of codification and development of international law. Although of great importance in supplementing the rules of general international law, and sometimes known as international legislation,[2] international treaties do not provide a true process of legislation. The fundamental principle of *pacta tertis nec nocent nec prosunt* renders treaties binding only on states agreeing to be bound by them,[3] and there are very few treaties

---

[1] A recent tendency is that the concern with formal law-making sources is vanishing from contemporary approaches to the rôle and content of legal doctrine: see M. S. McDougal and W. T. Burke: *The Public Order of the Oceans*, 1962, wherein the processes associated with claims and authoritative decisions are perceived as the essential constituent of the international legal system. There has also been an increasing tendency to recognize the decisions of international organizations as being another source of international law: Tammes: 'Decisions of international organizations as a source of international law', *Hague Recueil*, 1958, p. 265; R. Higgins: *The Development of International Law through the Political Organs of the United Nations*, 1963, pp. 1–10; for a critical reinterpretation of the sources, see C. Parry: *The Sources and Evidences of International Law*, 1965.

[2] See Hudson, *International Legislation*, vol. I, p. 13.

[3] See for exceptions to this rule *ibid.*, vol. I, Introduction, p. xvii. Professor Jennings, while admitting that 'within very limited areas there may be beginnings of exceptions to that rule, but the exceptions are relatively unimportant and must not be allowed to obscure the basic fact that there is no process of true legislation available to the codifier of international law: that is to say, there is no authoritative body which can lay down general norms not sanctioned by the common agreement of states': 'Progressive development of int. law', *B.Y.B.I.L.*, vol. 24, 1947, pp. 303–4; P. E. Corbett: 'The consent of states and the sources of the Law of Nations', *B.Y.B.I.L.*, vol. 6, 1925, pp. 20–30.

having universal acceptance. However, international treaties have brought into existence certain norms as a result of the free acceptance of participant states which agree to abide by them in their mutual relations. The rules enacted by them may be either identical with the established customary law or may be new,[1] but the whole purpose of the international conventions has been to prescribe certain rules by which states agree thereafter to be bound. The convention method of codification of international law has been a traditional one by which states have sought to regulate their mutual relations through the adoption of a code. It was resorted to by both the Hague Conferences of 1899 and 1907 and by the Codification Conference of 1930 for stating positive international law as well as for reforming it. Similar to legislation within states, international conventions have been used to develop or override custom-created international law. But the marked difference between legislation and conventions has been that while the former can always change customary law for the whole community, the latter are regarded as binding only on those states which are parties to them.[2] Also, since it is impossible to have conventions by unanimous decisions in a multilateral conference, the authority of the conventions themselves is relative to the numbers and the importance of the states which effectively become parties.[3] In addition to the political difficulties arising in connection with any attempt to secure international agreement on general principles of international law, the method of codification by means of a convention involves the possibility of a legal contradiction within itself. When a well-established rule of customary international law is embodied in a convention, the question arises whether the binding force of that rule is derived from the fact that the particular article in the convention is truly a statement of existing law or from the fact that the particular rule is binding because it appears in an international convention.[4] The necessity for obtaining governmental

[1] See for the study of inevitable repercussions of the change of source from custom to treaty, Jennings: *op. cit.*, pp. 304–7; T. Gihl: *International Legislation*, 1937, p. 64.
[2] Professor Jennings warns against the temptation to identify legislation and codification, *op. cit.*, p. 304.
[3] See Resolution adopted in 1927 by the Assembly of the League of Nations concerning the future Codification Conference stating that 'although it is desirable that the Conference's decisions should be unanimous, and every effort should be made to obtain this result, it must be clearly understood that, where unanimity is impossible, the majority of the participating states, if disposed to accept as among themselves a rule to which some other states are not prepared to consent, cannot be prevented from doing so by the mere opposition of the minority': L. of N. Offl. Rec., 1927, sp. supp. No. 55, p. 53; see also Minutes of the 3rd Session of the Committee of Experts 1927, pp. 11, 12.
[4] This question arose in connection with the Convention on Nationality adopted by the Hague Conference of 1930, and it was found necessary to provide in Article 18 of the Convention a specific clause to the effect that the inclusion of

approval, involved in the method of convention, has proved a major stumbling block in the work of codification.

Restatement method

The other possible method is that of the scientific restatement of law in the form of authoritative declaration of law by the jurists and other experts. The example of the highly successful restatement of American municipal law—a purely American venture initiated by the American Law Institute[1]—demonstrated great possibilities of this method, as one full of potentialities in promoting the clear statement of the law and to make it better adapted to social needs. In the field of international law, eminent jurists and publicists, such as Lieber, Bluntschli, David Dudley Field and scientific organizations like the Institute of International Law, the American Institute of International Law, or the Harvard Law School, have made most significant contribution in producing draft codes or projects on various subjects of international law.[2] The immense utility of a restatement of law undertaken in the fashion of the American Law Institute by private groups, such as the Harvard Research in international law, in clarifying the international law and indicating the right line of advance to be followed for its improvement,[3] has opened up new possibilities of a similar venture under international auspices and on official initiative. In view of the disappointing results of the Codification Conference at The Hague in 1930 which highlighted the difficulties inherent in attempting to codify international law by the convention method, the scientific restatements of law, compiled by an international body of jurists under the auspices of the UN, seemed to have in it some possibility of winning a special position in the hierarchy of the sources of law as recognized by Article 38 of the Statute of the ICJ.[4]

---

certain rules in the convention should in no way be deemed to prejudice the question whether they do or do not already form a part of international law.
[1] See for the history of the American Law Institute and the first restatement of the law, William Draper Lewis: 'How We Did It' in *History of the Institute and the Restatement*, American Law Institute Publication, entitled *Restatement in the Courts*, 1945, pp. 1–23.
[2] See above, chap. II, pp. 37–75.
[3] Just as the restatements prepared by the American Law Institute have frequently been referred to in court decisions, and extensive use has been made of them in law schools and law offices throughout the United States, in the field of international law, the drafts prepared by the Harvard Research have been widely used by statesmen, jurists and students of international law; see Memorandum by the Secretary General, Ways and Means of Making the Evidence of Customary International Law more readily available, U.N. Doc. A/CN.4/6/corr. 1, pp. 79–84.
[4] At San Francisco, the question of explicitly empowering the GA itself to initiate draft conventions was decided in the negative, and Article 13 of the Charter only

The method of scientific restatements was first suggested at the first session of the League Committee of Experts in 1925 by Mr. G. W. Wickersham of the U.S.A. He drew attention to the work of the American Law Institute and the Commissioners of Uniform State Legislation, in the United States, whose restatements of various topics of customary law were being treated by the American courts as reliable statements of the existing law.[1] He recommended that the preparation of statements on international law might perhaps be less difficult a method than one which sought the assent of governments to formal agreements of international law, to be embodied in treaties.[2]

Similarly, the value of the preparation of restatements of international law by the consensus of publicists was reiterated when the United Nations contemplated the appointment of a body of experts in connection with the codification work.[3] The Committee on the Development and Formulation of International Law, which was appointed by the International Law Association under the chairmanship of Sir Arnold McNair, in its report adopted by the Association at its Prague Conference in September 1947, advocated the appointment of a Restatement Commission of legal experts by the GA with the duty of preparing a comprehensive programme for the restatement of the existing rules of international law. According to the Committee, the restatements would fulfil two objects: i. they would soon begin to have an influence upon tribunals, national and international and upon teachers, writers and all other persons concerned with international law; and ii. they would pave the way for the codification of international law by a series of multipartite conventions at a later date.[4] Similarly, the Institute of International

---

implicitly does not preclude the GA from recommending drawing up of international conventions. See Summary Report of Twelfth Meeting of Committee, II/2 Doc. 571 (English) II/2/27, May 25, 1945. UNCIO Docs., vol. 9, pp. 79–81.

[1] See Minutes of the First Session, 1925, p. 7.

[2] See also Philip Marshal Brown: 'The Codification of International Law', *A.J.I.L.*, vol. 29, 1935. Speaking of the monumental task of the restatement of international law by publicists, the author said: 'We would thus have eventually a scientific statement of the law, a compilation, a suitable digest, a virtual code comparable in value to the monumental labours of those great jurisconsults who at the behest of Justinian rendered such memorable service to the cause of universal jurisprudence': p. 39.

[3] See Hurst: 'Plea for codification . . .', *Trans. Grotius Soc.*, vol. XXXII, 1947, pp. 135–53. Professor Jennings also thought that, where the aim was merely to declare or consolidate existing customary law, for that aspect of codification a very suitable vehicle might be found in the scientific restatement: *B.Y.B.I.L.*, vol. 24, 1947, pp. 309–10. See also Yuen Li-Liang: 'Methods for the encouragement of the progressive development of international law and its codification', *Year Book of World Affairs*, vol. 2, 1948, pp. 268–71; *idem*, 'Development and codification of international law', *Proc. Am. Soc. Int. Law*, 1947, pp. 36–40.

[4] See I.L.A. Report of 42nd Conference, Prague, 1947, Annex 1, pp. 108–10, para. 55; for discussions, *ibid.*, pp. 64–81.

Law (which resumed its activity after the war, at its first meeting in August 1947 at Lausanne) resolved that it, without discarding the method of international conventions which entails a risk of weakening and shattering the very law which codification has for its objective to render precise and firm, 'believes that, for the moment, the most important contribution to the work of codification would consist in carrying out, on the national and international planes, research activities of a scientific character with a view to arriving at an exact statement of the actual condition of international law. This inventory would serve as a basis at once for a scientific effort and also for official action undertaken according to methods deemed best suited to filling the gaps of international law and remedying its imperfections'.[1]

The Memorandum on Methods prepared by the UN Secretariat in 1947 for facilitating the work of the Committee on Development and Codification of International Law had also directed the attention of the Committee to the two methods: international conventions, and scientific restatements of law. While pointing out the many drawbacks and inherent difficulties of the convention method for securing international agreement on general rules and principles of international law, the Memorandum emphasized that the preparation of scientific restatements 'might be considered as a useful preliminary step which would prepare the ground for the eventual codification of international law by international agreement'. In its view such restatements drawn under the mandate of the UN and issued from time to time under its *imprimatur*, though lacking the imperative authority of legislative enactments or treaty stipulations, 'would commend themselves by their own intrinsic value, and exercise a persuasive influence of an effective and constructive nature. Their authority will be increased if they are adopted by resolutions of the General Assembly at any time when the General Assembly, on the proposal of a Member State or Member States, considers it desirable to do so.'[2]

The suggestions made by the Secretariat were prompted by the necessity emphasized in the report of the Sixth Committee for a 'fresh approach to the problem' in view of 'the difficulties encountered in past efforts to promote the progressive development of inter-

---

[1] See for the resolution passed by the Institute on the codification of international law, *A.J.I.L.*, vol. 42, 1948, pp. 168–9. The resolution was circulated as a document of the Sixth Committee at the request of the U.K. delegation, U.N. Doc. A/C.6/152. Attention was also drawn to the resolution adopted by the I.L.A. at its Prague Conference in 1947, circulated as a document of the Sixth Committee, A/C.6/154, in which 'general approval' was given to the recommendation contained in the I.L.A. Report.

[2] U.N. Doc. A/AC.10/7 corr. 1 and 2 (reproduced in *A.J.I.L.*, vol. 41, 1947, suppl. pp. 111–16).

national law and its codification'. The fact that the results of the Hague Codification Conference of 1930 seem to have produced profound scepticism as to the future use of the convention method was evident in the deliberations of the Committee of Seventeen. However, recognizing the necessity of concluding multipartite conventions for the extension of the law into new fields, the Committee had recommended the use of both methods. According to the majority view, the convention method only should be used for the progressive development of international law, but for codification other methods were allowable.[1]

Combination of both methods in the Statute

The Statute of the ILC has been drawn up with due regard to the reasons for the failure of earlier attempts at codification which had been directed solely towards the immediate conclusion of international conventions, and to the necessity for reconciling the work of scientific preparation with political requirements and the need to take the interests of states into account. While recognizing the antithesis between progressive development and codification 'for convenience', Article 15 of the Statute assumes that certain work might relate exclusively to the progressive development, or to the codification, of international law; and also, that other work might relate to both at the same time. It therefore prescribed: i. 'the preparation of draft conventions on subjects which have not yet been regulated by international law or in regard to which the law has not yet been sufficiently developed in the practice of States'. In other words, for creation of new rules of international law and for reframing of rules on subjects already regulated by international law, but the regulation of which is unsatisfactory or fragmentary, the method deemed suitable by the Statute is that of preparing conventions; ii. 'the more precise formulation and systematization of rules of international law in fields where there already has been extensive State practice, precedent and doctrine', is the method which is akin to consolidation of established customary rules. It means, in effect, resorting to the restatement method in regard to well-established customary international law.

Simultaneous recognition of restatement method in Article 15 of the Statute side by side with the traditional method of conventions, the result of past experience relating to codification and of the work on the restatement of international law by the Harvard Law School, reflects a compromise between those who favoured the

[1] See pp. 155–6, above for account of the recommendations of the Committee of Seventeen.

restatement method for codification and those who advocated the employment of the multipartite treaty in every case.[1]

The Commission is placed in a better position than the codifiers of The Hague or Geneva because if governments are not inclined to embody the rules in a convention, other ways remain open, for example, restatements embodying recommendations. Thus, the work formerly performed by individual publicists, or national and international scientific organizations can henceforward be more authoritatively undertaken by the ILC.[2] There is no need for the Commission to restrict itself to the formulation of universally accepted traditional rules. Its restatements may fill the gaps in existing law, settle dubious interpretations and even make amendments where necessary in the light of new developments. Moreover, since the Commission is to continually devote itself to its work, aided by the resources of the UN as a whole, regardless of how much of it will materialize in the form of convention, the cumulative product of its pronouncements cannot fail to influence States, and may be a sub-sidiary means of the determination of rules of law under Article 38, para. 1(d) of the Statute of the ICJ. Thus, the additional method of restatement has opened up for the Commission new prospects of presenting the prescriptions of international law which, in the full-ness of time, may be woven into the fabric of the entire *corpus juris* of international law.

PROCEDURES OF THE COMMISSION'S WORK

The Statute of the Commission has prescribed two sets of procedures for two distinct functions assigned to it.

Procedure for progressive development

Articles 16 and 17 of the Statute describe the procedure for pro-gressive development. They give no power to the Commission to

---

[1] Dr. Liang summarized the situation before the Commission as to how the different methods and procedures had been arrived at in the provisions of the Statute: *Y.B.I.L.C.*, 1951, vol. I, 97th mtg., pp. 133–4, paras. 138, 144. Dr. Brierly, who acted as the Rapporteur of the Codification Committee of 1947, expressed with all requisite clarity the position which led to the recognition of the 'statements' or 'restatements' of the law as a necessary or preliminary step in the process of eventual codification in the form of conventions—a view shared by various governments represented on the Codification Committee: U.N. Doc. A/AC.10/35, pp. 3–4.

[2] Sir Gerald Fitzmaurice, acknowledging the value of the Commission's work said: 'Never before had there been a body like the Commission which was official in the sense that it had been set up by an intergovernmental institution. The impact of the quantity of real codification which the Commission was producing was now perhaps being felt for the first time. That was a matter for congratulation, and neither the General Assembly nor Governments should feel that the Com-mission's work was wasted': *Y.B.I.L.C.*, 1958, vol. I, 464th mtg., p. 177, para. 23.

initiate progressive development, and clearly limit it to subjects recommended by the GA, other intergovernmental official bodies and specialized agencies, and the principal bodies of the United Nations and its members. The reason for depriving the Commission of its initiative in this matter appears to be political. Whether a project of progressive development should be undertaken, whether the need for new rules is clear, whether an agreement on a proposed project is possible; all these questions involve political implications, and their solution depends upon an explicit consensus of opinion prevailing in the GA.[1] The very fact that the consummation of the work of progressive development can only be achieved by international agreement, adequately demonstrates the political character of progressive development.[2] Moreover, a perusal of questions referred to the Commission by the GA, whether selected for codification or otherwise, shows that they have invariably been initiated by single states and presumably had a political object in view.[3] Since it is impossible for the GA to label a topic as being either belonging to the category of progressive development or of codification unless an extensive and thorough study of the subject has been made by the experts, the GA has initiated several projects without any clear definition whether they were meant for progressive development or codification or a mixture of both.

Article 16 requires the following procedure for progressive development. Having received a proposal from the GA, the Commission is required to appoint one of its members as a Rapporteur on that subject. This is to be followed by the formulation of a plan of work and the circulation of a questionnaire to the governments, inviting them to supply within a fixed period of time, data and information relevant to items included in the plan. After the appointment of a sub-committee of members to work with the

[1] As observed by Mr. Evans (U.K.), the Commission's members were experts sitting in their personal capacity, and it was a legal, not a political, body. Had the General Assembly intended the Commission to have a political function, it would have established a committee composed of representatives of states or governments: UNGAOR 16th sess. 1961, 6th Com., 717th mtg., p. 135, para. 4.

[2] Spiropoulos justified the distinction, in respect of progressive development, in that the Assembly alone had the initiative. It was for the GA, a political body, to instruct the Commission to prepare a legislative text for its use: *Y.B.I.L.C.*, 1951, vol. I, 97th mtg., p. 133, para. 151. See also François's views on the need for consultation with governments, *ibid.*, p. 133, para. 141.

[3] For instance, GA Res. 374(IV) of December 6, 1949, relating to the study of the régime of territorial waters, was initiated by Iceland. GA Res. 685(VII) of December 5, 1952, relating to the study of the topic of diplomatic intercourse, was sponsored on the initiative of Yugoslavia, which was at the time involved in a political controversy with the U.S.S.R. GA Res. 799(VIII) of December 7, 1953, relating to state responsibility, was moved on the initiative of Cuba. GA Res. 1400(XIV) of November 21, 1959, was initiated by Salvador, which called for the study of the rules of international law relating to the right of asylum.

Rapporteur on an interim draft, pending receipt of the replies from governments on the questionnaire, there is to be periodical consultation by the Commission with scientific institutions and individual experts, whether or not nationals of members of the UN. Following this will be a consideration of drafts proposed and, if satisfactory, the Secretary General will be asked to issue the drafts as a Commission document along with appropriate explanatory and supporting material and information relating to replies of the governments to the Commission's questionnaire. The whole of this work is to be given the widest possible publicity and the governments are to be asked to submit comments within a reasonable time. The Rapporteur and his sub-committee will reconsider the draft in the light of comments received, and will prepare a final draft and explanatory report for submission to the Commission. Finally, the Commission is required to submit drafts adopted by it, along with its recommendations, to the GA through the Secretary General.

Article 17 requires that, when the proposals or draft conventions emanate from the principal organs of the UN other than the GA, specialized agencies and intergovernmental bodies, or from the members of the UN, the Commission, if finding it appropriate to proceed with such proposals, must follow a procedure similar to one described above, save that comments are first to be invited from such members of the UN or organs, agencies, or official bodies as are concerned with the question.

Procedure for codification

Articles 18 to 24 of the Statute deal with the procedure set forth for the work of codification of international law. In the matter of codification the Commission has been authorized to initiate studies by surveying 'the whole field of international law with a view to selecting topics for codification, having in mind existing draft whether governmental or not' (Article 18(1)). Article 18(3) of the Statute is interpreted as authorizing the Commission to initiate projects of codification, while requiring it to give priority to requests of the GA. This conceals an ambiguity. Para. 2 of this article stipulates that 'when the Commission considers that the codification of a particular topic is necessary or desirable, it shall submit its recommendations to the GA'. This may mean that the Commission's decision regarding the selection of a topic according to the criteria laid down, i.e. desirability or suitability of a topic for codification, is subject to confirmation by the General Assembly, and that whether the codification of a particular topic is 'necessary or desirable' must await instructions from the GA before proceeding to the work of codification. Another interpretation could mean that, in regard to codification, the Commission is free to go forward not only with the selection of topics but also with the preparation of drafts codifying such topics and is only bound to report to the GA when it has prepared 'a final draft and explanatory report' (Article 22). These alternative interpretations were the subject of exhaustive discussion in the Commission in 1949.[1] Recourse was had to the summary records of meetings of the sub-committee of the Sixth Committee in which the draft Statute of the ILC was debated to discover only that both proposals had been made in that body with a view to clarification of the ambiguous paragraph, each reflecting the alternative constructions outlined above, and that neither had been adopted.[2] François, the then Rapporteur of the Sixth Committee and a member of the ILC, recollected that in his opinion Article 18(2) was intended to bear a meaning intermediate between the widest and the narrowest interpretations, and that the Commission did not require the approval of the GA before embarking on the study of a given question. It could even continue that study to a very advanced stage in order to be able to submit well-founded recommendations to the GA, but it could not consult governments, nor send them questionnaires without first securing the assent of the GA.[3] Ultimately, the Commission decided to carry out its work on its own initiative without awaiting the GA's decision on the recommendations submitted by the Commission under Article 18, para. 2.[4]

Thus, the initiative in the matter of codification may come directly from the Commission or from the GA, but precedence is to

[1] See *Y.B.I.L.C.*, 1949, 2nd–4th mtgs., pp. 14–32. A compromise solution proposed by Alfaro was that the Commission, after surveying the whole field of international law and choosing the topics realizable for codification, should address recommendations to the GA, while at the same time proceeding with the work of codification (p. 25, paras. 16–18). Divergence of views as to the interpretation of Article 18 were expressed in three different ways: i. that the Commission should submit the topics chosen by it for the GA's approval and await its reply before beginning codification; ii. that the Commission was not obliged to have its selection of topics confirmed by the GA nor was it required to make recommendations to the GA without completing a very searching study in order to request the Assembly's authorization to undertake the codification of a topic; iii. that the topics should be submitted to the GA, but the Commission would have the right to begin the codification without awaiting the Assembly's reply (pp. 31–2, para. 8).

[2] *Ibid.*, p. 23, paras. 2, 3. Also *Survey of Int. Law, op. cit.*, p. 63, para. 106 and n. 75.

[3] *Y.B.I.L.C.*, 1949, pp. 23–4, paras. 6–12.

[4] *Ibid.*, p. 32, para. 15. Dr. Parry commented that the Commission did not take sufficient account of the history of Articles 16 and 17 in arriving at its conclusion: 'Constitutions of international organizations', *B.Y.B.I.L.*, vol. 26, 1949, p. 513, n. 1. But the Commission's conclusion is justified since, both in the order of procedure envisaged by the Committee of Seventeen for 'codification' and 'progressive development' and in the procedure retained in the ILC Statute in respect of the latter, the stage of circulation of questionnaire to governments preceded that of report to the GA, and thus presumably did not call for prior assent of that body.

be given to the GA's requests. Once a project is chosen for codification, the machinery of Rapporteur, sub-committee and questionnaire is similar to that for the progressive development. Governments
are to be approached through the Secretary General with a request
to furnish the text of laws, decrees, judicial decisions, treaties, diplomatic correspondence and other documents relevant to the topic and
deemed necessary by the Commission (Article 19). The Commission
is required to prepare its reports in the form of draft articles of multipartite conventions, and each article is to be followed by a commentary containing: *a.* Adequate presentation of precedents and
other relevant data, including treaties, judicial decisions and doctrine; *b.* conclusions relevant to i. the extent of agreement on each
point in the practice of States and in doctrine; ii. divergencies and
disagreements which exist, as well as arguments invoked in favour
of one or another solution' (Article 20). This procedure implies that
the Commission is not to confine its work to a mere registration of
the present law or to ascertainment of the extent of the agreement
and of the divergencies. On the contrary, the commentaries of the
Commission accompanying its draft must contain its conclusions
relevant to the extent of agreement or divergencies. Such a task
entails not only critical appreciation and balancing the causes of
prevailing divergencies, it also requires an expression of decisive
judgment as to what is the proper rule of law.

The Commission is to satisfy itself with the preliminary drafts,
having found out what the law is on a given topic and presented it
in a form which is precise, systematic and as detailed as the overriding principle of the necessary generality of the law allows, before
such drafts are issued as Commission documents by the Secretary
General. The preliminary drafts are to be published along with an
explanation supporting material, information supplied by governments, and opinions expressed by scientific institutions or individual
experts (Article 21). This implies that the work of the Commission
has to be accompanied and aided by scientific activity in various
countries. Finally, in the light of the criticism and observations of
governments, of scientific bodies, of private scholars and of its own
members, the Commission is to prepare a revised draft and explanatory report for submission to the GA (Article 22).

In contrast to the procedure laid down for progressive development, which stops short at this point, the procedure for codification
goes further to provide that the final draft of the Commission shall
be accompanied by either of the following recommendations: '*a.* to
take no action, the report having already been published; *b.* to take
note of or adopt the report by resolution; *c.* to recommend the draft
to Members with a view to the conclusion of a convention; *d.* to

convoke a conference to conclude a convention' (Article 23).[1] This provision of the Statute, characterized by its deliberate elasticity, offers possibilities of various kinds with regard to which action may be taken by the GA in the matter of drafts produced by the Commission. On the other hand, the Commission's work is no longer handicapped by the necessity of producing only such drafts as are intended to materialize as conventions to be adopted by a considerable number of governments. It may submit a complete draft on a subject which is not likely to secure the acceptance of the majority of States, because of the existing divergencies and uncertainties. Nevertheless such a draft, stating accurately the existing law on matters on which agreement exists, or clarifying the position in other respects and offering solutions in regard to conflicting views and practices, to the extent of proposing changes in the existing law, may be allowed simply to remain in the form of a model codification and only to have the influence its quality warrants. Such a draft might serve as a model code if the GA takes no action, or has merely taken note of the draft as recommended by the Commission. It could however be adopted by the GA by resolution as a restatement of a law which has its approval.

The procedure laid down in regard to drafts not meant for immediate conclusion as conventions has three advantages. Firstly, if there exists no likelihood of securing a sufficiently wide measure of support from Governments, it can be saved from the risk of being remitted to the limbo of unratified conventions. Secondly, as a restatement of a rational law on the subject, it may influence the International Court of Justice as a subsidiary source of law (Article 38 of the Statute of the ICJ). Thirdly, it may be a contribution to the eventual codification of international law by convention.

When, however, the Commission recommends conclusion of a convention, Article 23 of the Statute conceives of a two-fold procedure for the GA—one leaving the initiative for calling a conference to the Governments themselves, and the second entitling the GA to convene and organize a conference for the purpose of concluding a convention. The former leaves a free scope for the continuation of working of the existing machinery in matters which have been traditionally organized by particular governments, such as the Netherlands government convening conferences for codification of private international law, the Belgian government convening Mari-

---

[1] This article, as pointed out by Dr. Liang, the Secretary of the ILC, had been adopted in 1947 after a lengthy and detailed discussion and was the keystone of the Statute. In his view, the intention of the framers of the Statute had been to make the procedure flexible, and to avoid the necessity of convening a conference or adopting a convention: *Y.B.I.L.C*, 1951, vol. I, 97th mtg., p. 133, para. 140.

time conferences, and the British government taking initiative regarding the safety of Life at Sea.

When initiative is taken by the GA, international conventions may be concluded in one of the three following ways. The first is to hold a conference of plenipotentiaries as was done in the case of the Law of the Sea, or the Law of Diplomatic Relations and Consular Relations.[1] The second is to draft a final text of a convention to be recommended to member states for signature. The third way is simply to recommend the Commission's draft to member states for their own action.

Two alternative procedures prescribed by the Statute for 'progressive development' and for 'codification' provide for a fairly flexible drafting machinery. But the major defect of this part of the Statute lies in the fact that it assumes that a given topic can at the outset be labelled as belonging to either a project for 'progressive development' or a project for 'codification'. The Statute seems to have supposed that not only the choice of procedure can be finally made when the subject matter is first chosen but also that it is always possible to make a clear distinction between the progressive development and codification and to commit a given subject to one or other of these procedures.

After several years of practical application the ILC formulated its views when, in its introduction to the chapter on the Law of the Sea, which is regarded as its most monumental work, it observed that in the domain of the law of the sea at any rate, the two functions of the Commission, namely the codification and progressive development were interrelated.[2] Having selected a subject originally for codification, the Commission has often found itself drifting towards progressive development of international law. This is a fact which is illustrated well by its work on the régime of the high seas[3] and on the law of treaties which shows much determination to improve the law.[4] Also, the Commission found that the various special assignments from the GA, such as the Draft Declaration of Rights and Duties of States, Formulation of Nuremberg Principles, and Draft Code of Offences against the Peace and Security of Mankind, were on the borderline between codification and progressive

---

[1] See below, pp. 302, 312, 315.
[2] *Y.B.I.L.C.*, 1956, vol. II, pp. 255–6, para. 26.
[3] Dr. Liang also drew attention to the overlapping of the work of legislation and codification: *Y.B.I.L.C.*, 1951, vol. I, 97th mtg., p. 135, para. 173. See also *Y.B.I.L.C.*, 1953, vol. I, pp. 357–61, paras. 43–87.
[4] For the final draft of the Commission see Report of ILC covering work of 2nd part of its 17th and 18th sess., UNGAOR suppl. no. 9, U.N. Doc. A/6309/Rev. 1.

development. Consequently, the question of bringing the two distinct procedures laid down by the Statute, one for progressive development and the other for codification, more into line with each other has constituted a most important problem with which the Commission has had to deal. Since the Commission found it impossible to label beforehand the topics selected for study, it had to apply a single consolidated procedure to both types of work.

In 1950, on an invitation from the GA[1] to revise its Statute, the Commission had an opportunity to consider what was the most appropriate procedure from the point of view of accelerating its work.[2] General views emerging from the discussion were: that the existing procedures were cumbrous and complicated enough to delay a solution for a long time; that, during the course of its work, not only was the Commission held up by doubts as to whether it was dealing with the codification or the progressive development, but also in regard to several matters it felt that the procedures laid down in the Statute need not necessarily be applied and that there were too many provisions requiring consultations with governments, at times a source of embarrassment to them, and the inability of the Commission to initiate proposals for promoting the development of international law hampered the Commission's work. Solutions conceived by different members were as follows: i. the complete elimination of the artificial distinction between progressive development and codification, followed by a complete amalgamation of the existing distinct procedures into one, provided for codification;[3] ii. while retaining the distinction between the two functions of the Commission and leaving the existing procedures unaltered, to grant authority to the Commission to take initiative in proposing to the GA draft proposals for the progressive development of international law, and allowing it to choose in each individual case what procedure was to be applied;[4] and iii. to minimize the distinction between the various processes and make the existing procedures more flexible and simple.[5]

The review of the Statute with a view to introducing greater flexibility in the procedure prescribed did not help the Commission to say unequivocally whether the lack of clarity in the statutory

[1] GA Res. 484(V) of December 12, 1950.
[2] See, for debate in the Commission, *Y.B.I.L.C.*, 1951, vol. I, 83rd, 96th, 97th, 112th and 113th mtgs.
[3] Hudson, *ibid.*, p. 132, para. 133.
[4] El Khoury, *ibid.*, p. 133, para. 145; he suggested an amendment of Article 1 of the Statute (which was not clear about the Commission's right to encourage progressive development): 'The Commission may discuss and submit to the General Assembly proposals of a legislative character.'
[5] Spiropoulos, *ibid.*, p. 133, para. 151; and Kerno, p. 134, para. 165. Both thought that the distinction provided by the Statute was necessary.

provisions, or the inflexibility of the procedures, would interfere with its achievement of rapid and positive results.[1] The impossibility of detaching 'codification' from 'progressive development' did not obstruct the Commission's work, because the Commission found the procedure relating to codification quite flexible, Article 19 providing that 'the Commission shall adopt a plan of work appropriate to each case'.

<h2>THE SELECTION OF TOPICS</h2>

The procedural side of the Commission's work is directly related to the question of the selection of topics. The selection of topics has two aspects: (i) the organs responsible for the selection of topics, and (ii) the guiding principles regarding the selection of topics.

Organs responsible for the selection of topics

Articles 16 and 17 allow the Commission to undertake progressive development on the proposals referred to it by the GA, or by the members of the UN and its principal organs, but Articles 18 to 23 relating to codification concede to the Commission the right of initiative, subject to a certain amount of control by the GA, in as much as the Commission cannot consult governments or send them its questionnaires, or draw up its draft proposals without first securing the approval of the GA. The question of the right of the Commission to issue questionnaires is governed by Article 19 of the Statute. In a debate on the application of Article 19(2) it was recognized that it was doubtful whether the Commission was in a position to address detailed questionnaires to governments, even in relation to the topics selected for codification at an early stage in its work. Koretsky opposed Spiropoulos' proposal to send a questionnaire to governments until the GA had approved the Commission's recommendations regarding selection of the topics. But in view of the possibility of delay in replies it was then decided that appropriate questionnaires be sent at once.[2] However, in the light of its liberal interpretation of Article 18 para. 2, the Commission is no longer handicapped in seeking information from governments before its programme of work has been sanctioned by the GA.

Article 18 of the Statute authorizes the Commission to 'survey the whole field of international law with a view to selecting topics for codification, having in mind existing drafts whether governmental or not'. But the same article in para. 2 adds that 'when the Commission considers that the codification of a particular topic is

---

[1] *T.B.I.L.C.*, 1951, vol. II, p. 139, para. 71.
[2] *T.B.I.L.C.*, 1949, 34th meeting, pp. 238–9, paras. 15–27.

necessary or desirable, it shall submit its recommendations to the General Assembly'. This article leaves to the Commission a substantive responsibility for the task of selection of topics. And, although its interpretation has been made so as not to restrict the Commission to the mere selection of topics pending the approval by the GA, the Commission, as a subsidiary organ of the Assembly, must inevitably report regularly to the parent body. This, in fact, the Commission has done, so that criticism, or even the veto of its selection of topics for codification is possible at a relatively early stage of any particular project of the Commission.

The first programme of work of the Commission, established in 1949, included in addition to the specific tasks assigned to it by the GA the basic question of the selection of topics of international law for codification. This was drawn up by the Commission itself at its first session.[1] The Commission examined the important preparatory memorandum submitted by the Secretary General entitled *Survey of International Law in Relation to the Work of Codification of the International Law Commission*,[2] and on this basis it drew up a provisional list of fourteen topics selected for codification; the list was provisional in the sense that additions or deletions could be made after further study by the Commission, or in compliance with the wishes of the GA.[3] The Commission decided to give priority to three topics, namely, the law of treaties, arbitral procedure and the régime of the high seas.[4] The General Assembly, through its Sixth Committee,

---

[1] *Y.B.I.L.C.*, 1949, 2nd to 7th mtgs., pp. 14–59.

[2] U.N. Doc. A/CN.4/1/Rev. 1, undertaken by the Secretary General in pursuance of GA Resolution 175(II) of November 21, 1947. Part II of the Document surveying a great many, though not all, topics of international law has served as a guiding light to the codifiers of international law. The Commission considered this document at its first session and was much influenced by it not merely on the selection of topics for codification but also on the whole question of the range and organization of its task of codification. See pp. 205–9, above.

[3] All taken from the *Survey of International Law*, these were:
   1. Recognition of states and governments;
   2. Succession of states and governments;
   3. Jurisdictional immunities of states and their property;
   4. Jurisdiction with regard to crimes committed outside national territory;
   5. Régime of the high seas;
   6. Régime of territorial waters;
   7. Nationality, including statelessness;
   8. Treatment of aliens;
   9. Right of asylum;
   10. Law of treaties;
   11. Diplomatic intercourse and immunities;
   12. Consular intercourse and immunities;
   13. State responsibility;
   14. Arbitral procedure.
   See *Y.B.I.L.C.*, 1949, 6th meeting, p. 53, para. 69, and p. 281, para. 17.

[4] It appointed Brierly, Scelle and François as Special Rapporteur on the three respective subjects: *ibid.*, p. 281, paras. 20 and 21.

has performed its guiding rôle by selecting topics already on the ILC's agenda or on its provisional list, and by requesting the ILC to give priority to its choice. For instance, the GA asked the Commission to give priority to the régime of territorial waters,[1] and subsequently insisted upon a comprehensive treatment of the vast topic of the law of the sea, linking together problems relating to the high seas, territorial waters, contiguous zones, the continental shelf, and the superjacent waters.[2] The guidance provided by the GA stressed the unity of the theme and this bore fruitful results in the Conference on the Law of the Sea in 1958.

From time to time the GA has asked the Commission to deal with other topics on its provisional list, sometimes with, and sometimes without, a call for priority. For instance, it asked for priority treatment, in 1952, for the topic of diplomatic intercourse and immunities;[3] it requested, in 1953, the codification of the principles of international law governing state responsibility as soon as the Commission considered it advisable;[4] and it desired, in 1959, the codification of law relating to the right of asylum, without calling for any priority.[5] It had also requested the Commission to study the question of the juridical régime of historic waters, including historic bays—a matter which arose out of a resolution adopted by the Law of Sea Conference of 1958.[6] In 1959, the GA directed the Secretariat to carry out a preliminary survey of the legal problems pertaining to the utilization and use of international rivers, as a preliminary to a decision whether the subject was appropriate for codification.[7] In 1961, the GA, in its Resolution 1686(XVI), whilst recommending the Commission to continue its studies of the law of treaties and of

[1] GA Res. 374(IV) of December 6, 1949, on the initiative of Iceland: UNGAOR 4th sess. 1949, 6th Com., p. 134. The Commission accordingly included it in its priority list in its 1950 session: *Y.B.I.L.C.*, 1950, vol. II, p. 366, para. 18.

[2] GA Res. 798(VIII) of December 7, 1953, and Res. 899(IX) of December 14, 1954. The Commission acknowledged that the various sections of the law of the sea were closely interrelated: *Y.B.I.L.C.*, 1956, vol. II, p. 256, para. 29.

[3] GA Res. 685(VII) of December 5, 1952. The Commission postponed the decision until its 6th session when it appointed Sandström as Special Rapporteur: *Y.B.I.L.C.*, 1953, vol. II, p. 231, para. 170, and 1954, vol. II, p. 162, para. 73.

[4] GA Res. 799(VIII) of December 7, 1953. The Commission took note of it and, in view of its heavy agenda, postponed its decision for its next session: *ibid.*, para. 74. At its 7th session, the Commission appointed Garcia Amador as Special Rapporteur for the topic: *Y.B.I.L.C.*, 1955, vol. II, p. 42, para. 33.

[5] GA Res. 1400(XIV) of November 21, 1959. The Commission took note of the resolution and deferred its consideration: *Y.B.I.L.C.*, 1960, vol. II, p. 180, para. 39. The topic was included for study in its 14th session: *ibid.*, 1962, vol. II, p. 190, para. 60.

[6] GA Res. 1453(XIV) of December 7, 1959. The Commission requested the Secretary General to undertake its study and deferred the matter to a future session: *Y.B.I.L.C.*, 1960, vol. II, p. 180, para. 40. For discussion on its inclusion in the programme see *ibid.*, 1962, vol. II, p. 190, para. 60.

[7] GA Res. 1401(XIV) of November 21, 1959.

state responsibility, requested it to include the topic of succession of states and governments on its priority list.[1] By Resolution 1687 (XVI) of December 18, 1961, the Commission was requested to study further the subject of special missions as soon as it considered it advisable.[2]

By the end of 1963, codification had been initiated in ten out of fourteen topics originally selected in 1949.[3] Of these—régime of territorial waters, diplomatic intercourse and immunities, state responsibility, the right of asylum, and succession of states and governments, had been referred to the Commission by the GA, always on the deliberative initiative of single states.[4]

The Assembly's requests for the study of such matters as relations between states and intergovernmental organizations,[5] the juridical régime of historic waters,[6] special missions,[7] and extended participation in multilateral treaties concluded under the auspices of the League of Nations,[8] arose out of the prior consideration of topics included in the provisional list for codification.

The Commission at the instance of the GA formulated the Nuremberg Principles, the Draft Code of Offences against the Peace and Security of Mankind, the Question of International Criminal Juris-

---

[1] For the Commission's decision see *Y.B.I.L.C.*, 1962, vol. II, pp. 189–90, paras. 49–54. A sub-committee under the chairmanship of Lachs was appointed to prepare a preliminary report on the subject.

[2] The Commission included it in its programme of study at the 14th Sess., see *ibid.*, p. 190, para. 60.

[3] The four remaining topics to be studied by the Commission are: i. recognition of states and governments, ii. jurisdictional immunities of states and their property, iii. jurisdiction with regard to crimes committed outside national territory, and iv. treatment of aliens.

[4] See above, p. 226.

[5] This question was adopted by the GA in connection with the Assembly's consideration of the draft and report on diplomatic intercourse and immunities: UNGAOR 13th sess. 1958, Annexes.

[6] This question arose out of the resolution adopted by the UN Conference on the Law of the Sea, 1958, on April 27: see I UNCLSOR, vol. II, pl. mtg. 20th, p. 68; see for the background, U.N. Doc. A/CN.4/143, study prepared by the Secretariat, *Y.B.I.L.C.*, 1962, vol. II, pp. 1–26. It was included on the Commission's agenda at the 14th Sess.: *ibid.*, p. 190, para. 60.

[7] The question arose out of the resolution adopted by the UN Conference on Diplomatic Intercourse and Immunities on April 10, 1961: U.N. Doc. A/Conf. 20/10/Add. 1, Resolution 1, UNCDIIOR, vol. II, Annexes. The Commission included this question on the agenda in 1962 session: *Y.B.I.L.C.*, 1962, vol. II, p. 190, para. 60.

[8] See GA Res. 1766(XVII) of November 20, 1962. The Commission's commentary on Articles 8 and 9 of its Draft articles on the Law of Treaties contained in the Report of its fourteenth session raised the problem of the accession of new states to general multilateral treaties concluded in the past whose participation clauses were limited to specific categories of states. See *Y.B.I.L.C.*, 1962, vol. II, pp. 168–9. The question was studied by the ILC at its 15th Session. See U.N. Doc. A/5509, UNGAOR 18th sess. 1963, Supp. no. 9, chap. III, pp. 30–5, paras. 18–50.

diction, and the Draft Declaration on the Rights and Duties of States. None of these was listed in the Commission's provisional list and they may be regarded as matters on which the GA decided to initiate projects without being certain whether they required codification or progressive development. In two instances, the Assembly referred a question at the instance of its Political Committee rather than of the Legal or Sixth Committees. One was the question of defining aggression, referred by GA Res. 378B(V) of November 17, 1950,[1] and the other was the question relating to a complaint of violation of the freedom of navigation in the area of the China seas, referred by GA Res. 821(IX) of December 17, 1954.[2]

Five topics out of the original list of fourteen were taken up by the Commission on its own initiative: the régime of the high seas, the law of treaties, arbitral procedure, consular intercourse and immunities, and nationality including statelessness.

In 1960, the GA took an initiative in its Resolution 1505(XV) of December 12, 1960, by discussing 'Future work in the field of the codification and progressive development of international law . . . in order to study and survey the whole field of international law and make necessary suggestions with regard to the preparation of a new list of topics for codification and for the progressive development of international law.'[3] This resolution called upon the member states to submit their views and suggestions with regard to the preparation of a new list of topics for the codification and progressive development of international law. This was of great importance in the history of codification under the auspices of the UN. Twelve years had elapsed since the Commission had adopted its original programme of work. The resolution acknowledged that the new developments in international law and the appearance of a number of new independent states, which had thus far had no opportunity of expressing their viewpoint in regard to the formulation of international standards, necessitated a review of the Commission's programme.

By emphasizing the idea that the change in the pattern of international relationships and in the requirements of the international community warranted a complete overhauling of the programme of codification, the resolution recognized the impact of social, economic and political conditions on the content and formulation of the norms of international law, as well as on the method of work

[1] *Y.B.I.L.C.*, 1951, vol. II, p. 131, para. 35.
[2] *Y.B.I.L.C.*, 1955, vol. II, p. 21, para. 16. On this question the Commission decided that it was not competent to examine the charges referred to in the complaint.
[3] UNGAOR 15th sess. 1960, Annexes, vol. 2, Ag. it. 65; also for debate on ILC Report, 6th Com., 664th–672nd mtgs.

relating to their codification. This showed a renewal of the GA's active interest in the codification and progressive development of international law.[1]

Another circumstance which led to the adoption of Resolution 1505(XV) was that the Sixth Committee had an agenda extremely limited in comparison with that of other main committees of the GA. The reports of the Commission during 1959 and 1960 were themselves of an interim character, and the Sixth Committee found itself with hardly any agenda at all.[2]

The states which had taken the initiative[3] in the adoption of the Resolution 1505(XV) had maintained from the outset that the progressive development and codification of international law must primarily be the responsibility of the GA, and the Commission must fulfil its functions as part of the general policy laid down by the GA. For that reason the original draft of the Resolution proposed the setting up of a special committee to make preliminary studies to facilitate the Assembly's task of selecting topics for codification, but the final resolution, while ignoring the Commission, preferred to leave the work of the future programme of the Commission to the governments and to a political body like the Sixth Committee.

Notwithstanding the fact that Resolution 1505(XV) did not ask the Commission to comment or to take any decision on it, the Commission did discuss the question, so that the views of its members were taken into account by the GA. The Commission approved of the spirit of the resolution, stressing the increasing importance of the rôle of international law in international relations, and underlining

[1] See for the general welcome given to the GA resolution at the Commission's 614th, 615th and 616th meetings: *Y.B.I.L.C.*, 1961, vol. I, pp. 206–23.

[2] In contrast to other main committees of the GA, the Sixth Committee had no regular flow of administrative or political matters. The Agenda of the Sixth Committee was very limited, mainly to the annual reports of the ILC which did not always require immediate and substantial decision. A lack of balanced distribution of work and a rather rigid approach to the question of distribution of items to the Committees not in conformity with GA Res. 362(IV) of October 22, 1949, may perhaps be said to have caused the decline in the work of the Sixth Committee. In this connection the paradox may be recalled that at the time when the Statute of the ILC was in preparation, anxiety was expressed that the Sixth Committee would be unable to give adequate consideration to the reports of the ILC owing to its anticipated enormous agenda.

See observations by Ernest L. Kerley of the Department of State of the U.S.A. at the Fourth Session of the Am. Soc. of Int. Law in 'United Nations contribution to developing international law', *Proceedings*, 1962, pp. 99–105.

Several members in the Sixth Committee expressed anxiety about the paucity of the Committee's agenda: U.N. Doc. A/4605 report of the Sixth Committee, UNGAOR 15th sess. 1960, Annexes, vol. 2, Ag. it. 65, paras. 35, 36 and 37.

[3] The original draft, U.N. Doc. A/C.6/L467, was sponsored by Afghanistan, Argentina, Brazil, Canada, Ceylon, Ghana, Iraq, Mexico, the United Arab Republic, Venezuela and Yugoslavia. See UNGAOR 15th sess. 1960, Annexes, vol. 2, Ag. it. 65.

the urgent need for the re-examination and revision of international law under the changing conditions. However, some of the Commission's members expressed doubts as to the appropriateness of the Assembly's selecting topics for the Commission. Some members seemed to fear that, by assuming the rôle of guide, legally conferred upon it, the GA was exceeding its powers and at the same time transgressing the rights of the Commission. Other members, however, recognized the competence of the Assembly in the matter which was based on Article 13(a) of the Charter and which was not abdicated upon the establishment of the Commission.[1] In their view the GA had the right to propose to the Commission, a body essentially a creature of the GA, subjects to be considered for codification, and could also suggest a programme of its work. For the justification of this view it is worthwhile to quote fully what the Indian member Pal said:

it was most desirable that a politically aware body should select topics to meet the demands of the new developments. The new tension would necessarily be experienced by those shouldering the responsibility of working the state machinery: they it was who would feel and know where the real conflict arose and once they would specify the fields of tension and the extent and character of such tension, the experienced jurists would usefully come in with their formulations to relax, remove or release them. . . . The states members of the international community life alone were essentially and justly qualified to specify the field of tension in each sphere. That was essential to determine which way to direct law-making energy. The preparation of a list would not go further.[2]

The Commission on the whole recognized the importance of the Assembly's directing rôle through its Sixth Committee in regard to codification work, and welcomed the renewal of the Assembly's interest in international law which was considered to strengthen the rôle of the Commission as its main subsidiary organ for the codification and development of that law.

In the Sixth Committee debates at the sixteenth session of the GA in 1961, opinions differed as to which body was competent for the selection of topics for codification. Some members favoured the system established in 1949, namely, that the Commission itself should select topics of study, its procedure and method of work, others preferred that the GA and, more particularly, the Sixth Committee should undertake this task, the political aspects of which

[1] For instance, Garcia-Amador referred to the past practice of the League of Nations and the Hague Conferences of 1899 and 1907 being guided by the Institute of International Law, and pleaded that the experienced jurists should provide states with carefully thought-out legal instruments: *Y.B.I.L.C.*, 1961, vol. I, p. 207, para. 45; also p.280, para. 60. See also Humphrey Waldock, *ibid.*, p. 217, paras. 62 and 63 and Yaseen, p. 210, paras. 3 and 4.   [2] *Ibid.*, p. 213, para. 19.

could not be ignored. However, a compromise solution prevailed which provided for co-operation between the Sixth Committee and the ILC. On the recommendation of the Sixth Committee, the GA adopted Resolution 1686(XVI) of December 18, 1961,[1] which, expressing appreciation of the Commission's valuable work already accomplished, and taking note of the discussion in the ILC on the matter, recommended the Commission in para. 3: '*a.* to continue its work in the field of the Law of Treaties and of State Responsibility and to include on its priority list the topic of Succession of States and Government'; and *b.* to report to the GA its views on the future programme of work bearing in mind the discussion in the Sixth Committee at its 15th and 16th sessions and the observations of member states[2] submitted pursuant to GA Resolution 1505(XV).

The Commission complied with the directive of the above resolution by continuing its work on the law of treaties and giving priority to the topics of state responsibility and of succession of states and governments.[3] In compliance with para. 3(b) of the resolution the Commission appointed a Committee of eight members to consider its future programme of work.[4] The Committee acknowledged that, since 1949, when the provisional list had been prepared by the Commission, several topics had become important; and some recent occurrences had brought to light insufficiency of treatment, and yet in others, new circumstances were demanding new rules. It recommended that the Commission, considering its resources, should limit its programme of work for the time being to the three main topics referred to in para. 3(a) of the GA Res. 1686(XVI) (i.e. law of treaties, state responsibility, and succession of states and governments) and four additional topics of more limited scope: special missions, relations between states and intergovernmental organizations, the right of asylum, and the juridical régime of historic waters, including historic bays. The Commission agreed to limit the future

---

[1] See U.N. Doc. A/5036, Report of the Sixth Committee, UNGAOR 16th sess. 1961, Annexes, vol. 3, Ag. it. 70, paras. 17, 18; for debate, *ibid.*, 6th Com., 713th–730th mtgs. The Resolution was adopted at 1081st plenary meeting of the GA.

[2] See U.N. Doc. A/4796 and add. 1–8 for Note by the Secretary General and observations by governments on future work in the field of codification and progressive development of international law: UNGAOR 16th sess. 1961, Annexes, Ag. it. 70; in pursuance of operative para. 2 of Res. 1505(XV), the Secretary General received observations from only 17 governments: see U.N. Doc. A/C.6/L491, *ibid.*, Annexes, vol. 3.

[3] U.N. Doc. A/5209, Report of the ILC on the work of its 14th session, *Y.B.I.L.C.*, 1962, vol. II, pp. 159–92.

[4] The Committee considered the question on the basis of the working paper prepared by the Secretariat (U.N. Doc. A/CN.4/154) which in its introduction enumerated the topics referred to the Commission by the GA and in parts I and II set out topics proposed for codification by governments in their replies. The Committee formulated a number of suggestions and submitted them at the 668th mtg. of the Commission: U.N. Doc. A/5209, *op. cit.*, p. 190.

programme of work for the time being to topics suggested by the Committee of Eight. Since these alone were likely to keep it occupied for several sessions, the Commission thought it inadvisable to add anything further to the already long list of topics on its agenda.[1]

The Sixth Committee, at the seventeenth session of the GA in 1962, endorsed the programme of work and order of priorities adopted by the Commission, and agreed for the time being not to add any new topics which might overload the Commission's work programme.[2] A great many members of the Committee expressed satisfaction that the Commission, in preparing its work programme, had followed the directives and recommendations of the GA.[3]

The entire debate on the future programme of the Commission relating to the GA Res. 1505(XV), whether in the Commission or in the Sixth Committee, throws ample light on the relations between the GA and the Commission, in particular on the selection of topics. It makes it abundantly clear that, notwithstanding the fact that the codification and progressive development of international law was a prerogative of the GA, which was entitled to take initiative in the matter, the selection of topics for codification was both a political and a technical question.[4] The political aspect of the question required the establishment of priorities in order to meet the needs of the international community which could best be done by the GA or its Sixth Committee. On the other hand, the technical aspect of any question made it necessary to ascertain whether that question was suitable for codification. The suitability or desirability of a given topic from the technical viewpoint, and the possibility of codifying that matter in juridical terms to achieve a wide measure of agreement are interrelated aspects of the same question.[5] So that this interrelationship might not become a source of difficulties,[6]

---

[1] U.N. Doc. 5209, *op. cit.*, p. 190, paras. 60–61.

[2] U.N. Doc. A/5287, UNGAOR 17th sess. 1962, Annexes, Ag. it. 76, para. 40.

[3] GA Res. 1765(XVII) of November 20, 1962, expressed the viewpoint of most of the representatives when, without giving rigid directions to the Commission, it recommended it to continue its work, taking into account the views expressed at the 17th session of the GA and the comments which may be submitted on the topics under its study: *ibid.*

[4] See Gros, *T.B.I.L.C.*, 1961, vol. I, p. 218, para. 6.

[5] For conflicting approach and debates in the General Assembly over the question of the codification of the principles of peaceful co-existence and eventual adoption of GA Res. 1686(XVI), which achieved a compromise in substituting the term 'peaceful co-existence' by the more acceptable phrase 'friendly relations and co-operation among states', see U.N. Doc. A/5036, UNGAOR 16th sess. 1961, Annexes, vol. 3.

[6] As pointed out by Ago, the GA was in an excellent position to deal with the political implications of the selection of topics for codification, but the Commission was most suited to decide on the question of priorities. 'In drawing up a list of topics, a political body might easily reach the result of establishing too long a list, with the consequences that the Commission would be given a task which it would

R

the closest collaboration between the ILC and the GA is needed. But, what considerations should govern the selection of topics for codification?

Guiding principles for the selection of topics for codification

The technical and political aspects of the question of selection of topics for codification have been given due consideration in the Statute of the Commission. The Commission is directed 'to survey the whole field of international law with a view to selecting topics for codification, having in mind existing drafts whether governmental or not' and 'when the Commission considers that the codification of a particular topic is necessary or desirable, it shall submit its recommendations to the General Assembly' (Article 18(1) and (2)). Since the expression 'necessary or desirable' is not self-explanatory, this provision of the Statute leaves a large measure of responsibility with the Commission in the task of the selection of topics for codification so that it might examine fully the technical aspect of the question. Furthermore, by directing the Commission to give priority to the requests of the GA, the same article of the Statute enables the GA to examine the political aspect of selection of a topic and thereafter to establish priorities in dealing with the codification work (Article 18(3)). As we have seen, before the Commission first met to consider the question of selection of topics for codification, it had at its disposal the Secretariat's *Survey of International Law*.[1] This document was a remarkable achievement, which has since served as a guide to codifiers of international law. In its first part, it made clear that the meaning of the term 'codification', as employed in the Statute, would have a determining effect upon the choice of topics for codification.[2] It advanced the constructive thesis that Article 15 of the Statute conceived 'codification' which may embrace the reframing of rules on 'subjects which have been regulated by international law, but the regulation of which is unsatisfactory or fragmentary'. For 'the law with regard to these subjects has sufficiently developed, but it has not developed in a manner compatible with the requirements of a peaceful and neighbourly intercourse of States'.[3] Such subjects, according to the Survey, fell within the category of codification of international law as envisaged in Article 15 of the Statute.

With a view to assisting the Commission in solving the difficult

---

be unable to perform if it were not free to make a choice to establish priorities.' *T.B.I.L.C.*, 1961, vol. I, p. 214, paras. 29–30.

[1] See pp. 205–9, above.
[2] *Survey of Int. Law*, p. 3, para. 2.
[3] *Ibid.*, p. 9, para. 13.

and intractable problem of the selection of topics for codification, the Survey attempted to suggest a correct interpretation of the expression 'necessary or desirable' used in Article 18(2) of the Statute, which prescribed the standard for the choice of subjects. It pointed out that Article 18(2) seemed to favour a broader and more flexible approach than that of the League of Nations because the criterion of codification of a topic set forth for the Commission constituted a marked advance on the situation under the League of Nations when proofs of 'feasibility' were required.[1] Besides, in its view, the task of the ILC is of an entirely novel character, not confined to the narrow limits of the choice of subjects fit for immediate codification in the form of international conventions, as was the limitation in the case of the League of Nations. Since the Commission is expected to produce drafts of varying degrees of formal authority, evidently, it has a wider scope, almost unlimited, inasmuch as it is directed to select subjects the codification of which is 'necessary or desirable'.

According to the Survey, 'the decisive criterion must be not the ease with which the task of codifying any particular branch of international law can be accomplished, but the need for codifying it'.[2] It saw the possibility of the Commission interpreting the term 'desirable' as not differing substantially from 'necessary' as apparently indicated by the natural meaning of these words. It visualized that the Commission will tend to select topics the codification of which is considered 'necessary or desirable' because of the importance of their subject matter having regard to international interest, the requirement of peaceful international intercourse, and the authority of international law'.[3]

The Memorandum of the Secretariat further believed that the codification of a topic is necessary or desirable 'not in the sense of overwhelming and immediate urgency, but in the sense of appropriateness for international regulation made desirable by the necessity of removing uncertainty productive of confusion and friction, by the necessity of preventing waste of international resources, by

[1] *Ibid.*, p. 60, para. 101ff.
[2] Referring to topics eventually selected by the League Committee of Experts and the Assembly for codification, the Survey said that 'they were topics with regard to which the practice had previously registered a distinct measure of disagreement, with regard to which the divergencies had reference to political and economic interest of apparent importance, and in relation to which divergent traditions of national law and jurisprudence had indicated from the outset the difficulties of codification. The statement may sound paradoxical, but the affirmative criterion of "ripeness" as eventually acted upon seemed to have been not the ease with which the subject could be codified, but the difficulty, as expressed in existing divergencies and in the need for regulation, of regulating it by way of codification', *ibid.*, p. 12, para. 16.
[3] *Ibid.*, p. 59, para. 100.

the necessity of filling gaps and meeting the new conditions of international life, and, generally, by the necessity of enhancing the authority of international law'.[1] It is from this point of view that the Survey in Part II examined a great many, though not all, of the topics of international law. It surveyed the field of international law of peace and enumerated in a comprehensive and satisfactory way, a good number of topics in that field on which the Commission, in years to come, relied heavily.[2]

The Memorandum realized that it might be difficult to discover a working test of preference, but said that the Commission should 'proceed to some selection for the reasons both that it is instructed to do so by the Statute and that it cannot possibly codify all subjects at once—if we bear these factors in mind then the problem of selection no longer appears as one of perplexing and arbitrary choice'.[3] It saw the task of selection of topics for codification as one of assignments of priorities or of fitting the Commission's work at any particular time into the orbit of a comprehensive plan—a matter to be determined by 'considerations of convenience, of available means and personnel, of classification, and of scientific symmetry'.[4]

The Commission's members, however, could not agree to any commonly acceptable criteria concerning the selection of topics for codification.[5] The Commission eventually adopted Scelle's suggestion of considering briefly the topics listed in Part II of the Survey, and choosing topics by the elimination of those which the Commission deemed unnecessary or undesirable. By resorting to this method the Commission avoided the need for a precise definition of the criteria of 'necessity' and 'desirability' laid down by Article 18(2) of the Statute.

---

[1] *Survey of Int. Law*, p. 61, para. 102.
[2] *Ibid.*, pp. 19–58.
[3] *Ibid.*, p. 61, para. 103.   [4] *Ibid.*, p. 14, para. 19.
[5] Spiropoulos thought that the choice would necessarily be purely subjective, rather than logical. Sandström thought that it should be subjective but based on practical considerations, upon the relative value of which the Commission would have to be the judge. François preferred to choose topics the codification of which was easily realizable, in that results could be obtained almost immediately. Cordova favoured preparation of a general plan, to be followed by selection of topics which the Commission considered realizable for immediate codification. Scelle opposed the drawing up of a general plan of codification and thought that 'the only possible solution was to choose a limited number of topics, after having decided whether they would be of a general or specific character. Such a procedure was actuated by an essentially pragmatic and not a scientific conception: the Commission must produce concrete results as soon as possible.' Garcia-Amador recommended that it would be better to have an exchange of views on the different criteria which influenced each member of the Commission to select a particular topic: *Y.B.I.L.C.*, 1949, 4th mtg., pp. 32–5. Scelle also pointed out that 'readiness' was not a relevant test and cited, as an example, a number of topics which the *Code Napoléon* had codified at a time when they had not been ripe for codification: *ibid.*, p. 36, para. 61.

The Commission rejected as unnecessary and undesirable the following topics out of the list of the Survey.[1] The topic of 'subjects of international law' was dismissed because a majority of the Commission did not find it 'ready' for codification; the topic of 'sources of international law' was likewise rejected on the ground that its codification was of no practical interest and 'would have more disadvantages than advantages'. The question of 'obligations of international law in relation to the law of the State' (i.e. incorporating the provisions of international law and of validly concluded treaties in the national law of states) was regarded as irrelevant, unripe and perhaps better dealt with by way of a statement by the Commission affirming the priority of international law over the law of states. The topic of 'the fundamental rights and duties of States' was postponed, to be examined in connection with the specific item on the Commission's agenda of a draft declaration on the rights and duties of States. The 'recognition of the acts of foreign states', which in the words of the Chairman actually meant 'the effect given in a State to the acts of another State', was not selected because it appeared to belong less to the field of public than to private international law. The topic of 'obligations of territorial jurisdiction', which included various aspects of the question of damage caused by one state to the property of another, was not retained because it embraced many unconnected matters, and it appeared difficult to codify them. Similarly, the question of 'territorial domain of States', covering acquisition and loss of territory, was also rejected since it lacked clarity, raised various matters unconnected with each other, and was unsuitable for codification. The topic of 'pacific settlement of international disputes' was also rejected as its codification was felt to be premature, pointless and possibly a duplication of the work of the Interim Committee of the GA. Finally, the topic of 'extradition' was rejected as unnecessary and undesirable for codification as the subject was deemed more properly regulated by bilateral treaties.

The Commission selected on its provisional list fourteen topics from the Survey, thought to be suitable, or 'necessary or desirable' for codification. It was, however, conceded that fresh topics might at any time be added to the provisional list so that the 'whole field of international law' could ultimately be at least explored.[2]

Apart from the topics taken from the Survey, three topics were proposed independently by the Commission's members. Yepes drew attention to the question of 'domestic jurisdiction' which was omitted by the Survey submitted by the Secretary General. The

[1] *Y.B.I.L.C.*, 1949, 4th mtg., pp. 35–7, 40–4, 47.
[2] See above, p. 234, n. 3.

Secretariat defended the omission on the ground that the topic formed a part of many other topics considered in the Survey.[1] The Commission, acquiescing in this matter dropped the subject. François had suggested the question of the laws of war. Although this topic was omitted from the Survey, it was mentioned in paragraph 14 of the working paper (A/CN. 41 W1) prepared by the Secretariat on the basis of that document, expressing the view that concern with it was incompatible with the status of the Commission as an organ of the UN and with the Charter.[2] Some members of the Commission thought that the topic should be examined since war was still a physical possibility as long as employment of force in international relationships was not entirely ruled out.[3] But the majority were opposed to the study of the problem[4] because 'if the Commission, at the very beginning of its work, were to undertake this study, public opinion might interpret its action as showing lack of confidence in the efficiency of the means at the disposal of the United Nations for maintaining peace'. The proposal was dropped. Similarly, the third proposal regarding study of the subject of neutrality which was merely a consequence of war, was also rejected.[5]

The Commission never returned to the question of the selection of topics for codification until it debated the GA Resolution 1505(XV) of December 12, 1960 on 'future work in the field of the codification and progressive development of international law' at the 614th, 615th and 616th meetings at its thirteenth session in 1961. During the debate, Professor Verdross suggested that four general principles should guide the planning of the Commission's future work: i. that the Commission could codify only the law concerning topics of universal importance; ii. that it could not codify the law concerning extremely controversial topics; iii. that the codification should already be in progress as reflected in generally established practice, since the Commission was not competent to make entirely new international law; and iv. that the Commission's work should not overlap with that of other competent international organs such as the Commission on Human Rights.[6] Endorsing these four criteria, as a basis for the choice of topics, François added a fifth criterion,

[1] *Y.B.I.L.C.*, 1949, 5th mtg., p. 39, paras. 16–19 and 25.
[2] *Ibid.*, 6th mtg., p. 51, paras. 45–46.
[3] See views of Scelle, Spiropoulos and Hsu, *ibid.*, pp. 51–2, paras. 47–49, 51, 52, 61–63. See for reiteration of the proposal by Hsu, *Y.B.I.L.C.*, 1961, 615th mtg., p. 211, para. 8.
[4] Koretsky, supported by Brierly, Sir Benegal Rau, and Yepes were opposed to the study of the laws of war: *Y.B.I.L.C.*, 1949, pp. 51–3, paras. 53–54, 55–56, 60, 64, 66.
[5] *Ibid.*, p. 53, para. 68.
[6] *Y.B.I.L.C.*, 1961, vol. I, 614th mtg., pp. 206–7, para. 44.

namely, that the Commission should select for codification only topics of restricted scope, so that their consideration could be completed within the limited time available.[1] These views gave rise to considerable discussion and to certain objections. Some members held that the Commission should not be afraid to take up broader and controversial topics which usually raised more important issues pertaining to the law of nations than more restricted topics.[2] The general opinion in the Commission failed to support the view that the Commission should evade controversial and complex questions relating to important aspects of contemporary international relations.

The viewpoint of governments in response to the GA Resolution 1505(XV) on the future work of the Commission was summarized by a working paper prepared by the Secretariat.[3] In Austria's view special account of recent sociological developments in the international community should be taken, so that a new survey would call for the progressive development of international law rather than codification proper.[4] In Czechoslovakia's view emphasis should be on such measures in the field of law as would render a positive contribution to the consolidation of peace and international security and to the peaceful existence of states, irrespective of their social systems.[5] Denmark stressed the desirability of combining progressive evolution with the preservation of indispensable elements of stability in international relations, and of encouraging the compulsory jurisdiction of the International Court of Justice.[6] The United Kingdom was opposed to the creation of new laws under the guise of progressive development where the subject is so novel that it is a matter for agreement between states rather than for progressive development based on the foundation of known and accepted rules, and it disapproved of reference to highly controversial topics which aimed to further political aims and policies of particular governments, or which undermined the authority of the existing law.[7] Yugoslavia favoured selection of topics which took cognizance of new trends in world affairs, strengthened international relations among the nations, led to the settlement of disputes by peaceful means, and advanced economic and social progress throughout the world.[8]

---

[1] *Ibid.*, p. 209, para. 61. He argued that the Commission could not be expected to discuss broad topics exhaustively; 'its discussions would either be too hasty or would be prolonged beyond the five year term of the Commission's membership, in which event there would be the additional difficulties of a change of membership and of a change of special rapporteurs'. His views were endorsed by Bartos, *ibid.*, p. 211, para. 12.

[2] *Ibid.*, 615th mtg., p. 212, para. 17; p. 215, para. 48.

[3] U.N. Doc. A/C.6/L491, UNGAOR 16th sess. 1961, Annexes, Ag. it. 70.

[4] U.N. Doc. A/4796/Add. 6, UNGAOR 16th sess. 1961, Annexes, Ag. it. 70.

[5] U.N. Doc. A/4796/Add. 3.   [6] *Ibid.*, Add. 1.

[7] *Ibid.*, Annex 6.   [8] *Ibid.*, Annex 7.

When the Commission reconsidered at its fourteenth session its future programme of work, it had before it the working paper summarizing the observations of governments, the report discussion of the Sixth Committee[1] and a working paper prepared by the Secretariat (A/CN.4/145), which consisted of a summary, topic by topic, of the ideas expressed in the replies of governments and in statements made in the Sixth Committee at the fifteenth and sixteenth sessions of the GA.[2] The two considerations which influenced the ILC in its selection of topics for future programme of work were: firstly, that its agenda items be kept to a minimum to allow it sufficient time to consider the reports on various topics submitted by the Special Rapporteurs; and secondly, that it should, in drawing up its programme of work, take account of its resources, namely, its limited term of five years and the nature of the materials which it could formulate in legal terms. Since topics of broad scope require considerable time for discussion and study which might continue over a period of years, the Commission preferred to confine its work to the study of only three broad topics and four additional topics of limited scope referred to it by the GA.[3] It is gratifying to note that the GA has tended to rely on the Commission's experience and judgment in the matter of selection of topics, its programme of work and priorities.

During its 19th session, in 1966, the Commission again considered its future programme of work. The topics of right of asylum and historic waters, including historic bays, suggested by the General Assembly,[4] were not favoured by the Commission since in its opinion they raised political problems and were of considerable scope, so that they might severely delay the completion of work on important topics already under study. Various other topics considered by the Commission were: the effect of unilateral acts; the use of international rivers, international bays and international

---

[1] U.N. Doc. A/5036. In the Sixth Committee, the following topics were suggested: the question of the peaceful co-existence of states, consideration of legal aspects of friendly relations and co-operation among states in accordance with the United Nations Charter; the pacific settlement of international disputes; the question of ratification of and accessions to multilateral conventions concluded under the auspices of the United Nations and for which the Secretary General acted as depository; the question of the acceptance of compulsory jurisdiction of the International Court of Justice; a legal study of disarmament, and the question of the establishment of an international tribunal for the protection of human rights.

[2] This document has two parts: Part I deals with the possibility of codifying topics enlisted in the provisional list drawn up by the Commission in 1949; Part II examines the possibility of codifying new topics in the sense that the Commission had never considered making a study of them: *Y.B.I.L.C.*, 1962, vol. II, pp. 84–100.

[3] See above, pp. 230–1.

[4] GA Res. 1400(XIV) of November 21, 1959, on right of asylum, and Res. 1453(XIV) of December 7, 1959, on historic waters.

straits; draft declaration on the rights and duties of states; question of criminal jurisdiction; question of international procedures; and drawing of the statute of a new United Nations body for fact finding in order to assist the General Assembly. All these topics were found by the Commission either controversial or of too broad scope. The Commission unanimously agreed to select the topic of most-favoured nation clauses in the Law of Treaties because it had remained uncovered by the general Law of Treaties and the GA had also urged the Commission to deal with it.[1]

The decisive factor in the selection of topics for codification, should, indeed, be the needs of the international community. The GA is certainly the most suitable forum for deciding upon these needs and their priorities so as to guide the Commission in computing those realities for formulation of rules of international law. The initiative of the will of states expressed through the GA can facilitate the Commission's work even though there exist no already known and accepted rules on a topic, or even if the given subject is highly controversial. This fact is well demonstrated in the case of two important matters, namely, the question of the continental shelf, and of the fisheries and the conservation of living resources of the sea. In both cases, notwithstanding the lack of a general practice, uniform doctrine, or a body of treaties, the idea of progressive development took precedence over a mere code of the pre-existing law. Thus, the 'necessity' or 'usefulness' of a subject can best be indicated by the GA. The GA is also better qualified than the Commission to deal with such subjects which are important but essentially dominated by political considerations, e.g. disarmament, regulation of outer space, recognition of states and governments.

On the other hand, the Commission is the best judge of the technical possibility of codification which requires extensive research into treaty law, judicial decisions, state practice and learned writings. It would be advisable for the Commission to utilize fully the services of the Legal Department of the UN Secretariat concerning the preparatory work,[2] similar to that undertaken in 1949, on the basis of which it may periodically make its selection of topics. In drawing up its future programme of study the Commission[3] should judge objectively various proposals in the GA by getting back to the policies which support them, and to the changing conditions in economic and social structure, to the demands, the expectations and

[1] U.N. Doc. A/6309/Rev. 1, ILC Report, UNGAOR suppl. no. 9, chap. III, paras. 45–46.
[2] As in U.N. Doc. A/CN.4/145, working paper of the Secretariat prepared in 1962.
[3] See for ILC's review in 1968, U.N. Doc. A/7209/Rev. 1, *op. cit.*, pp. 3–33.

the aspirations of peoples the world over. It should also examine the canonized doctrines of international law, which ignore the kind of world in which we live. It should consider whether their purification is enough to achieve what the peoples are demanding. Since it is conflicting interests which the institution of law tries to harmonize should not the Commission first try to determine what are those conflicting interests and what are their values in the light of the debates in the GA or the Sixth Committee? Should it not gather information from governments, before attempting to harmonize these interests in the form of codified rules?

The nature of the materials which it could utilize in formulation of its drafts might well be the principal criterion in determining the Commission's selection of topics for codification. And, if the limitation of time, in view of its five-year term and annual sessions of only ten weeks' duration, were removed by giving the Commission a full-time status, the Commission could be free, because its membership would remain undisturbed, to take up the topics of broad scope as well as the controversial ones which entail work for longer periods.

Since the General Assembly and the International Law Commission are fully competent to determine respectively the usefulness or necessity and the technical suitability of a subject for codification, the collaboration between the two bodies should continue unhindered. If the ILC continues to draw up its programme guided by the opinions expressed in the GA and with the latters' approval, both technical and political criteria would thus be secured.

TECHNIQUE AND WORKING METHODS OF THE COMMISSION

In view of the concern expressed from time to time about the slow rate of progress in the Commission's work,[1] a study of the technique and working methods of the Commission deserves some attention.

It is clear from the account of the procedures set forth in articles 16 to 22 of the Statute that the codification work is not entirely a one-sided and exclusive concern of the Commission alone. The Commission's final draft proposals are the product of the mature consideration of various opinions, and of extensive preparatory work based upon the material and comments received from governments and other bodies. Any examination of the technique and working methods of the Commission, therefore, requires a study of three

[1] See for the criticism in the Sixth Committee in one session after another, particularly the debates of 11th and 12th sessions, UNGAOR 11th sess. 1956, 6th Com., 483rd to 485th mtgs., U.N. Doc. A/3427, Annexes, Ag. it. 59. *Ibid.*, 12th sess. 1957, 6th Com., 509th–513th mtgs.; and reiteration of similar views at 16th sess. 1961, 713th–730th mtgs.

principal aspects: i. The Commission's methods of preparatory work; ii. its relations with governments during the preparation of a project; and iii. its co-operation with other bodies concerned with the development of international law.

Methods of preparatory work

The Commission may (and it does in practice) entrust the preparatory work of a preliminary nature to the UN Division for the Development and Codification of International Law. This Division of the Secretariat has submitted a number of valuable working papers and documents on various subjects in response to GA resolutions and requests from the Commission. But its important services, which are lesser known, consist in extending to the Special Rapporteurs, throughout their work, its full professional collaboration through the regular members of the staff as well as through such special research assistants and consultants as may be required. In fact, at the request of the Special Rapporteur concerned, the Codification Division assumes full responsibility, in the language of Article 19(2) of the Statute, for collecting 'the text of laws, decrees, judicial decisions, treaties, diplomatic correspondence and other documents relevant to the topic being studied and which the Commission deems necessary'. Yet the main part of the preparatory work on each subject under study by the Commission is performed by the Special Rapporteur.

The *Survey of International Law*, the Memorandum prepared by the Secretary General in 1949, had advocated the appointment of a sub-committee of three or four of the Commission's members on each particular topic under study in order 'to guide and assist the Special Rapporteur in the preparation of the preliminary version of the draft and the commentary'.[1] But the Commission preferred to leave entire responsibility regarding preparation of the preliminary draft of the articles and of the commentary to the Special Rapporteur concerned, and until recently did not resort to the regular practice of appointing sub-committees in such a way as to generalize or extend this as one of the Commission's normal methods of work. Although it has made some use of sub-committees purely on an *ad hoc* basis, it has apparently relied on the principle that the actual preparation of the drafts and commentaries must be the responsibility of one person, and that it would be incompatible with the scientific character of the work of codification to encourage any system of collective drafting at this first stage, a practice that has resulted in a heavy burden being laid on the Special Rapporteurs. It has been the subject of some criticism in the GA and has been

[1] U.N. Doc. A/CN.4/1 Rev. 1, *op. cit.*, p. 69, para. 116.

regarded by some as one of the factors contributing to the delay in the drafting of articles.[1] In the Commission itself suggestions have been made in favour of giving precise directives to the Special Rapporteurs, and of employing two Special Rapporteurs instead of one, or of forming a Committee of Three, to draft proposals on a given subject.[2] The Commission did issue detailed instructions to Sir Humphrey Waldock, the newly appointed Special Rapporteur for the Law of Treaties,[3] but it was probably for the reason that he was the fourth Rapporteur on the subject and the Commission had changed the scheme of its work on the law of treaties from a mere expository statement of the law to the preparation of draft articles capable of serving as a basis for a multilateral convention.

Difficulty has been encountered by the Commission owing to the quinquennial change of membership and the consequent anxiety as to whether or not topics entrusted to certain Special Rapporteurs might have to be shelved.[4] Had the Commission been placed on a full-time basis with a staggered term of office—a certain fraction of membership retiring at intervals—the Commission could withdraw from routine retirement those members working as Special Rapporteurs whose reports had not been completed or adopted by the Commission. When the Commission discussed its future plan of work at the 13th session in 1961, the general views which emerged were: that the delay in codification of given topics was due to changes of Special Rapporteurs; that completion of draft conven-

---

[1] Several delegations in the Sixth Committee at the 17th session of the GA favoured the view that clear and detailed directions should be given to the Special Rapporteur as a general practice as was done in case of Law of Treaties in 1961 on the appointment of a new Special Rapporteur. See for the views of Coomarswamy (Ceylon), 735th mtg., para. 4; Genser (Canada), 737th mtg., para. 1; Movchan (U.S.S.R.), 738th mtg.: UNGAOR 17th sess. 1962, 6th Com.; also U.N. Doc. A/5287 Reports of the Sixth Committee, *Ibid.*, Annexes, Ag. it. 76, para. 53.

[2] Spiropoulos, *Y.B.I.L.C.*, 1949, 32nd mtg., p. 236, para. 64; Garcia-Amador and Tunkin, *ibid.*, 1961, vol. I, p. 250, paras. 24, 45; Hsu and Sandström, p. 211, para. 9. For Tabibi's suggestion (Afghanistan), UNGAOR 16th sess. 1961, p. 127, para. 28.

[3] *Y.B.I.L.C.*, 1961, vol. I, Report of the Commission, U.N. Doc. A/4843, chap. III, p. 128, para. 39.

[4] Pal clearly pointed out that 'The absurdity of the present position of the Commission would be easily visualized if it were remembered that even with its extended term of five years no complete work was possible. During the first year, the Commission would take up the study of a subject and would appoint a Special Rapporteur who would be expected to produce a draft during the second year. After the first reading of the draft the matter would get two years for that purpose, and in that way the second reading of the draft would never be possible before the fifth year.' He admitted that 'it was indeed lucky that Special Rapporteurs such as Dr. François, Dr. Sandström, and Dr. Zourek had been re-elected and it was thus sheer luck that the Commission had been able to finish the work undertaken with their help as Special Rapporteurs': *Y.B.I.L.C.*, 1961, vol. I, 615th mtg., p. 213, para. 21.

tions on some topics had only been possible owing to the chance re-election of Special Rapporteurs; that outside experts should be at the disposal of the Special Rapporteurs, or that more than one Special Rapporteur be appointed on each subject.[1] In case no change in the Statute is contemplated to ensure the continuity of the Special Rapporteur, the Commission should find the suggestion of having associate Special Rapporteurs, who are also members of the Commission, quite workable.

Another improvement which has often been suggested to speed up the Commission's work is that the Commission should divide itself into two or even more sub-commissions working independently or along parallel lines on different topics.[2] The Commission considered the questions of re-organization of the methods of work at the 10th session when Zourek's working paper on the subject recommended some changes in methods in such a way that less would be done in the plenary meetings of the Commission and more in committees or sub-commissions, of which greater use would be made.[3] Zourek favoured the idea of referring details of work to smaller, but sufficiently representative working parties. According to him any draft prepared by a Special Rapporteur should be the subject of a general discussion in a plenary meeting of the Commission, followed by a review of articles of the drafts and the amendments submitted by members, without any votes being taken at that stage unless absolutely necessary. The next stage after the preliminary discussion of the draft should be a full discussion over it and the amendments thereto in a sub-commission of not more than ten members, comprising the Special Rapporteur concerned, the representatives of all the legal systems of the world and such members of the Commission as were most interested in the particular subject. Lastly, the draft articles prepared by the sub-commission should then be submitted to the full Commission for possible discussion and adoption.[4]

This procedure would have the advantage of increasing the output of the Commission without placing an extra burden on its members, for the reason that the sub-commissions would meet at a time when the full commission was not sitting. The Commission

---

[1] *Ibid.*, pp. 206–23.
[2] See for Mr. Holmbäck's (Sweden) suggestion UNGAOR 11th sess. 1956, 6th Com., 483rd mtg., para. 4; *ibid.*, 12th sess. 1957, 513th mtg., para. 43. The delegations of the U.K. (511th mtg., para. 13); India (510th mtg., para. 29); Afghanistan (511th mtg., para. 41), The Federation of Malaya (512th mtg., para. 29) supported the idea of sub-commissions: UNGAOR 12th sess. 1957, 6th Com.
[3] See U.N. Doc. A/CN.4/L76, Zourek's working paper on future work of the Commission, *Y.B.I.L.C.*, 1958, vol. II, pp. 74–6; for discussion, *ibid.*, vol. I, pp. 174–80.
[4] *Ibid.*, vol. II, p. 76, para. 26.

would thus be enabled to submit one draft regularly to the GA every year, instead of no drafts at all, or two drafts at once as has sometimes been the case.

The Commission was not inclined to constitute sub-commissions on a formal basis because, apart from budgetary and other implications of a practical character entailing the proposed facility of simultaneous interpretation and summary records of the sub-commissions, it would tend to deprive the sub-commissions of precisely that informality and conversational atmosphere which helped quick disposal of difficult and controversial problems. Secondly, the Commission felt that it would reintroduce much of the deliberate character of the plenary meetings of the Commission.[1] However, the Commission accepted other proposals of Zourek which it felt should 'be kept in mind and acted upon as occasion might require or render desirable'. It did not think it necessary to take a definite decision in advance to the effect that the Commission would always (or even usually) adopt the proposed method of work, but was prepared to use it on an *ad hoc* basis, particularly, in the initial stages of drawing up a draft on a difficult and complex subject.[2] The Commission decided formally to constitute its Drafting Committee to which could be referred, as the practice was, not merely pure drafting points, but also points of substance which the full Commission had been unable to resolve, or which seemed likely to give rise to unduly protracted discussion.[3]

A standing drafting committee has been used since 1952.[4] Since 1955 the Chairman has been the ILC's first Vice-Chairman and the General Rapporteur is customarily the member of the Committee.[5] Special Rapporteurs participate in its work when the draft articles relating to their topics are considered. But it was only after there was some criticism in the Sixth Committee debates, at the 15th and 16th sessions of the GA, of working methods of the Commission,[6] that the Commission decided, at its own 14th session, to appoint two sub-committees which were to meet between the sessions for the purpose of undertaking the necessary preparatory work on the topics of State Responsibility and the Succession of States and Governments. This departure from its previous practice has been welcomed by several delegations in the Sixth Committee at

---

[1] *Y.B.I.L.C.*, 1958, vol. II, Report of the Commission, chap. V, p. 108, para. 63.
[2] *Ibid.*, para. 62.   [3] *Ibid.*, para. 65.
[4] *Y.B.I.L.C.*, 1952, vol. I, 144th mtg., para. 62.
[5] *Ibid.*, 1955, vol. I, 295th mtg., para. 13; 1954, vol. I, 250th mtg., para. 61.
[6] See U.N. Doc. 4/4605 Report of the Sixth Committee, UNGAOR 15th sess. 1960, Annexes, vol. 2, Ag. it. 65; and U.N. Doc. A/5036, Report of the Sixth Committee, *ibid.*, 16th sess. 1961, Annexes, vol. 3, Ag. it. 70, paras. 26, 27.

the 17th session of the GA.[1] Some members, although accepting the justifiability of the sub-committees in view of the unique complexities of the subjects concerned, did not consider their establishment necessarily desirable as a regular practice. The delegation of the U.S.A. said that 'the Commission must weigh the potential benefits of establishing such sub-committees against the disadvantage that their creation delayed for a year the appointment of the Special Rapporteur'.[2] Preliminary preparatory work on certain subjects may well go a long way to help the Special Rapporteur and to expedite completion of the Commission's work. It is likely that the Commission would consider the appointment of a sub-committee on the merits of a subject rather than as a normal practice. This is abundantly clear from the Commission's debate on the method of work on state responsibility and succession of states and governments, that it was owing to the difficulty and complexity of these subjects that the ILC decided to vary its practice and to appoint a small sub-committee on each to submit a report not on the substance of the matter but on purely preliminary questions.[3] Work done through sub-commissions or sub-committees might result in the Commission's losing its *esprit de corps*. The Drafting Committee meeting frequently has in practice worked successfully because every matter, before being referred to it, is thoroughly discussed in the full Commission.

In controversial matters the Commission has tended to avoid voting and has resorted to the practice of leaving such matters to the Drafting Committee to find a solution which is satisfactory for the majority of the members. The Commission has often unanimously adopted the proposals of the Drafting Committee and, sometimes, even without discussion. This practice has been adopted with a view to ironing out most serious differences of opinion at the preparatory stage so that eventually when diplomatic conferences are held they can proceed with their work in an atmosphere of unanimity. However, on this method of reaching agreement there was an interesting debate in the Commission at its 11th session in 1959. Some members thought that exhaustive discussion in the plenary Commission was necessary in order to reach an agreement on the

[1] UNGAOR 17th sess. 1962, 6th Com., 735th mtg., para. 6. See for general welcome given to the appointment of sub-committees, U.N. Doc. A/5287, Report of 6th Committee, *ibid.*, Ag. it. 76, para. 50.
[2] UNGAOR 17th sess. 1962, 735th mtg., para. 14; see for debate in the Commission and for different views expressed concerning the method of work to be adopted regarding the consideration of the question of state responsibility, *Y.B.I.L.C.*, 1962, vol. II, Report of the Commission, Doc. A/5209, pp. 188–9.
[3] *Ibid.*, pp. 188–9, paras. 41–48, p. 191, paras. 68, 72. See below, pp. 324, 325.

substance by voting or by obtaining consensus before texts were referred to the Drafting Committee. Others considered that discussion at plenary meetings should be briefer and, when a certain measure of agreement, or at least a majority view had emerged, the question could be referred to the Drafting Committee.[1] Again, in the 12th session in 1960, the issue was raised by a member of the Commission as to whether it was desirable for the Commission to refer all articles to the Drafting Committee without itself taking a decision on the substance, or without first settling matters of principle on the basis of a consensus or a majority opinion of its members.[2] The crux of the whole problem here lies not in choosing between voting and not voting, or between a majority decision and a consensus, but in evolving a method of producing an agreed draft. In fact each question has different characteristics. Whilst some problems need discussion at length others may be easily decided by vote. Perhaps it is not practicable for the Commission to have a rigid system. Indeed the Drafting Committee should not be referred prematurely the matters involving deep-seated differences and it should be enabled on the basis of the debates in the Full Commission to discover a consensus or a majority view so that the resulting texts would find a widest possible support. For this reason, the principle the Commission has adhered to is that the representative character of the Commission should be adequately reflected at all stages of its work and this is likely to remain the most important factor to condition the successful outcome of its future endeavours.

Indeed, the records of the Commission fail to reveal well-defined methods of work. The Commission has to proceed with deliberation and caution in view of the great difficulty and complexity of its work, and, therefore, it cannot commit itself to any rigidly laid down method of work. The flexibility of the Commission's methods, despite their drawbacks, has enabled the Commission to adjust to the requirement of producing a detailed commentary in most cases as well as well-drafted articles, or occasionally a general report on the subject concerned. This has resulted in the finalization of one complete piece of work every year for submission to the General Assembly. In 1958, the Commission reviewed its work of the last ten years and pointed out that in fact it had done better than this in having produced no fewer than fifteen or sixteen final and completed pieces of work, which it listed in its report.[3]

Those who call for accelerating the Commission's work are not

---

[1] *Y.B.I.L.C.*, 1959, vol. I, pp. 161–4.
[2] *Y.B.I.L.C.*, 1960, vol. I, p. 137, para. 56.
[3] *Y.B.I.L.C.*, 1958, vol. II, Report of the Commission Doc. A/3859, chap. V, part II, p. 109, para. 68(a) and n. 39 and 40.

certain that even if the Commission were to produce drafts more quickly, governments, and the GA itself would be able to keep pace with them, since further action would be required on the Commission's completed piece of work—in some cases an international conference, which for administrative and technical reasons cannot be held frequently.[1]

Relations with governments during preparation of a project.

The experience of the past shows that success in codification work largely depends upon the co-operation of governments.[2] The failure of the Hague Conference of 1930 has been partly attributed to the insufficient collaboration with governments with a view to the clarification of their attitudes on the problems selected for the Conference.[3] Hence, to attain success, the Commission must discover whether conflicting interests can be harmonized, or whether a new set of norms can be evolved by a compromise which will take into account all the interests, or whether it may be wiser to wait until a change in the international atmosphere permits the modification of some of the interests involved.

In the Commission's Statute much concern has been shown to enable the Commission to take account of the viewpoints of governments individually as well as collectively. The importance of bringing the collective influence of governments to bear on the Commission's work has been recognized in the rôle assigned to the GA in relation to the Commission, which is discussed above. It may be noted that apart from the comments made by the delegations of governments during the annual debates of the Sixth Committee of the GA, a digest of which is made available for the use of the Commission, the resolutions of the GA are of greater significance inasmuch as they embody the collective attitude of governments in regard to the Commission's work. The Commission's Statute also contains a number of provisions designed to give governments ample opportunities to transmit to the Commission any data relating to their practice at the early stages of the Commission's work on a project; they can submit their comments on the Commission's drafts at subsequent

[1] As the Commission explained 'it was doubtful whether, on the average, such conferences could be held oftener than once a year, or more probably once in two years. For administrative and technical reasons, they could not usually be held concurrently with either the meetings of the Assembly or of the Commission itself. This meant that, in practice, the only time of the year at which such conferences could be held, unless they were very short, was between January and April': *ibid.*, pp. 109-10, para. 68(c).

[2] See Visscher: *Theory and Reality in Public International Law*, pp. 144-5.

[3] See Historical Survey of Development of International Law and its Codification by International Conferences, U.N. Doc. A/AC.10/5, (*A.J.I.L.*, vol, 41, 1947, pp. 85-6).

s

stages of the works.[1] In addition, Article 24, directs the Commission to 'consider ways and means for making the evidence of customary international law more readily available, such as the collection and publication of documents concerning state practice and of the decisions of national and international courts on questions of international law'.[2] This article, however, does not preclude the consideration of other ways and means nor does it exclude other sources. All these provisions of the Statute attach much importance to state practice.

Obtaining the necessary data or comments from the various governments has not proved to be easy. The Commission employs the questionnaire technique for the collection of information. This was the mode of consultation used not only in the preparation for the Hague Codification Conference of 1930, but also at the Universal Postal Congresses and at the Conferences for the Unification of Private International Law, and in a modified form, at the ILO. The questionnaires[3] are sent to governments for reply within a fixed period of time through the Secretary General without the latter having to await the GA's decision.[4] But the questionnaire method for collecting data or information from governments does not appear to have been effective. Some members of the Commission have doubted 'whether satisfactory results would be obtained by sending a questionnaire to governments. Generally-speaking, governments did not reply to questionnaires, or sent replies which were of little use.'[5]

---

[1] Articles 16, 17, 19, 21 and 22; see outline of procedures at pp. 225–32ff above. While Articles 16(c) and 17(b) refer to circulation of a questionnaire to governments, Article 19(2) binds the Commission to address to governments 'a detailed request to furnish the text of laws, decrees, judicial decisions, treaties, diplomatic correspondence and other documents relevant to the topic' under study. Articles 16(h), 21(2) and 22 require the Commission to procure and take account of the comments from governments in preparing its draft.

[2] For the history of this text see the Memorandum of the Secretary General: Ways and Means of Making the Evidence of Customary International Law More Readily Available, U.N. Doc. A/CN.4/6 1949.

[3] For example, the Secretary General's communication to Governments LEG/291/10/YLL of July 11, 1949, referred to in Doc. A/CN.4/19 containing replies from governments to the questionnaires of the ILC concerning topics for codification, namely régime of the high seas, and law of treaties: *Y.B.I.L.C.*, 1950, vol. II, p. 52, para. 3; p. 196, para. 3.

[4] When, at the 63rd mtg. of the Commission, France's Special Rapporteur on régime of the high seas proposed that the questionnaire prepared by the General Rapporteur and the Special Rapporteur should first be discussed by the Commission and incorporated in its report to the GA, and, when approved by the GA, be circulated to governments, Dr. Liang pointed out that there was nothing in the Statute 'to prevent detailed questionnaires being sent to governments through the Secretary General without the latter having to await the General Assembly's decision., *Y.B.I.L.C.*, 1950, vol. I, 63rd mtg., paras. 1(g) and 2(a).

[5] See *Y.B.I.L.C.*, 1950, vol. I, 63rd mtg., p. 181, para. 15 for Alfaro's statements, Hudson, para. 4, and Hsu, para. 9, for similar views.

It may be that the Commission has not formulated sufficiently detailed questionnaires under Articles 16(c) and 19(2) of its Statute to elicit precise replies.[1] This can only be inferred from some of the replies of governments as illustrated in the French Government's caustic note that it 'unfortunately cannot consider communicating all the documentary material which has appeared on these three classic topics (Treaties, arbitral procedure, and the régime of the high seas), representing as it does several tons of its archives'.[2] Obviously, the lack of response of governments to the Commission's inquiries is unfortunate.

The publication of the United Nations Legislative series prepared by the Secretariat in co-operation with governments is, however, a compensatory development. Mention may also be made here of the compilations of state practice on international law. Official digests of international law compiling materials, official or others, relating to the practice of the United States have been prodigious undertakings. Francis Wharton's *International Law Digest* in three volumes (1886) set the pattern of succeeding American digests, such as John Bassett Moore's *International Law Digest* (1906) in 8 volumes and Hackworth's *Digest of International Law* (1940), also in 8 volumes. The latest are M. M. Whitman's *Digest of International Law* (1963) and Clive Parry's *British Digest of International Law* (1965), which is the first British digest on international law. Such undertakings at national level constitute a valuable development worth following by other governments.

The Commission has had similar experience in collecting the comments of governments on its own circulated documents. Although requests for comments have not been unduly numerous, the results have not been encouraging, either in content or in quantity. According to an analysis of the period 1947–53[3] governments were requested to provide information on six topics and to make comments and observations on six draft proposals. Of 60 members of the UN, 14 made no reply at all to any of the twelve requests; 12 governments replied to only one of the twelve requests, in many cases very briefly and without official comment. No government replied to all of the requests, and only 3 replied to eleven

[1] There is no evidence of the nature of these questionnaires since these materials are not available in the printed records, except in the case of depository practice in respect of reservations: Doc. A/5687, *Y.B.I.L.C.*, 1965, vol. II, pp. 103–4, Annex I.

[2] U.N. Doc. A/CN.4/19, *Y.B.I.L.C.*, vol. II, p. 206; also the replies from Denmark, *ibid.*, p. 206, and from the U.K., p. 221.

[3] H. W. Briggs: 'Official interest in the work of the International Law Commission: Replies of governments to requests for information or comment', *A.J.I.L.*, vol. 48, 1954, pp. 603–12.

requests.[1] The replies in many cases contained little or no substantial information or comment.

Recently, on the question of the future work in the field of codification and progressive development of international law, although the delegations of governments in the GA evinced a very lively interest, only seventeen governments out of more than a hundred members of the United Nations cared to reply to the Secretary General's *note verbale* of January 25, 1961, in pursuance of the GA Resolution 1505(XV) requesting the views of governments.[2]

The Israeli government's reply perhaps expressed the opinion of many other governments when it said that

the experience of the government of Israel—and it believes that this experience is shared by other new and small states—is that adequate preparation for discussions of questions of codification and progressive development (both discussions in the General Assembly and discussions in the *ad hoc* political conferences) imposes a considerable burden on the personnel of the different ministries concerned. This subjective factor may militate against too rapid an acceleration in the completion of projects by the International Law Commission and against too great a proliferation within a short period of time of substantive discussions leading to the completion of the codification process on a given topic.[3]

The replies of the French and Israeli governments, as well as of other governments, only reflect the difficulties faced by the various chancelleries, which are already overburdened in coping with the demands made by the Commission. Comments on the Commission's communications cannot be left to subordinate officials. Moreover, these communications require interdepartmental consultations and decisions at the high level of governments. But, apart from these difficulties, perhaps there are two other factors which tend to make governments reluctant to reply to the Commission's enquiries. Firstly, it is likely that governments think that their replies embodying the official view of states as to the understanding of the law on a given topic, may involve a question of their committing themselves in advance to what they give in writing, or to some change in the law. Secondly, they may hesitate, lest their replies may be relied upon by an opponent against them in some future dispute.[4]

[1] The records of Belgium, Canada, India, Israel, the Netherlands, Norway, Philippines and Sweden were comparatively good with five or six replies each, usually of interest and value. Of 15 states having nationals serving on the International Law Commission, two did not reply to any requests, three replied to one request, and four replied to two requests each: *ibid.*, pp. 610–11.

[2] U.N. Doc. A/C.6/L491, UNGAOR 16th sess. 1961, Annexes, Ag. it. 70, para. 3.

[3] U.N. Doc. A/4796, Annex 4, UNGAOR 16th sess. 1961, vol. 3, Annexes, para. 8.

[4] See Rosenne, 'International Law Commission, 1949–59', *B.Y.B.I.L.*, vol. 36, 1960, p. 146.

Besides, it is probable that more pressing international issues demanding urgent attention seem to leave insufficient time for governments to extend full co-operation in the undertaking of codification.[1]

However, the fault may not lie entirely with the various governments. Zourek pointed out:

Governments were hardly in a position to begin to study drafts submitted to them until September, when the General Assembly began. Since the draft came up for reconsideration in the following April, there were only seven months in which to complete the whole process of study and transmission of comments by governments, translation of the comments, study of the replies and preparation of his conclusions by the Special Rapporteur, translation and distribution of his memorandum by the individual members of the Commission. As a result, the number of replies from governments was relatively small, and many were received so late that they could not be considered either by the Special Rapporteur or by the Commission during the session when the draft articles were examined in the light of the comments by governments.[2]

Zourek further explained that the effective period at the disposal of governments to make comments, from the time of the receipt of the Commission's report to the date by which their replies were supposed to be sent in, was not only insufficient but also inconvenient, since it was during this period that a number of the officials concerned would be absent from their respective countries to attend the General Assembly's session at New York with their national delegation. He proposed, therefore, to give more time to governments to comment on the Commission's first drafts by reviewing them, not at the session immediately following their adoption, but at the subsequent one, by which time such comments should be conveniently available.

The Commission, admitting 'that its work tended to suffer because of defects in the process of obtaining and dealing with the comments of Governments', decided in principle to adopt Zourek's proposal. But, even after this method had been applied in the case of draft articles on consular intercourse and immunities,[3] comments were received from only nineteen governments to enable the Special Rapporteur to prepare his final draft on the subject.[4]

[1] What Elihu Root observed at the beginning of this century still holds good: 'Every Foreign Office is fully occupied with questions that it must decide and, as a rule, foreign offices will not concern themselves with any other questions unless they are moved by some special impulse of external pressure or by the promptings of exceptionally far-sighted policy': 'The function of private codification in international law', *A.J.I.L.*, vol. 5, 1911, p. 580.

[2] *Y.B.I.L.C.*, 1958, vol. I, 464th mtg., p. 175, para. 11.

[3] *Y.B.I.L.C.*, 1958, vol. II, pp. 107–8, paras. 57, 61; *ibid.*, 1959, vol. II, Report of the Commission, Doc. A/4169, chap. III, p. 109, para. 27.

[4] *Y.B.I.L.C.*, 1961, vol. II, Report of the Commission, Doc. A/4843, chap. III, pp. 129–70, Annex 1.

The system of consultation with governments remains a cardinal feature of the procedural side of the codification of international law; without active governmental collaboration codification would be operating in a vacuum and it is vitally important to improve the system. Codification is conceived of as a systematic long-range effort, and if governments are genuinely keen to make it part of their effort, it is suggested that they should collaborate with the Commission in two ways. Firstly, a special section in the legal departments of the foreign offices might be established to enable them to maintain a sustained collaboration with the Commission; such a step would be indicative of the measure of importance they attach to the Commission's work and their responsibilities in this regard. Secondly, the Commission should have at its disposal adequate resources in terms of time and personnel to be in a position to make full use of the material made available by governments as well as other bodies.

Co-operation with other bodies

Several articles of the Commission's Statute recognize the importance of bringing other bodies, national and international, into some relationship with the work of the ILC. Firstly, Article 16, para. (e), authorizes the Commission to consult 'scientific institutions and individual experts' and Article 17 enables it to consider proposals from, and 'to circulate a questionnaire' in connection with its work to the principal organs of the UN, specialized agencies, and intergovernmental bodies established to encourage progressive development of international law. Again, the third chapter of the Statute is entitled 'Co-operation with Other Bodies'. Under it, Article 25 enables the Commission to consult with any organs of the UN on any subject which is within the competence of that organ, and Article 26 confers on the Commission a general power of consulting any international or national organizations, both official and unofficial, if it believes that such a procedure might aid in the performance of its functions. The latter article enjoins the Secretary General to draw up a list of international and national organizations concerned with international law.

Organs of the United Nations. Apart from the General Assembly, the Economic and Social Council is the only organ of the UN which has figured in relation to the activities of the Commission. It will be recalled that the Committee of Seventeen had unanimously recognized the right of the ECOSOC to propose conventions. The ECOSOC took some initiative in the matter of the Genocide Convention when by its Resolution 47(IV) of March 28, 1947, it requested the Secretary General to consult the Committee of Seventeen regarding the preparation of a draft convention on the crime of genocide. The Committee, however, viewed such a function as different in kind from those for which it was constituted. After the Commission was established, it was only in connection with two aspects of the law of nationality that the ECOSOC came into relationship with the ILC, first on the status of women, and, second, on the question of statelessness.[1] The Commission initiated work on both topics in 1951 under the general topic of nationality including statelessness.[2]

There is no other instance of any relationship with any other organ. But several problems (such as the whole question of Charter law; the place in the system of international organizations of various kinds, of individuals and of public and private corporations; the use of international rivers; and the use of outer space) might be suitably studied by the various organs of the UN, so as to move the ILC to formulate a code of general principles and jurisprudence.

Co-operation with non-governmental organizations. The consideration of the application of the provisions relating to international and national organizations was postponed in the first session of the Commission, but, while examining a tentative list[3] of such organizations, prepared by the Secretary General under Article 26, paras. 2 and 3, of the Statute, the Commission then decided against Koretsky's interpretation that the paragraphs 1 and 2 of the above article were closely linked and that the sole purpose of the distribution of documents for which the list was provided 'was to supply the organizations with the necessary documentation so that they could submit their opinion with a full knowledge of all the facts'.[4] In the opinion of the Commission, paragraphs 1 and 2 of Article 26 of

---

[1] ECOSOC Res. 304D(XI) of July 14, 1950, requesting the Commission to undertake drafting of a Convention on the Nationality of Married Women embodying the principles recommended by the ILC on the status of women: Doc. E/1712, ECOSOC, Offl. Records, 11th sess. 1950, Ag. it. 20; also Doc. A/CN.4/33, *T.B.I.L.C.*, 1950, vol. II, p. 363. And Res. 319B(XI) of August 11, 1950, urging the ILC to prepare the necessary draft documents relating to the elimination of the problem of statelessness: Doc. E/1618 and corr. 1, ECOSOC, Offl. Records, 11th sess. 1950, Ag. it. 32; also Doc. A/CN.4/47, *T.B.I.L.C.*, 1951, vol. II, pp. 121–2.

[2] See Report of the Rapporteur, U.N. Doc. A/CN.4/50, *T.B.I.L.C.*, 1952, vol. II, pp. 4–24; *ibid.*, Report of the Commission, U.N. Doc. A/2163, chap. III, pp. 67–8, paras. 25–34; U.N. Docs. A/CN.4/81, A/CN.4/83, A/CN.4/84, *ibid.*, 1954, vol. II, pp. 26–111; *ibid.*, Report of the Commission, Doc. A/2693, chap. II, pp. 141–9, paras. 10–40.

[3] U.N. Doc. A/CN.4/8 (mimeographed only). There were some suggestions for additions to this list at the first session of the Commission, but Kerno (Asst. Secty. Gen.) indicated that further additions could be made at any time and the Secretariat would endeavour to formulate the list in such a way as to include national organizations of all states. *T.B.I.L.C.*, 34th mtg., paras. 85–90; U.N. Doc. A/CN.4/14 (mimeographed only)—another list was issued by the Secretariat.

[4] *T.B.I.L.C.*, 1949, 34th mtg., p. 247, para. 81.

the Statute were not related, and the list referred to in paragraph 2 was meant only for the distribution of the Commission's documents.[1] The matter of co-operation with other bodies came before the Commission again in the 3rd session in 1951 when the Commission's members appreciated the response of many international and national organizations concerned with international law to the Commission's appeal for co-operation in its work. Recognizing the value of such co-operation in preparatory work, the Commission in its report said that 'reports and studies supplied to the Commission by a number of such organizations have been of great value in the Commission's work, particularly that on the régime of the high seas. It has become apparent that in the future the Commission will need to rely even to a greater extent on the contributions which are being made by non-official groups.'[2]

It seems that in the succeeding years the Commission's interest in the co-operation of non-governmental organizations diminished, for it has mentioned them but briefly. Only the memoranda prepared by the Secretariat or the reports submitted by Special Rapporteurs give reference to the work done by private authorities —individuals or groups.[3] The only non-official scientific body with which some collaboration materialized has been the Harvard Law School. It was in connection with the preliminary work on the topic of state responsibility, and largely owing to the initiative of Dr. Liang, the Director of the Codification Division of the Secretariat, that the co-operation with the Harvard Law School Research Centre began. The Secretariat had suggested to the Law School that the Harvard Draft of 1929, prepared in anticipation of the Hague Codification Conference of 1930, might be revised and that a new draft would be of great service to the Commission.[4] Accordingly, the Law School undertook the work under the general super-

[1] *Ibid.*, paras. 82–83. Another question which arose under this article was a request from Mr. Belaunde, Chairman of the Peruvian delegation to the GA to be heard by the ILC, particularly on the Draft Declaration on Rights and Duties of States on which subject Mr. Belaunde had been Rapporteur at the Ninth International Conference of American States at Bogota (1948). The Chairman referred to Article 16, para. (e) and Article 26, paras. 1 and 4 of the Statute in this connection. The Commission decided to invite him for informal discussion rather to establish a precedent of allowing a private individual to participate in the work of the ILC: *ibid.*, 9th mtg., pp. 69–70, paras. 1–8.

[2] *Y.B.I.L.C.*, 1951, vol. I, 124–125th mtgs., pp. 358–9, paras. 56–61, 362, paras. 1–2; vol. II, Report of the Commission, Doc. A/1858, chap. VIII, p. 141, para. 90.

[3] For example, see U.N. Doc. A/CN.4/98, Memorandum by the Secretariat on Diplomatic Intercourse and Immunities, *Y.B.I.L.C.*, 1958, vol. II, pp. 146–52; and U.N. Doc. A/CN.4/23, First Report by J. L. Brierly, Special Rapporteur on Law of Treaties, *Y.B.I.L.C.*, 1950, vol. II, pp. 243–8.

[4] *Y.B.I.L.C.*, 1956, vol. I, 370th mtg., p. 228, para. 16; U.N. Doc. A/CN.4/96, Special Rapporteur's report on State Responsibility, *ibid.*, vol. II, p. 176, paras. 13–14.

vision of Professor Milton Katz and assisted by a distinguished advisory committee composed of professors and practising lawyers. The Special Rapporteur on State Responsibility, Garcia-Amador, and the Harvard School collaborated, and Professor Louis B. Sohn, one of the authors of the Harvard Draft, 'Convention on the International Responsibility of States for Injuries to Aliens (1959), attended the sessions of the Commission in 1959, 1960, and 1961 during the debates on the subject.

The collaboration of the Commission with the Harvard Law School was unfortunately the subject of some criticism in the Sixth Committee at the 15th session of the GA. The initiative of the Secretariat in this matter, the method of preparing the reports and even their substance, the visit of the Special Rapporteur to Harvard and his co-operation with the Law School and the Legal Office of the Pan-American Union, were severely censured by the Russian delegate Morzov.[1] But the co-operation with the School was certainly not incompatible with the relevant provisions of the Statute. Occasion for criticism would perhaps not have arisen if similar institutions, having resources and willingness to co-operate with the ILC, had also been approached. The Institute of International Law and the International Law Association had put on their programme topics which the Commission had selected for codification. Similarly, the Union of International Law of the University of Vienna had encouraged preparation of theses on topics which the Commission planned to study.[2]

The provisions of the Statute regarding co-operation with non-governmental organizations, both national and international, have not been fully made use of by the Commission. Organizations like the Harvard Law School Research Centre, the Institute of International Law, the International Law Association and the American Institute of International Law are capable of preparing studies and drafts which could be of great assistance to the Commission. Besides, in contrast to official organizations, they are more free to take a world perspective and to rise above particular, and frequently

[1] UNGAOR 15th sess. 1960, 6th Com., 657th mtg., paras. 27–28. The main points of criticism were: i. that the collaboration with the School was made without authorization from the Commission, and on the sole initiative of the Secretariat; ii. that it was more objectionable because only one institution was approached and other similar institutions or universities of other countries were ignored; iii. that eight out of ten members of the Commission participating in the debates on the Harvard Draft criticized the text vigorously as it was entirely one-sided work; and iv. that the Secretariat, by taking such initiative, violated the provisions of Article 100, para. 1 of the UN Charter.

[2] Prof. Verosta (Austria) stated this at 743rd mtg. of the Sixth Committee, and proposed that a new list of official and non-official international organizations and national bodies concerned with international law be prepared by the Secretariat: UNGAOR 17th sess. 1962, 6th Com., 743rd mtg., para. 4.

temporary, national interests. In view of the entry of many states from Asia and Africa into the community of nations, and the consequent increasing importance of comparative law studies as a source of international law, the private scientific organizations can be better relied upon for deducing 'the general principles of law recognized by civilized nations'. They have freedom to avail themselves of the services of persons from all over the world, with the knowledge of various national systems of law as well as of international customs and precedents. In the words of Professor Quincy Wright, 'The field of international relations is today complicated and dangerous, but the dynamic ingenuity of private judicial groups, co-operating with experts in all the international disciplines, aware of mankind as a whole, and exerting influence on official international organizations and governments, may, as did the founders of international law in the sixteenth century, gradually create an image of the world of nations capable of influencing decisions towards peace, justice, and progress.'[1] Furthermore, it is submitted that, in our era of science when the successful conduct of scientific projects in certain fields demands a degree of regulation and control, the rôle of scientific organizations in the development of international law cannot be ignored.[2] By seeking co-operation of the private organizations, the Commission would be relieving itself of considerable labour concerned with preparatory work.

CO-OPERATION WITH INTERGOVERNMENTAL ORGANIZATIONS

The intergovernmental organizations regularly mentioned in the Commission's reports from 1954 onwards are the Inter-American Council of Jurists, and the Asian-African Legal Consultative Committee. These two bodies and the Commission have established consultative relationships in the matter of the codification of international law.

The Inter-American Council of Jurists

It may be recalled that the Committee of Seventeen had specially named the organs of the Pan-American Union for consultation by the ILC, and Article 26 para. 4 of the Statute incorporated the same recommendation. The Inter-American Council of Jurists[3] is a com-

---

[1] Wright: 'Activities of the Institute of International Law', *Proc. Am. Soc. Int. Law*, 1960, pp. 199–200.
[2] See J. A. Johnson: 'Scientific organizations and the development of international law', *ibid.*, pp. 206–13.
[3] See above, p. 139.

ponent part of the regional Organization of the American States which has replaced the Pan-American Union. Article 61 of the Charter of the Organization of American States and Article 4 of the Statute of the Inter-American Council of Jurists provide for establishing co-operative relations with the corresponding organs of the UN. The Council of Jurists serves as an advisory body on judicial matters, to promote the development and codification of public and private international law, and to study the possibility of attaining uniformity in the legislation of the various American countries. It was after the Inter-American Council of Jurists had taken some preparatory action in 1950 to establish co-operation with the ILC that the ILC took appropriate steps first in 1954[1] and then in 1955, requesting the Secretary of the Commission to attend the 1956 meeting of the Council of Jurists and to report to the Commission 'concerning such matters discussed by the Council as are also on the agenda of the Commission'.[2] As a result, two matters were reported on: i. system of territorial waters and related questions; and ii. reservations to multilateral treaties.[3] The Inter-American Council of Jurists reciprocated by sending its representative to attend the 8th session of the Commission.[4] Since then, it has been almost a regular feature that the ILC and the Inter-American Council of Jurists reciprocally send observers to attend their respective sessions.[5] Although the value of such representation cannot be measured in concrete terms, and notwithstanding the difference in the scope of their work since one body is regional and the other world-wide, collaboration between them on the topics of common study[6] must be further developed and strengthened so as to attain the common objective, namely the development and codification of the same branch of law.

Asian-African Legal Consultative Committee

The Asian-African Legal Consultative Committee, established originally with the title 'Asian Legal Consultative Committee' in

[1] See, for Garcia-Amador's resolution, *Y.B.I.L.C.*, 1954, vol. II, Report of the Commission, Doc. A/2693, chap. V, pp. 162–3, para. 77.
[2] *Y.B.I.L.C.*, 1955, vol. II, Report of the Commission, Doc. A/2934, p. 42, para. 36.
[3] *Y.B.I.L.C.*, 1956, vol. II, U.N. Doc. A/CN.4/102, chap. I, pp. 238–47. This document includes a brief history of the Inter-American Council of Jurists.
[4] *Ibid.*, Report of the Commission, Doc. A/3159, p. 302, para. 46.
[5] See *Y.B.I.L.C.*, 1960, vol. II, U.N. Doc. A/CN.4/124, Report by the Secretary of the Commission on the proceedings of the Fourth Meeting of the Inter-American Council of Jurists held in 1959, pp. 120–2.
[6] For example, the topics discussed at the Fourth Meeting of the Inter-American Council of Jurists which were on the agenda of the ILC were: i. reservations to multilateral treaties; ii. principles of international law that govern the responsibility of the state; *Y.B.I.L.C.*, 1960, vol. II, U.N. Doc. A/CN.4/124, pp. 124–40.

1956,[1] is an intergovernmental committee of legal experts. The statutory basis for co-operation between the Committee and the ILC is to be found in the provisions of Article 3 of the Statute of the Committee. According to it, one of the objects of the Committee is 'to examine questions that are under consideration of the International Law Commission and to arrange for the views of the Committee to be placed before the Commission; to consider the reports of the Commission and to make recommendations thereon to the governments of the participant countries'.[2] Another function of special interest to the UN and the ILC is 'to communicate, with the consent of the governments of the participating countries, the points of view of the Committee on international legal problems referred to it, to the United Nations, other institutions and international organizations'.[3]

The Committee requested, in 1957, co-operation with the Commission, and directed its Secretary to take certain steps in order to establish consultative relations with the Commission. The Commission placed the Committee on the list of organizations which receive the Commission's documents and expressed its willingness to receive the Committee's observations on the questions under study of the Commission. In 1958, and again in 1959, the Committee invited the Commission to send its observer to its second and third sessions respectively, but, owing to the lateness of the invitation and the closeness of the dates of those sessions, the Commission expressed its inability to send an observer. However, on both occasions the Commission expressed its interest in the reports of the activities of the Committee, particularly those related to the Commission's work. It was for the fourth session of the Committee, held in 1961 at Tokyo, that the Commission, considering that among the topics on

---

[1] It was founded by the Governments of Burma, Ceylon, India, Indonesia, Iraq, Japan and Syria. On the suggestion of Pandit Nehru, the Prime Minister of India, other countries agreed to amend the Statutes of the Committee to enable countries from the African continent to become members as from April 1958 and the Committee's title was changed to the present one. Originally founded for five years by a resolution adopted at the fourth session, member governments were recommended to make it a permanent body, or, at all events, to extend its term for a further period of five years, and at the end of this to reconsider the question. Its permanent secretariat is at New Delhi and the Committee meets yearly in different member countries. See Report of Garcia–Amador, Observer for the Commission for the fourth session of the Asian-African Legal Consultative Committee: U.N. Doc. A/CN.4/139, *Y.B.I.L.C.*, 1961, vol. II, p. 78.

[2] This article 3(a) was amended at the fifth session of the Committee by adding the last part of the article quoted above to the original one with a view to extending the power of the Committee regarding co-operation with the ILC: see Report of Radhabinod Pal, Observer for the Commission at the fifth session of the Committee in 1962 at Rangoon, U.N. Doc. A/CN.4/146, *Y.B.I.L.C.*, 1962, vol. II, p. 152.

[3] See U.N. Doc. A/CN.4/139, *op. cit.*, pp. 79–80, Article 3(d).

the agenda of the Committee was state responsibility, a subject which the Commission itself was discussing at its next session, designated its Special Rapporteur on that subject as its observer.[1] It also decided that appropriate steps were to be taken by the Secretariat to ensure that the organizations with which the Commission was in consultative relationship supplied their documentation to all the members of the Commission. Since then, observers from the Commission as well as from the Committee have been reciprocally invited by both bodies to their respective sessions.

Some members of the Commission have been doubtful of the value of such representation as a whole.[2] The Chairman of the Commission said at the thirteenth session of the Commission that he did not think the Commission 'could establish the principle of regular representation, in view of the considerable expense involved, which was, moreover, all the less justified in view of the extensive exchange of material. Every case should therefore be decided on its own merits and in the light of such possibilities as sending members who happen to be near the locality of the session' (of the regional body).[3] But the question of reciprocal representation between the regional bodies and the Commission should be looked upon as a symbol of co-operation existing between the scientific bodies at the regional level and the one at the international level. Besides, it is common knowledge that the regional movement in Latin America at one stage of its history made a deep impact on the prevailing notions and principles of international law,[4] and the value and importance of the codification efforts in America had also been recognized by the United Nations General Assembly, when it adopted the Statute of the ILC by Resolution 174(II).

Its historic parallel—the regional movement in Asia and Africa —can also make a valuable contribution to the inescapable task and goal of adapting international law to the needs and interests of the international community. The opinions of these regional bodies represent the interests of non-European and new nations and,

[1] For the reports and discussions on these events, see *Y.B.I.L.C.*, 1957, vol. I, p. 172, paras. 1–4, vol. II, p. 144, para. 24; 1958, vol. I, pp. 200–1, paras. 9–17, vol. II, p. 110, para. 73; 1959, vol. II, p. 123, para. 46; 1960, vol. I, pp. 222–3, para. 95, p. 297, paras. 47–49, vol. II, p. 181, para. 43.

[2] See for the views of Tunkin and Padilla Nervo (Chairman), *Y.B.I.L.C.*, vol. I, 1960, 571st mtg., p. 296, paras. 33, 34.

[3] *Y.B.I.L.C.*, 1961, vol. I, 597th mtg., p. 97, para. 5. For the reason of the nearness of a member to the place of the session of a regional body, the Chairman of the Commission, Dr. Tunkin, deputed Mr. Radhabinod Pal as the observer for the Commission at the 5th session of the Asian-African Legal Consultative Committee held at Rangoon in 1962.

[4] See pp. 133–9, above.

through them, the ILC and other organs of the UN may become aware, better than by any other means, as Garcia-Amador appropriately expressed it, 'of the trends which really reflect the new needs and legitimate interests of the countries composing the United Nations'.[1] As regards Europe, the Council of Europe set up, in 1963, a special body, the European Committee on Legal Co-operation, for its members to work together in the legal field. This committee, composed of the delegations of eighteen states and of three delegates of the Consultative Assembly of the Council of Europe, had under consideration various topics which appeared to be connected with the work of the ILC. The Commission has established a relationship with the European Committee like that existing with the juridical bodies of America and Asia.[2] These regional bodies can render valuable services to the Commission because their objectives are those also of the ILC—the codification and development of international law. As far as the common subjects of study are concerned these bodies are capable of doing much preparatory work and of creating a consensus of opinion among the governments at regional level, which may not only facilitate the task of the ILC but also expedite its work. For that reason, the Commission, at its 15th session, expressed the hope that 'the relevant regulations of the United Nations would be so adapted as to ensure a better exchange of documentation between the Commission and the bodies with which it co-operates', and recommended the Secretariat to make whatever new arrangements were needed for the purpose.[3] Indeed, apart from the mere exchange of representatives and documents, some kind of co-ordination of the work and consultations with these regional official organs is still necessary to make their co-operation with the Commission more fruitful.

[1] See statement by Garcia-Amador at the 4th session of the Asian-African Legal Consultative Committee held at Tokyo in 1961: *Y.B.I.L.C.*, 1961, vol. II, pp. 84–5, Annex 2 to Doc. A/CN.4/139. Also Letter of Hafez Sabek, observer for the Asian-African Legal Consultative Committee, addressed to the Chairman of the ILC, dated June 26, 1961, *ibid.*, p. 85.

[2] U.N. Doc. A/6309/Rev. 1, *Y.B.I.L.C.*, 1966, vol. II, Report of the ILC, pt. II, chap. IV, para. 78, p. 278.

[3] U.N. Doc. A/5509/Report of the 15th sess. of the ILC, UNGAOR 18th sess. 1963, suppl. no. 9, p. 38, para. 70.

CHAPTER SIX

THE ACHIEVEMENTS OF
THE COMMISSION

How optimistic one may be about the future prospects of the general codification of international law may be judged from an assessment of the achievements of the International Law Commission after some two decades of its work. A review of that work, made in the context of contemporary conditions and problems and seen against the history of the codification movement during the past hundred years, will also indicate the rate of progress in codification that has so recently been achieved.

WORK COMPLETED

The work already completed by the Commission may for convenience of study be divided into two categories: i. matters specially referred to the Commission by the General Assembly; ii. matters forming part of the Commission's own programme of codification as drawn up at its first session in 1949, or subsequently directed by the G.A. for priority treatment.

SPECIAL ASSIGNMENTS BY THE GENERAL ASSEMBLY

A considerable amount of the Commission's time has in fact been taken up by the special assignments referred by the General Assembly for opinion, report or proposals rather than for codification as such. Very often, those who demand quicker progress in the production of texts for submission to international conferences fail to take account of the Commission's work in this category. These special assignments have consisted of: Draft Declaration on Rights and Duties of States; Formulation of the Nuremberg Principles; Draft Code of Offences against the Peace and Security of Mankind; Question of Defining Aggression; Question of International Criminal Jurisdiction; Making Evidence of Customary International Law more readily available; Question of Reservations to Multilateral Conventions; Question of Extended Participation in General Multilateral Treaties concluded under the auspices of the League of Nations.

Draft Declaration on Rights and Duties of States

This, the first of the tasks specially assigned by the GA, was taken up by the Commission at its first session. The Commission was to prepare a 'Draft Declaration on the Rights and Duties of States' on the basis of the draft presented by Panama, taking into consideration the other documents and drafts on the subject.[1]

The Panama draft, which consisted of 24 articles in the form of a convention, was claimed by Dr. Ricardo J. Alfaro, the Minister for Foreign Affairs of the Republic of Panama and a member of the Commission, to be based upon various leading official and unofficial drafts prepared in the past, the Covenant of the League of Nations and the UN Charter.

It was examined article by article by the Commission and subjected to three readings.[2] Each of the articles adopted embodied the preponderant support of the Commission's members. The Commission reduced the Panama Draft to 14 articles, and made them very brief and shorn of titles.[3]

The draft Declaration adopted by the Commission was governed by four guiding considerations: i. that it should be in harmony with the provisions of the Charter of the UN; ii. that it should be applicable only to sovereign states; iii. that it should envisage all sovereign states of the world and not only the members of the UN; iv. that it should embrace certain basic rights and duties of states.

The draft Declaration declared four rights of states—of independence comprehending the right to exercise freely all their legal powers, including the choice of their own form of government; of jurisdiction over state territory in accordance with international law; of equality in law; and of self-defence, individual or collective, against armed attack.

Ten duties of states, expressed at greater length, were as follows: of conducting international relations in accordance with international law and of observing their legal obligations; of settling disputes by peaceful means and in accordance with law and justice;

---

[1] U.N. Doc. A/AC.10/53 of June 16, 1947, Report of the Committee of Seventeen, *A.J.I.L.*, vol. 41, 1947, suppl. pp. 27–8. Also GA Res. 178(11) of November 21, 1947. For the entire previous history of the project see Preparatory Study Concerning A Draft Declaration on the Rights and Duties of States, U.N. Doc. A/CN.4/2 1947. This document contained virtually everything which the Commission could require on the subject.

[2] *Y.B.I.L.C.*, 1949, 7th, 16th, 19th–25th, 29th and 30th mtgs.

[3] *Ibid.*, 25th, mtg., pp. 178–9, The sub-committee on the draft Declaration in its draft proposed sixteen articles. Its preamble stressed the principle of universality and the obligatory character of the UN, see U.N. Doc. A/CN.4/W5 incorporated in U.N. Doc. A/CN.4/SR19, also *Y.B.I.L.C.*, 1949, 19th mtg., p. 135, n. 2; U.N. Doc. A/CN.4/W7 draft after second reading, U.N. Doc. A/CN.4/W8 for draft after third reading. *ibid.*, pp. 163–4, n. 1.

of refraining from assisting any state resorting to war or other illegal use of force, or any state against which the UN is taking preventive or enforcement action; of refraining from recognizing any territorial acquisition resulting from war or other illegal use of force; of refraining from fomenting civil strife in the territory of another state and of preventing the organized incitement thereof from within their own territory; of ensuring, in general, that conditions in their own territory do not menace international peace and order; and of treating all persons within their jurisdiction with due respect for human rights and fundamental freedom for all, without distinction as to race, sex, language or religion.[1]

Several of these duties seem to overlap each other as well as comprehend all others. The commentary following each article revealed that the text was derived from the Panamanian draft. Chiefly the Commission only selected what in that draft was *lex lata*, and stated it usually in the language of the Charter, which in itself is considered to constitute general international law.

The Commission's draft declaration, while it combined some of the articles of the Panamanian Draft which were somewhat tautologous, dropped two articles: one relating to the definition of a state (which in the opinion of the Commission was unnecessary), and another relating to a state's right to exist and preserve its existence and to have it recognized by other states (which was considered to be too delicate and too fraught with political implications).[2] Its important features were that, like a declaration of basic rights and duties, it formulated the rights and duties of states only in general terms, the extent and modalities of the application of which required to be determined by more precise rules. Secondly, unlike the original draft, it was not given the form of a convention or a system of binding rules, but rather a declaration to be adopted and proclaimed by the GA as a standard of conduct. Thirdly, it was deemed to be neither the work of progressive development nor of codification,[3] but a special kind of work which related to both at the same time. It was not thought necessary to send the draft to governments for

---

[1] Hudson voted against the draft because the last of the duties enumerated above and embodied in Article 6 of the draft 'went beyond the Charter of the United Nations, and beyond international law at its present stage of development'. Koretsky also dissented because, apart from other shortcomings, the draft did not protect the interests of states against intervention within their domestic jurisdiction by international organizations or groups of states, and ignored some of the important duties of states: *Y.B.I.L.C.*, 1949, Report of the Commission, U.N. Doc. A/925, pt. II, p. 287, n. 21.

[2] *Ibid.*, p. 289, paras. 49–50.

[3] A long debate followed on the procedure after the adoption of the draft declaration at the Commission's 25th mtg., Koretsky dissenting from the Commission's decision to leave it to the GA whether or not to transmit the draft to member governments for comments.

T

comments in accordance with Articles 16 and 21 of the Statute, which course was left to the GA to decide.

The draft was considered by the Sixth Committee of the GA at its 4th session which led to Resolution 375(IV) of December 6, 1949, requesting member states to give their comments and suggestions, particularly on whether the Assembly should take any further action on the draft declaration and, if so, the nature of such action.[1] But, by 1950 only 11 replies had been received, and the GA deferred this item until its sixth session in 1951, when, again because of the insufficient number of replies, it decided by Resolution 596(VI) on the basis of its Sixth Committee's report (A/1982) to postpone the consideration of the matter until the requisite number of states had made comments.[2]

The Nuremberg principles

The GA previously, by Resolution 95(1) of December 11th, 1946, affirmed the principles of international law recognized in the Charter and judgment of the International Military Tribunal of Nuremberg, and, in accordance with the recommendation of the Committee of Seventeen,[3] by Resolution 177(11) of November 21, 1947, directed the Commission in rather imperative terms, to *formulate* these principles and prepare a draft code of offences against the peace and security of mankind.

When the Commission undertook a preliminary consideration of the subject at its first session, it found some inconsistency between the GA's affirming the relevant principles and its calling for their formulation. It also found some ambiguity in the term 'formulation'.[4] The questions which arose were: Whether the Commission was to analyse those principles and criticize them before deciding to what extent they were in conformity with international law; whether it was merely to transcribe those principles officially as principles of international law; whether it was to perform simple legal drafting of already recognized principles, or to confine its attention to only those parts of the Nuremberg Charter and Judgment which in the Commission's opinion constituted principles of international law as distinct from what the Charter and Judgment recognized as international law.[5]

[1] UNGAOR 4th sess. 1949, pl. mtgs., 270th mtg.
[2] U.N. Doc. A/1338, and Add. I, and A/1982, UNGAOR 6th sess. 1951–2, Annexes, Ag. it. 48.
[3] U.N. Doc. A/AC.10/52 of June 17, 1947 (reproduced in *A.J.I.L.*, vol. 41, 1947, suppl. pp. 26–7).
[4] See D. H. N. Johnson: 'The draft code of offences against the peace and security of mankind', *I.C.L.Q.*, vol. 4, 1955, pp. 446–7.
[5] *Y.B.I.L.C.*, 1949, 17th mtg., pp. 129–33.

The Commission had before it the preparatory work submitted by the Secretary General entitled 'The Charter and Judgment of the Nuremberg Tribunal; History and Analysis'.[1] This exhaustive document did not sufficiently help the Commission on the above questions, nor did it emphasize the historical connection between the project for the 'formulation' of the Nuremberg principles and that of the preparation of a somewhat wider code of international offences and the enshrinement of the former amongst the provisions of the latter. The Commission, however, adopted a cautious course by deciding that it was not asked to express an appreciation of the principles applied in the Charter and the Judgment of the Tribunal at Nuremberg as principles of international law; it was asked merely to give formulation to those principles without any indication of their authority.[2] The Commission also decided then that its task was to formulate principles of a substantial character and, in particular, those contained in Articles 6, 7 and 8 of the Nuremberg Charter. These two important decisions by which the Commission interpreted its terms of reference, determined the scope of this particular assignment.

A Sub-Committee appointed by the Commission submitted a working paper containing a formulation of Nuremberg principles[3] which served as a basis for the Commission's work. The Commission had at first adopted the course of dealing with the Nuremberg principles in isolation, but during the course of considering the revised draft of the sub-committee, it noted that the task of formulating the principles 'appeared to be so closely connected with that of preparing a draft code of offences against the peace and security of mankind that it would be premature for the Commission to give a final formulation to these principles before the work of preparing the draft code was further advanced'.[4] Spiropoulos, who was appointed

[1] U.N. Doc. A/CN.4/5. This document, in Part I paraphrased the Moscow Declaration of 1943, the London Agreement of 1945, the Charter, the indictment and the verdicts and sentences of the Tribunal; in Part II, it explained the historical background leading up to the entrusting of the Commission with the question of the Nuremberg principles; and in Part III, it gave an exhaustive analysis of the Charter, the indictment, the defence and the Judgment. In the Addendum it gave a comparison between the Charter and judgment of the International Military Tribunal for the Far East, and those of the Nuremberg Tribunal. See also U.N. Doc. A/CN.4/22, *Y.B.I.L.C.* 1950, vol. II, pp. 182–9.
[2] *Y.B.I.L.C.*, 1949. Report of the Commission, U.N. Doc. A/925, chap. III, p. 286, para. 26; *ibid.*, 17th mtg., p. 133, para. 35 (Chairman). This was approved by the GA in 1949. The question was re-opened by Hudson at the 44th mtg., *Y.B.I.L.C.*, 1950, vol. I, p. 29, para. 77. For divergent opinions in the Sixth Committee, see U.N. Doc. A/1639, UNGAOR 5th sess. 1950, Annexes, Ag. it. 52; pt. IV, paras. 23–34.
[3] U.N. Doc. A/CN.4/W16, *Y.B.I.L.C.*, 1949, 25th mtg., p. 183 n. 9; revised draft, U.N. Doc. A/CN.4/W2, *ibid.*, 31st mtg., p. 227 n. 8.
[4] *Y.B.I.L.C.*, 1949, Report of the Commission, chap. III, pp. 282–3, para. 29.

Special Rapporteur, worked during the interval between first and second session of the Commission and presented his report (A/CN/4. 22)[1] on the basis of which the Commission adopted a formulation of the Nuremberg principles of international law.

The text prepared by the Commission formulated seven principles and explained their basis in the commentary.[2] It does not represent a statement of all the principles in the Charter and Judgment of Nuremberg, but gives only a succinct restatement summarizing the main principles applied by the Court, particularly as derived from Articles 6, 7 and 8 of the Charter. It leaned heavily on the Nuremberg Charter in formulating the principles.[3]

In the Sixth Committee of the GA, too many contradictory opinions were expressed to permit conclusions on the Commission's formulation.[4] The GA neither approved nor disapproved the formulations as submitted, but, by Resolution 488(V) of December 12, 1950,[5] requested the Commission to take account in its final work on the draft code of offences against the peace and security of mankind of the observations of delegations at that session, and the further observations invited from governments of member states.

The Commission's formulation of the Nuremberg principles must be regarded as an accomplished fact. It is a document of international law deriving its significance as a succinct restatement of the law of Nuremberg from an authoritative legal body. If the Assembly Resolutions 95(I) and 177(II) be regarded as an affirmation of the Nuremberg Charter by the quasi-totality of states in the UN and as an expression of international law,[6] then there is much weight in the

---

[1] *Y.B.I.L.C.*, 1950, vol. II, pp. 182–95. Also vol. I, 44–49th and 54th mtgs.

[2] U.N. Doc. A/CN.4/L2 in the Commission's Report A/1316, pt. III, *Y.B.I.L.C.*, 1950, vol. II, pp. 374–8.

[3] By GA Resolution 499(V) of December 12, 1950, governments of member states were invited to furnish their observations on the principles formulated by the ILC. Only seven governments sent their observations: see U.N. Doc. A/CN.4/45 and Add. 1–2, *Y.B.I.L.C.*, 1961, vol. II, pp. 104–9. The repetition in Principle VI of the formulation of the Charter was the subject of criticism in the Sixth Committee of the GA: see UNGAOR 5th sess. 1950, 6th Com., 232nd, 233rd, 235th and 236th mtgs.; also U.N. Doc. A/1639, *ibid.*, Annexes, vol. II, Ag. it. 52, para. 27.

[4] See for summary of views expressed by delegations U.N. Doc. A/CN.4/44, Second Report by Spiropoulos on the draft code, *Y.B.I.L.C.*, 1951, vol. II, pp. 45–57, chap. 1.c. Also Yuen Li-Liang: 'The Second Session of the International Law Commission: Review of its work by the General Assembly', *A.J.I.L.*, vol. 45, 1951, pp. 519–22.

[5] UNGAOR 5th sess. 1950, pl. mtgs., 320th, p. 604. See U.N. Doc. A/1639, *op. cit.*, paras. 21–34.

[6] On the effect of these resolutions there has been considerable debate as to whether they confirm Nuremberg Law as a part of international law, or merely express moral support for the proceedings and their outcome, or depreciate the Charter by implying that as a *lex specialis* it could not become part of general international law until carefully produced into the form of formulation and generally approved and accepted; see C. Parry, 'Some considerations upon the content

submission that 'the majority of states are now estopped from denying that the substantive aspects of the Charter and Judgment of
Nuremberg have become part of the positive law'.[1]

Draft Code of Offences against the Peace and Security of Mankind.

This question, despite its interconnection with the formulation
of the Nuremberg principles, due both to the GA Res. 178(II)
and to the proceedings of organs of the UN which resulted in the
adoption of that resolution, was a distinct item of the agenda of
the ILC.[2]

At its first session, the Commission decided to classify the task
relating to the question of the preparation of a draft code of offences
against the peace and security of mankind, as one of 'progressive
development' rather than codification, and provided for the application to it of the procedure laid down in Article 16 of the Statute.
Realizing that the question appeared to be closely connected with
that of formulating the Nuremberg principles, the same member
of the Commission, Spiropoulos, was appointed as Rapporteur for
both the tasks. He was directed to prepare a working paper on the
subject, and a questionnaire was to be circulated to governments
inquiring what offences, apart from those defined in the Charter
and Judgment of Nuremberg should in their view be comprehended
in the draft code.[3]

At the second session of the Commission, in 1950 the Commission
considered the first report of Spiropoulos[4] and the replies received
from Governments to its questionnaire.[5] The report of Spiropoulos
made it clear that the task of preparing draft codes was, to a large
extent, of a speculative nature, and the determining factor was the
chance which each of the solutions would have of receiving the

---

of a Draft Code of Offences against the Peace and Security of Mankind', *I.L.Q.*
vol. 3, 1950, pp. 208–27; D. Johnson: 'Draft Code of Offences against the Peace
and Security of Mankind', *I. & C.L.Q.*, vol. 4, 1955, pp. 446–7; R. J. Woetzel:
The Nuremberg Trials in International Law, 1960, p. 233; C. A. Pompe: *Aggressive
War, an International Crime*, 1953, pp. 309–38.

[1] I. Brownlie: *International Law and the Use of Force by States*, 1963, pp. 193–4; see
chap. IX, pp. 167–94 for extensive references and discussion on the subject. G.
Schwarzenberger: 'The problem of an international criminal law', *C.L.P.*, vol.
III, 1950, p. 291.

[2] See for the historical background, particularly the correspondence between
Justice Biddle, American member of the Nuremberg Tribunal, and President
Truman which suggested drafting a code of international criminal law and
resulted in the GA Res. 95(I) of December 11, 1946, directing the Committee of
Seventeen to treat as a matter of primary importance plans for the formulation of
an International Criminal Code, U.N. Doc. A/CN.4/25, pp. 253–78.

[3] *Y.B.I.L.C.*, 1949, Report of the Commission, U.N. Doc. A/925, p. 283, paras.
30–31.

[4] U.N. Doc. A/CN.4/25, *op. cit.*, pp. 253–78.

[5] U.N. Doc. A/CN.4/19 and add. 1 and 2, *Y.B.I.L.C.*, 1950, pp. 249–53.

approval of governments. It presented the 'bases of discussion' derived from international practice, the Nuremberg Charter, the Charter of the UN, and the Draft Declaration on Rights and Duties of States elaborated by the ILC. The non-official text specially mentioned in the report was 'The Plan for a World Criminal Code' drawn up by Professor V. V. Pella which was used as a basis for the work of the International Association of Penal Law,[1] the Inter-Parliamentary Union and the International Law Association.[2] Since no preparatory work or specific material on the subject was presented by the Secretariat on the subject, this report greatly helped the Commission in accomplishing its task. The Commission appointed a drafting committee of three to prepare a provisional text (A/CN.4/R6), which was referred without discussion to Spiropoulos to prepare a new report on its basis.[3]

At the third session in 1951, the Commission adopted a definitive code of mankind on the basis of the second report of Spiropoulos[4] which contained a revised draft code and a digest of observations on the Commission's formulation of the Nuremberg principles made by delegations at the Assembly's 5th session. It had also considered observations from governments (A/CN.4/45, corr. 1 and add. 1 and 2).[5] The Draft Code presented by the Commission for the GA's consideration had five articles and listed many acts which were not punishable under Nuremberg law. It classified the crimes into the same general divisions of crimes against peace, war crimes and crimes against humanity, and declared illegal the conspiracy to commit any of those acts. It confined the meaning of the term 'offences against the peace and security of mankind' to offences which contain a political element and disturb peace and security, omitting such offences as piracy or counterfeiting, or conflicts of legislation and jurisdiction in international criminal matters. It limited the subject also to the criminal responsibility of individuals.[6]

The Commission refrained from proposing methods for imple-

[1] Professor Vespasien V. Pella, President of the Association Internationale de Droit Pénal and a noted Rumanian jurist, was requested, in anticipation of the second session of the ILC, by the Secretariat of the United Nations to prepare a memorandum on the Draft Code of Offences against the Peace and Security of Mankind and also a memorandum on the Establishment of an International Criminal Court. His Memorandum on the Draft Code of Offences was a document of 220 mimeographed pages, U.N. Doc. A/CN.4/39, *Y.B.I.L.C.*, 1950, vol. II, pp. 278-362. See also A. K. Kuhn, 'The Pella Memoranda relating to international crimes and criminal jurisdiction', *A.J.I.L.*, vol. 46, 1952, pp. 129-30.
[2] U.N. Doc. A/CN.4/25, *op. cit.*, p. 255, para. 3.
[3] *Y.B.I.L.C.*, 1950, vol. I, 54th-62nd and 72nd mtgs.; *ibid.*, vol. II, Report of the Commission, U.N Doc A/1316, pt. V, pp. 379-80, paras. 146-157.
[4] U.N. Doc. A/CN.4/44, *Y.B.I.L.C.*, 1951, vol. II, pp. 40-60.
[5] *Y.B.I.L.C.*, 1951, vol. II, pp. 104-9.
[6] *Y.B.I.L.C.*, 1951, vol. II, Report of the Commission, U.N. Doc. A/1858, p. 134, para. 52(a) and (c).

menting the code, and thought that its implementation as a transitional measure might be achieved through national courts pending the establishment of an international court.[1] It also did not try to incorporate the Nuremberg principles in their entirety in the draft code as it felt that it was not precluded from modifying them to an undefined extent in the interests of sound legislation.[2]

The GA postponed consideration of this draft in 1951, and for two consecutive years omitted it from its agenda in view of the Commission's continuing study in the light of the comments from governments.[3] The Commission produced a revised draft on the basis of the third report of Spiropoulos.[4]

The revised draft[5] contained four articles which defined offences against the peace and security of mankind as 'crimes under international law, for which responsible individuals shall be punished'. This omitted Article 5 of the previous text which provided for the punishment of the offences by a competent tribunal, as it felt that, at the present stage, only certain legal principles regarding criminal liability under international law should be attempted. It enumerated, in Article 2, 13 specific acts as offences; declaring that a person committing any of these offences could not be absolved from responsibility on the ground that he acted as Head of State or as a responsible government official, and held that a person charged with any of these offences could not be relieved of responsibility in international law on the plea of superior orders, provided that in the circumstances of time it was possible for him not to comply with the order.[6]

The General Assembly again postponed consideration of the Draft Code of Offences Against the Peace and Security of Mankind, in 1954 and then again in 1957, until the question of the definition of aggression was first considered by it. The failure of the Assembly to make further progress with the Draft Code of Offences has been largely due to political causes.[7] Like the League of Nations, the UN also has experienced that it is frequently impossible to make progress in one field without parallel and complementary progress in other fields. Just as the questions relating to disarmament, security, and pacific settlement of disputes are intimately interrelated, so the

---

[1] *Ibid.*, para. 52(d).   [2] *Ibid.*, para. 52(b).
[3] U.N. Doc. A/2162 and add. 1.
[4] U.N. Doc. A/CN.4/85, *Y.B.I.L.C.*, 1954, vol. II, pp. 112–22.
[5] *Y.B.I.L.C.*, 1954, Report of the Commission, U.N. Doc. A/2693, chap. III, pp. 151–2, para. 54.
[6] Lauterpacht, Pal and Edmonds regarded the draft as unpractical and abstained from voting: *Y.B.I.L.C.*, 1954, vol. I, p. 151, para. 20; pp. 176–7, paras. 24–29.
[7] See for Debate in the Sixth Committee, UNGAOR 9th sess. 1954, 6th Com., 396th and 420th–425th mtgs., U.N. Docs. A/3650 and A/3770, UNGAOR 12th sess. 1957, Annexes, Ag. it. 55.

question of international offences and their punishment is inextricably bound up with the proposed international criminal law, which
is linked with the values which it is designed to protect.[1] Hence, by
the 9th Session of the GA, the question of the Draft Code of Offences
was seen to be completely merged in the question of defining
aggression, over which the majority of states remain seriously
divided.

However, the Draft Code has also been criticized. The distinction
between offences 'which contain a political element' and those
which do not, and the exclusion of the 'non-political' crimes from the
international crimes are regarded as unfortunate and harmful.[2]
Suggestions have been made for the change of the title from the
present one, which has limited connotations, to a more comprehensive one such as 'the Code of Crimes against Mankind'—a title
thought to be consistent with the aims and objects of the GA Resolution 178(II). This change would enable the codifying body to aim
at including eventually all the offences detrimental to the unity and
integrity of mankind, whether they are political or non-political.[3]
Secondly, the Draft Code has erred in dealing with the criminal
responsibility of individuals only, and not with that of states.[4] The
central crime against peace mentioned in the Draft Code is the act
of aggression which can be normally committed by an individual
only by obtaining control of the agencies of a state. Considering that
the Commission's work on the Draft Code is regarded as *lex ferenda*,
it would seem desirable for the Commission to carry one stage
further the development of international criminal law by emphasizing that the responsibility of states and individuals for international crimes is not necessarily exclusive.[5] Moreover, both the

---

[1] See Parry, 'Some considerations upon the content of a Draft Code of Offences
. . .', *I.L.Q.*, vol. 3, 1950, p. 208.
Professor Pella's notion of the functions of the proposed code was expressed in
his memorandum: 'Just as in order to protect the existence of the individual,
criminal law punishes all offences against human life, bodily integrity, health,
etc., and as in order to protect the existence of the state, criminal law treats as
criminal all acts directed against the independence or integrity of the state,
including the institutions governing political, economic and social life, so, in order
to protect the peaceful existence of the international community, criminal law
should punish all acts which endanger peaceful relations between states': U.N.
Doc. A/CN.4/39, *op. cit.*

[2] As Dr. Johnson has appropriately observed 'It serves to preserve the notion,
otherwise contradicted by the Code, that crimes committed in the sphere of
relations between states are of a different order from other crimes. The maintenance of this distinction would strike a blow, not merely at the unity and integrity
of the Code but also at the unity and integrity of mankind itself': *I. & C.L.Q.*,
vol. 4, 1955, pp. 456–7. See also Parry, *op. cit.*, p. 208; Pompe, *op. cit.*, p. 338 ff.

[3] Johnson: *op. cit.*, pp. 458, 460.

[4] See D. W. Bowett: *Self-Defence in International Law*, 1958, p. 268.

[5] Johnson: *op. cit.*, pp. 460–5; see also opening address of Sir Hartley Shawcross
before the International Military Tribunal on December 4, 1945, *Trial of the*

inclusions as well as exclusions in the definition of aggression given in Article 2 of the Commission's draft tend to be too vague and inexhaustive and leave scope for wide diversity of interpretations. The solution of the definition of aggression is a *sine qua non* of any further progress with the Code. But it raises most serious questions in the context of 'cold war' when the character of the political system of a country is a matter of grave concern and rivalry for 'super powers'.[1]

The Draft Code further involves the problem of its implementation. Since the crimes against peace are necessarily committed by the authorities of state, the question of their trial by national courts obviously remains largely theoretical. The conditions of impartial administration of justice, and of fair and effective implementation of the Code in punishing the authorities of a state or their accomplices, can be guaranteed only by the establishment of a permanent international criminal tribunal.[2]

The Draft Code was intended to establish well-written rules of international criminal law. At present it represents only the opinion of the Commission on the form the international criminal law should take in the future. It does not contain an element of positive law. The content of the draft codes drawn up by the Commission represents the law applicable when jurisdiction is obtained by *ad hoc* consent or by treaty, or when states incorporate such provisions in their internal law. Until and unless accepted by the states and enacted in the form of a treaty or a Statute between them, it is the Nuremberg law which would continue to retain its validity as case law for the international community.

Question of Defining Aggression

With regard to the definition of aggression the United Nations has found itself on the horns of a dilemma since its very inception. Although the Charter of the UN used the words 'act of aggression'

Major War Criminals, H.M.S.O., 1947, vol. III, pp. 104–5. Also the main operative provisions of the Draft Code contained in Article 2. The first nine paragraphs are directly or indirectly concerned with the question of aggression and no fewer than nine instances are of acts constituting 'offences against the peace and security of mankind' which can be committed only by 'the authorities of a state': *Y.B.I.L.C.*, 1954, vol. II, Report of the Commission, U.N. Doc. A/2693, p. 151, paras. 1–9. In paras. 10 and 11 are the offences which may be committed by 'the authorities of a state or by private individuals'.

[1] See C. G. Fenwick: 'Draft Code of Offences against the Peace and Security of Mankind', *A.J.I.L.*, vol. 46, 1952, pp. 98–100. With reference to the U.S. Mutual Security Act of 1951 the author observed that the terms of that law made the consideration of the Draft Code by the GA wholly impracticable. See also P. B. Potter: 'Offences against the peace and security of mankind', *ibid.*, pp. 101–2; Pompe: *Aggressive War*, pp. 338–53; Bowett: *Self-Defence in Int. Law*, pp. 46–50.

[2] See Brownlie: *Int. Law and Use of Force*, pp. 195–213; Pompe: *Aggressive War*, pp. 356–7.

in Article 39, it left the determination of their meaning to the Security Council.[1] But the logical conclusion of the 'affirmation' of the Nuremberg principles and their formulation, and the decision to prepare a Code of Offences in which those principles would be accorded a place, led the General Assembly at its 5th session in 1950 to refer the question of defining aggression to the Commission.[2]

In pursuance of Resolution 378B(V) of the GA, the ILC considered the question at the 3rd session in 1951. The majority of the Commission interpreted the resolution as a request to attempt to define aggression and report results. The Commission had before it the report by Spiropoulos entitled 'The Possibility and Desirability of a Definition of Aggression' which concluded that a legal definition of aggression would be an artificial construction, which could not be comprehensive enough to comprise all imaginable cases of aggression, since the methods of aggression are in a constant process of evolution.[3] It considered two types of definitions, one using general terms, and the other proceeding by enumeration.[4] It soon abandoned enumeration, not only because thereby the concept of aggression could not be exhausted, but also because the judgment of organs applying the Code in future might thereby be unduly limited.[5] The Commission, however, could not agree even on any general definition. The definition, finally formulated but not adopted, ran: 'Aggression is the threat or use of force by a State or Government against other State, in any manner, whatever the weapons employed and whether openly or otherwise, for any reason or for any purpose other than individual or collective self-defence or in pursuance of a decision or recommendation by a competent

---

[1] The San Francisco Conference had decided not to include a definition of aggression in the Charter of the UN: UNCIO, 1945, vol. 12, chap. 8, sect. B, p. 505.

[2] It was felt that if aggression were not defined it would not be possible to prepare a satisfactory code of offences against the peace and security of mankind in which the Nuremberg principles would be enshrined. The GA Resolution 378B(V) of November 17, 1950 was adopted as a result of a proposal by the U.S.S.R. in connection with the agenda item 'Duties of States in the Event of an Outbreak of Hostilities': *Y.B.I.L.C.*, 1950, vol. II, Report of the Commission, U.N. Doc. A/1316, p. 131; also Doc. A/CN.4/44. Second Report by J. Spiropoulos, Special Rapporteur on the Draft Code of Offences, *ibid.*, p. 60, paras. 132–133. This document gives an historical account of the attempts made in the past to define aggression. See also U.N. Doc. A/AC.10/52. Report of the Committee of Seventeen of June 17, 1947, reproduced in *A.J.I.L.*, 1947, vol. 41, suppl. pp. 26–7, para. 2.

[3] U.N. Doc. A/CN.4/44. *op. cit.*, p. 69, paras. 165–170.

[4] Memoranda submitted by Amado (A/CN.4/L6); Yepes (A/CN.4/L7); Alfaro (A/CN.4/L8); Scelle (A/CN4/L19); Proposals by Cordova (A/CN.4/L10); and Hsü (A/CN.4/L11); and Yepes (A/CN.44/L12): *Y.B.L.I.C.*, 1951, vol. 2, pp. 28–42; *ibid.*, vol. I, 92nd–96th, 108th, 109th, 127th–129th, and 133rd mtgs.

[5] *Y.B.L.I.C.*, 1951, Report of the Commission, U.N. Doc. A/1858, chap. IV, p. 132, paras. 45–46.

organ of the United Nations.'[1] By way of compromise, Article 2 of the Commission's Draft Code of Offences has declared an 'act of aggression' criminal without defining aggression.

The failure of the ILC to define aggression, and also of the GA to arrive at an agreed notion of aggression,[2] is illustrative of the result of attempting to legislate prematurely before the law is allowed to crystallize through international practice.[3] But so long as aggression is considered the supreme international crime, there is a case for continuing the attempt to clarify it.[4] In fact, similar to crimes in municipal law, international crimes require meticulous definition in order to avoid the charges of retroactivity in the absence of a single authoritative international legislature, and to prevent discrepancies when international criminal law is applied by municipal or *ad hoc* international tribunals pending the establishment of an international criminal court. However, the difficulty in enclosing the concept of aggression in any legal definition in the present state of international relations is due to the fact that in any concrete case the finding involves political and military judgments and a subjective weighing of motives which in the context of ideological differences and the cold war renders the problem all the more complicated.[5] Nevertheless, as Dr. Bowett has pointed out, the problem of the definition of aggression has become intractable because it has been treated without regard to the purpose for which the definition

[1] *Ibid.*, para. 49, This definition was based on the draft definition of Alfaro (A/CN.4/L8). See C. H. M. Waldock: 'The regulation of the use of force by individual states in international law,' *Recueil des Cours*, II, 1952, chap. V., pp. 506–14. The author throws light on the three main schools of thought that have appeared in the debates in the UN: i. the enumerative school led by the Soviet Union; ii. the general definition school led by France; and iii. The No-definition school led by the U.S.A., the U.K. and Greece. See also Bowett, *Self-Defence in Int. Law*, pp. 249–68, for criticism of the emphasis generally placed upon the inter-relation of the two concepts of self-defence and aggression.

[2] The GA has entrusted to one committee after another, ever since 1952, the procedural task of studying the replies of governments and determining the time when the question of defining aggression could be appropriately dealt with by the Assembly. The special committee which met in 1959, 1962 and 1965 on each occasion found itself unable to reach a decision and so has adjourned its deliberations each time: see A/AC.91/2, 91/3 and 91/5, mimeographed documents, for the reports of the committee.

[3] For extensive critical analysis of attempts defining aggression under the UN, see Bowett: *op. cit.*, pp. 267–8. Also Julius Stone: *Aggression and World Order*, 1958, pp. 41–77; at p. 79, he presents a case against definition. For the reasons of failure see Stone: *Legal Controls of International Conflict*, 1954, pp. 330–1.

[4] Brownlie is not discouraged by the failure of various bodies to formulate a definition of aggression which according to him 'indicates the difficulty of the problem but no more': *Int. Law and Use of Force*, p. 355; see also Q. Wright: 'The prevention of aggression', *A.J.I.L.*, vol. 50, 1956, pp. 514–32.

[5] For the practice of the UN in assessing the claims to the use of force by sovereign states, and the new problems arising out of the various controversies, see R. Higgins: *Development of International Law Through the Political Organs of the United Nations*, 1963, pp. 167–239.

is required. It is 'essentially a problem connected with the development of a system of collective security. The need for definition is the need for knowing the circumstances in which the machinery of the collective security system will operate and the conditions upon which intervention in the collective interest in the maintenance of international peace and security will be warranted.'[1] It might be possible to arrive at agreement on the definition of aggression if the purpose were to determine a question of fact (whether a situation constitutes a threat to international peace and security) rather than to allocate responsibility for a conflict.

Question of International Criminal Jurisdiction

The question of international criminal jurisdiction has occupied the attention of the organs of the UN at different times and in different contexts. Apart from the proposal of the Committee of Seventeen stressing the desirability of the existence of an international judicial authority to exercise jurisdiction in connection with the implementation of the Nuremberg principles and the punishment of other international crimes,[2] the Secretary General's draft of a convention on genocide submitted in 1947, both to the Committee of Seventeen and, subsequently, to the GA at its second session, provided for exclusive jurisdiction of an international tribunal over persons charged with committing acts of genocide whilst acting as state organs or with the support and toleration of states.[3] Similarly the *Ad Hoc* Committee on Genocide established by the Economic and Social Council, provided for international jurisdiction over crimes of genocide.[4] The GA Resolution 260(III)B of December 11, 1948, was framed on the basis of all such suggestions, and it directed the Commission to study the whole question of international criminal jurisdiction.[5]

In that resolution the conviction was expressed that 'in the course of development of international community, there will be an in-

[1] Bowett: *Self-Defence in Int. Law*, p. 251.
[2] U.N. Doc. A/AC.10/52 Report of the Committee of Seventeen of June 17, 1947, reproduced in *A.J.I.L.*, vol. 41, 1947, suppl. p. 27, para. 3.
[3] U.N. Docs. A/AC.10/41 and A/AC.10/42, Rev. 1.
[4] See Article VII of Draft Convention prepared by the *Ad Hoc* Committee on Genocide, U.N. Doc. E/794. Prior to the approval of the Genocide Convention the Sixth Committee of the GA, on October 14, 1948, considered 'the need for the establishment of an appropriate international tribunal': UNGAOR 3rd sess. 1948, 6th Com., p. 103.
[5] See Historical Survey of the Question of International Criminal Jurisdiction, Memorandum prepared by the Secretary General U.N. Doc. A/CN.4/7/Rev. 1, UN. Publ. Sales No. 1949. V.8. This document gives the history of the question of the establishment of an international jurisdiction in some detail. One part dealt with the proposals, official and unofficial, prior to the United Nations, and another part dealt with further developments leading to the GA Resolution 260(III)B. The appendices presented in convenient form various texts relevant to the subject.

creasing need of an international judicial organ for the trial of certain crimes under international law', and the Commission was asked to 'study the desirability and possibility of establishing an international judicial organ for the trial of persons charged with genocide or other crimes over which jurisdiction will be conferred upon that organ by international conventions', and 'to pay attention to the possibility of establishing a Criminal Chamber of International Court of Justice'.

The Commission's members noted that the resolution did not call upon them to present any plan, but only to report on the desirability and possibility of international criminal jurisdiction. Since this matter was a special question, in no way related to the progressive development or codification of international law, and required a study merely from a theoretical point of view, the Commission at its first session appointed two rapporteurs to prepare one or more working papers on the subject.[1]

At the second session the rapporteurs submitted their reports which presented opposite points of view. Alfaro's report[2] concluded that it was both desirable and possible to establish an international criminal court. Sandström's report[3] expressed the opinion that in the actual organization of the international community an international court would be impaired by such practical defects as the absence of any effective organization for bringing the accused before the court, and that it would do more harm than good. In his view the time was not yet ripe for the creation of such a court. But both the reports agreed that the establishment of a criminal chamber of the International Court of Justice, vested with power to try persons accused of certain crimes, would necessarily require an amendment of the Statute of the Court which, in Article 34, provides that only states may be parties in cases before the Court.

The Commission decided that the establishment of an international court was desirable as well as possible. It did not recommend the alternative of the creation of a criminal chamber within the International Court of Justice.[4]

Upon consideration of the Commission's report the General Assembly, by Resolution 489(V) of December 12, 1950, called for the intergovernmental committee to meet at Geneva to prepare 'one or more preliminary draft conventions and proposals relating

---

[1] *Y.B.I.L.C.*, 1949, 30th mtg, pp. 219–21, see also Report of the Commission, U.N. Doc. A/925, *ibid.*, p. 283, chap. IV, para. 34.

[2] U.N. Doc. A/CN.4/15, *Y.B.I.L.C.*, 1950, vol. II, pp. 1–18.

[3] U.N. Doc. A/CN.4/20, *ibid.*, pp. 18–23.

[4] See for discussion in the Commission, *Y.B.I.L.C.*, 1950, vol. I, 41st–44th, 79th and 81st mtgs, see Report of the Commission, U.N. Doc. A/1316, *ibid.*, vol. II, p. 379, paras. 141 and 145.

to the establishment and the Statute of an international criminal court'.[1] The Committee presented a Draft Statute.[2] The GA thereafter appointed a Special Committee on International Criminal Jurisdiction, composed of Seventeen Member States, to explore the implications and consequences of establishing an international criminal court and of the various methods by which this might be done.[3] This Committee presented a revised draft for an international criminal court, and recommended the method of convention drawn at an international diplomatic conference for establishing the Court.[4] The General Assembly's resolutions 898(IX) of December 14, 1954, and 1187(XII) of December 11, 1957, referred to the connection between the question of defining aggression, the draft code of offences against the peace and security of mankind and the question of an international criminal jurisdiction. Since then, linked as it is with the intractable question of defining aggression, no further progress has been made with regard to the establishment of an international criminal court.[5]

Making Evidence of Customary International Law more readily available

In connection with the Commission's responsibility, under Article 24 of the Statute, for considering and reporting on ways and means of making the evidence of customary international law more readily available, the Secretariat had presented a scholarly and comprehensive memorandum on the subject.[6] This document offered a number of suggestions for the improvement of present literature of international law and how the authority of governments and of the

[1] U.N. Doc. A/1639, Report of the Sixth Committee, UNGAOR 5th sess. 1950, Annexes, Ag. it. 52, pt. V, paras. 35–43. The intergovernmental committee met at Geneva from August 1 to 31, 1951; *YB of the UN*, 1950, pp. 857–61.
[2] U.N. Doc. A/AC.48/1; for comments see Notes by Q. Wright, Yuen Li-Liang, G. A. Finch, in *A.J.I.L.*, vol. 46, 1952, pp. 60–98.
[3] GA Res. 687(VII) of December 5, 1952, *YB of the UN*, 1952, pp. 806–7.
[4] U.N. Doc. A/2645, Report of the Committee, UNGAOR 9th sess. 1954, Annexes. For summary see *YB of the UN*, 1953, pp. 683–6.
[5] Professor Quincy Wright has well observed 'if . . . half of the members of a society believe that the other half is actually or potentially criminal, conditions are unfavourable for the functioning of a system of criminal law, and the society is likely to disintegrate': 'Proposal for an International Criminal Court of Justice', *A.J.I.L.*, vol. 46, 1952, p. 65.
[6] U.N. Doc. A/CN.4/6, U.N. Publ. Sale no. 1949. V.6. In Part II of the document the suggestions made are clear from the following headings: Collections of documents on the state practice of particular countries; Digests of the practice of particular countries; Digests of state practice in general; Collections or reports of decisions of international tribunals; General registers of decisions of international tribunals; Reports and digests of decisions of municipal courts on questions of international law; National legislation relating to international law; Collections and opinions of international organizations on questions of international law; and Suggestions of organizations and publicists for the improvement of documentation of customary international law. This document also set forth the history of the drafting of Article 24 of the Statute, pp. 3–5.

Commission, the services of non-governmental organizations and the resources of government departments, the Secretariat, and of individual scholars might be appropriately harnessed for the production of 'a systematic and comprehensive compilation of evidence of customary international law'.[1]

The Commission's discussions at its first session showed that it thought that the preparation of a comprehensive collection of all the existing evidence of customary international law was rather impracticable.[2] It invited its chairman Manley O. Hudson, to prepare a working paper[3] on the basis of which the Commission concluded, at its second session (1950), that, since customary and conventional international law need not be mutually exclusive, materials of conventional international law could be considered in connection with this question.[4] Without finding it necessary to give a precise definition of customary international law, the Commission dealt with the scope of customary international law which later gave rise to some criticism in the Sixth Committee.[5] It made the following practical recommendations: Firstly, 'that the widest possible distribution be made of publications relating to international law issued by organs of the United Nations, particularly the *Reports* and other publications of the International Court of Justice, the *United Nations Treaty Series* and the *Reports of International Arbitral Awards*'. Secondly, that the General Assembly should authorize the Secretariat to prepare and issue: (*a*) a Juridical Yearbook; (*b*) a Legislative Series containing the texts of current national legislation on matters of international interest; (*c*) a collection of the constitution of all states; (*d*) a list of the publications issued by the governments of all states containing the texts of treaties concluded by them, supplemented by a list of the principal collections of treaty texts published under private auspices; (*e*) a consolidated index of the League of Nations Treaty series; (*f*) occasional index volumes of the United Nations Treaty series; (*g*) a *repertory* of the practice of the organization of the United Nations with regard to questions of international

---

[1] *Ibid.*, pp. 103–4.

[2] *Y.B.I.L.C.*, 1949, 31st and 32nd mtgs., pp. 228–35. It discussed the working paper submitted by the Secretariat, U.N. Doc. A/CN.4/W9, *ibid.*, 31st mtg., pp. 228–9, n. 10.

[3] U.N. Doc. A/CN.4/16 and add. 1, *Y.B.I.L.C.*, 1950, vol. II, pp. 25–33. See also U.N. Doc. A/CN.4/27, Secretariat's Comments on Hudson's working paper, *ibid.*, pp. 33–5. For discussions see *ibid.*, vol. I, 40th mtg., pp. 4–8.

[4] *Y.B.I.L.C.*, 1950, vol. II, Report of the Commission U.N. Doc. A/1316, chap. II, p. 368, para. 29. It may be noted that Hudson's working paper (Doc. A/CN.4/16) with slight changes, became Part II of the Commission's report to the GA, *ibid.*, pp. 367–74.

[5] See observations made by delegations of Israel, Peru, India and France: UNGAOR 5th sess. 1950, 6th Com., 230th, 231st mtgs. See also U.N. Doc. A/1639, UNGAOR, *ibid.*, Annexes, vol. 2, Ag. it. 52, pt. III, para. 18.

law; and (*h*) additional series of the Reports of International Arbitral Awards. Thirdly, that the General Assembly should call to the attention of governments the desirability of their publishing digests of their diplomatic correspondence and other materials relating to international law.[1]

These recommendations were on the whole favourably received and GA Resolution 487(V) of December 12, 1950,[2] invited the Secretary General to report upon them in the light of the discussions in the Sixth Committee, since they involved administrative and financial implications. Other recommendations of the Commission were not referred to the Secretary General. The suggestion contained in para. 92 of the Commission's Report that the Registry of the ICJ should publish occasional digests of the Court's Reports was considered superfluous since such digests were already published in the Court's Yearbook. Another suggestion made in para. 94 that the GA should give consideration to the desirability of an international convention concerning the general exchange of official publications relating to international law and international relations was not considered as ripe for decision.[3]

On the basis of a number of reports subsequently presented by the Secretary General[4] and by the Sixth Committee, the GA has authorized the issue of most of the publications suggested by the Commission.[5]

Question of reservations to multilateral conventions

This question had received the attention of the Commission during the course of its study of the law of treaties at its second session in 1950. It had some preliminary discussion on the question of reservations to treaties on the basis of Brierly's report (A/CN.4/23). It had then felt that, notwithstanding a large measure of agreement on general principles, particularly regarding the requirement of consent of all parties to a reservation, the application of those principles

[1] See U.N. Doc. A/1316, *T.B.I.L.C.*, 1950, vol. II, Report of the Commission chap. II, pt. II, p. 373, paras. 90, 91 and 93.
[2] UNGAOR 5th sess. 1950, pl. mtgs., 320th mtg.; *TB of the UN*, 1950, pp. 850–1.
[3] U.N. Doc. A/1639, *op. cit.*, para. 19.
[4] U.N. Docs. A/1934, A/2170. For reference to the documents see *TB of the UN*, 1951, pp. 849–51, and 1952, pp. 797–800.
[5] UN Juridical Yearbook (published since 1962); UN Legislative Series (13 vols. have been issued); List of Treaty Collections (published in 1955); Cumulative Index of the UN Treaty Series; Repertory of the Practice of the Security Council (first published in 1954 with supplements); Repertory of the Practice of the UN Organs (first published in 1955, with supplements); and Reports of International Arbitral Awards. The General Conference of UNESCO also adopted in 1958 two conventions: one concerning the exchange of official publications and government decisions between states, and the other concerning the international exchange of publications, see U.N. Tr. Ser., vol. 398, p. 9, and vol. 416, p. 51.

to the great variety of situations arising in the making of multi-lateral treaties required further consideration.[1]

Again the subject was referred to the Commission by GA Resolution 478(V) of November 16, 1950, which asked it to study the question from the point of view both of its codification and progressive development. Furthermore, the Commission was asked to give it priority especially in regard to multilateral conventions of which the Secretary General was the depositary. The same resolution also sought advisory opinion of the ICJ concerning the reservations to the Convention on Genocide.[2]

The justification for referring the question to the International Law Commission and to the International Court of Justice lay in the fact that attention had been called by the Secretariat to the lack of unanimity both as to the procedure to be followed by a depositary in obtaining the necessary consent to a proposed reservation of other parties to a convention, and as to the legal effect of an objection made by one of the parties. But, whereas the task of the ICJ in this regard was restricted in scope, that of the ILC was much broader. The questions submitted to the ICJ by GA resolution related solely to reservations to the Convention on Genocide, and it gave its advisory opinion on the basis of the interpretation of the existing law.[3] The Commission, on the other hand, was aksed to study the question more broadly and in general, both from the point of view of codification and from that of the progressive development of international law.

The Commission considered the matter at its third session in 1951 on the basis of two reports presented by Brierly, Special Rapporteur.[4] The Commission's careful analysis[5] of the question of reservations led it to arrive at the following conclusions. It noted that the

[1] *Y.B.I.L.C.*, 1950, vol. II, Report of the Commission, U.N. Doc. A/1316, chap. I, p. 381, para. 164.
[2] The question had acquired certain practical urgency principally in connection with the Convention on the Prevention and Punishment of the Crime of Genocide which certain states had ratified with reservations, to which some other states had objected: UNGAOR 6th sess. 1951, 6th Com., 272nd mtg, paras. 12 and 13 (statement of the Assistant Secretary General of the Legal Department of the UN).
[3] See Reservations to the Convention on Genocide, Advisory Opinion: ICJ Reports, 1951, pp. 29–30. See also for the questions referred to the ICJ by the resolution and for the answers given by the Court, *Y.B.I.L.C.*, 1951, vol. II, Report of the Commission U.N. Doc. A/1858, chap. II, pp. 125–6, para. 15.
[4] U.N. Doc. A/CN.4/41, First Report, *Y.B.I.L.C.*, 1951, vol. II, pp. 1–17. This report gave an account of the views of writers, the state-practice, the practice of the Pan-American Union, and of the various clauses in multilateral conventions regarding reservations: see Annexes A, B, C and D. Annex E presented draft articles giving a flexible series of options adaptable to varying situations. The Second Report, U.N. Doc. A/CN.4/L18, with drafting modifications, was incorporated in the Commission's report to the GA: *ibid.*, pp. 125–31, paras. 12–34.
[5] U.N. Doc. A/1858, *op. cit.*, paras. 20–24, 26, 28, 33.

criterion of the compatibility of a reservation with the object and purpose of a multilateral convention, as enunciated by the Advisory Opinion of the ICJ on Reservations to the Convention on Genocide, was not suitable for application to multilateral conventions in general. It held that the practice of the Pan-American Union, which stimulated the offering of reservations, perhaps appropriate in the case of states having common historical traditions and close cultural bonds, would tend to split up a multilateral convention and reduce its effectiveness in view of the diversity of reservations and the divergent attitude of states regarding them. The Commission also did not favour the principle of excluding the possibility of reservations as followed in regard to international labour conventions by the International Labour Organization. It recognized the importance of reconciling the desirability of the widest possible acceptance of a multilateral convention by states with the maintenance of uniformity in the obligation of all the parties. However, it noted that multilateral conventions were so diversified in character that no single rule uniformly applied could be wholly satisfactory. It recommended that the organs of the UN specialized agencies and states should, in the course of preparing multilateral conventions, consider the insertion therein of provisions relating to the admissibility or non-admissibility of reservations and to the effect to be attributed to them. This recommendation went beyond the practice followed by the Secretariat, which followed substantially the practice of the League of Nations in permitting a state to make a reservation only with the consent of all states which have ratified or acceded to the convention up to that time, in requiring that the proposed reservation be accepted also by the signatory states which have not yet ratified, either before the convention enters into force or after. The GA Res. 598(VI) of January 12, 1952, endorsed the Commission's recommendation regarding insertion of reservation clauses in future conventions and asked the Secretary General to act as depositary of documents containing reservations and objections to future UN conventions without passing on their legal effects. The main foundations of the régime of reservations to multilateral treaties were laid down by the ILC in its final Draft Articles on the Law of Treaties.[1]

Question of extended participation in general multilateral treaties concluded under the auspices of the League of Nations

Another question which the Commission studied in connection with multilateral treaties was the problem of the accession of new states to general multilateral treaties concluded in the past, whose participation clauses were limited to specific categories of states. This

[1] Now Articles 19–23 of the Vienna Convention on the Law of Treaties, Doc. A/CONF. 39/27, 23 May 1969.

question was raised by the Commission in para. 10 of the commentary to articles 8 and 9 of the Commission's draft articles on the law of treaties presented to the GA in its report of the 14th session (1962). It had pointed out that certain technical difficulties stood in the way of new states which may wish to become parties to some of these treaties, and suggested that consideration should be given to some more expeditious procedures than through the medium of the draft articles on the law of treaties which were under preparation, for finding a speedy and satisfactory solution of the problem.[1]

On the basis of the discussion in the General Assembly and its Resolution 1766(XVII) of November 20, 1962, and a report of the Special Rapporteur on the subject, the Commission considered the Question of extended participation in general multilateral treaties concluded under the auspices of the League of Nations, at its 1963 session.[2] It also had at its disposal a working paper submitted by the Secretariat setting out the multilateral agreements concluded under the auspices of the League of Nations in respect of which the Secretary General acted as depositary and which were not open to new states.[3]

The Commission examined the question of extended participation generally with reference to the 26 treaties which, concluded under the auspices of the League of Nations, have entered into force. In its view a number of them might be of no interest to states and, therefore, required re-examination with a view to determining what actions may be necessary to adapt them to contemporary conditions. It pointed out that only five of these 26 treaties were closed treaties because of rigid participation clauses, but the rest of them were open and were in effect rendered closed treaties by the dissolution of the League of Nations and its Council, and the absence of any organ of the UN exercising the powers previously exercised by the Council under the treaties to enable participation of any state.[4]

In the considered opinion of the Commission the General Assembly was the appropriate organ of the UN to exercise the functions of the League Council. It suggested that, since a number of treaties concerned might hold no interest for states, they be examined with a view to determining what action might be necessary to adapt them

---

[1] *Y.B.I.L.C.*, 1962, vol. II, Report of the Commission, U.N. Doc. A/5209, chap. II, p. 169.
[2] U.N. Doc. A/CN.4/159 and add. 1, a note by the Secretariat, summarized the discussions of the Sixth Committee. See U.N. Doc. A/5509, Report of the Commission, UNGAOR 18th sess. 1963, suppl. no. 9, chap. III, para. 19.
[3] U.N. Doc. A/CN.4/162, *Y.B.I.L.C.*, 1963, vol. I, pp. 267–76.
[4] U.N. Doc. A/C.6/L498, UNGAOR 17th sess. 1962, Ag. it. 76. Part A of this paper gave a list of 26 agreements already entered into force while Part B gave five agreements which had not done so.
[5] See U.N. Doc. A/5509, *op. cit.*, p. 31, para. 23.

to contemporary conditions.[1] The GA agreed and asked the Secretary General to examine them and report. On the basis of his report the GA Resolution 2021(XX) of November 5, 1965 recognized that nine treaties listed in the annex 'may be of interest for accession by additional states' and drew the attention of the parties to the desirability of adapting the remaining treaties to contemporary conditions, particularly in the event that new parties should so request.[2] This has offered a reasonable accommodation between the necessity for change resulting from altering conditions and the advantages of continuity, both to the new and older states, in respect of treaties in question.

MATTERS FORMING PART OF THE COMMISSION'S OWN PROGRAMME OF CODIFICATION

The Commission's own programme of work drawn up at its first session in 1949, consisted of the following topics: Arbitral Procedure; Nationality, including Statelessness; Law of the Sea relating to Régime of the High Seas and the Régime of Territorial Waters; Diplomatic Intercourse and Immunities; and Consular Intercourse and Immunities.

Codification of all these topics has been completed except in the case of Nationality; within that item statelessness has been codified.

Arbitral Procedure

This subject was selected by the Commission at its first session as one of the items accorded priority for codification, and was the subject of progressive study until 1958 when a draft of model rules on arbitral procedure was presented by the Commission to the GA. Georges Scelle acted throughout the study as the Special Rapporteur on the subject and submitted several valuable reports.[3] The Commission's 1953 draft on arbitral procedure which at that time was intended to be a final draft, was submitted to the fifth session of the GA.[4] It contained *inter alia* the recommendation of the Commission,

---

[1] Reference was made to the Resolution of the League dated April 18, 1946, recommending that the members of the League should facilitate in every way the assumption, without interruption, by the UN of functions and powers entrusted to the League under international agreements of a technical and political character which the UN was willing to maintain (L. of N. Offl. Jrnl., sp. suppl. no. 194, p. 57). The GA Resolution 24(1) of February 12, 1946, (A/CN.4/154) declared its willingness in principle to assume the exercise of certain functions and powers previously entrusted to the League; also *Y.B.I.L.C.* 1963, vol. II, pp. 217–33.

[2] For conclusions of the Commission, see U.N. Doc. A/5759 and Add. 1 UNGAOR, 20th sess., 1965, Ag. it. 88.

[3] U.N. Docs. A/CN.4/18, *Y.B.I.L.C.*, 1950, vol. II, pp. 114–51; A/CN.4/46, *ibid.*, 1951, vol. II, pp. 110–20; A/CN.4/57, *ibid.*, 1952, vol. II, pp. 1–2; A/CN.4/109, *ibid.*, 1957, vol. II, pp. 1–15; A/CN.4/113, *ibid.*, 1958, vol. II, pp. 1–15.

[4] U.N. Doc. A/2456, Report of the Commission, *Y.B.I.L.C.*, 1953, vol. II, chap. II, pp. 201–12. See for the comments received from eleven governments Annex I

in accordance with Article 23, para. 1(C), of its Statute, that the GA should 'recommend the draft to members with a view to the conclusion of a convention'.[1]

During the 8th session the GA was unfavourable to the adoption of a convention incorporating the draft's principles and articles, since the majority thought that it would distort the traditional institution of arbitration, which was diplomatic in character, by turning it into a quasi-compulsory jurisdictional procedure. It took the view that the Commission had exceeded its terms of reference by giving preponderance to its desire to promote development of international law instead of concentrating on its primary task of codification of custom.[2] Two years later GA Resolution 989(X) of December 14, 1955 expressed no view as to the desirability of convening a codification conference to conclude a convention and postponed the decision on that point to its next session. But the same resolution in its preambular paragraphs suggested a solution which referred to 'a set of rules on arbitral procedure (which) will inspire states in the drawing up of provisions for inclusion in international treaties and special arbitration agreements'.

The Commission was not able to take the matter until its 9th session (1957) when it appointed a committee of nine of its members[3] which concluded that the full Commission must decide whether the ultimate object should be a convention or simply a set of model rules for inclusion in international treaties and special arbitration agreements. The Commission decided in favour of the latter alternative.[4] On the basis of Scelle's report, the Commission finally submitted a text of a set of Model Rules on Arbitral Procedure at its 10th session in 1958.[5] The Commission's Model Rules on Arbitral Procedure consisted of a preamble and 38 articles followed by a general commentary prepared by Sir Hersch Lauterpacht the General Rapporteur for the year.[6] The new draft did not introduce fundamental alterations of the structure or concept of the 1953 draft, but increased the original number of articles from 30 to 38 in order to

---

to the report, pp. 232–41. For Memorandum prepared by the Secretariat at the Second Session of the Commission, see U.N. Doc. A/CN.4/35, *Y.B.I.L.C.*, 1950, vol. II, pp. 157–80. U.N. Doc. A/CN.4/19 contained replies from eleven governments to questionnaires of the ILC, *ibid.*, pp. 151–6.

[1] U.N. Doc. A/2456 *op. cit.*, p. 208, para. 55. Para. 56 of the document gave reasons why the ILC considered conclusion of a convention on arbitral procedure important and highly desirable.

[2] U.N. Doc. A/CN.4/109, *op. cit.*, Scelle's Report of April 24, 1957, paras. 6 and 7, briefly summarized the points of criticism in the GA.

[3] *Y.B.I.L.C.*, 1957, vol. I, p. 104.   [4] *Ibid.*, pp. 181–5.

[5] *Y.B.I.L.C.*, 1958, vol. I, 433rd–448th, 450th, and 471st–473rd mtgs.

[6] U.N. Doc. A/3859. Report of the Commission, *Y.B.I.L.C.*, vol. II, chap. 2, pp. 83–8.

include a number of provisions relating to routine conduct of arbitral proceedings, such as are normally inserted in the *compromis d'arbitrage*. The principal innovation was that the text was presented not as a prospective general arbitration convention, but as a set of model draft articles which states could draw upon as they might see fit in concluding bilateral or multilateral arbitral agreements, *inter se* or in submitting particular disputes to arbitration *ad hoc*.

The Commission's Model Rules on Arbitral Procedure had drawn its inspiration directly from the doctrine of the jurists—such as Moore, Lammasch, Politis, Lapradelle, Van Vollenhoven and Renault—all of whom advocated making arbitration jurisdictional.[1] For this reason, although it ensured the fundamental principles of the autonomy of the disputing parties regarding the adoption of procedure or rules, the provisions regarding automatic procedures for filling in any gaps created by action or inaction of the parties prevented the frustration of the arbitration agreements. In consequence, any arbitration agreement once entered into legally bound the parties to take all steps necessary to enable the arbitration to take place. The emphasis on the overriding principle of non-frustration led many representatives in the Sixth Committee to maintain that, by destroying the flexibility—one of the most valuable features of international arbitration—the Commission had established a system half-way between arbitration and judicial settlement.[2]

The GA Resolution 1262(XIII) of November 14, 1958, expressing the appreciation of the Commission's work, took note of the Model Rules on Arbitral Procedure, and drew 'attention of Member States for their consideration and use, in such cases and to such an extent as they consider appropriate, in drawing up treaties of arbitration'.[3] The Model Rules serve as a guide rather than as a straitjacket international convention creating new obligations.[4]

The Commission's work on arbitral procedure shows an unusual boldness in embodying a concept of judicial as opposed to diplomatic arbitration. It is declared to contain predominantly the element of progressive development. But in an environment surcharged with ideological and serious political differences, members of the UN tend to be averse to the idea of judicial settlement of disputes whether through the International Court or through arbitra-

---

[1] See U.N. Doc. A/CN.4/113, *op. cit.*, Scelle's Report of March 6, 1958, para. 4.
[2] See for debates in the Sixth Committee, UNGAOR 13th sess. 1958, 6th Com., 554th–567th mtgs; see also U.N. Doc. A/3983, Report of the Sixth Committee, *ibid.*, Annexes, Ag. it. 57, paras. 15–23.
[3] UNGAOR 13th sess. 1958, pl. mtg., 780th.
[4] The model rules are governed throughout by paragraph 4 of the preamble which provides that 'the procedures suggested to States parties to a dispute by these model rules shall not be compulsory unless the States concerned have agreed, either in the *compromis* or in some other undertaking, to have recourse thereto'.

tion.[1] Nevertheless, it is a task of the science of international law to explore ways and means for bringing international differences more and more to arbitration and judicial settlement, and to create universal confidence in these methods by evolving procedures which in the eyes of the parties guarantee a just trial and an adequate consideration of their claims.

Nationality, including Statelessness

This subject, although selected for codification in 1949, was taken up by the Commission at the instance of ECOSOC,[2] which urged the Commission to draft international conventions on the status of Women and on the elimination of statelessness. The study of this broad topic eventually subsumed individual studies of such subjects as the Status of Stateless Persons; the problem of Statelessness; Reduction of Future Statelessness; and Elimination of Future Statelessness.

The Commission formally initiated work on this topic in its third session (1951) by appointing Manley O. Hudson as Special Rapporteur and deciding that both questions referred to it by the Council formed an integral part of the whole subject of nationality, including statelessness.[3] Hudson submitted a comprehensive report containing two working papers;[4] one, a draft of a convention on the nationality of married persons, embodying the terms proposed by ECOSOC, suggested that the Commission should draft the convention without expressing its own views on them. The other paper dealt with statelessness, listing 19 points for the Commission's discussion. The Commission refused to confine itself to the drafting of a text on the nationality of married persons to embody principles which it had not itself studied and approved. It favoured preparation of a draft convention on elimination of statelessness and one or more draft conventions on the reduction of future statelessness. New Special Rapporteur Cordova replaced Hudson and was given general directions not to work on the broad subject of nationality but to confine himself to the question of statelessness.[5]

[1] See Rosenne: 'Int. Law Commission, 1949–59', *B.Y.B.I.L.*, vol. 36, 1960, p. 151.
[2] ECOSOC Res. 304D(XI) of July 17, 1950; see pp. 262–3, n. 1, above.
[3] *Y.B.I.L.C.*, 1951, vol. II, Report of the Commission, U.N. Doc. A/1858, chap. VIII, p. 140, para. 85; U.N. Doc. A/CN.4/47, Note by the Secretariat on Elimination of Statelessness, *ibid.*, pp. 121–2; Discussion in the Commission's 124th mtg., *ibid.*, vol. I, pp. 354–8.
[4] See U.N. Doc. A/CN.4/50, *Y.B.I.L.C.*, 1952, vol. II, pp. 3–24. The substance of the report is contained in the three annexes to it. Annex I gives a general historical and analytical review of the major problems connected with nationality, II and III contain two working papers.
[5] *Y.B.I.L.C.*, 1952, vol. I, 160th mtg., paras. 32 and 45. The records of the Commission have deleted the parts dealing with Hudson's resignation which could have explained the reasons for his replacement by Cordova. See *ibid.*, p. 224,

At its fifth session in 1953, the Commission provisionally adopted a draft convention on the Elimination of Future Statelessness and a draft convention on the Reduction of Future Statelessness, on the basis of two reports by the Special Rapporteur.[1] They were transmitted to governments for comment, as the Commission thought that one of the two drafts (which were identical save for the last sentence of the preamble and Articles 1 and 7) ought eventually to become part of international conventional law.[2] These drafts were inspired by the Universal Declaration of Human Rights which had proclaimed that everyone had a right to a nationality—an expression of compelling moral principle and a realizable standard of action for states in the sphere of human rights and fundamental freedoms. The Commission regarded statelessness as being inconsistent with one of the basic principles of international law, inasmuch as it rendered impossible in many cases the operation of a substantial portion of international law. Hence, in formulating its drafts, the Commission was fulfilling to a large extent the function of developing international law. Both conventions recognized that it was only through international agreement that the amelioration of the existing position concerning statelessness could be brought about, and both purported precisely to impose upon states the obligation of conferring in future a nationality on every individual, and to restrict their right of withdrawing it in a manner inconsistent with the real interest of the international community as well of the individuals concerned.[3]

In 1954, in the light of the comments received from 15 countries[4] on the 1953 Drafts and the third report on the elimination or reduction of statelessness submitted to the Commission by the Special Rapporteur,[5] the Commission adopted revised draft conventions of

paras. 47–52 and p. 227, paras. 6–9 concerning resignation of Hudson deleted from records.

[1] U.N. Docs. A/CN.4/64, Report on the Elimination of Statelessness, and A/CN.4/75, Second Report, *Y.B.I.L.C.*, 1953, vol. II, pp. 167–96. The Commission also had at its disposal Kerno's memorandum on national legislation concerning ground for deprivation of nationality: U.N. Doc. A/CN.4/66 (mimeographed); and two reports of the Secretary General, namely A Study of Statelessness (E/1112 and add. 1) and The Problem of Statelessness (A/CN.4/56 and add. 1); also Kerno's Memorandum on Analysis of Changes in Nationality Legislation of States since 1930, U.N. Doc. A/CN.4/67 (mimeographed).

[2] *Y.B.I.L.C.*, 1953, vol. II, Report of the Commission, U.N. Doc. A/2456, chap. IV, pp. 221–2, paras. 121 and 125. Comparative texts are presented on pp. 228–30. Both drafts were based upon points 1–19 contained in section 6 of Annex II to Hudson's report, U.N. Doc. A/CN.4/56.

[3] U.N. Doc. A/2456, *op. cit.*, paras. 126–132.

[4] U.N. Doc. A/CN.4/82 and add. 1–8 (incorporated in U.N. Doc. A/2693 Annex), *Y.B.I.L.C.*, 1954, vol. II, pp. 163–73.

[5] U.N. Doc. A/CN.4/81, Third Report by Cordova, *Y.B.I.L.C.*, 1954, vol. II, pp. 26–42.

18 articles each on the elimination of future statelessness and the reduction of future statelessness.[1] It also gave proposals in the form of articles relating to present statelessness which governments may take into account when attempting a solution of that urgent problem.[2]

The two conventions provided for the general application of the *jus soli* (the law of the soil) to all persons who would otherwise be stateless at birth, and also covered such specific cases as foundlings and children born at sea or on an aircraft. They aimed at preventing anyone from losing one nationality unless he thereby acquired another.[3] Provisions were made for the establishment, within the framework of the UN, of an agency empowered to act when necessary on behalf of stateless persons involved in controversies with governments. Also, provisions were made for a tribunal competent to decide complaints referred to it by the proposed agency and to consider disputes between signatory states concerning the interpretation or application of the Conventions.

The GA, on December 4, 1954, adopted Resolution 896(IX) regarding the elimination or reduction of future statelessness. It requested the Secretary General to communicate the Commission's drafts to governments, inviting them to give consideration to the merits of a multilateral convention on the elimination or reduction of future statelessness. It expressed its desire that an international conference of plenipotentiaries should be convened to conclude such a convention, as soon as at least 20 States had communicated their willingness to participate. Such a United Nations Conference first met in Geneva from March 24 to April 18, 1959, but no agreement could be reached at that time as to how to limit the freedom of states to deprive citizens of their nationality.[4] The second part of the Conference met in New York from August 15 to 28, 1961, and adopted a Convention on the Reduction of Statelessness; this was open for signature subject to ratification from August 30, 1961 until May 31, 1962, but it has not yet come into force.[5]

[1] U.N. Doc. A/2693, *ibid.*, pp. 143–7. The text of both revised draft conventions is produced in parallel columns for easy comparison, and variations from the 1953 text are given in italics.

[2] The key suggestion proposed by the Commission was that countries should grant stateless persons resident in their territory the special legal status of 'protected person' except in cases where an applicant 'constitutes a danger to public order or to national security': *ibid.*, pp. 148–9, para. 37, Articles 1 and 2.

[3] Both drafts contain the same basic 18 articles but the 'reduction' instrument attenuates the principle stipulating against depriving an individual of his nationality by way of penalty, by citing certain instances in which exceptions may be made.

[4] *YB of the UN*, 1959, pp. 413–14.

[5] *YB of the UN*, 1961, pp. 533–4. The Convention will enter into force after the date of the deposit with the Secretary General of the Sixth instrument of ratification or accession.

In view of the conflicting tendencies in approach both in the Commission[1] and in the GA[2]—the national and international tendency—the Commission concentrated only on the problem of Statelessness.[3] While it did not attempt to impose general limitations on municipal nationality laws except so far as they are productive of statelessness, it has boldly recognized that the question of the solution of conflicts of nationality laws as well as of the further development of international law relating to nationality is in fact closely linked to the question of the establishment of international judicial control of individual claims relating to nationality. The tendency underlying attempts at codifying the law of nationality seems to involve the question of the validity of nationality rules which are not consistent with international law and which may be invalidated by international tribunals.

Law of the Sea. Among the items in the Commission's provisional list of topics of 1949 were the régime of the high seas and the régime of the territorial sea. The Commission, at its first session, selected the régime of the high seas among the topics to be given priority and appointed Professor J. P. A. François[4] as Special Rapporteur for it. Subsequently, at its 1951 session, the Commission also decided, in

[1] In the Commission, Kozhevnikov and Zourek were opposed to the preparation of multilateral conventions since according to them questions of nationality 'fell almost entirely within the domestic competence of States' (Kozhevnikov, 162nd mtg., para. 60) or 'the solution lay in measures taken by governments within the framework of their domestic legislation' (Zourek, 211th mtg., para. 43): *T.B.I.L.C.*, 1952, vol. I and 1953, vol. I respectively. Lauterpacht declared statelessness as evil and offensive to human dignity. He wanted the Commission to be bold; *ibid.*, 211th mtg., para. 16. François and Garcia-Amador warned that the Commission should not go too far: *ibid.*, 211th mtg., paras. 23, 36. On the draft Convention finally adopted Edmonds abstained and Zourek voted against it: *T.B.I.L.C.*, 1954, vol. II, p. 142, n. 2.

[2] See, for debate in the Sixth Committee, UNGAOR 8th sess. 1953, 6th Com., 401st mtg. Fitzmaurice, para. 17; 402nd mtg., Castañeda, para. 26.

[3] It may be noted that on the question of statelessness the bodies of ECOSOC had continued their work, and, in 1954, in accordance with the Council's resolution a UN Conference of Plenipotentiaries met at New York from September 13 to 23 which was attended by representatives of 27 countries. It adopted a 42-article 'Convention Relating to the Status of Stateless Persons' which put stateless people on an equal footing with nationals of a contracting state with regard to enumerated matters. This left to the Commission the task of preparing conventions for the elimination and reduction of future statelessness. See P. Weiss: "The Convention Relating to the Status of Stateless Persons', *I. & C.L.Q.*, vol. 10, 1961, pp. 255–64.

On the Status of Women the ECOSOC decided in 1953 to prepare the convention itself and eventually submitted the draft to the GA, which, in turn, allocated it to the Third Committee. The work completed by the Third Committee on the Convention at the 11th session of the GA was adopted by GA Resolution 1040(XI) of January 29, 1957.

[4] It may be noted that François had a prior experience as a Rapporteur of the Second Committee of the Hague Conference of 1930, which was appointed to study the question of the territorial sea.

pursuance of GA Resolution 374(IV) of December 6, 1949, to initiate work on the régime of the territorial sea, and appointed Professor François as Special Rapporteur for that topic as well. Thus it undertook the codification of the law of the high seas and of the territorial sea separately. But, eventually, in pursuance of GA Resolution 899(IX) of December 14, 1954,[1] the Commission at its 8th session (1956) grouped together systematically all the rules it had adopted concerning the high seas, the territorial sea, the continental shelf, the contiguous zone and the conservation of the living resources of the sea, into a comprehensive project, since the various sections of the law of the sea were found to be closely inter-dependent.[2]

The Commission's final draft code of the law of the Sea—one of the great documents in the history of international law—was the outcome of work at its successive sessions on the basis of several reports of the Special Rapporteur and of extensive consultation with governments.

Régime of the High Seas. On the Régime of the High Seas six reports were submitted by the Special Rapporteur.[3] Having narrowed this field of study to only 11 selected subjects,[4] the Commission prepared draft articles on four of them, the provisions of which were related to jurisdiction over the sea bed and subsoil of the continental shelf, resources of the sea, sedentary fisheries, and contiguous zones for purposes of customs, fiscal, or sanitary regulations.[5] It adopted draft

---

[1] See below, p. 301, n. 6.

[2] *Y.B.I.L.C.*, 1956, vol. II, Report of the Commission, U.N. Doc. A/3159, chap. II, pp. 255–6, paras. 22, 29.

[3] i. U.N. Doc. A/CN.4/17, First Report, set out the various subjects which might be studied for the codification or progressive development of maritime law: *Y.B.I.L.C.*, 1950, vol. II, pp. 36–52; ii. U.N. Doc. A/CN.4/42, Second Report, covered a list of eleven selected subjects. It gave concrete proposals on the continental shelf and related subjects, on the nationality of ships, on penal jurisdiction in matters of collision on the high seas; on the right of approach of warships to foreign merchant vessels, on submarine telegraph cables, and on the subject of hot pursuit: *Y.B.I.L.C.*, 1951, vol. II, pp. 75–103; iii. U.N. Doc. A/CN.4/51, Third Report, dealt with six of eleven subjects discussed in the previous report: *Y.B.I.L.C.*, 1952, vol. II, pp. 44–9; iv. U.N. Doc. A/CN.4/60, Fourth Report, submitted draft articles with detailed commentaries on continental shelf and contiguous zones: *Y.B.I.L.C.*, 1953, vol. II, pp. 1–51; v. U.N. Doc. A/CN.4/69, Fifth Report, was specially devoted to penal jurisdiction in matters of collision, *ibid.*, pp. 51–3; vi. U.N. Doc. A/CN.4/79, Sixth Report, contained draft articles on the régime of the high seas, *Y.B.I.L.C.*, 1954, vol. II, pp. 8–18.

[4] At the second session, the ILC decided to leave aside subjects which were, because of their technical nature, not suitable for study, or were being studied by other UN organs or specialized agencies. The selected subjects were: nationality of ships; collisions; safety of life at sea; right of approach; slave trade; submarine telegraph cables; resources of the sea; right of pursuit; contiguous zones; sedentary fisheries; and the continental shelf: *Y.B.I.L.C.*, 1950, vol. II, Report of the Commission, U.N. Doc. A/1316, pt. VI, chap. III, pp. 383–5.

[5] *Y.B.I.L.C.*, 1951, vol. II, Report of the Commission, U.N. Doc. A/1858, chap. VII, pp. 139–40, pp. 141–4, Annex.

articles at its 5th session on the continental shelf, fisheries, and the contiguous zone.[1] A provisional draft on the régime of the high seas with commentaries adopted at its 7th session (1955) was transmitted to governments for observation,[2] and the chapter on the conservation of living resources of the sea, which was prepared in the light of the Report of the International Technical Conference on the Conservation of the Living Resources of the Sea held at Rome,[3] was communicated to the organizations represented in that Conference. Thus, having studied separately the isolated aspects of the subject, the Commission finally adopted 38 provisional articles concerning the régime of the high seas as a whole, followed by comments and an annex containing nine articles relating to the conservation of the living resources of the sea.[4]

Régime of the Territorial Waters. On this topic the Special Rapporteur submitted in all three reports.[5] In pursuance of GA Resolution 374(IV) of December 6, 1949, the Commission began the consideration of certain aspects of the régime of the territorial sea; in particular, the question of base lines and bays at the 1952 session, on the basis of the first report by the Special Rapporteur. While deciding to seek the opinions of governments in regard to the delimitation of the territorial sea of two adjacent states, and necessary information regarding their practice, the Commission further authorized the Special Rapporteur to consult with experts on certain technical aspects of the problem.[6] The second and third reports of the Special Rapporteur submitted respectively at the 1953 and

---

[1] *Y.B.I.L.C.*, 1953, vol. II. Report of the Commission, U.N. Doc. A/2456, chap. III, pp. 212–20. Draft articles were followed by exhaustive comments. The Commission derived considerable assistance from two publications of the Codification Division entitled *Laws and Regulations on the Régime of the High Seas*, in 2 vols., U.N. Leg. Ser. No. 1, 1951 and No. 2, 1952 (ST./Leg/Ser. B/1 and 2).

[2] *Y.B.I.L.C.*, 1955, vol. II, Report of the Commission, U.N. Doc. A/2934, chap. II, pp. 21–34.

[3] The GA, by its Resolution 900(IX) of December 1954, had recognized the importance of the question of the conservation of the living resources of the sea in connection with the work of the ILC and provided for convening this conference which met at Rome from April 18 to May 10, 1955. According to this resolution the report of the conference was to be referred to the ILC 'as a further technical contribution to be taken into account': *Y.B.I.L.C.*, 1955, vol. II, pp. 28–9, Commentary to Article 24.

[4] U.N. Doc. A/2934, *op. cit.*, pp. 21–34.

[5] i. U.N. Doc. A/CN.4/53, First Report, *Y.B.I.L.C.*, 1952, vol. II, pp. 25–43. It contained a project of 23 articles and exhaustive commentary on each article; ii. U.N. Doc. A/CN.4/61 and add. 1, Second Report, *ibid.*, 1953, vol. II, pp. 57–79. It was a revised draft accompanied by an annex of the report of the Committee of experts on technical matters concerning the territorial Sea; iii. U.N. Doc. A/CN.4/77, Third Report, *ibid.*, 1954, vol. II, pp. 1–6.

[6] *Y.B.I.L.C.*, 1952, vol. I, 164th–172nd mtgs.; *ibid.*, vol. II, Report of the Commission, U.N. Doc. A/2163, chap. IV, p. 68, paras. 37–40.

1954 sessions of the Commission, took into account the observations of the experts as well as the comments of governments concerning the delimitation of the territorial sea between two adjacent states. The Commission, at its 6th session (1954), adopted revised provisional articles on the basis of these reports and invited the comments of governments particularly about their attitude concerning the question of the breadth of the territorial sea.[1] At the next session (1955), the Commission further amended several draft articles in recognition of the cogency of many of the comments from governments,[2] and proposed articles on questions concerning the breadth of the territorial seas, bays, groups of islands, and the delimitation of the territorial sea.[3]

Finally, at the 8th session in 1956, the Commission drew up its project on the régime of the high seas as well as on the régime of the territorial sea on the basis of a report by the Special Rapporteur,[4] incorporating a number of changes deriving from the replies of 25 governments.[5] Moreover, in accordance with the desire of the GA affirming the idea of the unity of the whole subject of the law of the sea and its related problems,[6] the Commission had to recast all the rules it had adopted at different times concerning the high seas, the continental shelf, the contiguous zones, the conservation of the living resources of the sea, and the territorial sea, so as to constitute a single co-ordinated and systematic body of rules. To that end, some articles had to be revised with a view to harmonizing the provisions and avoiding repetition.

The Commission's final report on the subject was submitted to the GA in two parts—the first dealing with the territorial sea and the second with the high seas which was further subdivided into three

[1] *Y.B.I.L.C.*, 1954, vol. II, Report of the Commission, U.N. Doc. A/2693, chap. IV, p. 153, paras. 69–70; for draft of 27 articles on the Régime of the Territorial Sea, pp. 153–62.
[2] See U N. Doc. A/CN.4/90 add. 1–6, containing comments by 18 governments, incorporated as annex to Doc. A/2934, *op. cit.*, pp. 43–62.
[3] U.N. Doc. A/2934, *op. cit.*, pp. 34–41.
[4] U.N. Doc. A/CN.4/97, Report by J. P. A. François on Régime of the High Seas and Régime of the Territorial Sea, *Y.B.I.L.C.*, 1956, vol. II, pp. 1–12.
[5] *Y.B.I.L.C.*, 1956, vol. II, U.N. Doc. A/CN.4/99 and add. 1–9, pp. 37–101; A/CN.4/97 add. 1–3, pp. 13–37; A/CN.4/100, p. 102; A/CN.4/103, pp. 102–3.
[6] During the discussions in the GA, the delegation of Iceland had raised the question of the unity of the topic, stressing the inadvisability of considering any of its various aspects separately. The GA Res. 798(VIII) of December 7, 1953, accepted this view and decided not to deal with any of the problems until the ILC had studied and reported upon all of them. However, at the next session the GA partly modified this decision in order to deal with some of the problems on which the Commission had already completed its study. See U.N. Doc. A/2849, UNGAOR 9th sess. 1954, Annexes, Ag. it. 64. For the Commission's view see *Y.B.I.L.C.*, 1956, vol. II, U.N. Doc. A/3159, chap. II, p. 256, para. 29.

sections: i. general régime of the high seas; ii. contiguous zone; iii. continental shelf.[1] It contained 73 articles, each accompanied by a commentary.

The Commission very clearly pointed out that in regard to the work of developing and codifying the international law of the sea, it was convinced that the distinction between the two activities, as envisaged by the Statute could hardly be maintained. It observed:

Not only may there be wide differences of opinion as to whether a subject is already 'sufficiently developed in practice', but also several of the provisions adopted by the Commission, based on a 'recognized principle of international law', have been framed in such a way as to place them in the 'progressive development' category. Although it tried at first to specify which articles fell into one and which into the other category, the commission has had to abandon the attempt, as several do not wholly belong to either.[2]

For that reason the Commission concluded that in order to give effect to the project as a whole, it was necessary to have recourse to conventional means. It, therefore, recommended the GA, in conformity with Article 23 para. 1(d) of the Statute, to convene an international conference of plenipotentiaries 'to examine the law of the sea taking account not only of the legal but also of technical, biological, economic and political aspects of the problem, and to embody the results of its work in one or more international conventions or such other instruments as it may deem appropriate'. It further cautioned that the disagreement over the breadth of the territorial sea need not dissuade governments (as was the case at the Hague Codification Conference of 1930 from attempting to conclude a convention on the points on which agreement had been reached.[3]

In accordance with the above recommendation and object the GA Resolution 1105(XI) of February 21, 1957, provided for the convening of a conference on the law of the sea which was also requested 'to study the question of free access to the sea of land-locked countries, as established by international practice or treaties'.

The Geneva Conferences on The Law of the Sea, 1958 and 1960. The Law of the Sea Conference which met in Geneva from February 24 to

---

[1] U.N. Doc. A/3159, *op. cit.*, pp. 256–301.
[2] *Ibid.*, pp. 255–6, para. 26.
[3] U.N. Doc. A/3159, *op. cit.*, p. 256, paras. 28 and 30. For criticism of the Commission as to its failure to make any noticeable effort to clarify the factors which might guide the Conference in attempting to understand and apply its suggested rules, see M. S. McDougal and W. T. Burke: *The Public Order of the Oceans. A Contemporary International Law of the Sea*, 1962, pp. 6–8.

April 27, 1958, was preceded by considerable preparatory work.[1] It was attended by the unusually high number of 86 states,[2] as well as by observers from seven specialized agencies and nine intergovernmental organizations.[3] Being composed of national delegations which included experts not only in law but also in geography, oceanography and on technical and fishery problems, the Conference was well equipped to deal with the practical maritime problems confronting the world sea-faring community.[4] It adopted the Secretariat's recommendation in setting up four main committees for the allocation of the ILC draft articles which served as the basis of its work: First Committee (Territorial Sea and Contiguous Zone)—Articles 1 to 25 and 66; Second Committee (High Seas; General Régime)—Articles 26 to 48 and 61 to 65; Third Committee (Fishing); (Conservation of the Living Resources of the High Seas)—Articles 49 to 60; Fourth Committee (Continental Shelf)—Articles 67 to 73. In all these committees the countries attending the Conference were entitled to be represented. But another Special Committee, which became known as the Fifth Committee, having the status of a Main Committee, was also constituted to study the question of free access to sea of land-locked countries in pursuance of the recommendation of the preparatory group. It differed from other committees in that it was less essential for all countries to be represented on it than for the land-locked countries and their neighbours.[5] This Committee, unlike the other committees, lacked the benefit of any preliminary work by the International Law Commission. As regards procedure, whereas in the committees the decisions on questions of procedure and the recommendations were made on the basis of a simple majority, the decisions of the Conference itself on questions

[1] UN Conference on the Law of the Sea, Official Records (I UNCLSOR), vol. I, Preparatory Docs. 1958, pp. v–vii give a list of documents (UN Pubn. A/CONF. 13/37); See D. H. N. Johnson: 'The preparation of the 1958 Geneva Conference on the Law of the Sea', *I.&C.L.Q.*, vol. 8, 1959, pp. 122–45.

[2] All members of the UN at that time were represented save Ethiopia and Sudan. The non-members of the UN attending the Conference were: Federal Republic of Germany, Holy See, Republic of Korea, Monaco, San Marino, Switzerland and the Republic of Vietnam.

[3] See U.N. Doc. A/CONF. 13/L.58, Final Act of the Conference, for list of specialized agencies and intergovernmental organizations, I UNCLSOR, 1958, vol. II, pl. mtgs., pp. 146–7, paras. 4, 5.

[4] U.N. Doc. A/CONF. 13/11, I UNCLSOR, 1958, vol. I, pp. 172–5. It may be noted that, in contrast, the Hague Conference of 1930 was largely a lawyers' conference.

[5] For the documents of these five committees, see I UNCLSOR, 1958: vol. III, A/CONF.13/C.1/L1–168, First Committee; vol. IV, A/CONF.13/C.2/L1–153, Second Committee; vol. V, A/CONF.13/C.3/L1–93, Third Committee; vol. VI, A/CONF.13/C.4/L1–67, Fourth Committee; vol. VII, A/CONF.13/C.5/L1–27, Fifth Committee.

See P. C. Jessup: 'The United Nations Conference on the Law of the Sea', *Col. L. Rev.*, vol. 59, 1959, pp. 239–41.

of substance required a two-thirds majority of the representatives present and voting—a practice followed by the San Francisco Conference of 1945. This was perhaps a recognition of the overwhelming importance of the political element.[1]

The Conference adopted four separate conventions, based in large part on the draft of the ILC: The Convention on the Territorial Sea and the Contiguous Zone, the Convention on the High Seas, the Convention on Fishing and Conservation of the Living Resources of the High Seas, and the Convention on the Continental Shelf.[2] In addition, it adopted an Optional Protocol of Signature Concerning the Compulsory Settlement of Disputes,[3] and nine resolutions relating to matters raised by, or not dealt with conclusively in the conventions.[4] Each Convention corresponded to the separate instrument prepared by the Committees. But, as regards the work of the Fifth Committee, instead of adopting a separate convention on the right of land-locked countries to have access to the sea, the Conference decided that several of the key draft articles formulated by the Commission should be amended so as to apply to both coastal and non-coastal states. It approved a new article which, in essence, recognized the right of land-locked states, by common agreement and in conformity with existing conventions. These provisions were included in two of the four Conventions adopted by the Conference.

In contrast to the Hague Conference of 1930 where the territorial sea was the sole subject discussed, at Geneva the whole law of the sea was dealt with. Each of the four conventions adopted by the Geneva Conference constitutes a general code of law. Briefly speaking, their accomplishment was:

[1] See A. H. Dean: 'The Geneva Conference on the Law of the Sea: What was Accomplished', *A.J.I.L.*, vol. 52, 1958, pp. 607–28; also Johnson, 'The Geneva Conference', *Y.B.W.A.*, 1959, pp. 68–94, for some idea of the political factors working in the Conference and in the committees. The authors had personal experience as delegates of the U.S.A. and U.K. governments respectively. Mr. Dean described the political undercurrents in 'Freedom of the seas', *Foreign Affairs*, vol. 37, 1958, pp. 83–94; Max Sorenson, 'Law of the sea', *Int. Con.*, 1958, no. 520, pp. 195–255.

[2] For the Conventions see I UNCLSOR, vol. II, 1958, U.N. Doc. A/CONF.13, respectively: L.52 (32 articles), pp. 132–5; L.53 (37 articles), pp. 135–9; L.54 (22 articles), pp. 139–41; L.55 (15 articles), pp. 142–3. The Conventions were adopted on April 26 and 27, 1958, see I UNCLSOR, 1958, vol. II, pp. 57, 59, 61 and 73.

[3] *Ibid.*, L.57 (7 articles), pp. 145–6.

[4] U.N. Doc. A/CONF.13/L56, 1958, *ibid.*, pp. 143–5. The nine resolutions related to: nuclear tests on the high seas; pollution of the high seas by radioactive materials; international fishery conservation conventions; co-operation in conservation measures; human killing of marine life; special situations relating to coastal fisheries; the régime of historic waters; convening a second United Nations Conference; tribute to the International Law Commission for its preparatory work for the Conference.

The Convention on the High Seas, very largely based on the work of the ILC, upheld freedom of access to the high seas to all states, coastal or land-locked, and regulated the responsibility of a state towards the ships flying its flag.[1] The four freedoms—of navigation, fishing, laying submarine cables and pipelines and of flying over the high seas—were required to 'be exercised by all States with reasonable regard to the interests of other States in their exercise of the freedom of the high seas'.[2] The Convention on Fishing and Conservation of the Living Resources of the High Seas followed very closely, not only in substance but also in form, the text of the Commission's draft.[3] It did not lay down specific rules but only attempted to specify what conservation rules countries may lawfully enact and apply either by statute or agreements. In fact it sought to safeguard adequately the interests of the coastal states and of those states carrying on overseas fishing operations, and to indicate the circumstances and conditions under which conservation rules may be applied. It embodies a set of declaratory principles to be followed, providing a framework for future agreements rather than constituting a complete agreement in itself, and stressing the need for international co-operation in preventing over-exploitation of the living resources of the high seas.[4]

The Convention on the Continental Shelf incorporated a new concept in international law which had never before been recognized in a multilateral treaty.[5] It gave to coastal states exclusive rights to the exploitation of mineral and other non-living resources of the continental shelf, which was defined as the extension into the high seas of the sea-bed and sub-soil of the territorial sea to a depth of two hundred metres, or beyond that limit, to a depth allowing for the exploitation of natural resources.[6] It specified that these

[1] See U.N. Doc. A/CONF.13/L11, Report of Fifth Committee, I UNCLSOR, 1958, vol. II, pp. 85–8.
[2] See Article 2, Doc. A/CONF.13/L53, *op. cit.* These four freedoms of the high seas appeared first in a resolution adopted by the Institute of International Law in 1927.
[3] See U.N. Doc. A/CONF.13/L21, Report of Third Committee, I UNCLSOR, 1958, vol. II, pp. 102–9.
[4] See Johnson, 'Geneva Conference', *Y.B.W.A., op. cit.,* p. 91; Garcia-Amador: *Exploration and Conservation of the Resources of the Sea,* 2nd edn., 1963, pp. 134–200; W. W. Bishop Jr.: The 1958 Geneva Convention on Fishing and Conservation of the Living Resources of the High Seas', *Col. L. Rev.,* vol. 62, 1962, pp. 1206–29.
[5] See U.N. Doc. A/CONF.13/L12, Report of Fourth Committee, I UNCLSOR, 1958, vol. II, pp. 89–92. Also J. A. C. Gutteridge: 'The régime of the continental shelf', *Trans. Grotius Soc.,* vol. XLIV, 1958–9, pp. 77–89.
[6] For criticism of the definition see Johnson, *op. cit.,* p. 92. For its appreciation, Sorenson, 'Law of the sea', *Int. Con., op. cit.,* pp. 228–9. See also L. C. Green: 'The Geneva Conventions and the Freedom of the Seas', *C.L.P.,* vol. 12, 1959, pp. 224–46; R. Young: 'Sedentary fisheries and the Convention on the Continental Shelf', *A.J.I.L.,* vol. 55, 1961, pp. 359–73.

x

rights, however, should not affect the superjacent waters which continued to be regarded as high seas. The Convention followed closely the text of the corresponding articles prepared by the ILC.[1] It represents perhaps one of the most outstanding achievements of international codification in disposing of many of the controversies that had raged round the subject ever since the famous Truman Proclamation was made on September 28, 1945.[2] It is to be borne in mind that in this comparatively new field, tinged with politics, the considerations of general utility provided a sufficient basis for constructive progressive development of international law as treaties were conspicuously non-existent.[3]

Of all the conventions, that on the territorial sea and the contiguous zone[4] was the least complete, for the reason that the ILC itself had not formulated a precise rule concerning the maximum breadth of the territorial sea and the fishing limits, and had left the solution of these issues to the political decision of a conference of plenipotentiaries.[5] In the Conference no agreement could be reached on any definite limit of the territorial sea, and no express provision was made in the Convention on the Territorial Sea and Contiguous Zone on the question whether warships have a right of innocent passage through this sea.[6] Nor could a precise breadth of the exclusive fishing zones be settled. Nevertheless, the achievements of the convention were by no means insignificant. It recognized the general system of the straight base lines, as distinguished from normal base lines, and, thereby sought to embody the guiding principles laid down in the judgment of the ICJ in the Anglo-Norwegian

[1] See M. M. Whitman: 'Conference on the Law of the Sea: a Convention on the Continental Shelf', *A.J.I.L.*, vol. 52, 1958, pp. 629–59.

[2] C. H. M. Waldock: 'International law and the new maritime claims', *International Relations*, vol. 1, 1956, p. 187; Garcia-Amador, *op. cit.*, pp. 116–33; J. L. Kunz: 'Continental shelf and international law: confusion and abuse', *A.J.I.L.*, vol. 50, 1956, pp. 828–53.

[3] For critical comments on the Convention see B. B. L. Auguste: *The Continental Shelf: The Practice and Policy of the Latin American States with special reference to Chile, Ecuador and Peru*, 1960, pp. 94–103, 353–6.

[4] The Commission preferred the term 'territorial sea' to 'territorial waters' to denote the maritime belt of coastal waters, because the latter term might include inland waters; see Doc. A/2163, *Y.B.I.L.C.*, 1952, vol. II, p. 68, para. 37.

[5] See for the criticism of the Commission for having disavowed attempts at recommendation because the problem involved extra-legal factors, and for having adopted an extremely narrow view of its functions, M. S. McDougal and W. T. Burke: *Studies in World Public Order*, 1960, pp. 849–50 and n. 19.

[6] See Articles 1 and 14–23 of the Convention, Doc. A/CONF.13/L.52, *op. cit.* On innocent passage the relevant articles provide only the general rules applicable to all ships warranting the conclusion that warships have the same rights in this respect as other ships, although this did not seem to be the intention of the majority of delegations. For details of conflicting claims regarding the territorial sea, see U.N. Doc. A/CONF.13/L.28/rev. 1, Report of the first Committee, I UNCLSOR, 1958, vol. II, pp. 115–25.

Fisheries case.[1] It recognized and gave effect to the doctrine that the coastal states may have rights for limited purposes—preventive and protective control—in a belt of the high seas contiguous to its territorial sea. By limiting the contiguous zone to twelve miles from the base line from which the breadth of the territorial sea is measured, it was left to be presupposed that the breadth of the territorial sea is less than twelve miles.[2]

The Conference on the Law of the Sea focused attention on various problems relating to the vast areas of the globe covered by the sea which have been a source of friction and conflict. It fulfilled both the function of codifying customary rules of law and of achieving new agreement on various controversial issues. Its significant contribution was the clarification of various issues in reaching a wide area of agreement[3] which led to a codification of rules embodying such principles as the freedom of the high seas, rights of innocent passage for surface vessels through international straits and territorial waters, the right of vessels of all states to fish the high seas, the right of every costal state to exploit the resources of its continental shelf contiguous to its coast, and the right of access of land-locked states to the sea. It formulated comprehensive provisions for the settlement of fishing disputes and conservation matters through the offices of an independent commission. Its noteworthy achievement was that it brought about profound transformation in the traditional law of the sea to settle a number of issues which had risen as a result of technical progress and of its economic and social repercussions.[4] Its success proved the worth of the ILC, without whose carefully prepared draft, the Conference could never have accomplished its task.[5]

The Conference failed to reach agreement on only two questions, namely the breadth of the territorial sea and the width and rights in the contiguous exclusive coastal fishing zone. But it had requested the GA to convene a second international conference for further

---

[1] ICJ Reports, 1951, pp. 128–9; also Waldock, *B.Y.B.I.L.*, vol. 28, 1951, pp. 114 ff., and Article 4 of the Convention, U.N. Doc. A/CONF.13/L.52.

[2] Dean: 'Freedom of the Seas', pp. 89–91; Garcia-Amador: *Exploration and Conservation*, pp. 22–85.

[3] See P. C. Jessup: 'The United Nations Conference on the Law of the Sea', *Col. L. Rev.*, vol. 59, 1959, pp. 234 ff.; and Sir G. Fitzmaurice: 'Some results of the Geneva Conference on the Law of the Sea', *I. & C.L.Q.*, vol. 8, 1959, p. 74.

[4] The Law of the Sea Conference, however, did not cover the entire body of maritime law. It did not concern itself with such matters as the legal relations between shippers and carriers, salvage, marine insurance, regulation of safety at sea, and rules of the road at sea, which have had a long historical development and many of which are covered by widely ratified international conventions.

[5] See for tributes to the Commission at the end of the Conference I UNCLSOR, 1958, vol. II, p. 78, paras. 59–62, U.N. Doc. A/CONF.13/L.48, para. 60; also U.N. Doc. A/CONF.13/L.56, Res. IX, I UNCLSOR, 1958, vol. II, p. 145.

consideration of unresolved questions.[1] The General Assembly by its Resolution 1307(XIII) of December 10, 1958, called for a second conference to study two specific questions of the breadth of the territorial sea and fishery limits.[2]

The second conference met in Geneva from March 17 to April 26, 1960, and was attended by 88 states. It worked in two stages; the discussion on substance took place first in the Committee of the Whole formed by all the states present which could, by a simple majority rule, adopt a report and proposals for the Plenary Session of the Conference. At the second stage of the Plenary Session an official convention could be adopted by the same delegates upon the affirmative votes of two-thirds of the states present and voting and not abstaining.[3]

At the second conference there was no proposal for a maximum of a three mile limit of the territorial sea. There were two camps, one seeking twelve miles[4] and another six miles as the maximum limit.[5] The 'twelve-milers', mainly Afro-Asian, but also Latin-American and Socialist countries, favoured a flexible formula of the twelve-mile permissible, not obligatory, limit, leaving every state the option of choosing any limit of their territorial sea within twelve miles. They sought truly exclusive fishing rights up to a limit of twelve miles, whatever the width of territorial sea adopted by the coastal state, and were opposed to the interests of the long-range fishing states. Their eighteen-power proposal was rejected at the 28th meeting of the Committee of the Whole by 39 votes to 36 with 13 abstentions. The 'six-milers', principally the western maritime powers, succeeded in getting the joint Canadian–U.S. proposal adopted by 43 votes to 33 with 10 abstentions in the Committee of the Whole. The joint proposal, the result of a compromise, offered a 'six-plus six' formula, which would authorize the coastal state to extend its

---

[1] U.N. Doc. A/CONF.13/L.56, Res. VIII, *op. cit.*, p. 145.

[2] See U.N. Doc. A/4034, Report of the Sixth Committee for debate on the question, UNGAOR 13th sess. 1958–9, Annexes, Ag. it. 59.

[3] For summary records of plenary meetings and meetings of the Committee of the Whole see Second UN Conference on the Law of the Sea, Official Records (II UNCLSOR). Among the latest documents furnished to the Conference were Synoptical Table concerning the Breadth and Juridical Status of the Territorial Sea and adjacent Zones, U.N. Doc. A/CONF.19/4, II UNCLSOR, 1960, pp. 157–63, and Supplement to Laws and Regulations on the Régime of the Territorial Sea, U.N. Doc. A/CONF.19/5 and add. thereto (mimeographed only); also Suppl. to Bibliographical Guide to the Law of the Sea, U.N. Doc. A/CONF.19/6 and add. (mimeographed).

[4] 18-power proposal of April 11, 1960, sponsored by Mexico, Indonesia, Philippines, Ethiopia, Ghana, Guiana, Iraq, Iran, Jordan, Lebanon, Libya, Morocco, Saudi Arabia, Sudan, Tunisia, U.A.R., Venezuela and Yemen: U.N. Doc. A/CONF.19/C.1/L.2/Rev. I, II UNCLSOR, 1690, pp. 165–6.

[5] U.S.A.–Canadian compromise 'Joint proposal', U.N. Doc. A/CONF.19/C.1/L.10, *ibid.*, p. 169.

territorial sea up to a maximum breadth of six nautical miles, and to establish a fishing zone contiguous to its territorial sea up to a maximum limit of twelve nautical miles from the base-line. It recognized the same rights of the coastal state in respect of fishing and the exploitation of the living resources of the sea in the contiguous zone as in its territorial sea. It provided for the automatic disappearance of the limitation to the coastal state's exclusive fishing rights in this additional six-mile zone put by 'historical rights', after a period of ten years. But at the plenary session this proposal failed to be adopted just because of the shortage of a single vote in obtaining the required two-thirds vote in favour.[1]

Another issue which occupied the Conference was the claim to 'preferential' fishing rights beyond the territorial sea, or any other 'exclusive' fishing zone with due regard to the special requirements of a state from the point of view of the livelihood and economic development of its people.[2] The Conference rejected the proposal embodying such claims.

The Conference failed to adopt any proposal on the two questions before it, which were left unsettled by the first conference. These issues clearly demonstrated that they involved security and economic problems.[3] The emphasis on military considerations[4] naturally led to strengthening opposition to the three miles rule by those states belonging to the Soviet and the Afro-Asian groups, which seem suspicious of the naval supremacy of the western powers. This, in conjunction with the economic interests of many coastal states,[5]

[1] See A. H. Dean: 'The Second Geneva Conference on the Law of the Sea: the fight for freedom of the seas', *A.J.I.L.*, vol. 54, 1960, pp. 751–89; D. W. Bowett: 'The Second United Nations Conference on the Law of the Sea', *I. & C.L.Q.*, vol. 9, 1960, pp. 415–35.

[2] Iceland, Cuba, Brazil and Uruguay tabled their proposals: see II UNCLSOR, 1960, pp. 168, 169, 171, 173, 174; also Report of the Committee of the Whole, *ibid.*, pp. 169–71.

[3] See for the analysis of these problems Bowett: 'Second UN Conference on Law of the Sea', *op. cit.*, pp. 415–21.

[4] See Dean: 'Freedom of the Seas', *op. cit.*, where the author, the leader of the U.S. delegation, stressed the military implication of an extension of the territorial sea to twelve miles, and described the defeat of that proposal at the first Conference as an important U.S. achievement. See also C. M. Franklin: *The Law of the Sea: Some Recent Developments*, U.S. Naval War College, Int. Law Studies, vol. 53, (1959–60), 1961, pp. 116–23.

For opposite view emphasizing security of coastal states against non-coastal states' warships operating in adjacent seas, see speeches of Shukairy (Saudi Arabia) and Sen (India) in plenary mtg., and the Committee of the Whole, II UNCLSOR, 1960, pl. mtgs., 11th mtg., para. 12, and 12th mtg., paras. 19–22; Verbatim Records of the Committee of the Whole (A/CONF.19/9) 1st mtg., pp. 12–13, 10th mtg., pp. 190–4.

[5] Latin-American countries and countries like Iceland were motivated by the desire to protect the fisheries off their coasts against overfishing by foreigners employing modern and efficient equipment. See Gudmundsson (Iceland), Verbatim Records of the Committee of the Whole, *ibid.*, 11th mtg., pp. 203–10; for

militated against any agreement. The old fishing nations, which are also the leading maritime nations of the world, were not inclined to shape the law to suit the interest of smaller and less developed nations. Consequently, any attempt to produce a convention by a process of tug of war of innumerable votes or procedural manoeuvres was not likely to give entire satisfaction to many states.[1] The only concrete achievement of the Conference was the technical assistance resolution which called for studies and technical assistance by the UN and its specialized agencies to foster the development of fisheries and fishing industries.[2] Besides, the voting on the main issues clearly indicated that a substantial majority of states favoured the maximum limit of six miles for the territorial sea, and that there was substantial support for an extension of exclusive fishing rights beyond the outer limit of the territorial sea, whilst partially recognizing the 'general interest' and the need for allowing gradual accommodation of conflicting interests.[3] But the failure of the Conference need not be regarded as a set-back to the codification movement. As Dr. Bowett remarks: 'it brings home the obvious truth that no movement of this kind can take place, at least via international agreements, unless states are willing to view their own interests in the larger context of the interests of international society as a whole; that is the essence of the compromise which will invariably be needed to secure general acceptance of a rule on any controversial issue'.[4] Indeed, a gradual adjustment of conflicting interests is likely to take place as is indicated by the conclusion of bilateral agreements on fishing rights, such as those between the U.K. on the one hand and Denmark, Iceland and Norway on the

---

Latin American point of view, See Garcia-Amador, *Exploration and Conservation*, *op. cit.*

[1] See editorial comment by P. C. Jessup: 'The Law of the Sea around us', *A.J.I.L.*, vol. 55, 1961, pp. 105 ff., as to variety of positions taken by states according to local interests.

[2] See Ethiopia–Ghana–Liberia Proposal, U.N. Doc. A/CONF.19/L8, adopted without change, II UNCLSOR, 1960, Annex II, p. 176.

[3] The Commission itself, though taking no decision, had enunciated two principles which should be borne in mind in considering the question of the breadth of the territorial sea: first that 'international law did not justify an extension of the territorial sea beyond 12 miles', implying thereby that extension up to that limit could not be overruled; and second that 'the extension by a state of its territorial sea to a breadth of between three and 12 miles was not characterized by the Commission as a breach of international law': see commentary on Article 3 of its draft, U.N. Doc. A/3159, *Y.B.I.L.C.*, 1956, vol. II, pp. 256–6, paras. 3 and 4.

[4] Bowett, 'Second Conference on Law of the Sea', *op. cit.*, p. 435; McDougal and Burke's treatise, *The Public Order of the Oceans. A Contemporary International Law of the Sea*, 1962, stresses the common interest in the continued maintenance of an international law of the sea and rejects all claims of special interests and exclusive interests.

other.[1] This trend can be further strengthened by the conclusion of multilateral conventions at regional or broader level, and by assisting less developed nations in the modernization of their fishing industries. The variety and complexity of conflicting claims can only aggravate the crisis of the law of the sea, and requires a continuous balancing in terms of reasonableness under community criteria.[2]

Diplomatic Intercourse and Immunities

This subject, although selected for codification in 1949 by the Commission, did not receive priority until 1954 when, in accordance with the priority request of GA Resolution 685(VII) of December 5, 1952,[3] the Commission initiated work on the subject and appointed Sandström as Special Rapporteur.[4] The Commission was unable to take up the subject until its 9th session in 1957, when on the basis of the report by the Special Rapporteur containing a draft for the codification of the subject, and a memorandum prepared by the Secretariat,[5] it adopted a provisional set of draft articles each with a short commentary, on the provisional assumption that it would form the basis of a convention.[6] This draft, circulated to governments for comment, dealt only with permanent diplomatic missions, and did not cover missions accredited to, or staffs of, international organization for *ad hoc* diplomatic purposes. Finally, at the 10th session in 1958, the Commission adopted a revised draft[7] on the basis of the observations of governments and conclusions drawn from them by the Special Rapporteur.[8] It recommended to the GA that the draft articles on diplomatic intercourse and immunities be referred to member states with a view to the conclusion of a convention.[9]

[1] See D. H. N. Johnson: 'Developments since the Geneva Conferences of 1958 and 1960: Anglo-Scandinavian Agreements concerning the Territorial Sea and Fishing Limits', *I. & C.L.Q.*, vol. 10, 1961, pp. 587–97.
[2] McDougal and Burke conclude: 'The choice before the states of the world in the present crisis of the law of the sea is whether, for the illusory mess of pottage obtainable in an uneconomic extension of exclusive right, they will forego their heritage of inclusive rights and its promise of even great future achievement in community and particular values', *Public Order of Oceans*, p. 911.
[3] U.N. Doc. A/2252, UNGAOR 7th sess. 1952, Annexes, Ag. it. 58.
[4] *Y.B.I.L.C.*, 1954, vol. II, Report of the Commission, U.N. Doc. A/2693, chap. V, p. 162, para. 73.
[5] Respectively, U.N. Doc. A/CN.4/91, *Y.B.I.L.C.*, 1955, vol. II, pp. 9–17; and A/CN.4/98, *Y.B.I.L.C.*, 1956, vol. II, pp. 129–72.
[6] *Y.B.I.L.C.*, 1957, vol. II, Report of the Commission, U.N. Doc. A/3623, chap. II, pp. 133–43.
[7] *Y.B.I.L.C.*, 1958, vol. II, Report of the Commission, U.N. Doc. A/3859, chap. III, pp. 89–105.
[8] U.N. Doc. A/CN.4/116/add. 1 and 2, *Y.B.I.L.C.*, 1958, vol. II, pp. 16–19. Comments were received from only 21 governments; reproduced as Annex to U.N. Doc. A/3859, *op. cit.*, pp. 111–39.
[9] U.N. Doc. A/3859, *op. cit.*, p. 89, para. 50. Comments were received from 25 governments; *vide* GA Res. 1288(XIII) of December 5, 1958; see U.N. Doc. A/4164, UNGAOR 14th sess. 1959, Annexes, Ag. it. 56.

The General Assembly, by Resolution 1450(XIV) of December 7, 1959, decided to convoke a conference in order to embody the results of its work in an international convention or such ancillary instruments relating to the subject as might be necessary.[1]

The UN Conference on Diplomatic Intercourse and Immunities met at the New Hofburg in Vienna from March 2 to April 14, 1961. It was attended by 81 States and observers from several specialized agencies and intergovernmental organizations.[2] It worked mainly through a Committee of the Whole, and a sub-committee to deal specifically with the question of special missions.[3] It adopted three instruments: a Convention on Diplomatic Relations; Optional Protocol concerning Acquisition of Nationality; and Optional Protocol concerning the Compulsory Settlement of Disputes.[4] In addition it adopted four resolutions which were annexed to the Final Act.[5]

In the title of the main convention, formally named the Vienna Convention on Diplomatic Relations,[6] the term 'diplomatic intercourse' was replaced by 'diplomatic relations', as was suggested by the Commission in its final report.[7] The Vienna Convention, consisting of 53 articles[8] codifies the rules governing diplomatic relations

[1] U.N. Doc. A/4305, Report of the Sixth Committee, UNGAOR, *ibid.*

[2] Observers from ILO, FAO, UNESCO, International Atomic Energy Agency, League of Arab States and Asian-African Legal Consultative Committee participated: see U.N. Doc. A/CONF.20/10, Final Act (paras. 3, 4 and 5 give a list of states and the bodies represented). The Conference was presided over by Professor Alfred Verdross, the distinguished international lawyer. See United Nations Conference on Diplomatic Intercourse and Immunities Official Records (UNCDIIOR), 1961, vol. II, p. 81.

[3] For Rules of Procedure adopted by the Conference, *ibid.*, vol. I, pp. xxiii–xxvii.

[4] The Vienna Convention, U.N. Doc. A/CONF.20/13 and corr. 1; Optional Protocol concerning acquisition of Nationality, U.N. Doc. A/CONF.20/11; Optional Protocol concerning the Compulsory Settlement of Disputes, U.N. Doc. A/CONF.20/12, reproduced in *A.J.I.L.*, vol. 55, 1961, pp. 1064–81. See UNCDIIOR, 1961, vol. II, pp. 82–9.

[5] The Resolutions related to Special Missions; Consideration of Civil Claims; Tribute to the Commission; and Tribute to the government of Austria for hospitality: U.N. Doc. A/CONF.20/10/add. 1, UNCDIIOR, 1961, vol. II, pp. 89–90.

[6] The reference of the site of the Conference in the title was partly in recognition of the generosity of the host state and its historic rôle in the development of the law of diplomatic privileges and immunities, and partly in response to the efforts of communist states to designate the government of Austria as the depositary authority of the Convention, contrary to the normal practice of the Secretary General being the depositary of conventions concluded under the auspices of the UN. See for debate in the Committee of the Whole, *ibid.*, vol. I, 40th–41st mtg. Also E. L. Kerley, 'Some Aspects of the Vienna Conference on Diplomatic Intercourse and Immunities', *A.J.I.L.*, vol. 56, 1962, pp. 89–90. The Convention remained open for signature until October 31, 1961, at the Federal Ministry for Foreign Affairs of Austria and subsequently until March 31, 1962, at the UN Headquarters.

[7] See Report of the Commission U.N. Doc. A/3859, *op. cit.*, p. 89, and n. 24; U.N. Doc. A/CONF.20/L2, Report of the Committee of the Whole, UNCDIIOR, 1961, vol. II, p. 50, para. 17.

[8] Adopted on April 14, 1961, *ibid.*, vol. I, 12th pl. mtg., para. 36.

in general as well as diplomatic privileges and immunities, and covers a much wider field of diplomatic law than was done by the Regulation of Vienna on March 9, 1815, which merely settled the classification of the various classes of diplomatic agents. Although it largely incorporated the Commission's draft articles, it added a few new articles and paragraphs as well as a preamble which stressed the importance of the promotion of friendly relations among nations, irrespective of their differing constitutional and social systems. The preamble also affirmed, though not unequivocally, the theory of efficient performance of functions as the basis of the diplomatic privileges and immunities.[1] Besides this, two of the Commission's draft articles, having failed to find place in the Convention, emerged as the optional protocols. Article 35 of the articles drafted by the commission, which did not favour the view that a person enjoying diplomatic privileges and immunities should acquire the nationality of the receiving state solely by the operation of the law of that state and without his consent, was not adopted by the Conference, and was instead made a subject of a separate Optional Protocol concerning Acquisition of Nationality.[2] Similarly, Article 45 of the Commission's draft concerning compulsory settlement of disputes also emerged as Optional Protocol on the subject.[3]

Of the resolutions adopted by the Conference, one recommended to the GA that the question of special missions be entrusted to the Commission for further study and another recommended that the sending states should waive the immunity of the members of its diplomatic missions in respect of civil claims by persons in the receiving state, when this could be done without impeding the performance of the functions of the mission.[4]

In comparison with the Law of the Sea Conference, the Vienna Conference was more successful since it reached agreement on the totality of its subject matter.[5] The success is largely attributed to two

[1] Compare Report of the Commission, U.N. Doc. A/3859, *op. cit.*, pp. 94–5, commenting on Article 18 paras. 1 to 3 which equivocally placed emphasis on the theory of 'functional necessity'. The Convention also pays allegiance in a secondary degree to the 'representative character theory' but discards for all practical purposes the theory of 'exterritoriality'.

[2] U.N. Doc. A/CONF.20/11, *op. cit.*, pp. 88–9. It consists of eight articles but the central article is Article 2. Although Article 35 of the Commission's draft was adopted by the Committee of the Whole by 46 votes to 12 with 12 abstentions, in the plenary meeting of the Conference the article failed to obtain the required two-thirds majority and emerged as a subject of separate optional protocol.

[3] See U.N. Doc. A/CONF.20/12, *op. cit.*, p. 89.

[4] Respectively Resolutions no. 1 and no. 2, U.N. Doc. A/CONF./20/10/add. 1, *op. cit.*, pp. 89–90.

[5] See for a review of the achievements of the Vienna Convention, E. Castrén: 'Innovations in the Vienna Convention on Diplomatic Relations, 1961', *Legal Essays. A Tribute to Frede Castberg*, 1963, pp. 217–29.

major factors: first, that the subject matter itself was substantially less contentious than that of the Geneva Conference, for, except in isolated political incidents, the subject raised no deep-rooted conflicts of political, ideological or economic interest; second, that the experience and improved and mature handling of the Conference work by the Secretariat, and the parliamentary skill of the Chairman of the Committee of the Whole contributed largely to the creditable formulations of international law at Vienna.[1]

But it is unfortunate that the Convention has based the law of diplomatic immunity on the concept of reciprocity,[2] which, save in the unavoidable contingency of reprisals, in essence amounts to a denial of the existence of a rule of law and of a legal duty. The insertion in the Convention itself of a unilateral right to vary its application on the basis of a subjective determination that it is not reciprocally applied by another party, may encourage a tendency to generalize and perpetuate encroachment upon diplomatic immunities. Professor Briggs has rightly said that such a 'provision appears to enshrine reciprocity in place of law, to provide that the agreed rules of international law carefully defined in the treaty are legally binding only so long as states do not exercise their ill-defined treaty right to vary their application on the basis of unilateral determinations'.[3] Similar provision has also found its way into the Convention on Consular Intercourse and Immunities signed at Vienna on April 24, 1963, which was harmonized as far as possible with the Convention on Diplomatic Relations.[4] The Conventions which are intended to codify and develop international law and to set forth the mutual rights and obligations of the highly variegated states of the world by their agreement, should not contain provisions permitting any party to discriminate or retaliate against another party in the name of reciprocity, in applying its provisions. Should it not be assumed that reciprocity has been built into the Convention and its provisions are intended to be applied without discrimination?[5]

---

[1] See Kerley: 'Aspects of Vienna Conf.', *op. cit.*, pp. 128–9.

[2] See Article 47, U.N. Doc. A/CONF.20/13, *op. cit.*

[3] H. W. Briggs: 'Codification Treaties and Provisions on Reciprocity, Non-Discrimination or Retaliation', *A.J.I.L.*, vol. 56, 1962, p. 475. The author examines how the text of Article 47 of the Convention following closely Article 44 of the final draft of the ILC on diplomatic intercourse and immunities (1958), but not existing in the earlier drafts, came in because of the comments of certain governments on the Commission's provisional draft of 1957. See also E. Lauterpacht: 'The codification of the law of diplomatic immunity', *Trans. Grotius Soc.*, vol. 40, 1955, pp. 65–81. The author maintained that the codification of the law of diplomatic immunity must leave out of account the exceptional conditions of post-war international tension and eschew the idea of basing the law on reciprocity, p. 80.

[4] See below, pp. 316–17.

[5] See for debate in the Committee of the Whole, UNCDIIOR, 1961, vol. I, 37th mtg.

Consular Intercourse and Immunities

This subject did not receive the attention of the Commission until 1955, when Jaroslav Zourek was appointed as Special Rapporteur.[1] Zourek submitted a first report in 1957, a second in 1960, and a third one in 1961.[2] At the 1960 session, giving first priority to the subject, the Commission provisionally adopted 65 draft articles on Consular Intercourse and Immunities, and submitted them to governments for comments. The Commission adopted at the next session (1961) a revised final draft of 71 articles which was brought as far as possible into line with that on Diplomatic Intercourse and Immunities.[3] It recommended that the GA should convene an international conference to conclude one or more conventions on the subject. In accordance with GA Resolution 1685(XVI) of December 18, 1961,[4] a conference of plenipotentiaries met at Vienna from March 4 to April 22, 1963. It was attended by 92 states, and observers from the specialized agencies and interested intergovernmental organizations.[5]

The Conference divided the draft articles adopted by the Commission, and certain additional proposals, between two main committees, each composed of all the participating states. The Conference adopted the following instruments: Vienna Convention on Consular Relations; Optional Protocol concerning Acquisition of Nationality; Optional Protocol concerning Compulsory Settlement of Disputes.[6]

There was also a resolution on refugees requesting the Secretary General to submit to the appropriate organs of the UN all documents and records on the refugee question, and resolving meanwhile

[1] *Y.B.I.L.C.*, 1955, vol. II, Report of the Commission, U.N. Doc. A/2934, p. 42, para. 34.
[2] For these see respectively:
U.N. Doc. A/CN.4/108, *Y.B.I.L.C.*, 1957, vol. II, pp. 71–103.
U.N. Doc. A/4169, Report of the Commission, *Y.B.I.L.C.*, 1959, vol. II, pp. 111–22.
U.N. Doc. A/CN.4/131, *Y.B.I.L.C.*, 1960, vol. II, pp. 2–32, U.N. Doc. A/CN.4/ L86, *ibid.*, pp. 32–40, and U.N. Doc. A/4425, Report of the Commission, *ibid.*, pp. 146–9;
U.N. Doc. A/CN.4/137, *Y.B.I.L.C.*, 1961, vol. II, pp. 55–75.
[3] U.N. Doc. A/4843, Report of the Commission, *Y.B.I.L.C.*, 1961, vol. II, chap. II, pp. 91–128.
[4] U.N. Doc. A/5013, Report of the Sixth Committee, UNGAOR 16th sess. 1961–2, Annexes Ag. it. 69. There was much debate on the issue whether all states should be invited, or whether only members of the UN should be invited. The question of the participation of such nations as the People's Republic of China, the German Democratic Republic, the Democratic People's Republic of Korea and the Democratic Republic of Vietnam was really the issue at stake. The western view finally prevailed, to confine the invitation to members of the UN.
[5] See U.N. Doc. A/CONF.25/13, Final Act of the Conference, reproduced in *A.J.I.L.*, vol. 57, 1963, pp. 993–5, paras. 3–5.
[6] See respectively U.N. Docs. A/CONF.25/12, *A.J.I.L.*, vol. 57, 1963, pp. 995–1022; A/CONF.25/14, *ibid.*, pp. 1022–3; A/CONF.25/15, *ibid.*, pp. 1023–5.

not to take any decision on that question.[1] In this way steps were taken for further study of the subject before codification.

The Convention on Consular Relations is based on customary international law as well as on the material furnished by international conventions; especially consular conventions.[2] It contains 79 articles, and covers consular relations in general; facilities, privileges and immunities relating to consular posts, career consular officers and other members of a consular post; régime relating to honorary consular officers and consular posts headed by such officers, and other general provisions. The wording of the text has been strongly influenced by the Vienna Convention on Diplomatic Relations (1961). The convention has avoided an excessively detailed enumeration of consular functions in view of the differences in the legislation and practices of states (Article 5 of the Convention). The preamble stresses that the purpose of the privileges and immunities of consular officers is 'to ensure the efficient performance of functions' on behalf of their respective states. The achievement of the convention is that a subject, which was governed by a heterogeneous set of rules strongly influenced by economic and commercial considerations and found in national legislation, customary law and bilateral agreements, has been brought under a generally unifying concept. The Convention has also taken due account of the tendency to bring the status of the consul closer to that of the diplomat. To the extent that it has enlarged on existing trends it is a creative work. Since it might not altogether obviate the need for bilateral agreements, especially on matters of detail, it does not 'preclude states from concluding international agreements confirming or supplementing or extending or amplifying' its provisions (Article 73).

It is regrettable that, contrary to the Commission's opinion, Article 72 of the Convention, which deals with non-discrimination and which corresponds to Article 47 of the Vienna Convention on Diplomatic Relations once referred to as 'the worst paragraph in the Vienna Convention', has incorporated the provision for retaliation found in para. 2(a) of Article 47 of the Vienna Convention. The Commission's final draft on Consular Relations in 1961 had dropped the idea of a reciprocity clause,[3] since it had taken the view

---

[1] See U.N. Doc. A/CONF.25/13, *op. cit.*, p. 995, para. 16.

[2] The Special Rapporteur described the Commission's work on this subject as both codification and progressive development of international law. In his report he said: 'A draft set of articles prepared by that method will therefore entail codification of general customary law, of the concordant rules to be found in most international conventions, and of any provisions adopted under the world's main legal systems which may be proposed for inclusion in the regulations'. See U.N. Doc. A/CN.4/108, Zourek's Report, *Y.B.I.L.C.*, 1957, vol. II, p. 80, para. 84.

[3] The text of Article 70, of Draft Arts on Consular Relations submitted by the Commission in 1961 was as follows: '(1) In the application of the present articles,

that all the provisions would be equally binding on all the contracting parties, with the result that the parties would all be on equal footing which would make the reciprocity clause unnecessary.[1] This clearly demonstrates how political considerations may influence the shape of codification.

The Optional Protocols concerning Acquisition of Nationality and the Compulsory Settlement of Disputes have also been drafted to correspond to similar protocols adopted at the Vienna Conference on Diplomatic Intercourse and Immunities.

The conventions on Consular Relations and Diplomatic Relations have attempted to codify and standardize customary law in two major spheres of international relations. They are likely to contribute greatly to an economic, political and cultural *rapprochement* between nations.

The Geneva and the Vienna conferences mark an important step in the development of the United Nations' law-making techniques. The conventions adopted at these conferences do not automatically bring into existence a codified law on the subject concerned. In fact, the law-making technique of the UN involves seven stages to produce an operative document: i. initiative by the GA or the Commission to launch study of a subject for the purpose of codification; ii. successive drafts by the Special Rapporteur in the light of observations from governments and of discussions in the Commission; iii. adoption by the Commission of a final report; iv. consideration of the report by the GA, and its decision to convene a diplomatic conference of plenipotentiaries; v. further preparatory studies by the Secretariat to facilitate the work at the conference; vi. the holding of the diplomatic conference, resulting in adoption of a convention and other instruments; and, finally, vii. signature, ratification of or accession to the adopted instruments. Of these seven stages, the last is crucial.

Under international law and practice, states signify their consent to be bound by treaties in one of the two ways: by signature and ratification, or by accession. The former is a means of conclusion of a treaty *de novo*, the latter is the means whereby a third state, not a

---

the receiving State shall not discriminate as between the States parties to this convention. (2) However, discrimination shall not be regarded as taking place where the receiving State, on a basis of reciprocity, grants privileges and immunities more extensive than those provided for in the present Articles'; see *Y.B.I.L.C.*, 1961, vol. II, U.N. Doc. A/4843, Commission's Report, chap. II, p. 128.
[1] See U.N. Doc. A/CN.4/137, Zourek's Third Report on Consular Privileges and Immunities, *Y.B.I.L.C.*, 1961, p. 65, paras. 2, 3, 4; also, *Y.B.I.L.C.*, 1960, vol. II, Report of the Commission, U.N. Doc. A/4425, chap. II, p. 178 for commentary on Article 64 of the draft, para. 3.

participant in the negotiations or conference in case of a multilateral treaty, becomes bound by the treaty in existence between the contracting parties. But the law and practice of multipartite treaties is rapidly undergoing changes[1] and which the Commission has recently studied. However, interesting developments are: i. employment in the multipartite instruments of a formula giving to intending parties the option of contracting treaty obligations by bare signature, or by signature subject to ratification, followed by ratification, or by accession; ii. provision for a date of general entry in the texts of instruments; iii. stipulation of a 'quorum' of parties for entry into force of treaties concerned; and iv. assignment of depository functions to the Secretary General of the UN. These features are found in the codifying conventions adopted at Geneva and Vienna.[2]

All the codifying conventions—four on the Law of the Sea and others on diplomatic and consular relations—required a minimum of 22 ratifications or accessions to come into force. They have been ratified or acceded to by the requisite number of States and they have entered into force.[3] The problem is that the number of ratifications is rather limited and very tardy. Unless these conventions bind a group of States sufficiently numerous and representative of geographical distribution and importance, the object of laying down the general law on the subject may not be attained. What is needed is a highly effective system for speeding up ratifications.

[1] See C. Parry: 'Some recent developments in the making of multipartite treaties', *Trans. Grotius Soc.*, vol. XXXVI, 1951, pp. 149–89.

[2] See Advisory Opinion on Reservations to the Convention on the Prevention and Punishment of the Crime of Genocide, which also throws light on the rules of law relating to the effect to be given to the intention of the parties to multilateral conventions: ICJ Reports, 1951, pp. 27–9. Also U.N. Doc. ST/LEG/7, 'Summary of the practice of the Secretary General as Depositary of Multilateral Agreements'.

[3] By September 1968 the ratifications were:

	Number of parties at present	Date of entry into force
Convention on the High Seas	42	September 30, 1962
Convention on the Continental Shelf	39	June 10, 1964
Convention on the Territorial Sea and the Contiguous Zone	35	September 10, 1964
Convention on Fishing and Conservation of Living Resources of the High Seas	36	March 20, 1966
Convention on Diplomatic Relations	79	April 24, 1964
Convention on Consular Relations	39	March 19, 1967

These conventions do not provide for reservations, save the Convention on the Continental Shelf which authorizes any state to make reservations to articles of the Convention other than to Articles 1 to 3 at the time of signature, ratification or accession.[1] The obvious reason is that an excessive number of reservations tend to defeat the operation of the treaty and also subjects the contracting parties to a considerable uncertainty about the nature of treaty obligations.

The conventions on the Law of the Sea expressly provide for their revision, since the codified law embodied therein should not encumber future generations with the limited foresight of the present, nor should it be exposed to termination by reference to indeterminate doctrines such as the *clausula rebus sic stantibus*. The revision stipulations lay down that, after the expiration of five years from the date on which these conventions enter into force, a request for revision of any of them may be made at any time by any contracting party by means of notification in writing to the Secretary General of the UN, whereupon the General Assembly shall decide on the steps to be taken in this regard.[2] The Conventions on Diplomatic Relations and Consular Relations have no revision clause. It is submitted that codifying conventions should always make a provision for revision so that it becomes possible to reconsider the continuing obligations in the light of new changes or developments in the international community. Another alternative is suggested by Lord McNair when, stressing the need of some means of revision of law-making treaties, he hoped that the signatory states would sooner or later set up a standing commission of revision, which may perhaps receive power to make minor amendments upon its own responsibility and to submit major amendments to the signatories for their ratification.[3]

The conventions produced at the international codification conferences are invariably a product of a conglomeration of factors—the idealists' craving for a better law in the interest of mankind, the legalists' sceptical search for the existing law, the diplomatists' concern for the protection of national interests and for manipulating compromises where possible, and the politician's preoccupation with political and strategic considerations.

The codified rules of international law, proposed by the Commission and projected for adoption as authoritative prescription by

---

[1] Article 12, U.N. Doc. A/CONF.13/L55, I UNCLSOR, 1958, vol. II, p. 143.

[2] See Article 30 of Convention on Territorial Sea; Article 35 of Convention on the High Seas; Article 20 of Convention on Fishing and Conservation of the Living Resources of the High Seas; Article 13 of Convention on the Continental Shelf.

[3] *Law of Treaties*, p. 748, reproducing 'Functions and Differing Character of Treaties., *B.Y.B.I.L.*, 1930.

the general community of states, are today in a process of formulation in which most states of the world have for the first time an opportunity of participation. Newcomers in the international society are no longer in danger of being disregarded by the older states in the formulation and further development of the law of nations. In a way codification under the auspices of the UN embodies fulfilment of the aspirations and demands of newly independent nations, for fuller participation in the law-making process and in the revision of the international legal system that was developed by the older dominant ruling group of states. Consequently, it represents a widening of the international legal community, and this may ensure a greater faith and confidence in the codified legal norms.

UN CODIFICATION CONFERENCES

Since these legislative conferences act in reality for the international society as a whole, they almost inevitably tend to take the form of a legislative assembly and adopt the practices that parliamentary bodies all over the world have found to be essential in the conduct of their business. Since the establishment of the United Nations, six codification conferences have so far been convened: i. First UN Conference on the Law of the Sea, Geneva, February 24 to April 27, 1958; ii. Conference on the Elimination and Reduction of Future Statelessness, of which the first part was held in Geneva, March 24 to April 18, 1959, and the second part in New York, August 15 to 28, 1961; iii. Second UN Conference on the Law of the Sea, Geneva, March 17 to April 26, 1960; iv. Conference on Diplomatic Intercourse and Immunities, Vienna, March 2 to April 14, 1961; v. Conference on Consular Relations, Vienna, March 4 to April 22, 1963; vi. Conference on the Law of Treaties, held in Vienna in two sessions, the first session from March 26 to May 24, 1968, and the second from April 9 to May 23, 1969.

These conferences have set the pattern of the organization and procedure of future codification conferences. The division of the conference work into two or more committees (in addition to the Credentials, Drafting and General Committees) to consider in detail the draft articles proposed by the ILC before the texts are finally adopted by the plenary meetings, and of the procedure providing for voting rules (requiring decisions on matters of substance by two-thirds majority and on matters of procedure by a simple majority in the plenary meetings, and all decisions in the committees by a majority) and to divide proposals and amendments, are indicative of the fact that these conferences tend to adopt practices and procedures evolved by parliamentary bodies in order to produce solutions based on democratic decisions. Thus codification through the convention method tends to be a legislative process, which indeed is a compromise among conflicting interests and positions unlike the judicial process of victory and defeat; and for this reason it seems suitable for the progressive development of international law.

The conventions on the law of the sea and on diplomatic and consular relations have been adopted during the short period between 1958 and 1963, demonstrating that the Commission's researches, its objective search for the solution of ill-defined or conflicting rules of international law in the carefully selected fields, and its thorough preparation of documents, have just begun to bear fruit. Anyone familiar with the great amount of effort expended on the Commission's work on the law of the sea, or on the law of diplomatic and consular relations, could not countenance the facile way in which the critics of international codification tend to approach the whole problem.

TOPICS UNDER STUDY BY THE COMMISSION

In 1966 the Commission's programme of study had the following eight topics on its agenda, of which the first three mentioned formed the main topics and the rest additions of more or less limited scope: the law of treaties; state responsibility; succession of states and governments; special mission; relations between states and intergovernmental organizations; principles and rules of international law relating to the right of asylum; juridical régime of historic waters, including historic bays; and most-favoured nation clauses in the law of treaties.

Law of treaties

This subject was given priority by the Commission at its first session, and since then a number of important reports had been submitted by its successive Special Rapporteurs—Dr. Brierly, Sir. H. Lauterpacht, Sir G. Fitzmaurice and Sir H. Waldock.[1] Until 1962, the

---

[1] Three reports by Brierly: U.N. Docs. A/CN.4/23, *Y.B.I.L.C.*, 1949; A/CN.4/43, *ibid.*, 1951, vol. II, pp. 70–3; A/CN.4/54, *ibid.*, 1952, vol. II, pp. 50–5.
  Two reports by Lauterpacht: U.N. Docs. A/CN.4/63, *ibid.*, 1953, vol. II, pp. 90–162; A/CN.4/87, *ibid.*, 1954, vol. II, pp. 123–39.
  Five reports by Fitzmaurice: U.N. Docs. A/CN.4/101, *ibid.*, 1956, vol. II, pp. 104–28; A/CN.4/107, *ibid.*, 1957, vol II, pp. 16–70; A/CN.4/115, *ibid.*, 1958, vol. II, pp. 20–46; A/CN.4/120, *ibid.*, 1959, vol. II, pp. 37–81; A/CN.4/130, *ibid.*, 1960, vol. II, pp. 69–107.
  Six reports by Waldock: U.N. Docs. A/CN.4/144 and add. 1, *ibid.*, 1962, vol. II, pp. 27–83; A/CN.4/156 and add. 1–3, *ibid.*, 1963, vol. II, pp. A/CN.4/167 and add. 1–3, *ibid.*, 1964, vol. II, pp. 5–65; A/CN.4/177 and add. 1–2, *ibid.*, 1965, vol. II, pp. 3–72; A/CN.4/183, add. 1–4, *ibid.*, 1966, vol. II, pp. 1–50; A/CN.4/186 and add. 1–7, *ibid.*, 1966, pp. 51–103.

Y

Commission was unable to do much beyond adopting a special report (of 1951) on the subject of reservations to multilateral conventions,[1] and working on a substantial part of Sir G. Fitzmaurice's report on framing the conclusion and entry into force of treaties.[2] The Commission had contemplated, on Fitzmaurice's recommendation, a code of general character on law of treaties in view of possible difficulties in producing it in the form of a multilateral convention.[3] Fitzmaurice had therefore framed his draft reports in the form of an expository code rather than a convention. However, in 1961 the Commission changed the plan of its work on the law of treaties from a mere expository statement of the law to the preparation of draft articles capable of serving as a basis for a multilateral Convention.[4] Accordingly, Sir H. Waldock, the new Special Rapporteur, was given specific instructions to prepare a series of draft articles, to cover the whole subject in two years. The Commission gave two reasons for this change: first, that an expository code could not be so effective as a convention for consolidating the law of treaties, which is of particular importance when many new states have recently become members of the international community; second, a multilateral convention on treaties would give all new states the opportunity to participate directly in the formulation of the law which in the Commission's opinion is extremely desirable in order to place the law of treaties upon the widest and most secure foundations.[5] From 1962 to 1966 the bulk of the Commission's time was devoted to six successive reports by Waldock. The Commission tentatively framed each year's work as a separate draft and the decision on the final proposal on draft conventions was taken in the light of comments from governments.

The Commission's final draft of 75 articles on the Law of Treaties[6] was approved by the General Assembly for consideration by an international conference which was held in two sessions in 1968 and 1969 for the purpose of producing an international convention on the subject.[7]

---

[1] See pp. 289–90, above.

[2] See *Y.B.I.L.C.*, 1959, vol. II, pp. 92–109 for text of 14 articles adopted on the framing, conclusion and entry into force of treaties, on the basis of Fitzmaurice's First Report.

[3] U.N. Doc. A/4169, Report of the Commission, *Y.B.I.L.C.*, 1959, vol. II, p. 91, para. 18.

[4] U.N. Doc. A/4843, Report of the Commission, *Y.B.I.L.C.*, 1961, vol. II, p. 128, para. 39.

[5] For debate in the Commission, *ibid.*, vol. I, 620th and 621st mtgs.

[6] U.N. Doc. A/6309/rev. 1, Report of the Commission, *Y.B.I.L.C.*, 1966, vol. II, pp. 177–274.

[7] GA Resolution 2166(XXI), UNGAOR 21st sess. 1966, suppl. no. 16, p. 95.

The Vienna Convention on the Law of Treaties adopted on May 22, 1969 contains 80 articles, divided into seven parts. To them is added a 5-article part

State responsibility

This subject too has been on the agenda of the Commission since its first session. It received priority in response to GA Resolution 799(VIII) of December 7, 1953.[1] Garcia-Amador, the Special Rapporteur on the subject, submitted altogether six excellent reports in succession to the Commission between 1956 and 1961.[2] As pointed out elsewhere, the Harvard Law School was also actively associated with the Commission in the study of the subject. But these studies seemed to have assumed the international character of a state's responsibility for injuries to aliens, and on that assumption as a starting point sought an understandable basis of the imputation of responsibility to the state. In the Commission there was considerable difference of opinion on preliminary questions as to the approach to the subject as well as to the aspects which should be considered. The Commission in fact failed to give a clear directive whether it wanted to confine its study to one particular aspect of the question of state responsibility, namely a state's treatment of aliens and such related problems as denial of justice, the exhaustion of local remedies, and indemnification, or whether it contemplated a general study of the vast subject so as to enumerate certain general principles on all aspects of a state's responsibility in the light of recent developments in international life.[3] Again, there was debate on the problem of defining the scope of the subject when in compliance with para. 3(a) of GA Resolution 1686(XVI) of December 18, 1961, the Commission was requested to continue its study of the question of state responsibility.[4] Since the subject was found to be complex and ill-

VIII, dealing with final provisions, an annex relating to the settlement procedure provided in the Convention, two declarations and three resolutions, see for text U.N. Doc. A/CONF. 39/27 (May 23, 1969); for Summary Records of the plenary meetings and of the meetings of the Committee of the Whole, A/CONF.[39/S.R. 1–36 and A/CONF. 39/S.R. 1–105.

[1] UNGAOR 8th sess. 1953, suppl. no. 17, U.N. Doc. A/2630, p. 52.

[2] See his memorandum on the question, U.N. Doc. A/CN.4/80, *Y.B.I.L.C.*, 1954, vol. II, pp. 21–5. For his six reports: U.N. Docs. A/CN.4/96, *Y.B.I.L.C.*, 1956, vol. II, pp. 174–231; A/CN.4/106, *ibid.*, 1957, vol. II, pp. 104–30; A/CN.4/111, *ibid.*, 1958, vol. II, pp. 47–73; A/CN.4/119, *ibid.*, 1959, vol. II, pp. 1–36; A/CN.4/125, *ibid.*, 1960, vol. II, pp. 41–68; A/CN.4/134, *ibid.*, 1961, vol. II, pp. 1–54.

[3] U.N. Doc. A/5287, Sixth Committee Report, UNGAOR 17th sess. 1962, Ag. it. 76, paras. 44–47. A majority in Sixth Committee saw no reason to restrict codification to the traditional concept of responsibility for damages caused to aliens.

[4] See for account of the debate in the Commission at its 14th session in 1962, Report of the Commission U.N. Doc. A/5209, *Y.B.I.L.C.*, 1962, vol. II, pp. 188–9, paras. 33–48.

defined, before appointing a Special Rapporteur in succession to Dr. Garcia-Amador who was no longer a member of the Commission, the Commission appointed a sub-committee of ten members under the Chairmanship of Ago to study, primarily, the general aspects of the question and to report on the basis of specific memoranda submitted by its individual members.[1]

The report of the sub-committee[2] recommended to the Commission that it should give priority to the definition of the general principles governing state responsibility and consider possible repercussions which new developments in international law may have on state responsibility. It also outlined a programme of study of i. the origin of international responsibility, covering the international wrongful act, determination of the component parts of the international wrongful act (objective as well as subjective elements); the various kinds of violations of international obligations, and circumstances in which an act is not wrongful; ii. the forms of international responsibility, covering the duty to make reparation, forms of reparation, and sanction.[3] The report was unanimously approved by the Commission and Mr. Ago was appointed new Special Rapporteur on the subject.[4]

In accordance with the wish of the Commission the Secretariat prepared two working papers, one giving the summary of the discussions in various UN organs and resulting decisions, the other giving a digest of the decisions of international tribunals relating to state responsibility.[5] But, until the 1966 session, the Commission was engrossed in completing its draft on the Law of Treaties. During the 1967 session, the Commission accepting the viewpoint of Ago, Special Rapporteur on the subject, asked him to submit a substantive report at its 1968 session.[6]

Succession of states and governments

This subject was included in the provisional list of topics for codification by the Commission in its first session, perhaps because of the recommendation made in the Secretariat's Memorandum, *Survey of International Law*. It stated that 'Considerations of Justice and of economic stability in the modern world probably require that in any system of general codification of international law the question of

[1] U.N. Doc. A/5209 *T.B.I.L.C.*, 1962, vol. II, p. 191, paras. 67–68.
[2] U.N. Doc. A/CN.4/152, *T.B.I.L.C.*, 1963, vol. II, Annex 1, pp. 227–59.
[3] U.N. Doc. A/CN.4/152, *op. cit.*, p. 228, para. 6.
[4] U.N. Doc. A/5509, UNGAOR 18th sess. 1963, suppl. no. 9, p. 36, paras. 54–55.
[5] *T.B.I.L.C.*, 1964, vol. II, pp. 125–69.
[6] U.N. Doc. A/6709/rev. 1, Report of the Commission, of its 19th sess., UNGAOR 22nd sess. 1967, Suppl. no. 9, chap. III, para. 42.

State succession should not be left out of account' and that topic 'would seem to deserve more attention in the scheme of codification than has been the case hitherto'.[1] At the 13th session of the Commission, Bartos, Pal, Tunkin, Zourek and Padilla Nervo suggested that the topic should be codified.

In pursuance of GA Resolution 1505(XV) entitled 'Future Work in the field of the codification and progressive development of international law' of December 12, 1960, seeking suggestions from member states, eight governments favoured study of the topic.[2] Accordingly, GA Resolution 1686(XVI) of December 18, 1961, recommended the Commission, *inter alia*, 'to include in its priority list the topic of succession of States and Governments'.[3]

The Commission began the study of the subject at its 1962 session. In view of the complexity of the subject, its practical importance, and the difference of opinion amongst the members as to whether its study should be confined to the question of succession of states or should also take up the question of succession of governments; the Commission set up a Sub-Committee of ten of its members with Lachs as Chairman to suggest the scope of the subject, the method of approach for its study and the means of providing the necessary documentation.[4] This Sub-Committee after two meetings in 1962 decided that more thought should be given to the scope of the subject and its approach, and confined its suggestions to the preparatory work that would be required. According to its suggestions the Secretariat was requested by the Commission to submit the following three studies: (*a*) a memorandum on the problem of succession in relation to membership of the United Nations, (*b*) a paper on the succession of states under general multilateral treaties of which the Secretary General is the depositary, (*c*) a digest of the decisions of international tribunals in the matter of state succession.[5] These studies and the individual memoranda submitted by its members enabled the Sub-Committee to place its report before the Commission at its 15th session (1963).[6] The conclusions and recommenda-

---

[1] *Survey Int. Law.*, p. 32.

[2] See U.N. Doc. A/4796 and add. 1–8, UNGAOR 16th sess. 1961–2, Ag. it. 70.

[3] U.N. Doc. A/5036, Report of the Sixth Committee, UNGAOR 16th sess. 1961–2, Annexes, Ag. it. 70, para. 29.

[4] See *Y.B.I.L.C.*, 1962, vol. II, Report of the Commission, U.N. Doc. A/5209, p. 189, para. 54.

[5] *Ibid.*, p, 191, paras. 71–72.

[6] U.N. Doc. A/CN.4/160 and corr. 1, Report by Lachs, *Y.B.I.L.C.*, 1963, vol. II, pp. 260–300. The Secretariat prepared the following exhaustive documents for the Commission: U.N. Doc. A/CN.4/149 and add. 1, on the Succession of States in relation to Membership of the UN; A/CN.4/150, on the Succession of States in relation to general multilateral treaties of which the Secretary General is the depositary; A/CN.4/151, on Digest of Decisions of International Tribunals relating to state succession: see *Y.B.I.L.C.*, 1962, vol. II, pp. 101–51.

tions of the Sub-Committee were approved by the Commission. The objectives proposed were a survey and evaluation of the present state of the law and practice on succession and the preparation of draft articles on the topic having regard also to new developments in international law in this field; priority to be given to the study of the question of state succession, and the succession of governments, for the time being, to be considered only to supplement the study on state succession. In view of the modern phenomenon of decolonization, special attention was to be given to the problems of concern to the new states. Because of the interrelationship between the topic of state succession and other topics on the Commission's agenda, namely: the law of treaties and the responsibility of states, stress was laid on co-ordination between the Special Rapporteurs on the respective topics to avoid any overlapping in the codification of these three topics. Accordingly, in 1967, the Commission decided to divide the topic into three headings and appointed special rapporteurs for two of these: Sir Humphrey for 'Succession in respect of Treaties' and Mr. Bedjaoni for 'Succession in respect of Rights and Duties resulting from Sources other than Treaties'. The third topic 'Succession in respect of Membership of International Organizations' has been left aside for the time being.[1]

Special missions

This subject was studied by the Commission in connection with its work on diplomatic intercourse and immunities. At its tenth session the draft articles adopted by the Commission dealt only with permanent diplomatic missions. However, it was pointed out in the report of that session that diplomatic relations between states also assumed other forms, which could be grouped under the heading of '*ad hoc* diplomacy' covering itinerant envoys, diplomatic conferences and special missions sent to a state for limited purposes. Hence the Special Rapporteur on the subject of diplomatic intercourse, A. E. F. Sandström, was asked to submit a report on the topic of *ad hoc* diplomacy.[2]

The Commission had before it the report of the Special Rapporteur at its 12th session, a set of proposals and an explanatory memorandum by Jimenez de Aréchaga, a member, and an alternative proposal by Sandström regarding the privileges and immunities granted to special missions.[3] It adopted three draft articles on

---

[1] UNGAOR, 23rd sess. Supp. No. 9, A/7209/Rev. 1, pp. 23–24, paras. 40–42.
[2] *T.B.I.L.C.*, 1958, vol. II, Report of the Commission, U.N. Doc. A/3859, p. 89, para. 51.
[3] *Ibid.*, U.N. Doc. A/CN.4/129, pp. 108–15; A/CN.4/L87 and L88, pp. 115–17; A/CN.4/L89, p. 117.

special missions, together with a commentary and the following considerations were stated in the report of that session: that the question of 'diplomatic conferences' was linked not only to that of 'special missions', but also to that of 'relations between States and international organizations' which were governed largely by special conventions; that this link made it difficult for the Commission to undertake the subject of 'diplomatic conferences' in isolation; that, since in the Commission's view 'itinerant envoy' was one who carried out special tasks in the states to which he proceeded and to which he was not accredited as head of a permanent mission, the fact that his mission represented a series of special missions which were often linked together by a common objective, did not justify the adoption for itinerant envoys of rules differing from those which applied to special missions.[1] Whilst recommending its draft on special missions to be referred to the U.N. Conference on Diplomatic Intercourse and Immunities (1961) as supplementary to the articles on permanent missions, the Commission emphasized that because of the lack of time it could not give the topic of *ad hoc* diplomacy thorough study and, therefore, its draft articles and commentary were of a preliminary nature in order to put forward certain ideas and suggestions for the consideration of the Vienna Conference.[2]

The Vienna Conference on Diplomatic Intercourse and Immunities adopted a resolution recommending the GA to refer back to the Commission the subject of special missions for further study in the light of the convention to be concluded by the Conference.[3] In accordance with the GA Resolution 1687(XVI) of December 18, 1961,[4] the Commission placed the question of special missions on the agenda of its 1963 session.[5] The Commission, in 1963, appointed Milan Bartos as Special Rapporteur on the subject, and decided that he should prepare a draft of articles which should be based on the provisions of the Vienna Convention on Diplomatic Relations, 1961. The Special Rapporteur was directed to keep in mind that 'special

[1] *Y.B.I.L.C.*, 1960, vol. II, Report of the Commission, U.N. Doc. A/4425, p. 179, paras. 32–34.
[2] *Ibid.*, para. 37.
[3] U.N. Doc. A/CONF.20/10/add. 1, Resolution I, UNCDIIOR, 1961, vol. II, Annexes; See for the report of the Sub-Committee on special missions appointed by the Committee of the Whole, U.N. Doc. A/CONF.20/CL/L315, *ibid.*, pp. 45–6. For the recommendation of the Committee of the Whole, *ibid.*, vol. 1 Summary Records, 39th Pl. mtg. para. 63.
[4] U.N. Doc. A/5043, Report of the Sixth Committee, UNGAOR 16th sess. 1961–2, Annexes, Ag. it. 71.
[5] *Y.B.I.L.C.*, 1962, vol. II, Report of the Commission, U.N. Doc. A/5209, p. 192, para. 76; also U.N. Doc. A/CN.4/147, Working Paper prepared by the Secretariat, *ibid.*, pp. 155–6. U.N. Doc. A/CN.4/166 and A/CN.4/179, two reports of the special Rapporteur submitted respectively at 1964 and 1965 sessions of the Commission.

missions are, both by virtue of their functions and by their nature, an institution distinct from permanent missions'.[1] As to the scope of the topic it was decided that it should cover itinerant envoys but not the privileges and immunities of delegates to international conferences as part of the study of special missions.[2] In 1967, the Commission recommended to the GA a final Text of 50 draft articles and a preamble for a convention on special missions.[3]

Relations between states and intergovernmental organizations

Paragraph 52 of the report of the Commission on the work of its 10th session (1958) mentioned the question of relations between states and international organizations, and of the privileges and immunities of such organizations in connection with a preliminary examination of the various forms of *'ad hoc* diplomacy'.[4] The Commission found that these matters were, as regards most of the organizations, governed by special conventions. In the Sixth Committee of the GA, at its 13th session, France proposed that the subject of relations between states and international organizations be studied by the Commission, drawing a distinction between that part of the subject which could be codified and that which could be examined within the framework of progressive development.[5] The GA Resolution 1289(XIII) of December 5, 1958, based on the French proposal, invited the Commission to study further the question of relations between states and intergovernmental organizations after study of diplomatic and consular intercourse and immunities and *ad hoc* diplomacy.[6] The Commission discussed the subject in the 1960 session in connection with *'ad hoc* diplomacy' and noted that in view of the link of the question of 'diplomatic conferences' with the subject of 'relations between states and international organizations', it would not deal with the latter in isolation.[7]

This subject was also suggested by the governments of Austria and the Netherlands in their replies in pursuance of GA Resolution

---

[1] U.N. Doc. A/5509, *Y.B.I.L.C.*, 1963 vol. II, p. 225, paras. 62–65; also U.N. Doc. A/CN.4/155, Working Paper prepared by the Secretariat, *ibid.*, pp. 151–8.
[2] U.N. Doc. A/5509, *op. cit.*, para. 63.
[3] See U.N. Docs. A/6009 and A/6709/Rev. 1. Draft Convention on Special Missions has been considered by the GA at its twenty-third and twenty-fourth sessions.
[4] *Y.B.I.L.C.*, 1958, vol. II, Report of the Commission, U.N. Doc. A/3859, p. 89, paras. 51–52.
[5] U.N. Doc. A/C.6/L427 and a revised text, A/C.6/L427/Rev. 1, UNGAOR 13th sess. 1958, Annexes Ag. it. 56, and U.N. Doc. A/4007, Report of the Sixth Committee, *ibid.*, paras. 18–21.
[6] For the Text of the Resolution see, U.N. Doc. A/4007, *op. cit.*
[7] *Y.B.I.L.C.*, 1960, vol. II, Report of the Commission, U.N. Doc. A/4425, p. 179, paras. 32, 33.

1505(XV) of December 12, 1960, relating to 'Future work in the field of the Codification and Progressive Development of International Law'.[1] Also, the Working Paper prepared by the Secretariat in 1962 for the Commission's future programme of work (Doc.A/CN.4/145) included this topic under the heading 'Possibility of codifying "new" topics'.[2] It observed that 'the number of regional or universal intergovernmental organizations is continually increasing, and is now 150. Their relations among themselves and with governments raise complex legal problems which are not always settled satisfactorily. Almost a century has elapsed since the establishment of the Universal Postal Union, the ancestor of international organizations. An established practice has come into being and there are numerous texts.'[3] It regarded the law of international organizations as appropriate for codification which would meet a growing need. In the 1962 session of the Commission, 'Relations between States and Intergovernmental Organizations' was included in its programme of work as one of the additional four topics, and El-Erian was appointed as Special Rapporteur on it.[4] El-Erian submitted, in 1963, his first report (A/CN.4/161 and Add. 1), in 1967, second report (A/CN.4/195 and Add. 1), and, in 1968, third report (A/CN4/203 and Add. 1–5). The Commission, at its 986th meeting of the 1968 session, adopted a provisional draft of 21 articles which has been transmitted to governments for their observations.[5]

Principles and rules of international law relating to right of asylum

The topic of right of asylum was listed in the Commission's list of 14 topics selected in 1949. Since the Commission could not, for want of time, take up the subject for long, the representative of Colombia raised the question of giving priority to the right of asylum in connection with the debate on the question of priority for the codification of diplomatic intercourse and immunities at the 7th session of the GA.[6] The proposal was defeated on the ground that it constituted a separate topic. Again, in 1959, El Salvador proposed that the Commission be requested to codify the principles and rules relating to the rights of asylum since it was, with its twin aspects of territorial

---

[1] U.N. Doc. A/4796/add. 6 (Austria) and U.N. Doc. A/4796/add. 7 (Netherlands), UNGAOR 16th sess. 1961–2, Annexes Ag. it. 70.
[2] *Y.B.I.L.C.*, 1962, vol. II, p. 97, paras. 170–176.
[3] *Ibid.*, para. 176.
[4] *Y.B.I.L.C.*, 1962, vol. II, Report of the Commission, U.N. Doc. A/5209, p. 192, para. 75.
[5] U.N. Doc. A/7209/Rev. 1, *op. cit.*, pp. 2–21.
[6] U.N. Doc. A/C.6/L251, UNGAOR 7th sess. 1962, Annexes, Ag. it. 58. For Colombia's interest in the matter of the Haya de la Torre case (Colombia v. Peru), see ICJ Reports, 1951, pp. 71–84; Asylum Case, ICJ Reports, 1950, pp. 266–89.

asylum and diplomatic asylum, an ancient institution, accepted and applied in many parts of the world although it had not yet reached adequate uniformity. This proposal was adopted by the GA as Resolution 1400(XIV) of November 21, 1959.[1] The ILC could not take up the subject until 1962 when at its 14th session it was included in its future programme of work.[2] But independently from the work of codification on this topic to be further undertaken by the Commission in due course of time with a view to preparing a legal statement on the Right of Asylum, some progress has taken place on the elaboration of a series of broad humanitarian principles on territorial asylum. The General Assembly, by resolution 2312(XXII) of 14 December 1967, has adopted a Declaration on Territorial Asylum.[3]

Juridical régime of historic waters including historic bays

The Commission's draft articles on the law of the sea (A/3159, para. 33), which were used as a basis for the work of the Geneva Conference did not deal with the régime of historic waters.[4] The First Geneva Conference on the Law of the Sea, on the recommendation of its First Committee,[5] adopted Resolution VII (Doc.A/CONF.13/L.56) requesting the GA to arrange for the study of the juridical régime of historic waters, including historic bays, and for the communication of the results of such study to all member states of the UN. Accordingly, GA Resolution 1453(XIV) of December 7, 1959, asked the Commission to undertake the study of the subject and to make recommendations as it deemed appropriate.[6] The Commission included the subject in its future programme of work in 1962 as one of the four additional topics.[7]

During the 1967 session doubts were expressed by most members of the Commission about this topic, as well as about the right of

---

[1] U.N. Doc. A/C.6/L443, incorporated in Res. 1400(XIV) of U.N. Doc A/4253, Report of the 6th Com., UNGAOR 14th sess. 1959, Annexes, Ag. it. 55.
[2] See replies from governments in pursuance of GA Res. 1505(XV) relating to future programme of the Commission. Five countries favoured the study of right of asylum: UNGAOR 16th sess. 1961, Annexes Ag. it. 70. Also U.N. Doc. A/5209, *op. cit.*, p. 190, para. 60.
[3] U.N. Doc. A/6912, paras 64–65.
[4] Article 7, para. 4 of the draft articles had excluded historic bays from the scope of the general rules drawn up for ordinary bays: see *T.B.I.L.C.*, 1956, vol. II, p. 257.' Para. 6 of Article 7 of the Convention on the Territorial Sea and the Contiguous Zone is substantially the same as Article 7(4) of the Commission's draft: see U.N. Doc. A/CONF.13/L52.
[5] U.N. Doc. A/CONF.13/L28/rev. 1, Annex I, I UNCLSOR, 1958, vol. II, pl. mtgs. annexes.
[6] U.N. Doc. A/4333, Report of the Sixth Committee, UNGAOR 14th sess. 1959, Annexes Ag. it. 58.
[7] U.N. Doc. A/5209, *op. cit.*, p. 190, para. 60.

asylum, as to whether the time had yet been reached to proceed actively with either of them, because of their considerable scope and the political problems they raise. Moreover, the members thought that these topics might seriously delay the work of the Commission on important topics already under its study.[1]

Most-favoured nation clauses in the Law of Treaties

This topic was selected by the Commission at its 1967 session, amongst the additional topics for its future programme of work. The reasons given for its selection were: i. that it was not covered in the draft on the Law of Treaties, as the Commission had felt 'that such clause might at some future time appropriately form the subject of a special study'; ii. that several delegates in the Sixth Committee at its 21st session had urged the Commission to deal with the topic; and iii. that the clarification of its legal aspects might be of assistance to the UN Commission on International Trade Law which was to begin work in 1968.[2] The Commission appointed Endre Ustor as Special Rapporteur on the topic.

The positive achievements of the Commission, as shown by its reports, give us the idea of quality and quantity of its work. As Professor Jennings has rightly observed, 'if we can bring ourselves to cease following the mirage of international statute law, we may find that there is developing under our eyes the very machinery of international law-making that we have been looking for all these years'.[3] And if the critics of the Commission's work try to evaluate it in the context of the entire history of the codification movement traced in the preceding pages, they should not fail to see clear acceleration in the programme of the codification endeavour under the auspices of the United Nations.

Since the Commission has in practice abandoned the old futile search of the League days for topics 'ripe for codification' in view of the fact that all topics of international law need working up into something more than a set of vague principles, which means law-making, it should not be timid in turning its attention to some genuine new problems, such as law relating to international traversing river systems, law of outer space, law of international organization, law relating to economic and trade relations, international bays and international straits, international criminal jurisdiction

---

[1] See U.N. Doc. A/6709/rev. 1, *op. cit.*, para. 45.
[2] *Ibid.*, para. 48. Also, UN. Doc. A/7209/Rev. 1. *op. cit.*, chap. IV.
[3] R. Y. Jennings: 'Recent developments in the Commission', *I & C.L.Q.*, vol. 13, 1964, p. 397.

and legal procedure, model rules of conciliation.[1] The Commission has a vast amount of work to do, and the success of the work under its study depends not only upon the manner in which its members and those working with them perform their task, but also upon external factors beyond the sphere of the Commission itself. In fact, no draft prepared by the Commission would be viable unless it took account of the realities of contemporary international life and the changes which are taking place in the world.[2]

[1] For a list of new topics suggested by governments, see UN. DOC. A/CN.4/L 128 and ILC (XX) Misc. 2: Working Paper prepared by the Secretariat for the ILC to review its programme and methods of work in accordance with GA resolution 2272 (XXII) of 1 December 1967. See ILC Report on its 20th session, 1968 UNGAOR, 23rd sess. Supp. no. 9 (A/7209/Rev. 1) pp. 24–50, annex, at pp. 40–42.

[2] For a comprehensive study of the drafting of the Commission's Statute and of its application and evolution in practice see Herbert W. Briggs: The International Law Commission, N.Y., 1965.

CHAPTER SEVEN

FUTURE PROSPECTS

Early projects contemplated codification of the whole of international law, public as well as private, and also included the schemes of international organization—an assembly of nations, an international tribunal, and some executive authority. As time moved on the aim of codification changed from that of codifying the whole science of international law at one time to piecemeal codification, the method has also changed, from codification by one international lawyer to codification by a collegiate official organ under the auspices of an international organization.

In effect, the Charter of the United Nations, the Statute of the International Court of Justice, and the constitutional law of other international organizations themselves comprise a large part of codified law which, in rudimentary form, was found in most of the earlier projects for the codification of international law. Today, attempts at codification are not concerned so much with the problems of international organization, as with various segments of international law. In modern times, the idea of a single code incorporating the whole science of law is not possible to realize even in respect of municipal law. Codified law at the national level is a series of codes and statutes dealing with different aspects of the legal system and enacted from time to time by legislative bodies. In the field of international law, also, the idea of presenting a single comprehensive code at one time has been renounced. We notice that the progress of the codification of public international law has been achieved in parts, and without any international legislature. Progress has been slow but steady ever since the Hague Conferences of 1899 and 1907. Since the second World War, progress has certainly been accelerated owing to the highly organized efforts and resources of the United Nations, and a demand all over the world for the establishment of the régime of law in interstate relations. The results of codification may not have been spectacular, but is it not surprising that, notwithstanding grave obstacles to codification, it has been possible to achieve the results we have already examined in detail? Limited as they may be, do not these results establish the possibility of codification as an incentive for further efforts? In considering the future prospects for codification, thought might be given to methods and approaches involved in the work.

METHODS

It is not sufficient for the codifiers of international law to study the subject matter solely from the juridical aspect, or to rely only on the 'state practice, precedent and doctrine'. There is need also to make systematic studies of the problems of international law in their social, political, technological and psychological setting, of the nature and characteristics of interstate relations and the elements controlling these relations—such as motivations, observance or non-observance of obligations, official attitudes, and other forces underlying the challenges and demands in regard to particular segments of international law.[1] Taking cognizance of what Professor Julius Stone calls 'sociological substratum' is a necessary adjunct to the codifiers' duty of formulating international law. States are reluctant to seek juridical solutions which do not seem to them to conform to the realities of international life, and this may lead them to prefer solutions based on political expediency or compromise.

The creative effort of reconstructing international law can produce a general atmosphere of respect for it, if it is revised in such a way that, notwithstanding the differences of physical power and prestige or of economic strength between states, intercourse between them may be placed on a reasonable level of equality, but cutting down to an absolute minimum the factors likely in practice to destroy the theoretical equality of states. This requires the scrutiny of the basis and content of any legal rule in order to set it in the whole complex of social realities. The analysis and systematization of the available legal raw material, determining the social purposes served by the legal system, and censorial criticism *de lege ferenda*, should not only consider technical concepts, principles and the prevailing rules of law, but should also take account of the need of others to replace them. One finds oneself in complete agreement with Professor Stone's view that the systematic development of sociological inquiries concerning international law is 'indispensable for the human future, at any rate, insofar as the human future is deemed to depend

---

[1] Julius Stone: 'Problems confronting sociological enquiries concerning international law', *Recueil Des Cours*, vol. I, 1956, pp. 65–175. Professor Roscoe Pound, in his address on 'Legal education in a unifying world' to New York University, said that 'an effective understanding of comparative law involves much more than knowledge of legal precepts established or received in different bodies of law and of their derivation and historical development. It requires knowledge of the social and social–psychological and economic background on which the precepts must operate in their interpretation and application': *N.Y. Univ. Law Rev.*, vol. XXVII, 1952, pp. 12–13. Contrary to the analytical cry for the self-sufficiency of legal science, Pound's theory of sociological jurisprudence urges for an intimate knowledge of the social and economic factors shaping and influencing the law, see *idem*, 'Fifty years of jurisprudence'. *H.L.R.*, vol. 51, 1938, p. 812.

on the rôle of international law. It seems indispensable, moreover, not only for the development of international law *de lege ferenda*, but also for the clarification of its present content *de lege lata*.'[1] This need led the Latin-American jurist Alejandro Alvarez to suggest 'two new and closely interrelated sciences, the "science of international life" and the "science of national psychologies in international affairs" '.[2]

Professor Stone maintains that the International Law Commission is not destined to solve or transform the basic problems of international law and society, and its tasks under the present mandate will remain intractable unless it broadens its objectives 'to plan, to supervise, and, in part, to carry out a wide and flexible program aimed at extending our knowledge and understanding of the operation of international law as a means of social control'. For that he has suggested converting the International Law Commission into an International Research Centre with a reconstituted Secretary General's Division of Codification, manned with three Directors of Research, suitably qualified both in research and administration.[3]

It is beyond doubt that no worthwhile codification activity, whether at universal or regional level, can be effectively carried out without a vast extension of our understanding of international law in the full context of its contemporary operation; and so, the means should be found to make available to the international codifying agency knowledge wider than that of mere technical international law. If the International Law Commission were transformed into a full-time codifying agency, and were to confine itself to the task circumscribed within the technical legal ambit of its present terms of reference, i.e. the marshalling of the mass of materials of state practice and drawing out by induction the principles of binding custom thereby established, even then it seems doubtful whether the Commission could adequately cope with the weight of archives from the different states that comply literally with its requests.

Under its present mandate, the Commission is also assigned the task of 'progressive development', a term which has come to be construed in the development of new principles and rules of international

---

[1] Stone: *op. cit.*, p. 138. Lauterpacht stressed that political, economic and cognate factors were also factors of legal relevance as legitimate components of an eventual legal rule: 'Codification and development of international law' *A.J.I.L.*, vol. 49, 1955, p. 25. Similarly, as early as in 1908, Oppenheim emphasized the importance of the exposition of the existing recognized rules of international law as to their origin, development, and the extent of authority or weakness in theory or in practice, or in both, in order to find out whether they required to be conditioned by the milieu of the age: 'Science of international law' *A.J.I.L.*, vol. 2, 1908, pp. 317–19.
[2] Alvarez: 'The reconstruction and codification of international law', *I.L.Q.*, vol. 1, 1947, p. 473.
[3] Stone: 'On the vocation of the International Law Commission', *Col. L. Rev.*, vol. 17, 1957, pp. 49–51.

law to cope with problems that now lie beyond the reach of established doctrine. This is a sufficiently large and difficult undertaking, and there seems to be little more probability of the likelihood of states accepting the Commission's drafts now than there was at the time of the League of Nations. Professor Milton Katz of Harvard has suggested a new Commission parallel to, but distinct from, the International Law Commission, to bring international law more abreast of the fully developed and tested sectors of mature municipal legal systems by incorporating 'the general principles of law recognized by civilized nations' into the *corpus* of international law.[1]

The proposals, either to broaden the Commission's scope of work and composition in order to equip it with the extra-legal skills essential for the extension of knowledge concerning the operation of international law in the conditions of our mid-twentieth century world, or to create a new Commission parallel to the existing one, would undoubtedly involve great expense. However, it does not seem unreasonable to suggest the creation of a solid core of full-time members, including the president, serving for an indefinite or at least for a long term, and fully assisted by its own adequate permanent research staff, well-qualified in legal as well as in social sciences. It also seems reasonable for a Commission, required to deal with an enormous amount of material in well-defined preparatory work prior to arriving at final decisions in full session, to have its own secretariat. The heavy pressure of work on the Rapporteur and the Commission might be much reduced if the Commission had its own secretariat devoting itself continuously to research and even to the drawing up of preliminary draft codes. This would make it quite practicable for the Commission profitably to marshal the services of scholars in relevant areas of knowledge outside international law, and of learned societies within various states, and to encourage intensive research into the full historical contexts of selected segments of international law in order to put them in their social, political, technological and psychological setting. Moreover, universities, research centres, and scientific bodies national and international, can be excellent channels of communication of research projects on the 'sociological substratum' of the law of nations.[2]

The Commission should devise means for discussion, interpretation, co-ordination, and integration of results of research undertaken by the national and international scientific associations. The projects of the Commission based on thorough sociological inquiries, and on

---

[1] See for his Address given at the 54th Annual Mtg. of the American Soc. of Int. Law, *Proceedings*, 1960, pp. 254–60.
[2] The importance of research studies in paving the way for the development of law is well emphasized by Roscoe Pound, *op. cit.*, p. 19.

the recognition, measurement and adjustment of higher interests by reference to equal interests of all states and to those of the international community as a whole, would indeed supply the building material for shaping international law and for its ultimate victory over international anarchy.

To sum up, any task of fruitful codification entails (1) an accurate exposition of and a minute research into the existing rules of international law; (2) historical research in order to bring into view their growth and development; (3) sociological research taking cognizance of the external factors underlying the problems of international law; and (4) some reasonable criticism of existing legal norms in the context of these inquiries with a view to proposing modifications and additions necessitated by the conditions of the age.

Since the *raison d'être* of universal codification lies in acceptance of the projects of a code by all the governments of the world, the essence of the task of codification lies in the evaluation of national interests and their reduction to a common denominator of national and international interests. For this there is a great need to associate all states with the work of codification. The Commission's time-consuming questionnaire technique has not been entirely satisfactory and foreign offices do not seem to be able to respond fully to the inquiries. The question is: how can the Commission obtain a more effective co-operation with governmental and intergovernmental agencies?

Some improvement might be achieved by the General Assembly persuading states to appoint national committees to undertake the study of specific problems, on the lines adopted by the Pan-American Union.[1] The Commission might also make more use of the work of intergovernmental agencies, such as the Asian-African Legal Consultative Committee, the Inter-American Council of Jurists and the European Committee on Legal Co-operation. Similar bodies might also be constituted by the Communist countries to establish link with the Commission.

The Commission's recent practices of setting up working groups or sub-committees, of establishing relationships with intergovernmental bodies and with scientific bodies, and of holding additional winter sessions whenever necessary, seem to be steps in the right direction. Possibly regular meetings of the United Nations Codification Conference every second or third year, for approval, modification and revision of the Commission's projects, could present more concrete results than the Commission at present seems to achieve. The heart of the matter is that the whole problem of international law remains one of confidence. The codification process

[1] See pp. 136–38 above.

could be an opportunity and a method of creating universal confidence in an international legal system and of extending its scope.

The use of such terms as 'reconstruction' and 'progressive development' in connection with the codification of international law, does not necessarily mean creation *ex novo* of a new international legal order.[1] What is naturally required is addition to the present recognized rules, and in many points substitution, alteration, and even creation of new rules, without necessarily uprooting the entire system of existing international law. A system of law in quest of justice among men must be formulated with reference to the contemporary conditions and needs of that ideal, and to its historical experience. Whilst continuity with the past, in the words of Justice Oliver Wendell Holmes 'is only a necessity and not a duty',[2] the need for change is also secondary to the need for the reign of law. Conditions of excessive fluidity and chronic instability, resulting in day-to-day changes in the law, are incompatible with the idea of law. Stability and society are in themselves powerful elements of justice. The conflict between stability and change, conservation and innovation, contradictory forces of rest and mobility, has always been an inherent problem in the life of a developing society, and perhaps can never be obliterated.[3] But law, functioning as the cement to hold the social structure together, must link the past with the present without ignoring the pressing claims of the future. No law is an end in itself and its ultimate purpose is to serve its subjects. International law has developed for states in their totality rather than for the transient benefit of the individual state or group of states, and all states are made for human beings. It is by transforming international law into the law of a genuine community dedicated to universal welfare and justice, that the codification undertaken by the United Nations may

---

[1] There are many enthusiastic innovators who have rejected the very name 'international law', and whose problem is nothing less than to create a world legal order. They have used new names such as 'world law', 'common law of mankind', and 'transnational law', Professor Arthur Larson of World Rule of Law Center at the Duke Law School speaks of 'World Law' in terms of a new field of study wider than international law and universal, based on all legal systems; see his *International Rule of Law*, 1961; Grenville Clark and Louis B. Sohn also speak of 'world law' in their monumental work, *World Peace Through World Law*, Harvard Univ. Press, 1960, 2nd. ed.; Dr. C. Wilfred Jenks visualizes the present international law as 'the Common Law of Mankind' at an early stage of its development; see his *Common Law of Mankind*, 1958; Jessup conceives of 'transnational law' in *Transnational Law*, 1956.

[2] O. W. Holmes: 'Law in science and science in law', *H.L.R.*, vol. 12, 1899, pp. 443-4.

[3] As Roscoe Pound said, 'In every era of transition there is a time in which certainty seems to be lost. In the end the demands of the general security prevail and newer and better ways of attaining certainty are worked out': 'Jurisprudence', in Wilson Gee (ed.), *Research in the Social Sciences*, 1929. p. 200.

ensure peaceful change in the content and the scope of the law without disturbing universal stability and security.

EXTERNAL FACTORS BEARING ON CODIFICATION

While examining possible means of improving the processes whereby the codification of international law might be both facilitated and accelerated, one must not ignore those aspects of international life that have put difficulties in the way of the world community on its journey towards a universally stated public order. Four factors in particular have contributed to retarding the progress of the development and codification of international law.

First, the growth and the changing nature of the international community itself have, little by little, brought into the international conferences new countries with non-western antecedents, with consequent tensions and differences of approach to the problems of developing and codifying international law. These circumstances demand—and afford opportunity for—a fundamental rethinking of international law in the context of the diverse religions, civilizations and cultures of the whole world.[1]

Second, and related to the first factor, is the diversity of legal systems that now claim to be taken into account—Hindu, Buddhist, Islamic, Jewish, African, Communist—in determining what the Statute of the International Court of Justice describes as 'the general principles of law recognized by civilized nations'.[2] However, characteristic features of the present-day world are the interdependence of different communities and the interaction of legal systems.[3] Codification of international law will require a sustained effort to find the elements of a universal legal order in the major legal systems of the world and thus to promote a wider acceptance of the principles and rules embodied in codified and developed international law.

A third factor lies in the proliferation of sovereign states in the past half century, multiplying the number of units which may claim the traditional attributes of legal sovereignty in international law, and whose consent is necessary to the implementing of changes in that law. Conflicting national interests—*vide* the attitudes revealed

[1] Quincy Wright: 'The prospects of international law., *Proc. Am. Soc. Int. Law*, 1956, p. 11, and 'The strengthening of international law', *Recueil des Cours*, 1959, III, pp. 59–80 and 275–84.
[2] For a classification of the different legal systems into 16 broad categories see J. H. Wigmore: *A Panorama of the World's Legal Systems*, 1936. Also A. B. Bozeman: 'Representative systems of public order today', *Proc. Am. Soc. Int. Law*, 1959, pp. 10–21.
[3] Jenks: *Common Law of Mankind, op. cit.*, pp. 109–20, and 'International law in times of stress' in *Law, Freedom and Welfare*, 1963, pp. 68–9.

during the Geneva Conferences on the Law of the Sea—have proved to be a far greater obstruction in the development of international law and its effectiveness than have been the historical diversities of culture, religion and legal systems or political ideologies. Indeed, nations with widely differing cultural backgrounds but similar national interests have at times united in opposition to changes in international law that concerned those national interests. At the same time all the range of inequalities amongst nations—differences in power and material resources, the hierarchy of states in the international family, economic underdevelopment, and the economic and technological dependence of the developing nations on the more advanced—all these things contribute to conflicts of national interests and consequently to conflicting attitudes towards the norms of international law. Thus the enterprise of codifying that law becomes increasingly complicated.

The fourth factor—considered by some western jurists as a threat to international law and the fundamental values and premises of western public order[1]—is the emergence of communist ideology. Particularly since World War II, with the emergence of the U.S.S.R. as a world 'super power', the ideological division of the world has been viewed as a potential threat to the very existence of mankind. However, Soviet legal theorists have, time and again, compromised between abstract revolutionary Marxist theories and the concrete political necessities that have confronted Soviet Russia. The Soviet Union has acknowledged the importance, for instance, of Article 38 of the Statute of the International Court of Justice, the resolutions of the UN General Assembly, and the organization and functions of the International Law Commission, and has given special recognition to the codification of international law, and co-operated in the drawing up of draft codes in the ILC. A recent study of Soviet theory in practice in international law concludes that 'there is a fairly close similarity between Soviet and western views on the sources of order in international relations and that in both international treaties are of principal importance'.[2] Differences in honouring the prescriptions of international law and treaties have been revealed to be of degree rather than absolute.[3] Nevertheless, considering that the basic ideas of communism have gained wide currency in the world, particularly in the developing countries, international law can hardly afford to ignore them in the process of its revision.

[1] H. A. Smith: *The Crisis in the Law of Nations*, 1947, pp. 17–32.
[2] J. F. Triska and R. M. Slusser: *The Theory, Law and Policy of Soviet Treaties*, Hoover Institute Publication, 1962, p. 31.
[3] O. J. Lissitzyn: 'Western and Soviet perspectives on international law: a comparison', *Proc. Am. Soc. Int. Law*, 1959, pp. 21–5.

In sum, the conflicting attitudes that affect the work of the codifiers of international law are the product of historical factors and of the acceleration of the process of change in the international community. The phenomenal rise in the number of states; the rise of new ideologies and systems of public order; the growing demands for social reform; rapid technological progress; the consciousness of interdependence of states; and the fear of modern weapons of war threatening the very survival of humanity in the event of global conflagration: all these factors have tended to limit the operation or to decrease the relevance of some traditional norms of international law. They have also created new areas of need for legal regulation. As a result codification of international law is today looked upon by a large section of the international community less as a process of ensuring certainty and precision in the norms of international law than as a rightful opportunity to achieve a synthesis of different legal traditions into a generally acceptable common law of mankind. This embodies the will of the world community, recognizes the interdependence of states for peace, freedom, justice, prosperity and technological progress, and ensures the security and welfare of the international community. It has to be remembered, of course, that the task is being carried out by the International Law Commission in the context of the realities of international life, where the rubric of international relations includes not only political or diplomatic but also economic, commercial and financial relations, and even the conflict of such rival interests and ideologies as anti-colonialism and imperialism, capitalism and communism, dictatorship and liberal democracy. Moreover, consideration of the interest of the individual state plays an infinitely greater part in international society than does the interest of the individual in a municipal society. The codifiers of international law, therefore, are confronted with a very arduous task in formulating norms of a universal legal order in a society which lacks intensive international integration ideologically, culturally or in any other way.

SOURCES OF INTERNATIONAL LAW

In assessing the progress and prospects of codification one must examine the codifiers' problems concerning the type, the location and the availability of the source materials of international law. The traditional sources are restated in Article 38 of the Statute of the International Court of Justice. Treaties are important instruments of stability as well as of change in international relations; they are both tools of progress and catalysts of political forces in the international arena. The League of Nations and the United Nations

Treaty Series publications render available to the codifiers and to students of international law complete sets of treaty documents.[1]

State practice and custom, however, still constitute important factors in the evolution or modification of the principles of classical international law governing the adjustment of national sovereignties. But it has now become imperative to marshal the evidence of existing custom on a global basis, which requires a major effort of collective research involving substantial use of oriental and slavonic languages. Since customary rules are to be articulated and modified by the Commission by way of restatement of particular segments of international law, the major problem is the non-availability of the full material on the state practice or the diplomatic series of the several members of the United Nations.[2] A central repository of diplomatic precedents, the preparation of indexes of the precedents of the international experiences of governments, a substantial body of evidence of customary international law, and a regular publication of national legislation bearing on international law, are some of the essential requirements for anyone embarking upon the investigation of the practice of states relating to a question of international law.

The Memorandum submitted by the Secretariat in 1949, *Ways and Means of Making the Evidence of Customary International Law more readily available*, indicated the contemporary state of documentation and its shortcomings, and also gave a number of valuable suggestions for the improvement of the literature of international law, from the point of view of quantum and general availability.[3] The Commission, however, found the preparation of a comprehensive digest of the practice of states and the evidence of customary international law impracticable.[4] The entire question was thoroughly examined by M. O. Hudson in his Working Paper submitted to the Commission at its 2nd session in 1950. It suggested that early attention

[1] The texts of most of the treaties since 1920 have been published in the League of Nations and the United Nations Treaty Series. Prior to 1920, the British Foreign State Papers (published since 1841), de Martens' *Nouveau Recueil General de Traites* (published since 1843 in succession to earlier *Recueils* from 1791), Hertslet's *Commercial Treaties*, Rymer's *Foedera*, and Dumont's *Corps Universal Diplomatique du Droit de Gens* (the two last published in the eighteenth century), constitute the principal collections of the texts of treaties and conventions. They are supplemented by various national collections, published privately: see U.N. Doc. A/CN.4/16, Working Paper submitted by M. O. Hudson to the Commission, *Y.B.I.L.C.*, 1950, vol. II, pp. 26-7.

[2] For this reason see the emphasis given in Article 24 of the Statute of the Commission on the need to find ways and means of collecting evidence of customary international law. See an erudite monograph on the topic by Karol Wolfke: *Custom in Present International Law*, Warsaw, 1964.

[3] See p. 286 n. 6, above.

[4] See *Y.B.I.L.C.*, 1949, pp. 228-35; also, for Koretsky's vehement criticism, *ibid.*, pp. 229, 230, paras. 92-98.

be given to the possibility of concluding a multipartite convention providing for a comprehensive exchange of government publications on questions of international law and international relations, and also that a recommendation be made to governments to supply regularly to the United Nations Secretariat copies of all official publications bearing upon any phase of international law.[1] These were indeed good suggestions, worth implementing, and the Commission approved of them. Since they seem not to have been put into practice, perhaps the publication of a more comprehensive Juridical Yearbook of the United Nations and of international legal documents,[2] and the increasing liaison between the United Nations Secretariat with governments may to some extent solve the question of availability of material relating to national legislation, state practice, and diplomatic correspondence between governments.

The lack of working libraries on international law in many parts of the world has a considerable bearing on the general outlook for international law and consequently on its codification. The General Assembly Resolution 1968(XVIII) of December 16, 1963, on technical assistance to promote the teaching, study, dissemination and wider appreciation of international law is a positive step which is bound to contribute enormously to its progressive development.[3] Moreover, the continued accumulation of case law during the last three-quarters of a century, resulting from arbitral awards and judicial decisions of national and international tribunals, has in the words of Sir Arnold McNair 'completely transformed the international *corpus juris* from a system that rested very largely upon textbooks and diplomatic dispatches into a body of hard law'.[4] Article 24 of the Statute of the Commission recognizes the importance of judicial decisions when it refers to 'the collection and publication . . . of the decisions of national and international courts on questions of international law'. There are several valuable collec-

---

[1] U.N. Doc. A/CN.4/16, *Y.B.I.L.C.*, 1950, vol. II, p. 32.

[2] The American Society of International Law has been publishing International Legal Materials in six numbers every year since 1962. It produces documents such as Legislation and Regulations, Treaties and Agreements, Judicial and similar proceedings and Reports every two months.

[3] U.N. Doc. A/5672, UNGAOR 18th sess. 1963, Annexes, ag. it. 72; also Doc. A/5455 and add. 1 to 6, and Doc. A/5585, Doc. A/C.6/L/544 which throw ample light on existing conditions of teaching and study of international law in different countries. They contain many proposals given by different governments and international scientific organizations for the promotion of study and wider appreciation of international law. Mention may also be made here of GA Resolution 2054(XX) of December 8, 1965, in accordance with which the UN office at Geneva has been organizing seminars on international law for advanced students of the subject and for young government officials from different countries in conjunction with the Commission's sessions.

[4] Sir Arnold McNair: *The Development of International Justice*, 1954, p. 16.

tions, privately as well as officially published,[1] supplemented by a series of United Nations publications of Reports of International Arbitral Awards (*Recueil de Sentences Arbitrales*), the *Annual Reports* of the International Court of Justice, Documents and Records of the proceedings of each case published in *Pleadings, Oral Arguments and Documents*, and the *Yearbook* published by the Registry. But no attempt seems to have been made to assemble the decisions on questions of international law of the national courts of all states, or even of all members of the United Nations—undoubtedly a herculean task.[2] Decisions of the national courts of a state are of great value as evidence of that state's practice, and, in acquainting oneself well with the judicial opinions and law of more than a hundred states with different languages, an international lawyer is handicapped, unless one is a linguist, a historian, and a librarian with extraordinary resources. The United Nations *Juridical Yearbook* attempts to include a descriptive index of decisions of international and national tribunals as well as of administrative tribunals on questions relating to the United Nations and specialized Agencies.

'THE GENERAL PRINCIPLES OF LAW'

The fact that the 'general principles of law' are indeed a potentially fertile source of development in international law, in eliminating the problem of *non liquet*, has been universally recognized.[3] In the absence of a well-developed body of substantive principles of international law and, particularly, for the reconstruction and evolution of new branches of international law, where neither international treaties nor accepted custom nor international judicial precedent furnish a satisfactory rule of law, codifiers must look to this inexhaustible reservoir for a common source of substantial rules, namely, 'the general principles of law recognized by civilized nations'.[4]

But—what are these general principles and where can they be

---

[1] For instance, Stuyt's: *Survey of International Arbitrations, 1791–1938*; John Bassett Moore's work on *International Adjudications, Ancient and Modern* which began in 1929; idem., *History and Digest of the International Arbitrations to which the United States has been a party*, 1898, 6 vols.; James Brown Scott: *Hague Court Reports* (1916), second series in 1932; Hudson: *World Court Reports*, 4 vols. See Hudson's Working Paper, *op. cit.*, pp. 27–8, paras. 26–35.

[2] The most valuable collection in this field is the *Annual Digest and Reports of Public International Law Cases* inaugurated in 1919, London, which covers both national and international jurisprudence. Some international law periodicals regularly publish reports or digests of national judicial decisions.

[3] See B. Cheng: *General Principles of Law as Applied by International Courts and Tribunals*, 1953; Lord McNair, 'The general principles of law recognized by civilized nations', *B.Y.B.I.L.*, vol. 33, 1957, pp. 1–19.

[4] In the words of R. B. Schlesinger, 'the general principles mentioned in Article 38, if they can be concretely established, are a primary source, often the only

found? Is it possible to establish the foundations of a universal system of international law on the basis of general principles deduced from legal systems so varied as the civil law, the common law, the Buddhist law, the Hindu law, the Islamic law, the Jewish law, the African law, and the Communist law, all with their variants? These questions touch the heart of our contemporary problem. But the best solution is provided by the study of comparative law,[1] which shows us the distinction between what is universal in the problems of a world legal order and what is local because of geographical, economic and historical, social and political conditions; which exposes superficial contrasts sometimes making fundamental resemblances; and which separates ritualistic elements, virtually of no significance for contemporary international law, from certain common principles in the most varied legal systems which to a substantial extent have mutually influenced one another's growth. Comparative law studies help in the pragmatic examination of 'general principles of law recognized by civilized nations' with a view to extracting from the major legal systems of the world the maximum measure of agreement on the principles relevant to a given problem.[2]

Roscoe Pound has advocated proceeding in the building of an adequate international law 'by the method of an all-round comparative law in order to identify and bring out the universal element in experience of administering justice which will be usable for a world justice. Here is one function which of itself justifies a great, well-endowed centre for comparative law.'[3] By using comparative law as a guide such 'general' or 'universal' principles can be derived as are recognized in substance by all the main systems of law so that their incorporation would not be doing violence to the fundamental concepts of any of these systems, especially at a time when the subject matter of international legal relations is extending from the regulation of diplomatic interstate relations to a growing number of

---

source of international law in the absence of an applicable treaty': 'Research on the general principles of law recognized by civilized nations', *A.J.I.L.*, vol. 51, 1957, p. 735.

[1] There is a great abundance of comparative legal literature. For some idea of objectives and methods see R. B. Schlesinger: *Comparative Law*, 1960, 2nd edn., pp. xvi–xxi: 'the immediate objective of a comparative law study is to bring about a modicum of understanding among legal technicians'. He adds that one, 'possessing the desired "modicum of understanding" will find that in the process he has acquired a deeper knowledge of his own law, a sharpened sense for improving it, and an increased ability to bring it into line with foreign laws whenever he should be called upon to participate in the progress of domestic or international law making', *ibid.*, p. xxi; see also, H. C. Gutteridge: *Comparative Law*, 1949, 2nd edn.

[2] Gutteridge, *op. cit.*, pp. 64–5; *idem.*, 'Comparative Law and the Law of Nations', *B.Y.B.I.L.*, vol. 21, 1944, pp. 1–10.

[3] 'Legal Education', *op. cit.*, pp. 16–17. For Roscoe Pound's basic attitude towards law see his *Introduction to the Philosophy of Law*, 1954, rev. edn., p. 47.

social and economic relations.[1] Moreover, because of the intermingling of public and private law[2] in contemporary municipal as well as international law, as a result of a growing sphere of 'welfare' functions and responsibilities of the state at the national level, and their regulation at international level by a multitude of public international organizations,[3] the general principles of law may then be increasingly drawn from private as well as from public law. With the extension of public international law to new fields[4] formerly within the sphere of private international law, the scope of the applicability of such principles is constantly expanding, and this means in essence the application of a comparative study to the developing international law.[5] The significant use of 'general principles' in the developing of international law seems to be already proceeding through international contracts, concession agreements and other types of international transactions,[6] and through international administrative agencies as well as through the administrative and judicial organs of more closely knit communities like the European Economic Community.

Although it is difficult to enumerate these general principles,[7] Professor Friedmann has attempted a three-fold classification consisting of i. principles of approach and interpretation to legal relationships of all kinds; ii. minimum standards of procedural fairness;[8] and iii. substantive principles of law generally and firmly

---

[1] Dr. Cheng maintains that general principles of law are the cardinal principles of the legal system in the light of which rules of law are interpreted and applied. In default of specific rules they are applied to concrete cases. He points out that this is expressly provided for in a number of municipal codes, e.g. the Argentinian, Brazilian, Chinese, Guatemalan, Italian, Mexican, Peruvian, Siamese and Spanish Civil Codes. See 'General principles of law as a subject for international codification', *C.L.P.*, vol. 4, 1951, p. 39.

[2] H. Lauterpacht: *Private Law Sources and Analogies of International Law*; 1927, B. A. Wortley: 'The interaction of public and private international law today', *Recueil des Cours*, 1954, I, pp. 245–338. Professor Wortley in chap. IV of his lectures deals with some general principles common to public and private international law (pp. 313–26).

[3] C. W. Jenks: *The Proper Law of International Organizations*, 1962, pt. 2.

[4] W. Friedmann: *The Changing Structure of International Law*, 1964, pp. 152–87.

[5] *Ibid.*, pp. 186–7. See also Lord Asquith's award in the Abu Dhabi Arbitration, L. C. Green, *International Law Through Cases*, 1959, 2nd edn., pp. 390–7. Programmes of international legal studies by comparative method have been initiated at Harvard and Cornell. For the Cornell Programme see R. B. Schlesinger: 'Research on General Principles . . .', *op. cit.*, pp. 734–53.

[6] For example, in the international loan agreements of the World Bank, 'General principles' are assumed to be applied to the transactions; see A. Broches: 'International legal aspects of the operations of the World Bank', *Recueil des Cours*, 1959, III, pp. 301–408; see also F. A. Mann: 'The proper law of contracts concluded by international persons', *B.Y.B.I.L.*, vol. 35, 1959, pp. 34–57.

[7] For some references to efforts made to formulate certain 'general principles' especially in the area of human rights, see Schlesinger, *op. cit.*, pp. 750–1.

[8] For instances of procedural and evidentiary principles which are felt to be inherent in all civilized legal systems see Schlesinger, *op. cit.*, pp. 736–7, n. 10.

recognized in the legal systems of the world.[1] It is the last category
of general principles which can contribute much to the development
of international law in the new fields. It would also unfold the possibilities and prospects of future development of international law
aiming to secure on a world-wide basis the essential elements of a
world legal order which give reasonable expression to mankind's
sense of right and justice. If international law were codified and
developed from the common elements of major legal systems—the
European, Latin-American, Islamic, Hindu, Buddhist, Jewish,
African and Communist, all of which are still in a process of evolution—we may reasonably expect that by and large the great majority of the international community will accept codified international
law as an essential element in the community life of the universal
society.[2]

Usually the norms of law are practical compromises between the
rational moral ideals of what ought to be, and the possibilities of
the situation as determined by given equilibria of vital forces. The
form in which a system of law expresses the elements of ideals of
justice is a consequence of pressures and counter-pressures in a
living community. So law embodies, indeed, rationalization of competing expectations, or ordering of conduct developed by reason.
The theory of the law of nations, as we know it from the seventeenth
century to the world wars of the present century, was based on a
theory of the law of nature—a postulated ideal law of universal
validity and applicability—governing the conduct of all men at all
times and in all relationships, and derived from and demonstrated
by reason. In the modern science of international law also, natural
law has had a marked revival.[3] In the rapidly changing present
century, faced by wars, revolutions, rebellions, and by problems of
reforming and creating law, positivism has suffered. The profound

[1] Friedmann, *Changing Structure of Int. Law*, pp. 196–210, Dr. Jenks rightly
maintains that 'if we eliminate the ritualistic elements of certain legal systems,
the whole family law, virtually the whole law of real property and much of the
criminal law, we will find that we are left with an area within which the most
varied legal systems recognize certain principles and have to a substantial extent
mutually influenced one another's growth'. For his exploratory survey of such
principles see *Common Law of Mankind*, p. 109 and pp. 120–69; see also Cheng:
'General principles . . .', *op. cit.*, pp. 40–52.
[2] Roscoe Pound speaks of three requisites of world justice according to law:
i. international law adapted to the world as it is, or as we seek to make it, i.e., a world
of democratically organized societies; ii. an effective political organization equal
to making a system of world justice according to law possible; iii. sufficient cultural
unification to bring about an ideal universal background of universally received
ideals of right and justice behind the world legal order: see 'Legal Education',
op. cit., p, 14.
[3] J. L. Kunz: 'Natural law thinking in the modern science of international law',
A.J.I.L., vol. 55, 1961, pp. 951–8.

crisis of our times brought about by the abuse of law for purposes of injustice, torture and extermination, the threat of total war with thermo-nuclear weapons, and the ideological antagonism, has accelerated this trend of a return to natural law.[1]

It is submitted that the notion of natural law which has been so constructive and valuable to man, despite the lack of clarity as to the use of the term, has potentialities as a system of highest ethical principles. It may enable the codifiers to evaluate the norms of existing international law from an ethical point of view, to examine the ultimate foundation of their authority, and to guarantee by codified laws universal reasonable expectations involved in life in a civilized society. Since the quest for certainty of law is also the quest for clear and definite standards of valuation whenever action is involved, the notion of natural law, both as a recognition of a law common to humanity and as an assertion of the fundamental rights of man,[2] and also as a rational basis for social and political institutions, can serve as an instrument of stability as well as of change in the reconstruction of international law.

Furthermore, it can be said that the 'general principles of law recognized by civilized nations' are nothing but the fundamental and universal principles accepted for many centuries by jurists and philosophers as constituting the natural law, and thus their recognition by Article 38 of the Statute of the International Court of Justice is recognition of natural law without naming it.[3] It is submitted that fundamental legal principles and ideals which have a consensus[4] of the greater part of the whole world and which should

[1] A.J.I.L., vol. 55, 1961, pp. 954–6.

[2] Sir Hersch Lauterpacht is the most prominent name who returned to natural law, in his *An International Bill of the Rights of Man*, 1945, with regard to the problem of the international protection of human rights and freedoms. Amongst other international lawyers following the general trend of the revival of natural law may be mentioned Krabbe, Drost, Nicolas Politis, Georges Scelle, Charles de Visscher, Max Huber and Verdross. A substantial contribution to international law in regard to human rights is made by the European Convention of Human Rights; see A. H. Robertson: *Human Rights in Europe*, Manchester, 1963; also Gordon L. Weil: 'The evolution of European Convention of Human Rights', A.J.I.L., vol. 57, 1962, pp. 804–27.

[3] J. B. Scott: *Law, The State, and the International Community*, New York, 1939, vol. I, pp. 269–70.

[4] Two writers of distinction have recently drawn attention to a discernible trend from consent to consensus basis of international legal obligations and to the present-day need of a limited legislative authority to translate an overriding consensus among states into rules of order and norms of obligations despite the opposition of one or more sovereign states. See Falk and Mendlovitz: 'Towards a warless world: one legal formula to achieve transition', *Yale L.J.*, vol. 73, 1964, p. 399. The U.S. Supreme Court has recently relied upon the notion of consensus in the course of assessing the reality of an international legal obligation by holding that the traditional rules of international law requiring an expropriating government to pay an alien investor 'prompt, adequate, and effective compensation' were no longer supported by a consensus of sovereign states. See Banco Nacional de Cuba v.

govern the international law of the future need be stated in the form of a Declaration of the General Principles of Law. This alone would be the best codification which would not only serve to orient international law but also to assist the International Court of Justice in the application and development of the great principles of international law.[1] This pioneering experiment is worthwhile as the knowledge of a common core of legal principles may create a feeling of solidarity for a better community of nations and of men.

In conclusion, we may say that, since the idea of a code of international law that has stirred in man's mind for so long has crystallized itself into definite responsibility under the auspices of the United Nations, the conscious efforts to clarify and improve the content of international law is bound to continue in spite of the vicissitudes of world affairs. Although in the light of the complexities of modern international life it may be impossible to codify simultaneously the entire body of international law, the codification of parts of the law at any one time and in gradual stages will be a process of continuous adaptation to changing circumstances of international life. History bears testimony to the fact that interests which have been vital at one time gradually lose their importance, and time comes when a compromise becomes feasible to embody them in codification. Perhaps a longer and broader perspective of the older states which tend to regard international law as a projection of their own traditions and values, and a mature acceptance by the newer members of the international community of their full share of responsibility for upholding and promoting the development of the common legal standards, may open a new and more realistic era in the history both of that aspiration and of human organization generally. The obstacles in the way of complete codification are too serious to permit any facile optimism. An exhaustive code of rules of public international law can only, as we have seen, be built up step by step after prolonged research, followed by patient negotiation and widespread consultation. To succumb to a spirit of disillusion and defeatism and to regard the movement for codification as a mere pious aspiration would be a disaster. The contemporary achievements of the work of the International Law

---

Sabbatino, 376, U.S. 398, *A.J.I.L.*, vol. 58, 1964, p. 779; for interpretation, see Falks: 'The complexity of Sabbatino', *ibid.*, p. 935.

[1] As Professor Schlesinger observes: 'if it were possible to find and formulate a core of legal ideas which are common to all civilized legal systems, the effect might transcend the area of international law (however broadly defined) and of international organizations, and might go far beyond the goal—even though in itself it is an ambitious goal—of implementing Article 38 of the Statute. Tentatively . . . it is suggested that establishment of such a common core might lead to practical results in a number of areas of legal endeavor': 'Research on general principles of law', *op. cit.*, p. 739.

Commission—whether conventions signed and ratified, or the several projects which may not seem to amount to very much in concrete results for years to come—are the milestones of progress indicative of the present-day world's farthest points of agreement. We may repeat here Elihu Root's optimistic words after the two Hague Conferences in regard to their achievements which apply equally to those of the Commission: 'they are like cable ends buoyed in mid-ocean, to be picked up hereafter by some other steamer, spliced, and continued to shore. The greater the reform proposed, the longer must be the process required to bring nations differing widely in their laws, customs, traditions, interests, prejudices into agreement. Each necessary step in the process is as useful as the final act which crowns the work and is received with public celebration.'[1]

[1] *Addresses on International Subjects*, ed. Robert Bacon and J. B. Scott, 1916, p. 129.

INDEX

Abbé Grégoire, 44–46, 11n
Abu Dhabi Arbitration (1951), 346n
Achievements of the Commission, Chapter VI, 271–322: topics under study, 321–332; works completed, 271–321
Adams, H. B., 49n, 50n
Ad hoc diplomacy, *see* International law, special missions
Afghanistan, 171, 238n, 253n
Ago, Roberto (Italy), 241–242n, 324
Alabama Arbitration, 24
Alberoni, Cardinal, 11n
Alexander II, Czar of Russia, 84
Alfaro, Ricardo J. (Panama), 193n, 228n, 258n, 272, 282n, 283n, 285
Algeria, 171
Allen, William, 20
Alvarez, Señor Alejandro, 71n, 72n, 130, 135, 335n
Amado, Gilberto (Brazil), 282n
American Institute of International law, 62, 71, 72, 73, 135, 136, 221, 265
American Law Institute, 69, 221n
American Peace Society, 15, 20, 21n, 24, 25
American Society for the Judicial Settlement of Disputes, 62
American Society of International Law, 62, 198n, 343n; co-operation with the League, 73–75
American States, international conferences of: Bogota (1948), 264n; Habana (1928), 135–136; history of, 133; Lima (1938), 137; Mexico City (1901), 134; Montevideo (1933), 136–137; Rio de Janeiro (1906), 135; Santiago (1923), 135
Anglo-American Arbitration Treaty (1897), 24
Anglo-Norwegian Fisheries Case (1951), 306–307
Annuaire de l'Institut de Droit International, 65, 66
Appleton, L., 24n
Arbitration, international: draft regulations of Institute of International Law, 64; Fiore on, 55; Hague Conferences and, 95–97, 100, 104, 106; International Law Association and, 67; Model rules on arbitral procedure, 292–295; Pan-American Union on, 27; proposal of ILC as to reports

of awards, 287, 288n; Wave in legislatures of motions on, 24
Argentina, 152n, 171, 238n
Arnault, M., 62n
Asian-African Legal Consultative Committee; consultative relations with ILC, 267–269, 270n, 337; objects of, 268; origin of, 267
Asquith, Lord, 346n
Association for the Reform and Codification of International Law, *see* International Law Association
Asylum Case (Colombia v. Peru), (1950), 330n
Auguste, B. B. L., 306n
Australia, 152n, 168
Austria, 171, 247, 328

Bacon, R., 63n, 110n, 350n
Bailey, S. D., 175n, 188n
Balch, T. W., 7n
Baldwin, S. E., 86n, 102n
Ball, M. M., 175n
Banco Nacional de Cuba v. Sabbatino, (1964), 348n–349n
Bara, Louis, 47
Barker, Sir Ernest, 3n
Bartos, Milan (Yugoslavia), 247, 325, 327
Beales, A. C. F., 21n, 23n, 29n
Beckett, W. E. (U.K.), 163n
Bedjaoui, Mohammed (Algeria), 326n
Belaunde, Victor A. (Peru), 264n
Belgium, 230–231, 260n
Bellers, John, 5, 10
Bellot, H. H., 10n
Bellot, Hugh H. L., 78n
Bentham, Jeremy, 5, 13, 15, 21n, 45, 46, 53, codification movement and, 37–44
Biddle, Justice, 277n
Bingham, J. W., 69
Bishop, W. W., 305n
Bluntschli, Johann Caspar, 5, 54, 55, 57, 63, 66, 78n, 84, 111, 221; codification project, 49–51; peace plan, 17–18
Bolivar, Simon, 134
Bolivia, 171
Borchard, E. M., 11n, 53n, 54n, 56n, 60n, 61n, 69, 125n, 137n, 141n
Bosanquet, Helen, 23n
Bowett, D. W., 28on, 309n, 310; on definition of aggression, 283–284
Bowring, Dr. J., 38n

351

Bozeman, A. B., 339n
Brazil, 151n, 152n, 171, 238n, 309n
Brierly, James L. (U.K.), 116n, 129n, 130n, 152n, 189, 199n, 218n, 225n, 234n, 246n, 264n, 321n; on codification and progressive development, 204–205; report on reservations to treaties, 288–289
Briggs, Herbert W. (U.S.), 259n, 314, 332
Bright, John, 21, 23n
Britain (U.K.), 85n, 141, 152n, 171, 182n; agreements on fishing rights, 310–311; distinguishes codification from consolidation, 205n; initiation in convening London Naval Conference, 109, 110; and on safety of life at sea, 231
British Assn. for the Promotion of Social Sciences, 51, 52, 62
British Fabian Society, 29
British League of Free Nations, 29n
British Society for Promotion of Permanent and Universal Peace, 20
Broches, A., 346n
Brockhaus, F. A., 48n
Brown, H. B., 102n
Brown, P. M., 64n, 222n
Brownlie, I., 227n, 281n, 283n
Brussels Conference and Declaration (1974), 84–85, 90, 92, 93
Bryce, Lord, 6, 7n, 29
Burdick, C. K., 70
Burke, W. T., 219n, 302n, 306n, 311n
Burma, 268n
Burritt, Elihu, 15, 16, 21
Burton, J. H., 38n
Bustamente, Antonio S. de, 135n
Butler, G. G., 7n, 81n
Butler, N. M., 14n

Calvo of Buenos Aires, 63
Canada, 171, 238n, 260n
Carlyle, A. J., 4n
Carlyle, R. W., 4n
Carter, W. Horsfall, 8n
Castañeda, Jorge (Mexico), 298n
Castrén, Erik (Finland), 313n
Catherine II, Empress, 76, 77
Casual vacancies, see Members ILC, and Statute, art. 11
Central Organization for a Durable Peace, 29
Ceylon, 238n, 268n
Chamberlin, W., 147n
Charter, UN: art. 1, 148; art. 12, 185n; art. 13, drafting, purpose and implementation of, 148–152, 201; art. 39, 281–282
Cheng, B., 172n, 211–212n, 344n, 346n, 347n
China, 141, 152n, 171, 315

Choate, J. H., 104n
Clark, Sir George, 3n
Clark, Grenville, 338n
Clausula rebus sic stantibus, 319
Cobden, Richard, 7, 17n, 21, 23n
Code Napoléon, 244n
Codification of international law, see also International law topics and Progressive development:
Codification of international law: appraisal of, before World War I, 111–112; codification and progressive development:
  bearing of external factors, 339–341; concerned with sources of international law, 217–219; close interrelationship, 215, 231; defined, 203, 204–207; distinction made or queried, 149–150, 151, 154–155, 163, 203, 209, 211–213, 226, 231–233, 338; distinction blurred in practice, 209–211, 231, 302; distinguished from collecting evidence of customary international law, 202; factors retarding progress, 339–341; view of Survey, 207–209
  Committee of Seventeen on, 152–160; future prospects: Chapter VII, 333–350; Hague Conferences: of 1899 and 1907, 87–109, and of 1930, 121–133; importance of researches and sociological enquiries, 334–336, and other essentials, 337–339; individual countries' contribution, 76–79; initiative in, 201, 227–229, of General Assembly, 235–236, and of single states, 226n, 236; Inter-American System, 133–140; laws of war, 140–143; link with peace movement, 37; London Conference (1908–1909), 109–110; methods of: by conventions, 218–221, 230–231, by draft articles, 207, 229, by restatement, 221–224, Committee of Seventeen, 155–156, Statute, 219–225, view of survey, 208–209, 223; official efforts at, Chapter III, 76–143; private efforts at, Chapter II, 37–75; procedures, 157–159, 227–233; projects of individuals, 37–62; and of scientific organizations, 62–75; regulation of social and economic problems, 85–87; selection of topics, 233–250:
    controversial topics, 248–249, guiding principles, 242–251; list of topics in ILC provisional list, 234n, suggestions of governments, 240n, 248, of ILC members, 245–246; topics rejected, 245; topics worth considering, 332;

task of ILC in regard to, 201–202
United Nations Codification Conferences, 317–318, 320–321, and conventions, 318–320; work done on:
by individual scholars: Grègoire, 44–46; Bara, 47; Bentham, 37–44; Bluntschli, 49–51; Coline, 47; Domin-Petrushevecz, 48–49; Duplessix, 56–58; Field, 51–53; Fiore, 53–56; Internoscia, 58–61; Katchenovsky, 47–58; Paroldo, 47
by individual countries: America, 77–78; Britain, 79; Russia, 76–77
by inter-American System, 133–140
by international conferences, 81–112:
Brussels Conference (1874), 84–85; Congress of Vienna, 81–82; Declaration of St. Petersburg, 83–84; Geneva Convention (1864), 83; Hague peace conferences (1899, 1907), 87–109
by League of Nations, 112–113
by scientific organizations: 62–75: American Institute of International Law, 71–73; American Society of International Law, 73–74; Contribution of, 74–75, 125; Harvard Law School, 68–71; Institute of International Law, 63–66; International Law Association, 66–68
Cole, G. D. H., 30n, 59n
Coline, Lorenzo, 47
Colombia, 134, 152n, 171, 329, 330n
Colombos, C., 38n
Comité Maritime International, 117n
Committee on Progressive Development of International Law or Committee of Seventeen, 162, 164, 178, 204, 224, 266, 274, 284: establishment of, 151, functions, 152, report, 153–160; codification and progressive development explained, 154–155, 204; machinery of codification; 156–157; means of codification, 155–156, 224; problems examined 154; scientific bodies and codification, 159–160; 262–263; technique of work, 157–159, 160
Competence of the General Assembly for the Admission of a State to the United Nations, (1950), 197n
Conditions of Admission of a State to Membership of the United Nations, advisory opinion (1948), 197n
Convention, definition of, 91n
Convention on the International Régime of Maritime Ports (1923), 124n

Convention on the Nationality of Married Women, 263
Convention on the Reduction of Statelessness (1961), 297
Convention Relating to the Status of Stateless persons (1954), 298n
Corbett, P. E., 147n, 208n, 218n
Cordova, Roberto (Mexico), 182n, 188n, 191n, 224n, 282n, 293, 296n
Cory, H. M., 97n
Conservation of Living Resources of the Sea: Convention on Fishing and, 305; Rome Conference on, (1955), 300
Covenant of the League of Nations, *see* League of Nations; art. 14 of, 116; character as a higher law, 112–113; described as codification, 113–114; feeble reference to international law, 114
Cremer, W. R., 26n
Crimean War, 22, 82
Crucé, Emeric, 5, 7, 113n
Cuba, 171, 226n, 309n
Czar Nicholas II of Russia, 26, 89, 99
Czechoslovakia, 17, 247

Darby, W. Evans, 7n, 9n, 10n, 13n, 17n
Dante Alighieri, 5, 6, 7
Davis, G. B., 103n
Davies, Lord David, 12n
Dahomey, 171
Deak, Francis, 70
Dean, A. H., 304n, 307n, 309n
Declaration, defined, 91n
Declaration of London (1909), 102 109–110
Degras, Jane, 32n
De lege ferenda, 54, 109, 139, 201, 211, 334, 335
De Martens, Frederic, 99, 342n
De Nelidov, M., 99, 108
De Staal, M., 89
De Visscher, Charles, 208n, 257, 348n
Denmark, 247, 310
Dickinson, E. D., 70, 107n
Dickinson, G. Lowes, 29
Diena, Professor, 130n, 207n
Distribution of documents, 268, 269, 270, 287–288
Dodge, David Low, 20
Dogger Bank Case (1904), 100
Domin-Petrushevecz, 48–49
Drago doctrine, 100
Draper, G. I. A. D., 142n, 143n
Drost, 348n
Dubois, Pierre, 5, 6
Dumbarton Oaks Conference (1944), 147-148
Dumont, Etienne, 40, 342n
Dunant, Henri, 83

AA

Dunn, F. S., 106n
Duplessix, E., 56–58
Dutt, R. P., 30n

Economic and Social Council (ECOSOC): appoints *ad hoc* committee on genocide, 284; competence of initiative in codification, 158n, 159n; in relationship with ILC, 262–263; resolution 47 (IV), 1947, 152n, 262–263; resolution 678 (XXVI), 1958, 156n; resolution 304 D (XI), 1950, 263n, 295n; work on statelessness and status of women, 298n
Ecuador, 171
Edmonds, Douglas L. (U.S.), 279n, 298n
Edmunds, P. D., 168n
Effect of Awards of the United Nations Administrative Tribunal, Advisory Opinion (1954), 197n
Egypt, 152n, 166n, 171
El-Erian, Abdullah, 329
El-Khouri, Faris (Syria), 232n
El Salvador, 226n, 330
Emoluments of ILC members, under Statute of ILC, art. 13: comparison with those of *ad hoc* judges of ICJ, 184; honoraria, 182; inadequacy of, 183; secretariat report on, 183n; special allowance, 177–178; subsistence allowance, 182–183; travel allowance, 177, 182, 183
Encyclopaedia Britannica, 13, 47, 94n
Encyclopaedia of Social Sciences, 28n, 46n
European Committee on Legal Co-operation, 270, 337
Ethiopia, 141, 303n, 308, 310n
Evans, H., 26n
Evans, W. V. J. (U.K.), 226n
Everett, C. W., 39n

Fabian Society, 29
Falk, R. A., 218n, 348n, 349n
Feller, A. H., 70
Fenwick, C. G., 88n, 137n, 138n, 281n
Ferrater, Don Esteban, 47
Field, David Dudley, 25, 54, 57, 63, 66, 111, 202, 221; projection codification, 51–53
Field, H. M., 51n
Fifth Committee, General Assembly: appreciation lacked on emoluments of ILC members, 182; honoraria for Sp. Rapporteurs, 183
Finch, G. A., 286n
Fiore, Pasquale, 11n, 57, 60, 61n, 111; projection codification, 53–56
Fitzmaurice, Sir Gerald (U.K.), 174n, 180, 182n, 214n, 225n, 298n, 307n, 321n, 322n

Flournoy, Jr., R. W., 69, 122n, 127n
France, 84, 110, 141, 152n, 171, 258n, 328
Franco-Prussian War (1870), 23
François, M., 124n
François, J. P. A. (Netherlands), 189n, 195n, 209n, 226n, 234n, 244n, 252n, 298, 299, 301n; on guiding principles for selection to topics, 246–247
Franklin, C. M., 309n
Franco-German War, 84–85
French Civil Code, 203
French Revolution, 45, 46
Friedmann, W., 4n, 172n, 208n; on classification of general principles of law, 346–347
Fromageot (France), 116n
Fry, Ruth, 10n
Functions of the Commission and its methodology: Chapter V, 201–270: co-operation with intergovernmental organization, 266–270; functions, 201–216; defined in Survey, 208, 209; and in Statute, 201–202; methods, procedure etc., 217–266: difficulties of convention method, 219–221; utility of statement method, 221–222, 225
Future prospects: Chapter VII, 333–350; bearing of external factors, 339–341; general principles of law-potentialities, 344–350; methods, sources, 341–344

Garcia-Amador, F. V. (Cuba), 185n, 235n, 239n, 244n, 252n, 265, 267n, 268n, 270, 298n, 305n, 306n, 310n, 323
Garner, J. W., 53n, 70, 79n, 110n, 112n, 140n
Gee, Wilson, 338n
General Assembly, United Nations, *see also* Fifth and Sixth Committees: action of ILC drafts, 230; and request for priority to ILC, 235–236; approval for selection of topics and controversy, 227–228, 233–234; assignment of special problems to ILC, 203; election of ILC members, 173–177; initiative in asking ILC to study a topic, 201, 225–226, 235–236, 237, and for priority treatment, 228–229, at the instance of political committee, 237; resolution on future work of ILC, 237–241; resolutions referred: 24(I), 1946, U.N. willingness to exercise certain functions of the league, 292n
38 (I), 1946, rights and duties of states, 152n

94(I), 1946, appointing Committee of Seventeen on Codification, 151, 152, 153

95(I), 1946, affirming Nuremberg principles, 274, 276, 277n

174(II), 1947, establishing the ILC, 164, 269

177(II), 1947, asking ILC to formulate Nuremberg Principles and a draft code of offences, 274, 276

178(II), 1947, rights and duties of states, 272n, 277, 280

260(III) B, 1938, study of the questions of international criminal jurisdiction, 284–285

362(IV), 1949, distribution of items to the committees, 238n

374(IV), 1949, study of the régime of territorial waters, 226n, 235n, 299, 300

375(IV), 2949, requesting governments for comments on draft declaration on rights and duties of states, 274

378(V), 1950, question of defining aggression, 237, 282

478(V), 1950, requesting study of the question of reservation, 289

484(V), 1950, requesting ILC to review its Statute, 209n, 232n

485(V), 1950, special allowances for ILC members, 164n, 178n, 182n

486(V), 1950, extending terms of ILC Members, 178

487(V), 1950, evidence of customary international law, 288

488 (V), 1950, requesting ILC to take account of the draft code of offences in formulating Nuremberg principles, 276

489(V), 1950, establishing international criminal court, 285–286

499(V), 1950, requesting comments of governments on Nuremberg principles, 276n

596(V), 1951, postponing decision on draft declaration on rights and duties of states, 274

598(VI), 1952, reservation clauses in future conventions, 290

685(VII), 1952, study of diplomatic intercourse, 226n, 235n, 311

687(VII), 1952, international criminal jurisdiction, 286n

798(VIII), 1953, law of the sea, 235n, 301n

799(VIII), 1953, state responsibility, 226n, 235n, 323

821(IX), 1954, complaint of violation of freedom of navigation in China Seas, 237

896(IV), 1954, elimination and reduction of future statelessness, 297

898(IX), 1954, question of defining aggression, 286

899(IX), 1954, on the law of the sea, 235n, 299

900(IX), 1955, convening Conference on Conservation of Living Resources of the Sea, 300n

984(X), 1955, on amending art. 12 of the Statute of ILC, 164n, 185

985(X), 1955, five year term of ILC, 177n, 182

987(X), 1955, publication of ILC documents and records, 198

989(X), 1955, Draft Convention on Arbitral Procedure, 293

1040(XI), 1956, relating to Status of Women, 298n

1075(XI), 1956, approving rates of subsistence allowance for members of eligible bodies, 183

1103(XI), 1956, enlarging ILC to 21 members, 164n, 165n

1105(XI), 1957, convoking Conference on Law, 302

1106(XI), 1957, confirming special allowance of ILC members, 183

1187(XII), 1957, definition of aggression and its connection with other questions, 286

1202(XII), 1957, pattern of U.N. conferences, 186

1262(XIII), 1958, take note of Model Rules of Arbitral procedure, 294

1282(XIII), 1958, inviting comments on draft articles on diplomatic intercourse and immunities, 311n

1289(XIII), 1958, relations between states and intergovernmental organizations, 328

1307(XIII), 1958, convoking second Conference on the Law of Sea, 308

1400(XIV), 1959, right of asylum, 226n, 235n, 248n, 330

1401(XIV), 1959, utilization and use of international rivers, 235n

1450(XIV), 1959, convoking conference on diplomatic intercourse and immunities, 312

1451(XIV), 1959, publication of *Juridical Yearbook*, 200n

1450(XIV), 1959, juridical régime

General Assembly, resolutions (*contd*)
of historic waters, 235n, 248n,
330
1505(XV), 1960, future programme of the Commission, 215,
237–238, 240–241, 246, 247,
260, 325, 329, 330n
1588(XV), 1960, increasing of subsistence allowance of ILC members, 183
1647(XVI), 1961, enlarging membership of ILC, 164n, 165n, 173n
1685(XVI), convoking conference
on Consular Intercourse and
immunities, 315
1686(XVI), 1961, limiting ILC's
programme of work, 235, 240,
241n, 323, 325
1687(XVI), 1961, special missions,
236, 327
1765(XVII), 1962, future programme of ILC, 241n
1766(XVII), 1962, study of extended participation in multilateral treaties, 236n, 291
1814(XVII), 1962, publication of
juridical yearbook of United
Nations, 200n
1851(XVII), 1963, extending pattern of United Nations Conferences, 187
1968(XVIII), 1963, technical assistance to promote teaching and
study of international law, 343
2021(XX), 1965, League of Nations Treaties, 292
2054(XX), 1965, organizing seminars on international law, 343n
2116(XII), 1965, holding of ILC
sessions, 185n
2272(XXII), 1967, future programme and methods of work
of ILC, 332n
2312(XXII), declaration on territorial asylums, 330
General principles of law: natural law
and, 348; need of codifying,
349; potentialities as a source,
341, 344–346
Geneva:
Conference (1949) and conventions,
141–143
Conference on the Law of the Sea
(1958, 1960):
accomplishments, 305–307; adopts
conventions, 304, and resolutions,
304n; conflicting interests at conferences, 309–312; Conventions:
on Continental Shelf, 305–306, on
Fishing and Conservation of Living Resources, 305, on High Seas,

305, on Territorial Sea and Contiguous Zone, 306–307; failings,
307–308, 309–310; Issues at the
Second Conference (1960): preferential fishing rights, 309, six-
milers *v.* twelve milers, 308–309;
resolutions adopted, 304n; resolution on régime of historic waters,
330
Conventions on the Conduct of War-
fare (1864, 1868, 1906, 1929), 79,
90, 91, 92, 93, 141
Convention concerning the Treat-
ment of the Sick and Wounded
and Prisoners of War (1929), 141
Gas Protocol (1925), 141
Peace Society, 21
Genocide Convention: 152, 153n, in-
itiative of ECOSOC, 262; request
for ICJ Advisory opinion on, 289
Genser (Canada), 252n
German Peace Union (1894), 26n
Germany, 173n, 315n
Gesammelte Kleine Schriften, 17
Ghana, 238n
Gihl, T., 220n
Gilman, D. C., 49n
Goodrich, L. M., 32n
Grand Design of Henry IV, 8–9, 10
Green, L. C., 305n, 346n
Greenspan, M., 141n
Grégoire, Abbé, 44–46
Gregory, C. N., 44n, 102n
Gros, André (France), 241n
Grotius, Hugo, 5, 7–8
Gudmundsson (Iceland), 309n
Guerrero (Salvador), 116n–117n
Gutteridge, H. C., 168n, 345n
Gutteridge, J. A. C., 142n, 143n, 305n

Hackworth, G. H., 125n, 259
Hague Academy, 140
Hague Codification Conference (1930),
298, 303n, 304: appraisal of, 126–
133; confusion as to purpose, 129–
130, and as to codification, 203–204n;
defective preparatory work, 128–129,
221; influence on Montevideo Conference (1933), 136; insufficient collaboration with governments, 257;
instruments adopted, 122–126; preparatory work by Harvard Law
School, 69, 121, 122
Hague Congress of Women, 28
Hague Convention on Certain Questions relating to Conflict of Nationality Laws (1930), 122
Hague Peace Conference and Conventions (1899), 16, 19, 23, 26, 55, 56,
63, 64, 76, 79, 83, 84, 85, 239n;

achievements, 90–97; Czar's initiative in convoking, 88; influence of, 98; procedure adopted, 90, 105; programme, 89

Hague Peace Conference and Conventions (1907), 55–56, 63–64, 79, 80, 84, 96, 97, 98, 167n, 239n, 16: achievements, 99–104, meetings and programme, 99; Appraisal of Hague Conferences, 104–109, 220: failings in organization and procedures, 104–107, inherent limitations, 107–109, 112, preparatory work contrasted with 1930 Conference, 121, and with Panama Conference, 134

Hague Protocol relating to Military Obligations in Certain Cases of Double Nationality, 123, 126n

Hague Protocols relating to Statelessness, 123, 126n

Hale, R. W., 124n

Hammarskjöld (Sweden), 116n

Harley, J. E., 29n, 86n

Harvard Law School: collaboration with ILC and criticism of, 264–265; drafts presented as Research (1927–1939), 69–70; merit and influence, 70–71; organization of research in international law, 68–69; preparatory work for Hague Conference 1930, 121; restatement method, 221

Hastie, W., 14n

Haya dela torre case (Colombia v. Peru) (1951), 330n

Heemskerke, M., 121

Hemleben, Sylvester J., 6n, 7n, 9n, 11–12n

Henry, Aurelia, 6n

Hershey, A. S., 100n

Hertslet, 342n

Hicks, F. C., 107n

Higgins, R., 83n, 85n, 219n, 283n

Hindu Code, 203

Hinsley, F. H., 21n, 26n, 31n

Hobson, R. P., 103n

Holdsworth, W. S., 44n

Holland, T. E., 57n, 78n, 79n, 80n, 83n, 84n

Holls, George Frederick Williams, 87n, 88n, 89n, 94n, 95n, 98n

Holmbäck (Sweden), 253n

Holmes, Oliver Wendell, 338n

Holy See, 303

Honig, F., 177n

Hover, Jr., T., 147n

Hsu, Shuhsi (China), 246n, 252n, 258n, 282n

Huber, Max, 113n, 348n

Hudson, Manley O. (U.S.), 68, 71n, 112n, 114n, 127n, 128n, 129n, 132n, 166n, 167n, 168n, 186, 191n, 193n, 197n, 199n, 218n, 219n, 232n, 258n, 273n, 275n, 287, 295n, 296n 344; on preparing digests of practice of States, 342–343

Hugo, Victor, 21

Hull, W. I., 104n

Humphrey, A. W., 28n

Hurst, Sir Cecil, 121n, 129n, 133n, 222n

Hurst, J. W., 51n

Hyde, C. C., 103n

Iceland, 226n, 235n, 301n, 309n, 310

Ilbert, Sir Courtney, 39n

India, 141, 152n, 168, 171, 253n, 260n, 268n

Indonesia, 168n, 268n

Indus dispute, 74n

Instut ibérique de droit comparé, 117n

Institute of International Law: 25, 53, 62, 69, 71, 78, 85, 140, 198n, 239n; codification projects, 64–65; favours scientific statement, 163n, 222–223; founded, 63; guidance to the Hague Conferences and to the League of Nations, 239; limitations and procedures, 65–66; potentialities of service to ILC, 66, 68, 265; resolution on codification, 222–223

Instructions for the Government of Armies of the United States (1963); see also Francis Lieber, 77–78

Inter-American Council of Jurists, 149n, 152n: co-operative relation with ILC, 266–267, 337; formation of, 139

Inter-American Juridical Committee, 138, 139, 156n

Inter-American Neutrality Committee, 137–138

International Arbitration League, 17

International Arbitration and Peace Association of Great Britain (1880), 23n

International Code Committee of U.S.A., 25, 66

International Commission of Jurists, 135, 136, 137

International Conference of American States, Bogota (1948), 264n

International Conference on the Red Cross: Committee of Red Cross, 62; Convention (1906), 93, 102; Geneva Conventions (1949) and, 141; Seventh Conference, Stockholm (1948), 142n

International Court of Justice: 157, 176, 288, 339; compared with ILC, 166n, 180, 181n, 184, 195, 289; dissident opinion of judges, 194–195,

International Court of Justice (*contd*)
197; preparatory work, 197; statute of:
art. 2, 167n
art. 3, 157
art. 8–12, 157
art. 9, 167n–168n
art. 34, 285
art. 38, 172, 221, 230, 340, 341, 348
art. 57, 194n
International Institute for Unification of Private Law, 156n
International Labour Organization:
formation of, 31; legislation, 114, 115; labour conventions and reservations, 131, 290; mode of consulting governments, 258
International law: topics completed, considered or projected by ILC; *see also* Codification; Selection of topics; Progressive development
aggression:
assignment by GA, 203, 282; Charter of UN fails to define, 281–282; Commission attempts defining, 282–283; initiative of Political Committee, 237; main schools of definition, 283n; problem, 283–284; work of ILC, 281–284
arbitral procedure:
Commission adopts final draft on, 292–293; and favours Model Rules on, 293; and initiative in study of, 237, 292; and places in first provisional list, 234n; Models Rules on, 293–295; combination of codification and progressive development, 210; GA appreciates, 294; not favourable to a convention, 293
asylum:
declaration on, 330; initiative by Salvador, 226n, 236, 330; in the first provisional list, 234n; priority call by Colombia, 329; and by GA, 235
complaint of violation of the freedom of navigation in China Seas, 237
consular intercourse and immunities:
achievements of Vienna Convention, 316, 319; debate on inviting States, 315n; drafts articles adopted by ILC, 315; initiative of ILC on, 237; influence of Vienna Convention of diplomatic relations, 316; in the first provisional list, 234n; ratification position of the convention on, 318; reciprocity clause, 316–317; reports of Zourek, 315; resolution on refugee question, 315–316

Continental shelf:
convention on, 305–306; ratification position of convention, 318n; revision provision in the convention, 319
customary international law:
making evidence available, 286–288; ways and means, 201–202
diplomatic intercourse and immunities:
comparison with Geneva Conference on Law of Sea, 313–314; draft articles adopted by ILC, 311; in first provisional list, 234n; priority call by GA, 235; reciprocity clause in Vienna Convention on, 314; reference to the question of special mission, 313, 326, 327; Sandström reports, 311; Vienna Conference, and Conventions, 312–313, 314, 319; appraisal, 313–314, and observers attending, 312n, and ratification position, 318, resolutions adopted, 313; Yugoslavia's initiative in GA, 226n, 236
extended participation of multilateral treaties:
GA and the question of, 236, 291, 292; ILC raised the problem, 290–291; and examines, 291–292
future work:
first review (1961), 215, 237–239, 246, 248, 252–253; limits of, 240–241; second review (1966), 248–249; third review (1968), 249n; Verdross on, 246; views of governments, 247–248
high seas, régime of:
Convention on Fishing and Conservation of Living Resources of, 303, 304, 305; draft articles of ILC, 299–300, 301; Geneva Convention on, 305; and ratification position of, 318n; in the first provisional list of ILC, 234n, 235; initiative by, ILC, 237; Rapporteur's reports, 299
historic waters and bays, 235, 236:
Geneva Conference adopts resolution on, 304n, 330; initiative by GA, 238, 330; study by ILC, 330–331
international criminal jurisdiction:
initiative by GA, 236; study by ILC, 284–286
jurisdiction with regard to crimes outside national territory and jurisdictional immunities of states, 234n
making evidence of customary inter-

national law more readily available:
Commission's recommendations, 287–288; memorandum of the Secretariat, 258n, 286–287, 342; working paper of Hudson, 287, 342–343
most favoured nation clauses, 249, 331
nationality of married women, 263, 295
nationality, and problems connected with:
initiative of ECOSOC, 263, 295, and of ILC, 237; instruments adopted at Hague Conference (1930), 122–123; in the first provisional list of ILC, 234n; International Law Commission's work, 295–298, drafts of future statelessness, 296, revised draft conventions, 296–297; United Nations Conferences on (1959, 1961), 297
Nüremberg principles, 203, 278, 279, 282
and Committee of Seventeen, 152, 153n, 164; formulation by ILC, 274–277; fusion of codification and progressive development, 211; initiative by GA, 236
offences against peace and security of mankind:
and Committee of Seventeen, 152; and ILC, 203, 277–281, 282, 283; fusion of codification and progressive development, 211; initiative by GA, 236
recognition of States and governments, 234n
reservation to multilateral treaties:
Brierly report, 288, 289; on agenda of American Council of Jurists, 267; practice of ILO and Pan-American Union, 289n, 290; reference to ICJ for advisory opinion, 289; work of ILC, 288–290, 322, and recommendation, 290
rights and duties of states:
and Committee of Seventeen, 152, 153n, 272n; and sub-committee II, 164; Bogota Conference (1948), 264n; Commission's draft on, 272–274; Convention adopted by Montevideo Conference (1933), 136; difficulties, 209–210, 211; initiative by GA, 237; special assignment by GA, 203, 237
Sea, law af the:
Geneva Conferences (1958, 1960), 301–311, and conventions adopted,

304, 305–307, 318; reports of special rapporteurs, 299n; revision provision in the Conventions, 319; security and economic problems, 309–310; subjects left aside or selected for study, 299n, 307n
special missions:
connection with diplomatic intercourse and immunities, 326, 327; draft articles adopted by ILC, 327–328; GA asks ILC to study, 236; resolution at Vienna Conference on diplomatic intercourse and immunities, 313; sub-committee appointed, 327; study by the ILC, 326–328
statelessness: see nationality above
Convention:
on elimination of future, (1959), 297; on reduction of future, (1961), 296, 297; on status of, 1954, 298n
States and intergovernmental organizations:
GA request for study by ILC, 236, 328; linked with various forms of ad hoc diplomacy, 328; reports by El-Erian, 329; study by ILC, 328–329
State responsibility:
call for priority study by GA, 235; Hague Conference (1930) and, 125; initiative by Cuba, 226n; in first provisional list of ILC, 234n; preliminary work by Harvard Law School, 264–265, 323; report by Garcia-Amador, 323; study by ILC, 323–324; sub-committee appointed, 254, 324
succession in respect of membership of international organization, 326
succession in respect of rights and duties resulting from sources other than treaties, 326
Succession of States and governments:
call for priority study by GA, 236; in provisional list of ILC, 234n; memorandum of the Secretariat and, 324–325; study by ILC, 324–326; sub-committee on, 254, 255, 325, 326
Succession in respect of treaties, 326
Territorial sea, régime of:
convention on, 306–307; and position of ratification, 318n; initiative of Iceland, 226n; innocent passage in, 306n; in first provisional list of ILC, 234n, 235, 236; on agenda of American Council of Jurists, 267; principles and recommendations of Hague Conference (1930), 125–

International law—(contd)
  126; principles enunciated by ILC,
  310n; reports of special rapporteur,
  300n; six-milers v. twelve-milers,
  308–309; work of ILC, 300–302
treaties, law of:
  initiative of ILC, 237; instructions
  to special rapporteurs, 252; in the
  first provisional list of ILC, 234n,
  235; reports by successive rapporteurs, 321–322; Vienna Convention on, 322–323n; work by ILC,
  321–322
treatment of aliens, 234n
war, laws of, 246
International Law Association, 25, 53,
  62, 66, 140, 265, 278:
  aims, 67; codification work, 67–68;
  formation, 66–67; McNair Committee on development and formulation of international law, 222;
  resolution approving restatement
  method, 163n
International Law Commission:
  achievements of the Commission,
    Chapter VI, 271–332;
  criticism of slow progress, 250;
  topics under study, 321–332;
  works completed, 271–321
  Adoption of the Statute of, 160–164
  autonomy, 175, 176
  bureau, see 'officers' below
  comparison with ICJ, 166n, 180–
    181, 182n, 194, 195, 289
  Composition:
    membership, 165; principles re-
    garding, 165–166; qualification
    of members, 165–173, 175–176;
    tables, 170–171
  consultation of experts and spe-
    cialists, 336–337
  controversy as to full-time or part-
    time, 171–182, 184, 252
  co-operation with:
    governments, 257–262, 337–338;
    intergovernmental organiza-
    tions, 266–270, 337; other bodies,
    262–266, 357; regional bodies,
    267, 268, 269–270
  drafting committee of, 254–257;
  emoluments of members of, 177–
    178, 182–184
  establishment of:
    adoption of the statute, 160–164
    preludes to the, 147–160
    see Chapter IV, 147–200
  expansion of, 165, 169–172,176–177
  functions of the Commission and
    its methodology, see Chapter V,
    201–270; also Codification and
    Progressive development

  future prospects, Chapter VII,
    333–350:
    bearing of external factors on
    codification, 339–341; methods,
    333–339; sources of international
    law, 341–344; the 'general prin-
    ciples of law', 344–350
  members of, 165–173
  methods of work, 217–225, 251–
    266; see also Codification ob-
    jects:
    primarily public international
    law, 162–163, 202
    private international law not
    excluded, 202
  officers, 188–189
  organization of, Chapter IV, 147–
    200
  preludes to the establishment of,
    147–160
  procedure of meetings of, 187–188
  procedures and technique of work
    of, 217–266
  procedure for codification, 227–
    231 and for progressive develop-
    ment, 226–227
  productivity: limiting factors on,
    251–253
  proposals for increasing, 232–233,
    251–254
  publications of: recommentations
    relating to, 287–288, summary
    records, 198–199
  questionnaire technique, 258–259
  recommendations to GA, 229–
    230
  reports, 192–198
  representative character and prob-
    lems, 169–173, 176:
    emphasis on political factors,
    175
    'gentlemen's agreement', 169,
    171–172, 177
    importance of, 172–175
    tables, 170–171
  requests to governments, 257:
    difficulties in consultation, 258–
    260
    importance of consultation, 261,
    337
  Secretariat, 190–192
  selection of topics, 233–250
  sessions, 178, 184–187
  special assignments by GA, 203,
    271–292
  statute, see Statute of ILC
  sub-committees, 251–252, 253,
    254–255, 324, 325, 337
  working machinery of, 165–200
International League of Peace and
  Liberty, 23n

International League of Women for Peace and Liberty, 29
International Maritime Committee, 62, 111
International Peace Bureau, 26
International Sanitary Conference (1851), 86
International Technical Conference on Conservation of the Living Resources of the Sea, Rome (1955), 300
Internoscia, Jerome, 58–61, 202
Interparliamentary Conferences and Interparliamentary Union, 25, 26, 62, 140, 278
Iraq, 171, 238n, 268n, 308n
Iran, 171, 308n
Israel, 170, 171, 260
Italy, 141, 171

Japan, 171, 268n
Japanese house tax (1905), 96
Jay, William, 5, 16, 17, 21
Jenks, C. W., 31n, 55n, 172n, 209n, 338n, 339n, 346n, 347n
Jennings, R. Y., 159n, 160n, 177, 204n, 212n, 214, 217n, 219n, 220n, 222n, 331n
Jessup, P. C., 69, 70, 303n, 307n, 310n, 338n
Jimenez de Aréchaga, Eduardo (Uruguay), 326
Johnson, D. H. N., 274n, 276n, 277n 280n, 303n, 304n, 305n, 311n
Johnson, J. A., 266n
Jones, J. Walter, 4n
Jones, R. L., 24n
Judson, F. N., 44n
Juridical Society of London, 47–48, 62
Juridical Yearbook of UN, 199–200, 287, 288
Jus soli, 297

Kant, Immanuel, 5, 14–15, 113n
Katchenovsky, D. I., 47–48, 77n
Katz, Milton, 184, 265, 336
Keeton, George, 38n, 44n
Kelsen, Hans, 148n
Kellogg–Briand Pact (1928) (Treaty of Paris), 141n
Kerley, Ernest L. (U.S.A.), 238n, 312n, 314n
Karno, Ivan, 191n, 209n, 232n, 263n, 296n
Khoury, El, 232n
Klein, 57n
Knight, W. S. M., 6n, 8n
Knowles, G. W., 10n, 19n
Kopelmanas, Lasare, 218n
Koretsky, Vladmir (U.S.S.R.), 193, 213, 233, 246n, 263, 273n, 342n
Korea, 303n, 315n

Kozhevnikov, F. I. (U.S.S.R.), 298n
Krabbe, 348n
Krylov, S. B. (U.S.S.R.), 198n
Kuhn, A. K., 278n
Kunz, J. L., 139n, 140n, 142n, 306n, 347n

Lachs, Manfred (Poland), 236n, 325
Ladd, William, 5, 15–16, 21
Lammasch, 294
Lapradelle, 294
Lardy, M. C., 49n
Larson, Arthur, 338n
Latané, J. H., 29n
Lauterpacht, E., 314n
Lauterpacht, Hersch (U.K.), 8n, 113n, 129n, 176n, 180, 187, 193n, 194n, 195, 197n, 209, 216n, 279n, 293, 298n, 321, 335n, 346n, 348n; on nature of codification, 212–213
Law, legal systems: admixture of private and public, 168, 346; African, 170, 339, 345, 347; Buddhist (confucianist), 170, 339, 345, 347; Civil (Roman), 168, 170, 345; Common (Anglo-Saxon), 168, 170, 345; Communist, 168, 170, 339, 345, 347; Comparative, 168, 334n, and general principles of law, 345–346; Hindu, 170, 339, 345, 347; Islamic, 170, 339, 345, 347; Jewish, 339, 345, 347; natural, 347–348
Law of War, codification of: after two World Wars, 140–143; before World War I, 109–112; by governments acting individually: America, 77–78, its influence, 79–80, Russia, 76–77; by Institute of International Law, 64; by international conferences; Brussels Conference (1874), 84–85, Congress' of Vienna (1815), 81–82, Declaration of Paris (1856), 82–83, Declaration of St. Petersburg (1868), 83–84, Geneva Convention (1864); and of 1949, 141–143, Hague Conferences: of 1899, 91–98, of 1907, 99–104; Declaration of London (1908–09), 109–110; incompatibility with the status of ILC, 246; no place in projects of American Institute of International Law, 72; promulgation of municipal regulations, 78–79
Lawrence, T. J., 77n, 83n, 88n, 98n
League of Armed Neutrality (1780), 76, 77
League of Free Nations Association, 29
League of Nations, 6, 11, 15, 26, 30, 31, 32, 57: Codification efforts of: Committee of Experts, 116–120; Covenant as code, 112–114; Criteria for selecting topics, 243; Hague

League of Nations—(*contd*)
Conference of 1930, 121–133; Harvard Law School's association, 68, 69, 73, 98; International Labour Code, 115; preparatory committee, 120–121; quickened legislative process, 114–115; resolution on assumption by the UN of League functions, 292n; resolution on future codification conferences, 220n; work on nationality, 122–123; responsibility of states, 125–126; territorial waters, 124–125
League of Nations Society, 29n
League of Nations Union, 29
Levi, Leone, 5, 17, 53
Lewis, William Draper, 221n
Lewis, V. J., 9n
Liang, Yuen-Li, 149n, 150n, 188n, 209n, 211n, 213n, 217n, 222n, 225n, 230n, 231n, 258n, 276n, 286n
Lichtblau, G. E., 32n
Lieber, Francis, 49, 63; drafts first code on laws of war, 77–78; influence on other projects, 79, 84, 221
Lighthouses Cases (1934), 197n
Ligue de la Paix, 23n
Lijdphart, A., 175n
Lima Conference (1877), 134n
Lincoln, Abraham, 77
Lipsky, G. A., 142n
Lipstein, K., 39n
Lissitzyn, O. J., 340n
Livingstone, R. W., 4n
Lobingier, C. S., 46n
Loder (Netherlands), 117n
London Agreement (1945), 275n
London Convention dealing with Safety of Life at Sea (1914), 114
London Naval Conference (1908–09), 109–110
London Peace Society, 17
London Protocol relating to Rules of Submarine Warfare (1936), 141
Lorimer, James, 5, 13–19, 63
Lorwin, Lewis, 30n
Lotus case (1927), 197n
Lushington, Sir Godfrey, 79

Maccoby, S., 81n
Magalhaes, Barbozade (Portugal), 117n
Malkin, H. W., 83n
Mancine of Rome, 63
Mann, F. A., 346n
Marburg, Theodore, 29
Marvin, F. S., 4n
Massachusetts, 20, 21
Masters, Ruth D., 134n, 136n, 137n
Mastry (Czechoslovakia), 117n
Matsuda (Japan), 117n

McDougal, M. S., 208n, 219n, 302n, 306n, 310n, 311n
McKenna, C. H., 8n
McNair, Lord, 218n, 319, 343, 344n
McNair Committee in International Law Association, 70, 153n, 154n, 155n, 156n, 159n, 218n
Mead, E. D., 8n, 20n, 88n
Members, International Law Commission:
candidates' nomination, 173, 175; casual vacancies; filling of, 174, 184, *see also* Statute, art. 11; election by GA, 167, 173; criteria guiding, 169, 171, 172, 175; eligibility of, 165, 166; emoluments, see emoluments of members; exodus to the ICJ, 184; not representative of governments, 166; proposal for full-time service of, 179, 182, 184; qualifications of: nationality, 166, recognized competence in the international law, 165, 167, representative of principal legal systems, 165, 166, 167–168, 175–176; tables of representation, 170–171; tenure of, 177–182
Mendlovitz, S. H., 218n, 348n
Mexico, 134, 171, 238n, 308n
Meulen, Jacob ter, 5n
Meynier, Gustav, 83
Miall, C. S., 20n, 22n, 24n
Miles, J. B., 25, 66
Mill, James, 13, 47
Miller, D. H., 31n
Miller, Hunter, 129n
Minority Schools in Albania (1935), 197n
Model Rules on Arbitral Procedure, 293–294
Mohonk Conference on International Arbitration, 73
Monroe doctrine, 100, 113ʲ
Montevideo Conference (1888), 134n
Moore, John Bassett, 24n, 259, 294, 344n
Morocco, 308n
Morris, Clarence, 14n
Morrison, Stanley, 69
Morzov, Platon (U.S.S.R.), 265
Moscow Declaration, 275n
Movchan (U.S.S.R.), 252n
Muscat Dhows Case (1905), 96

Napoleonic Wars, 81
Natural law, influence of, 347–350
Nazis (Fascists), 159n
Nehru, Pandit (India), 268n
Netherlands, 23n, 121, 152, 156, 171, 192n, 328; codification of private international law, 112, 230
Nörsk Union against War (1882), 23n
Norway, 310

No-war movement, 28
Nuttall, E. M., 12n, 13n
Nussbaum, A., 7n
Non liquet, 43, 344
Nys, Ernest, 41, 44, 45n, 46, 47n, 49n, 61n, 78n, 79n

O'Brien, Helen, 14n
Observers, International Law Commission, 267, 268, 269
Official efforts at codification, Chapter III, 76–143: efforts of governments, 76–78; for the laws of war, 140–143; Hague Peace Conferences, 89–109; in the Inter-American System, 133, 140; other efforts before first World War, 109, 112; under the aegis of the League of Nations, 112–133
Ogden, C. K., 44n
Ogg, David, 8n, 9n
Olney, Richard, 73n
Oppenheim, L., 82n, 85n, 197n, 218n, 335n
Organization of American States: created by Bogota Charter (1948), 139; articles referred: art. 57, 139, art. 61, 267, art. 67, 139, arts. 68–70, 139

Pacta tertis nec nocent nec prosunt, 219
Padilla Nervo, Luis (Mexico), 269n, 325
Pal, Radhabinod (India), 181, 193n, 195n, 268n, 269n, 279n, 325; on charge of special rapporteurs, 252n; on selection of topics, 239
Panama, 152, 271
Panama Congress (1826), 134
Panama Draft on Rights and Duties of States, 272–273
Pan-American Union, *see also* Inter-American Conference of American States, Organization of American States: and American Institute of International Law, 72–73; codifying agencies, 138; co-ordination of various agencies, 137; committee of experts, 137n; conferences of, 134–137; efforts at codification, 134–139; foundation of, 134; Inter-American Council of Jurists, 139; Inter-American Juridical Committee, 138; Inter-American Neutrality Committee, 137; International Commission of Jurists, 135; practice in respect of reservations to treaties, 290; replacement by OAS, 267; special mention by Committee of Seventeen, 159–160, 266
Paroldo, Augusto, 47
Parry, Clive, 219n, 228n, 259, 276–277, 280n, 318n

Passy, M. Frederic, 66
Pauncefote, Sir Julian, 96n
Peace Committee of Berlin, 23n
Peace Congresses, 21–22, 23, 25–26
Peace movement: before the first World War, 27–28, and during war, 28–30, World War II and after, 30–33; from League to United Nations, 31–33; international labour movement and, 30–31; organized peace work: achievements, 26–27; first phase, 20–22, in England and U.S.A., 20–21, 23, 24, 25, in Europe, 21, 23n, 26–27, peace congresses, 21–22, 25, 26, second phase, 22–27, peace societies, 20–21, 23, 24, 25, 26, 27, 28–29; universal peace congresses, 25–26; visionaries of world organization, 5–19
Pearson, G., 3n
Pella, V. V., 278, 280n
Penn, William, 5, 9, 10, 113n
Permanent Court of Arbitration: established, 95–96, 98; improvement, 100; peace societies proposals, 26
Permanent Court of International Justice, 31, 114, 116, 167n, 181n, 197
Peru, 134, 33n
Pessoa, Epitacio, 57n
Phelps, Christina, 17n, 20n, 27n, 29n
Phillips, W. A., 9n, 11n
Phillipson, C., 5n
Pictet, J. S., 142n, 143n
Pious Funds case of the Californias (1902), 96
Plato, 4
Poland, 152, 171
Politis, N., 294, 348n
Pompe, C. A., 277n, 280n, 281n
Pollock, Sir Frederick, 5n, 29n
Pope, Leo XIII, 94n
Potter, P. B., 23n, 148n, 281n
Pound, Roscoe, 336n, 338n: on comparative law, 334n, 345; on requisites of world justice, 347n
Pratt, F. T., 77n
Private efforts at codification of international law: Chapter II, pp. 37–75: by individuals, 37–62; by scientific organizations, 62–75
Private international law: codification in Americas, 134, 136; Committee of Seventeen refers to, 156n; conferences for codifying, 87; Hague Conferences on, 192; initiative of Netherlands on, and, 112, 230; intermingling of public law with, 346; not excluded from ILC study, 202; sub-committee of GA and, 162–163; unification of, 111–112, 258

Progress of mankind towards world organization: Chapter I, 3–33: from the League to the United Nations, 27–33; individual visions of world organization, 5–19; the organized peace work, 19–27

Progressive development of international law, *see also* codification: distinction blurred in practice, 209–211, 231–233; distinguished from codification: Committee of Seventeen and, 154–155, in the Statute of ILC, 209–211, 231–233; initiative in, 201, 225–226; methods, 224; procedure for, 225–227

Quakers, 20

Radim, Max, 175n
Rafique, Sir Muhammad, 117n
Ralston, J. H., 20n, 24n, 96n
Rappard, W. E., 147n
Rapporteurs (general): appointment and functions, 188–189; members of the Drafting Committee of ILC, 254;
Rapporteurs (special): appointment of, 188, 189, 226; Committee of Seventeen's proposals, 157–158; heavy burden on, 251–252; honoraria, 183; personal contribution of, 189; proposal as to appointment of more, 253; the drafting and, 254
Rau, Sir Benegal (India), 180, 246n
Red Cross: Conventions, 93; International Conference (1948), 142; objection to adoption of, 93n
Reever, J. S., 69, 124n
Refugee question, 315–316
Reinsch, P. S., 27n, 73n, 86n
Renault, 102n, 294
Renault, M., 110n
Repertory of U.N. Organization, 288n
Reports of the ICL: annual, 192; controversy as to recording of dissenting opinion, 192–196; importance of various opinions, 196–198; publication of, 198
Reports of International Arbitral Awards, 288n
Re Piracy Jure Gentium (1934), 70n
Reservations to the Convention on Genocide (1951), 197, 289, 290, 318n
Resolution, defined, 91n
Richard, Henry, 20n, 21, 22n, 24, 66
Rie, R., 82n
Rights of the Nationals of the United States of America in Morocco (1952), 197n
Robertson, A. H., 348n
Robson, W. A., 168n
Rogers, J. G., 70
Rogers, T., 23n

Rolin-Jaequemyns, of Ghent, 63, 66
Rommen, Heinrich, A., 4n
Root, Elihu, 49n, 63n, 72n, 73, 78n, 104, 110n, 116, 167n, 261n, 261n, 350
Rosenne, Shabtai (Israel), 150n, 152, 160, 170n, 260n, 295n
Rousseau, Jean-Jacques, 5, 12–13, 59n
Rules of procedure of ILC, 187–188
Rundstein (Poland), 117n, 130n, 207n
Rymer, 342n
Russia, 76–77, 83–84, 85, 87n, 89, 99, 105, 152n
Russo-Japanese War, 97
Russo-Turkish War (1877), 85

Sabek, Hafez, 270n
Saint-Pierre, Abbé, 5, 10–12, 14n, 113n
Sandström, A. E. F. (Sweden), 244n, 252n, 285, 311, 326
San-Francisco Conference (1945): adopts art. 1 of UN Charter, 148; controversy as to meaning of codification in respect of art. 13; para 1(a) of the Charter, 204–205; drafting of art. 13, para 1(a), 148–149; initiative of GA as to draft conventions, 221n–222n; no definition of aggression in Charter, 282n
Scandinavian Peace Society (1882), 23n
Scelle, Georges (France), 189n, 193n, 234n, 244n, 246n, 282n, 292, 293, 348n
Schiffer, W., 33n, 113n
Schlesinger, R. B., 344n, 346n, 349n
Schücking, W., 88n, 97n, 98n, 117n
Schwarzenberger, G., 16n, 38n, 44, 168n, 172, 208n, 277n
Scott, G. W., 100n
Scott, James Brown, 8n, 9n, 47n, 63n, 64n, 65n, 71n, 72n, 77n, 85n, 87n, 88n, 89n, 92n, 93n, 94n, 96n, 99n, 100n, 101n, 102n, 104n, 105n, 107n, 108n, 110n, 122n, 127n, 133n, 134n, 135n, 136n, 344n, 348n, 350n
Secretariat, United Nations: assistance to Committee of Seventeen, 153n, and to special rapporteurs, 251; codification division of, and ILC, 190–191; 251; criticism of, 191–192; studies prepared on: arbitral procedure, 293n; digest of decisions of international tribunals relating to State succession, 325n; diplomatic intercourse and immunities, 264n, 311n; evidence of customary international law, 286n; for Law of Sea Conference, 308n; future programme of ILC, 329; *Guide to the Law of Sea*, 308n; Law

and régime of high seas, 300n; Law and régime of territorial seas, 308n; making evidence of customary international law available, 258n, 286n; methods of codification, 223–224; multilateral treaties under the League, 291; Nüremberg principles, 275; Question of extended participation in League treaties, 291; Question of international criminal jurisdiction, 284n; relations between States and governmental organizations, 328n; rights and duties of States, 272n; special missions, 327n; State responsibility, 324; succession of States and governments, 325n; survey of international laws, 205–207; Tables concerning breadth and juridical status of territorial seas, 308n; ways and means of making . . ., 258n, 342

Sellon, Count de, 21

Selection of topics, 233–250: controversial topics, 248–249; criteria for, 242–251, in art. 15, 242, in the Survey, 242–244, in the view of individual members of ILC, 244–247, and of governments, 247, and of ILC, 248; organs responsible for, 233–242; provisional list of ILC, 234n; suggestions of: governments, 240n, 248n, ILC members, 245–246, sixth committee, 248n; technical and political aspects, 249–251; topics rejected, 245; topics worth considering, 332

Sen (India), 309n

Sessions, International Law Commission: annual, 178, 184–187; date, 184; length, 185–186; overlapping with ECOSOC, 186–187; place, 184–185; proposal of winter sessions, 187; quorum, 187; voting, 187–188

Shawcross, Sir Hartley (U.K.), 280n

Shotwell, J. T., 22n

Shukairy (Saudi-Arabia), 309n

Singh, Sir Dalip (India), 152n

Sixth Committee, General Assembly: adopts ILC Statute, 160, 164, and amendments, 165; anxiety about paucity of its agenda, 238n; commission's membership and of, 188n; creation of ILC, 164; criticism of ILC, 250n, 254, 255; differs from report of Committee of Seventeen, 160–161; dissatisfaction with ILC composition, 171–172; distribution of additional ILC seats, 169; implementation of art. 13(1)a of the UN Charter, 150–151; on autonomy of ILC, 176; on directions to Special

Rapporteur, 252n, and its methods of work, 254–255, and selection of topics, 239–242, 248n; sub-committee of, 150, 155n, on composition of ILC, 162, 174n, on continuance of Committee of Seventeen, 164, on full-time ILC, 161, on functions of ILC, 162–163, on participation of non-members of UN in ILC, 173n

Slice, A. Vander, 30n

Slusser, R. M., 340n

Smith, E. Sherwood, 6n

Smith, H. A., 112n, 140n, 340n

Smith, J. A., 4n

Society of Comparative Legislation, 117n

Sohn, Louis B., 265, 338n

Sorenson, Max, 304n, 305n

Souleyman, Elizabeth V., 6n, 7n, 11n

Sources of international law: customs, 342; general principles of law, 344–349; judicial decisions, 343–344; treaties, 341–342

Spaak, P. H., 151n

Spanish Royal Academy of Moral and Pol. Sc. (1884), 23n

Spiropoulos, Jean (Greece), 179n, 180, 188n, 209n, 226n, 232n, 233, 244n, 246n, 252n, 275–276, 277, 278, 279, 282

Sprague, A. P., 51n

Starke, J. G., 218n

Status of Women, 298n

Statute of International Law Commission: adoption by GA, 164; amendments to, 164n; revision considered, 231–233; articles referred:
art. 1, 201
art. 2, 162, 165, 166, 173, 202
art. 3, 4, 5, 6, 7, 173
art. 8, 162, 165, 166, 167n, 173
art. 9, 166, 173n
art. 10, 177, 178, 182
art. 11, 174
art. 12, 184, 185
art. 13, 178, 182, 201, 210n, 214, 239
art. 14, 190
art. 15, 201, 203, 212, 213, 224–225, 242
art. 16, 157n, 158n, 188n, 189, 192n, 193, 201, 210, 225–227, 233, 258n, 259, 262, 264n, 274, 277
art. 17, 157n, 158n, 233, 258n, 262
art. 18, 157n, 158n, 192n, 193, 201; ambiguity in, 227–228; interpretation of, 233–234; political and technical aspects of codification, 242–243

Statute of International Law Commission—(*contd*)
  art. 19, 157n, 202, 229, 233, 251, 258n, 259
  art. 20, 156n, 157n, 192n, 193, 194, 196, 207, 229
  art. 21, 157n, 193, 229, 258n, 274
  art. 22, 157n, 192n, 193, 229, 258n
  art. 23, 157n, 158n, 192n, 229–230, 293, 302
  art. 24, 192n, 202, 258, 342n, 343
  art. 25, 159n, 262
  art. 26, 140n, 159n, 262, 263–264, 266
Stawell, F. Melian, 6n
Stockton, C. H., 101n, 110n
Stone, Julius, 208n, 283, 334, 335
Stowell, E. C., 100n
Stuyt, 344n
Suarez, Dr (Argentina), 117n, 130n, 207n
Suarez, Franciscus, 3n
Sully, Duc de, 8–9, 113n
Survey of International Law: defines task of ILC, 208–209; emphasis on legislative aspect of codification, 205–207; on selection of topics, 234 and critera for, 242–244; on subcommittees, 251; on succession of States and governments, 324–325
Sweden, 117, 152, 171
Swedish Peace and Arbitration Association (1883), 23n
Switzerland, 83, 142, 173n, 185
Syria, 166n, 171, 268n

Tabibi, Abdul Hakim (Afghanistan), 252n
Taft, William Howard, 29
Takahashi, S., 94n
Tammes, A. J. P. (Netherlands), 219n
Thailand, 17
Third Committee, GA, 298n
Travaux préparatoires, 197–198
Treatment of Polish nationals in Danzig (1932), 197n
Treaty of London (1930), 141
Treaty of Washington (1871), 24
Trimble, E. G., 140n
Triska, J. F., 340n
Trueblood, Benjamin F., 14n, 103n
Truman Proclamation, 277n, 306
Tryon, J. L., 104n
Tunkin, Grigory I. (U.S.S.R.), 252n, 269n, 325
Twiss, Sir Travers, 66

UNESCO, 288n
Union de la Paix, 23n
Union Juridique internationale, 117n

Union of Democratic Control, 29
Union of International Law, Vienna University, 265
United Arab Republic, 166n, 170n, 238n, 308n
United Nations, 33, 57, 98, 100 (*see also* Charter): election of ILC, 162; increased membership of, 165; initiative by GA, 221–222n; publications on ILC recommendation, 288n; use of term 'codification', 205n
United Nations Conference on: Consular Relations, Vienna (1963), 315–317, 320; Diplomatic Relations, Vienna (1961), 312–314, 317, 320, 327; Elimination or Reduction of Future Statelessness, (1959, 1961), 297, 320; International Organization (1945), 148–149; Law of the Sea, Geneva (1958, 1960), 302–311, 320: First Conference (1958): committees, 303; conventions, 304; position of ratification, 318; resolutions adopted, 304n; resolution on historic waters, 330; contribution of, 307;
  Second Conference (1960): conflicting attitudes, 339–340; causes of failure, 309–311; two camps at, 308;
  Law of Treaties (1968, 1969), 320
United Nations Juridical Yearbook, 199–200, 287, 288n, 343, 344
United Nations Legislative Series, 259, 287, 288n
United States of America, 52, 32, 152, 255, 283n
Universal Declaration of Human Rights, 296
Universal Peace Congresses, 25–26, 31, 62
Universal Peace Union (1866), 23n
Universal Postal Congresses, 258, 329
Uruguay, 309n
Ustor, Endre (Hungary), 331
U.S.S.R., 170n, 171, 282n, 340

Vaughan, C. E., 12n
Vaucher, P., 3n
Venezuela, 152, 238n, 308n
Venezuela Preferential Payment (1904), 96
Verdross, Alfred (Austria), 246, 312n, 348n
Verosta, Professor, 265n
Versailles, Treaty of, 31
Vesnitch, M. R., 11n
Vesey-Fitzgerald, 39n
Vienna Congress, 47, 81–82
Vienna Convention on Consular Relations, 315–317, 318n, 319

Vienna Convention on Diplomatic Relations, 312–314, 316, 318n, 319, 327
Vienna Convention on Law of Treaties, 322–323
Vietnam, 303n, 315n
Visscher, Auguste (Belgium), 66, 117n, 125n, 127n, 130n, 207n, 208n, 257n, 348n
Voeu, defined, 91n
Vollenhoven, Van, 8n, 294
Vreeland, Hamilton, 8n

Waldock, Sir Humphrey (U.K.), 189, 239n, 252, 283n, 306n, 307n, 321n, 322, 326
Walker, T. A., 85n
Wang, Chung-Hui (China), 117n
War Resisters' International, 28
Webster–Ashburton Treaty (1839), 20
Webster, Thomas, 66
Weil, Gordon L., 348n
Weis, Paul, 127n, 298n
Westlake, J., 107n
Wharton, Frances, 259
Wheaton, H., 11n
Whewell, William, 7n
White, T. R., 102n
Whitman, M. M., 138n, 139n, 259, 306n
Whitney, E. L., 24n
Whittück, E. A., 82n, 83n, 84n
Wickersham, G. W. (U.S.A.), 117n, 222
Wigmore, J. H., 339n
William, Sir John Fisher, 218n
Wilson, George, 41n
Wilson, G. G., 69, 101n
Wilson, President, 30
Woetzel, R. J., 277n
Woolf, L. S., 29n, 62n, 111n
Wolfke, Karol, 342n
Woolsey, T. S., 204n
Worcester, Noah, 20

Working methods, 251–266: collaboration with governments: 257–262, questionnaire method, 258–259, why not effective, 259–261; and with intergovernmental organizations, Asian-African Legal Consultative Committee, 267–269, European Committee on Legal Co-operation, 270, Inter-American Council of Jurists, 266–267; and with other bodies: non-governmental organizations, 263–266, organs of UN, 262–263; preparatory work, 251–257
World Court League, 29
World Society: concepts of unity, 3–4; individual's visions of organization of, 5–19; universal law, 4–5
World Wars:
First: codification before, 109, 111–112, and after, 112–133; marked close of an era of international legislation, 114
Second: codification of laws of war, 140–143; post-war reconstruction plans, 147
Wortley, B. A., 33n, 168n, 172n, 346n
Wright, Q., 64n, 69, 266, 283n, 286n, 339n

Yasseen, Mustafa Kemal (Iraq), 239n
Yearbook of ILC, 192n, 198
Yepes, Jesus M., (Colombia), 193, 245, 246n, 282n
York, E., 14n
Young, R., 305n
Yugoslavia, 152, 171, 226n, 238n, 247

Zimmern, Alfred, 113n
Zourek, Jaroslav (Czechoslovakia), 193n, 194n, 252n, 253, 254, 261, 298n, 315, 316n, 317n
Zurich Civil Code, 49